Dynamics of Virtual Work

Series Editors

Ursula Huws
De Havilland Campus
Hertfordshire Business School
Hatfield, United Kingdom

Rosalind Gill
Department of Sociology
City University London
London, United Kingdom

Technological change has transformed where people work, when and how. Digitisation of information has altered labour processes out of all recognition whilst telecommunications have enabled jobs to be relocated globally. ICTs have also enabled the creation of entirely new types of 'digital' or 'virtual' labour, both paid and unpaid, shifting the borderline between 'play' and 'work' and creating new types of unpaid labour connected with the consumption and co-creation of goods and services. This affects private life as well as transforming the nature of work and people experience the impacts differently depending on their gender, their age, where they live and what work they do. Aspects of these changes have been studied separately by many different academic experts however up till now a cohesive overarching analytical framework has been lacking. Drawing on a major, high-profile COST Action (European Cooperation in Science and Technology) Dynamics of Virtual Work, this series will bring together leading international experts from a wide range of disciplines including political economy, labour sociology, economic geography, communications studies, technology, gender studies, social psychology, organisation studies, industrial relations and development studies to explore the transformation of work and labour in the Internet Age. The series will allow researchers to speak across disciplinary boundaries, national borders, theoretical and political vocabularies, and different languages to understand and make sense of contemporary transformations in work and social life more broadly. The book series will build on and extend this, offering a new, important and intellectually exciting intervention into debates about work and labour, social theory, digital culture, gender, class, globalisation and economic, social and political change.

More information about this series at
http://www.springer.com/series/14954

Enda Brophy

Language Put to Work

The Making of the Global Call Centre Workforce

Enda Brophy
School of Communication
Simon Fraser University
Burnaby, BC, Canada

Dynamics of Virtual Work
ISBN 978-1-349-95772-9   ISBN 978-1-349-95244-1 (eBook)
DOI 10.1057/978-1-349-95244-1

© The Editor(s) (if applicable) and The Author(s) 2017
Softcover reprint of the hardcover 1st edition 2017
The author(s) has/have asserted their right(s) to be identified as the author(s) of this work in accordance with the Copyright, Designs and Patents Act 1988.
This work is subject to copyright. All rights are solely and exclusively licensed by the Publisher, whether the whole or part of the material is concerned, specifically the rights of translation, reprinting, reuse of illustrations, recitation, broadcasting, reproduction on microfilms or in any other physical way, and transmission or information storage and retrieval, electronic adaptation, computer software, or by similar or dissimilar methodology now known or hereafter developed.
The use of general descriptive names, registered names, trademarks, service marks, etc. in this publication does not imply, even in the absence of a specific statement, that such names are exempt from the relevant protective laws and regulations and therefore free for general use.
The publisher, the authors and the editors are safe to assume that the advice and information in this book are believed to be true and accurate at the date of publication. Neither the publisher nor the authors or the editors give a warranty, express or implied, with respect to the material contained herein or for any errors or omissions that may have been made. The publisher remains neutral with regard to jurisdictional claims in published maps and institutional affiliations.

Cover illustration: © Photo by Steve Dynie

Printed on acid-free paper

This Palgrave Macmillan imprint is published by Springer Nature
The registered company is Macmillan Publishers Ltd.
The registered company address is: The Campus, 4 Crinan Street, London, N1 9XW, United Kingdom

But beneath this apparent habituation, the hostility of workers to degenerated forms of work which are forced upon them continues as a subterranean stream that makes its way to the surface when the conditions permit, or when the capitalist drive for a greater intensity of labour oversteps the bounds of physical or mental capacity. It renews itself in new generations, expresses itself in the unbounded cynicism and revulsion which large numbers of workers feel about their work, and comes to the fore repeatedly as a social issue demanding a solution.
(Harry Braverman, *Labor and Monopoly Capital*, 1974)

The thing which gives us hope is that in the face of all of this, in the face of this "perfection" of the system which puts the call centre worker in the condition of not being able to carry out her job, she nonetheless manages to organize her subterranean battle... What is opposed to control is a lived autonomy which structures the operator's work: while on the one hand she is subject to pressure, on the other she is conscious that she herself has the capacity to run the call centre.
(Paolo Greco, *Analisi di un Call Center*, 2011)

Struggles are an infinite laboratory.
(Colectivo Situaciones, *¿Quién habla?* 2006)

Acknowledgements

This book is a product of the many encounters that informed, supported, and inspired my research. I'm especially indebted to the workers, trade unionists, and labour activists that shared their time and experiences with me. Thank you to the Communication Workers' Union in Ireland, the Communications, Energy and Paperworkers Union (now Unifor) in Canada, the Unite Union in New Zealand, and the Collettivo Precari Atesia and the Cobas in Italy for generously helping me out with this project. A number of people went above and beyond in connecting me to the varied contexts and histories I explored during field research on three continents. James Redmond, Paul Dillon, and Mark Malone put me in touch with call centre workers in Ireland and organized a memorable discussion on worker inquiry and call centre labour at the Seomra Sproi social centre in Dublin. In Italy I'd like to thank Giorgio de Rossi, Domenico Teramo, Antonio Sciotto, and especially Cristian Bosi, who not only gave me his perspective on the Collettivo's organizing, but provided regular updates on the situation in Italy and comments on my work in the years that followed. Much gratitude also to Omar Hamed for his crash course on the history of neoliberalism in New Zealand, for discussions on service sector work and postcolonial labour organizing, and even for his thoughtful critiques of autonomist politics. My thanks also to the collectives I have participated in, drawn sustenance from, or been in contact with, including Colectivo Situaciones, edu-factory, effimera, the Gruppo d'Inchiesta su Precarietà e il Comune, Kolinko, the Toronto School of Creativity and Inquiry, and uninomade 2.0.

Thanks to Vincent Mosco, for exemplary supervision from Carleton to Queen's; to Leah Vosko, for providing the space and time for me to work on this project at York; to Greig de Peuter, for suggesting I write a book on call centre labour and for his feedback and friendship throughout; to Ursula Huws, for valuable mentorship and support; to Benjamin Anderson, Mirjam Gollmitzer, Seamus Grayer, David Lavin, Rob Prey, and especially Paula Velázquez Lanzmaier, whose research labours improved this book immensely; to my students at Queen's, York, and Simon Fraser University, for allowing me to run ideas by them in various labour-oriented courses as the research progressed; to Rafael Alarcón Medina, Aneesh Aneesh, Franco Berardi, Ergin Bulut, Annette Burfoot, Nicole Cohen, Richard Day, Jodi Dean, Nick Dyer-Witheford, Andrea Fumagalli, Brian Green, Esin Gülsen, Liz Mason-Deese, Alice Mattoni, Heather Menzies, Gigi Roggero, Sid Shniad, Dan Schiller, Marcelo Vieta, Jamie Woodcock, and Steve Wright, for offering feedback on my research and support at different stages; to Gerard Goggin, Larry Haiven, Andrew Herman, and Delia Dumitrica, for inviting me to speak on this research at their institutions; to Harriet Barker, Amelia Derkatsch, and Dhanalakshmi Jayavel at Palgrave, for steering this book through the publication process; to this book's anonymous reviewers, for their time and their helpful suggestions; to Rosalind Gill and Ursula Huws, for including this book in the Dynamics of Virtual Work series; and to the Social Sciences and Humanities Research Council of Canada, Queen's University, and Simon Fraser University, for supporting my research.

My gratitude also goes to Emanuela Chiari and John Darroch for sharing their photos so that they could be included in the book, and to Steve Dynie for taking a cover photo which perfectly transmits work refusal in the call centre. Portions of Chaps. 1, 2, 3, and 4 have appeared in the journals *ephemera: theory & politics in organization; Journal of Communication Inquiry; Work Organisation, Labour & Globalisation;* and *Labour/Le Travail*. I thank the reviewers of those articles for their insights and suggestions.

In 2015 my teacher and friend Julian Bees passed away. His influence has shaped this book, and I am deeply saddened he won't be around to pick holes in it as he undoubtedly would have. Mi manchi, Julian.

As this project began to take shape my own story took a singularly fortunate turn when I met Julie Lapointe, my companion and facilitator of a life beyond work. More recently our relationship has expanded to include parenthood, as first Simona and then Nicola have joyously upended our lives. The girls remind me daily, in their own inimitable ways, of how resistance defines us. This book is dedicated to them.

Praise for *Language Put to Work*

"As we waited with baited breath for the arrival of the knowledge worker, we did not expect human communication to be turned into factory work. In this audacious book on call centre work, Brophy not only uncovers the subjugation of language to communicative capitalism, he also reveals the creative possibilities of labor resistance and alternate trajectories."
—A. Aneesh, *University of Wisconsin–Milwaukee, USA*

"This is a comprehensive, theoretically informed, lucidly written, beautifully researched and ultimately inspiring study of one the front lines of class struggle in digital capitalism—the call centre. Brophy gives us the living voices of workers on the tele-assembly lines speaking out against their managerial reduction to profitable, abstract communication; we should listen."
—Nick Dyer-Witheford, *University of Western Ontario, Canada*

"In a world tour that travels from Canada and Argentina, to Ireland and Italy, to Australia and New Zealand, Language Put to Work goes deep within the inner dynamics of call centers over the last decade. The analysis artfully synthesizes theorizations on communicative capitalism, immaterial labor, and virtual migration to shed light on the changing foundations and growing role of customer service phone work in the global economy. It documents with clarity, skill, and liveliness, the myriad ways that employee organizing endures: from self-organization, to digital sabotage, strikes and occupations, and cooperative alternatives."

—Winifred Poster, *Washington University, USA*

"This important work challenges existing streams of debate within labour studies and the role of communication therein."

—*Canadian Communication Association Book Prize Committee*

"*Language Put to Work* is a close inquiry into the nature of this digital assembly line, its implications for workers, and the possibilities for organized labor. [It] should be read by anyone who has an interest in understanding the future of work, which, despite current rhetoric about robots and full automation, will most likely look more like call center labor: highly managed, routinized, and entangled in various proprietary technologies and data-hungry software systems—yet also irreducibly human."

—Karen Gregory, *University of Edinburgh, UK*, review published in New Labor Forum

Contents

1 The Subterranean Stream — 1

2 Communicative Capitalism and Call Centre Labour — 29

3 Labour's Resistance in the Call Centre — 59

4 The Making of the Call Centre Cybertariat — 85

5 The Migration of Struggle — 131

6 The Organization of Autonomy — 169

7 The Making and Unmaking of the Global Call Centre Workforce — 213

Interviews Cited   263

References   265

Index   293

1

The Subterranean Stream

In 2010 a female employee at a Garanti Bank call centre in Istanbul had a conflict with management at her workplace. What caused the conflict is unclear, but in her account the industrial relations scholar Esin Gülsen (2015) suggests the employee was then isolated from her colleagues and barred from communicating with them. Managers cancelled her password for accessing the system, but still forced her to sit at her workstation each day without being able to do her job. Not long afterward she quit her position and eventually sued the company.

Workplace conflicts of this kind are hardly unusual, especially in call centres, but what happened next was remarkable. On the day the lawsuit was launched, call centre employees at Garanti began to receive a strange series of phone calls. Rather than the usual customers inquiring about the status of their chequing accounts, employees listened as one anonymous caller after another read a prepared message:

> Good evening, I am calling you on behalf of the Association of Call Centre Workers. According to the information I obtained from the Association, a worker who worked in the same call centre with you today just had a hearing for a lawsuit that is ongoing against the bank for which you work.

© The Author(s) 2017
E. Brophy, *Language Put to Work*, Dynamics of Virtual Work,
DOI 10.1057/978-1-349-95244-1_1

The bank imposed isolation upon this person for months and eventually forced her to resign. It did not allow her to talk to other people in the workplace. Other employees were warned not to communicate with her. She was forced to terminate her labour contract at the end of this process and then sued the bank.

It seems that the managers of your call centre want to threaten you, prevent you from defending your rights and suppress you with this kind of behaviour.

We, who support labour rights, are making this call to remind you that you are not alone. We know that your calls are being recorded and your managers will listen to these records. We do not expect you to answer right now.

Please contact the Association of Call Center Workers for a collectively organized working life where your rights are secured and you get compensated fairly in return for your labor.[1] (As cited in Gülsen, 2015, p. 144)

One employee noted that when the calls began to come in she was initially afraid and felt the need to hang up. Soon, however, workers at the call centre began to take their headphones off to discuss the calls among each other. Colleagues conversed across their workstations. As the day wore on, the Garanti call centre was so overrun by callers from the association that it could no longer receive calls from regular customers. The call centre had been shut down.

The example described by Gülsen offers a striking sketch of the contested and mutable social relations marking the relatively new and intensely communicative workplace that is the call centre. The dominant technological channels, communicative scripts, and labour processes engineered from above by management in the call centre had, in the short space of one afternoon, been suspended, reversed, and crowded out by incipient horizontal forms of communication developed from below. Instead of workers reading to customers from a text imposed by management, rank-and-file labour activists seized a direct channel for communication to their colleagues in order to read to them from an altogether different script—one that was both unsanctioned and subversive. Rather

---

[1] The translation has been slightly modified from the version offered in Gülsen's account. I would like to thank Esin Gülsen and Ergin Bulut for their assistance in going over this translation.

than call centre workers speaking to bank customers as they were paid to do, employees began to talk to each other about these strange phone calls and the lawsuit, bringing the labour conflict out into the open. Communication devoted to the production of profit came into open conflict with more horizontal forms of communication, ones that extended outward, among workers, and beyond the call centre walls.

A New Workforce

The events at the Garanti Bank underscore a critical transformation within capitalist economies and the rise of a newly communicative workforce. On the assembly line that dominated the Fordist factory, remarks the philosopher Paolo Virno, labour is silent (Virno, 2001). The soundtrack of a factory is the repetitive din of machines. As the economy has been transformed since the 1970s, however, Virno maintains, work has increasingly assumed the features of linguistic interaction. Communication has taken centre stage within post-Fordism, and labour now tends towards the production of intangibles, such as information, culture, services, or relationships.[2] Once admitted only grudgingly in the site of production, the human faculty of language has now comprehensively been put to work.

This book uses Virno's reflection on labour and language to describe the remarkable rise of the transnational call centre workforce and one of the fastest-growing and paradigmatic workspaces of our time. As a result of their steady meshing into the circuits of the global economy, the

---

[2] In using the term *post-Fordism*, Virno draws on the work of the French Regulation School to describe the political, economic, and cultural regime of accumulation that has asserted itself across developed countries out of the crisis of Fordism in the late 1960s. While this shift has taken different paths in different regions, post-Fordism is marked by shifts towards service sector employment, leaner and more flexible production processes, increasing financialization of the economy, unprecedented mobility for capital, the expansion and intensification of communications networks, and the increasing valourization of language, communication, and affect (see Virno, 2003). In this book I use the term *Fordism* to refer to the regime of accumulation (or stage of capitalism) that became ascendant in the post-World War II period. In using this term, I place a special emphasis on the logic of production which was the driving force of Fordism—a logic characterized by mass production, scientific management, and the assembly line. For a more in-depth discussion of this transition and the role of call centres within it, see Chap. 7.

growth of call centres over the last quarter century has produced notable shifts in the composition of labour forces across geographic regions both distant and diverse. If the factory was once symbolic of work within industrialized countries, call centres have taken their place alongside service occupations such as retail employment, food service, cleaning work, and care giving as one of the more likely forms of employment for new generations of workers.

The figures are striking. At the end of the twentieth century, global employment in these workspaces was swelling by 20% a year and 100,000 jobs were being added every 12 months (Deery & Kinnie, 2004). By 2006, some 15,000 call centres had opened in Europe alone, fuelling the continent's fastest-growing form of employment (Burgess & Connell, 2006; Huws & Paul, 2002). In the first decade of the twenty-first century, one out of every three new jobs in Ireland and the Netherlands was reported to be a call centre position, and in America over 4 million people, close to 3% of the working population, have been estimated to toil in one (Cugusi, 2005; Holman, Batt, & Holtgrewe, 2007). By 2010, call centre employment in the UK also stood at around 3% of the working population (or 950,000 people), and the industry had grown by 250% between 1995 and 2004 (Lloyd, 2013). In Canada, the most recent figures suggest that over half a million full- or part-time staff, or 3.4% of the working population makes a living in one of over 14,000 call centres in the country (Stevens, 2014, p. 59).

Employment growth has not been restricted to the Global North, as the call centre workforce has grown rapidly in Argentina, India, Barbados, South Africa, and many other countries. China has been estimated to have 400,000 workers employed in call centres (Qiu, 2010, p. 84). In the Philippines, 1.2 million people work in call centres, a sector which contributes 8% to the country's gross domestic product (*The Economist*, 2016). What's more, this form of workspace has been established in some of the most peripheral, seemingly disconnected areas of the global economy. Afghanistan, one of the most war-ravaged countries on earth, has a fledgling call centre sector supporting its own growing market for mobile phones: "Taleban call in and the women talk to them," says Zermina, a manager at one of Kabul's call centres, illustrating how the workplace has been translated into the most diverse settings, producing novel compositions of labour wherever it goes (as cited in Doucet, 2007).

This book explores the formation of a new workforce attached to capitalism's expanding communicative requirements. Picking up on the portrait of contemporary labour offered by Virno and other theorists of post-*operaismo* (in English, post-workerism, or autonomist Marxism), I describe this process as one in which language is *put to work* in the call centre.[3] The concept of language put to work designates capital's valourization of the human capacity to communicate through language. As a necessary precondition for this process of valourization, language put to work also references the production of an informational underclass whose purpose is to satisfy the economy's growing dependence on connectivity and communicative exchange with consumers. Borrowing a term from labour researcher Ursula Huws, I see this gendered and racialized class of workers as one part of an emerging and diverse *cybertariat* (Brophy & de Peuter, 2015; Huws, 2003).

While Virno's discussion could be taken to imply a sharp break between the characteristics of labour and value production characterizing Fordism and post-Fordism, the proliferation of call centres in the last quarter century also highlights the uncanny persistence of a world of work we are regularly told is a part of our past rather than our present. This book argues that forms of info-service work such as call centre employment create fatal problems for facile accounts of the end of the factory, the end of Taylorism, the end of disciplined and repetitive labour, the end of exploitation, the end of class, and other prematurely eulogized traits of Fordist capitalism. As a group of call centre workers in Calabria, Italy, put it, the story of call centres is one of new social subjects and also of old forms of exploitation (Cuccomarino & Pezzulli, 2012). The process of language put to work is one in which the working class is being

---

[3] Post-*operaismo* is usually referred to in English as autonomist Marxism. For a more detailed discussion of this tradition, see Chap. 2. The phrase which gives this book its title can be found in the writings of the philosopher Paolo Virno (2003), but it also signals the growing attention on the part of post-*operaismo*'s scholars to the ways in which capitalism has incorporated communicative, linguistic, and affective dimensions of life (see Fumagalli, 2007; Marazzi, 1999; Vercellone, 2007).

reconstituted in a manner that draws on the inherent communicative and relational capacities of populations across the planet.

As Virno's description of the contemporary relationship between labour and communication suggests, the first quality one is struck by when entering a call centre is the unbroken hum and buzz of conversation, of talk and affective connection. Despite long-standing and regularly refreshed predictions regarding the growth of highly skilled, upwardly mobile and intrinsically rewarding "knowledge work," however, the submission of language to the production of value in call centres tends to see the human capacity for relationality reduced to a limited set of allowable utterances, statements, and responses, all of them tailored towards the maximization of communicative productivity.

As Deborah Cameron (2008) has found, the communication produced in call centres tends to conform to what she calls "top-down talk," or interaction that is designed not by the participants themselves but by "superordinate agents" such as consultants or managers. A group of labour activists (Friends of Kolinko & Gurgaon Workers News, 2012) describes this communication as consisting "basically of industrialised mouth movements and Taylorised emotions," generating what Arlie Hochschild (2004, p. 5) called the "unexpected common ground" between the nineteenth-century factory and the twenty-first-century service sector.

Incorporating these insights and drawing on work by the post-workerist theorist Gigi Roggero (2011), I suggest that one of the call centre's defining features is that it tends to be geared towards the production of what we could call *abstract communication*, or communication that is instrumental, homogeneous, measurable, and thereby divorced from the concrete knowledge, abilities, or experience of those who enact it.[4] In this respect, call centres are important workplaces to examine not only because of their prevalence but because the labour relations that characterize them are a potent counter-example to recurring narratives of liberated

---

[4] The concept of abstract communication finds its antecedent in Karl Marx's (1990) discussion of abstract labour in Volume I of *Capital*. For a discussion of abstract and living knowledge, upon which I draw in developing the category of abstract communication in Chap. 4, see Roggero (2011).

knowledge workers, friction-free capitalism, and the growing creativity of labour (Drucker, 1996; Florida, 2002; Gates, Myhrvold, & Rinearson, 1996).

As the story that introduced this book suggests, such celebratory discourse is belied most forcefully by the many outbreaks of labour resistance provoked around the spread of this workspace over the last quarter century. Accordingly, this book's investigation of class formation in call centres begins with the conflicts, collective organizing and counter-subjectivities that have been produced along what the author Simon Head (2003) has called the "digital assembly lines." Moving beyond depictions of call centre labour as either entirely liberated or utterly subordinated, this inquiry explores the development of a resistant, antagonistic perspective among the ranks of an expanding transnational workforce. Materialized in the wide range of resistant practices that are its vernacular, this counter-perspective has signalled, contested, and disrupted the process of class formation unfolding in these workspaces.[5] Seen from this perspective, language put to work is also a process of struggle and the constitution of antagonistic subjectivities.

Communicative Capitalism and the Cybertariat

The point of departure for this study of class formation in call centres is Harry Braverman's classic indictment of labour's exploitation in a capitalist society, *Labor and Monopoly Capital* (Braverman, 1974). Writing at the twilight of Fordism, the American independent scholar detailed the widespread efforts of management to routinize, deskill, and debase the jobs of those performing what he called "mental labour."[6] Braverman's text lambasted the management theory and conservative industrial

---

[5] One could think of these resistant practices as constituting labour's *vernacular*, a culture of defiance that is produced from below in response to the submission of language to value in the call centre. The concept of the vernacular, as collective activity practiced in spite of and against attempts to control and homogenize the diversity of human expression, comes to me by way of the work of the anthropologist James C. Scott (2012).

[6] As a result, for Braverman "[m]ental labour" was reduced "to a repetitive performance of the same small set of functions" (Braverman, 1974, p. 220).

relations research of his day, noting the "apologetic purposes" they furthered in their attempt to reconcile workers with the drudgery of their toil (Braverman, 1974, p. 241). Against popular management thinkers such as Peter Drucker, who announced the rise of a liberated "knowledge worker," and liberal academics such as Daniel Bell, who foresaw growing labour harmony in the coming "post-industrial" society, the Marxist scholar painstakingly documented management's tightening grip over the labour processes of secretaries, clerks, and service workers (Bell, 1973; Drucker, 1996).[7] Far from being eliminated by the advent of new information technologies in the workplace, Braverman argued, through the spread of Taylorism class divisions were steadily being implanted within professions that had once occupied intermediate positions between capital and labour in the workplace hierarchy. In the process, the Marxist scholar concluded, mental labourers were beginning to feel the alienation of the factory as they joined the swelling ranks of the industrial working class. The outcome of this polarization of office work, for Braverman, was the creation of a "large proletariat in a new form" (Braverman, 1974, p. 355).[8]

Braverman's research was an ambitious attempt to investigate the structure of the working class in the United States and the manner in which it had changed during the first half of the twentieth century. Four decades after the publication of *Labor and Monopoly Capital*, the economy and the characteristics of work within it have indeed been transformed dramatically. Having passed away not long after his book's publication, Braverman never witnessed the intensive "informatization" of the workplace and of capitalism more broadly (see Castells, 1996; Schiller, 1999,

---

[7] Like Virno after him, Bell also underscored the central role of communication within labour in post-industrial society: "The fact that individuals now talk to other individuals, rather than interact with a machine, is the fundamental fact about work in the post-industrial society" (1973, p. 163).

[8] Braverman's inquiry into the transformation of labour was extended and shaped after his death by other scholars keen on understanding class dynamics on the factory floor. This research would become the foundation for a Marxist analysis of work known as "labour process" theory (see Burawoy, 1979; Edwards, 1979). Notable in this school is the work of sociologist Michael Burawoy (1979), who pointed out that, far from a simple affair, the securing of profit by owners resulted from diverse combinations of conflict and consent on the shop floor. Examining the way in which the tenuous relationship between management and workers unfolds, or as Burawoy put it, asking why "workers work as hard as they do" (p. xi) became one of the key concerns of this critical tradition.

2007).⁹ With the widely celebrated rise of networked, flexible work environments in telecommunications, high-tech and new media, to many observers his vision of an informational underclass subjected to the disciplinary rhythms of Fordist factory labour seems decidedly anachronistic. For its boosters, the high-technology workplace is now one of "seniors and juniors, not bosses and subordinates," as Peter Drucker (2006) put it. According to this well-rehearsed narrative, class differences and frictions are being irreversibly dissolved by the rise of information technology in the workplace.

Despite the dominance of celebratory discourse lauding the digital workplace as "cool, creative and egalitarian" (see Gill, 2002; Ross, 2004a), I argue in this book that Braverman's disquieting vision is altogether contemporary—albeit in a context significantly different from the one in which he wrote. Whereas he saw his era as one of monopoly capitalism, this book links the prodigious expansion of call centres over the last quarter century to the rise of a political, economic, and discursive regime the American political theorist Jodi Dean calls *communicative capitalism* (see Dean, 2009, 2010, 2012).

Dean uses the term "communicative capitalism" to designate a nascent twenty-first-century economic order that increasingly incorporates, depends upon, and justifies itself through the proliferation of "communicative access and opportunity" (Dean, 2009, p. 17). Adapting her concept, I use the term "communicative capitalism" to not only reference the economy's most communicative sectors (including telecommunications, new media, the cultural industries, advertising/public relations, and others) but also and especially to signal the growing *communicativity* of companies across the broader economy. This communicativity is produced by the increasing imperative to seek out and provide for regular informational exchange with consumers.¹⁰

---

⁹ Braverman's work foreshadows this transformation however: "In recent years, motion-time study (...) have had their logic and arithmetic assigned to computers, so that the time allowance for various job elements is worked out by the computer on the basis of standard data, perhaps supplemented for time study observations" (1974, p. 123).

¹⁰ For a more detailed discussion of communicative capitalism, see Chap. 2.

Call centres play a vital role in this scenario. An exploration of the social relations being forged inside these workspaces, where employees are plugged into digital networks and delegated the task of mediating capital's relationship with its customers, clearly reveals the highly unequal terms upon which subjects participate in what Drucker liked to call the "knowledge society" (2001, para. 5). Working in a call centre tends to include a well-established mix of low wages, high stress, gender inequity, precarious employment, disciplinary management, draining emotional labour, and pervasive electronic surveillance.[11] Labour researcher Guy Standing describes them as "ubiquitous, a sinister symbol of globalisation, electronic life and alienated labour" (2011, p. 16). Like many jobs attached to the spread of information technology, call centre work has not lived up to the rosy portraits that have been served up uninterruptedly for half a century by the sociologists, futurists, and management gurus for whom Braverman reserved his venom.

While these workspaces have been likened to everything from battery farms to Roman slave galleons, it is comparisons to the factory and its emblematic technology, the assembly line, which dominate critical discussion of call centres. By the late 1990s, Kim Moody of the rank-and-file labour publication *Labor Notes* maintained that the call centre was "becoming for some industries what the sweatshop is to garments and electronics" (Moody, 1999, p. 17). In an extensive study of the Taylorization of intellectual work in what he called the "new ruthless economy," Simon Head drew a direct line between call centres, scientific management, and the Fordist factory (Head, 2003, p. 100).[12] Labour process researchers Phil Taylor and Peter Bain named their classic investigation of scientific management in the call centre after a memorable description given by an employee, who suggested the experience was akin to having "an assembly line in the head" (Taylor & Bain, 1999). There can be little question that these workspaces are an uncanny embodiment

---

[11] For a summary of this research, see Chap. 2.
[12] This fact is also noted by Thomas Hastings, who notes of the call centres he studied in Scotland: "the pacing and direction of work was technically controlled across the majority of the cases—as in a factory production line—and this heavily impacted upon the autonomy of agents within each centre" (Hastings, 2011, p. 138).

of Braverman's predicted extension of the factory, its rhythms, and its class divisions into the "post-industrial" workplace.

Drawing inspiration from Braverman's analysis, my articulation of language put to work references a process of proletarianization, not professionalization. Against attempts by some management scholars and most call centre employers to cast call centre workers as "knowledge workers" who mostly see themselves as professionals and identify with the goals of management, I suggest that the global call centre workforce is part of an emergent and diverse class subject Ursula Huws has dubbed the cybertariat.[13] Toiling at the lower reaches of what political economist Dwayne Winseck calls the "network media industries" (2011), the cybertariat assembles the technology, organizes the information, tends the communication, delivers the products, maintains the consumer relationships, offers the support, and executes the sales communicative capitalism requires in order to secure its profits. A broad overview of the cybertariat would include warehouse sorters for e-commerce companies such as Amazon; assembly workers for outsourced electronics manufacturers like Foxconn; digital microtaskers hired by virtual temp firms such as Mechanical Turk, oDesk, and Fancy Hands; outsourced commercial content moderators for social media companies such as Facebook; journalists producing copy determined by algorithms for online content farms; retail employees at Apple Stores and wireless carrier storefront operations; data entry workers in Nepal, Barbados, or Brazil; delivery workers at UPS or FedEx, and many millions of others upon whose labour communicative capitalism depends daily, yet remunerates inadequately and sometimes not at all. While strikingly diverse in its composition, the cybertariat's labour processes tend to be mediated by information technology, routinized, disciplinary, and almost entirely devoid of the passion and autonomy one hears so much about in descriptions of work in the creative industries.

Noting the ascendance of this new labouring subject at the end of the twentieth century, Huws suggested in her analysis of the reorganization of work via information technology that a new cybertariat was "in the

---

[13] For a discussion of studies seeking to connect call centre work to the growth of "knowledge work" and post-industrialism, see Chap. 2.

making" (2003, p. 176). The category of the cybertariat was clearly opposed to neoliberal narratives of the IT-enabled end of class, but it also addressed some of the limitations of Braverman's own analysis. Through her research, Huws has provided a richer portrait of the informational underclass, paying particular attention to its global, gendered, and racialized composition.[14] Building upon her work, this book investigates the making of the global call centre workforce from a different perspective, offering a more sustained analysis of the *conflicts* generated within this process of class formation. The call centre cybertariat, as E.P. Thompson would have suggested, has without a doubt been "present at its own making," and has frequently acted to subvert the process. Taking call centres on three continents as my focus, I therefore investigate the making of the cybertariat as a *contested* process, one that is producing new subjectivities and new forms of collective organization within a sector that carries out an increasingly crucial set of functions within the capitalist economy.

Communication from Below

Braverman's study offers a sobering portrait of capital's subjugation of labour, but it notoriously ignores the question of how and when the latter resists. In explaining this analytical choice, the independent scholar maintained he was most interested in revealing the objective, technical qualities of the relationship between labour and capital (Braverman, 1974, p. 18). This approach allowed him to more comprehensively illuminate the techniques through which employers seek to subordinate labour (including the appropriation of workers' knowledge, the separation of conception from execution, and the application of monitoring and measurement), yet it necessarily dimmed the lights on the subjective, political dimension of "mental labour"—its resistances, refusals, and rebellions in the face of workplace transformation from above. "We are here omitting for the moment," Braverman acknowledged, "the fact that workers are

---

[14] This project has continued in the pages of the journal Huws edits, *Work Organisation, Labour and Globalisation*.

rebellious, and that the average pace of production is decided in a practice which largely assumes the form of a struggle, whether organized or not" (1974, p. 124). Labour's resistant vernacular is not permitted to surface in this story of class formation.[15]

In an uncharacteristic moment of his book, however, Braverman allows himself to reflect on the conflict produced by workers in the production process. Here he likens labour resistance to a "subterranean stream," which, he says, will emerge "when employment conditions permit, or when the capitalist drive for a greater intensity of labor oversteps the bounds of physical or mental capacity." Resistance, Braverman warns, is endemic to workers under capitalism. Their insubordination "renews itself in new generations, expresses itself in the unbounded cynicism and revulsion which large numbers of workers feel about their work, and comes to the fore repeatedly as a social issue demanding solution" (Braverman, 1974, p. 104). If management is compelled to ceaselessly reorganize and intensify the labour process to better exploit the communicative powers of its white-collar workforce, Braverman's threatening passage implies, the latter will surely generate its own varieties of organization.

This book locates the subterranean stream of labour resistance described by Braverman, plots the course of its diverse manifestations in the call centre, and engages with its protagonists. In privileging labour's agency and subjectivity as a means to illuminate the making of the call centre labour force, I draw on a different set of political and epistemological coordinates than those developed by the labour process tradition Braverman gave rise to. The approach adopted in the pages that follow takes its cue from a sentiment expressed five decades ago by the Italian theorist of *operaismo*, Mario Tronti, who in the 1966 text *Operai e Capitale* provocatively asserted that there was "no class without class struggle" (2005, p. 11).[16] For Tronti, the line separating labour and capital comes

---

[15] As Braverman (1974, pp. 26–27) readily admits, "this is a book about the working class as a class *in itself*, not as a class *for itself*."

[16] "Post-*operaismo*" names the incarnation of the tradition that emerged after the political repression of the Italian extra-parliamentary left at the end of the 1970s. Following this break, key figures within operaismo entered into a dialogue with French post-structuralism and the political economy

into the sharpest relief in the surfacing of the former's insubordination and search for autonomy, and to these moments he and other workerists accorded both analytic and political priority.[17] Class is not only an objective category, and it is certainly not a static social relationship, the Italian communist maintained. Rather, the working class is a subjective force, one that regularly arises against and provokes transformations within its antagonist. Locating the subterranean stream of labour's non-compliance and insubordination produces a different picture of class formation, one that foregrounds workers' capacity to oppose, frustrate, and transform the conditions they encounter in the contemporary workplace. What follows is a study of the cybertariat as seen through the "arts of resistance" (Scott, 1990) it deploys in the call centre.

Research undertaken for this book reveals the full extent to which the putting to work of language in call centres has been an uncertain and often conflictual process. Call centre workers have been the protagonists of collective bargaining through unions, transnational organizing drives, walkouts, demonstrations, workplace occupations, hunger strikes, "stand-up" strikes, and more subterranean forms of resistance, including digital sabotage, cheating, loafing, stealing, and quitting. In those moments when call centre workers have resisted their subjection in these high-technology workspaces, an opposition between two kinds of communication becomes apparent—that which is structured from above and that which is extended outward horizontally, among workers, from below.

---

of the French Regulation School, focusing increasingly on the role of language and communication in productive processes as well as emergence of new forms of resistance within them.

[17] According to this perspective, one that has been picked up by some of the more notable interpreters of Karl Marx in the informational era, classes come into being along with the struggles that produce them. Sergio Bologna (2014, para. 13) describes this approach to class analysis: "For the workerists ... the working class was an unexplored universe, extremely differentiated and complex, or, better, the point of arrival of a very long process, fraught with obstacles, in the course of which labor-power became aware of its own role and its own strength, and appeared on the scene of society as a protagonist, not as an appendage of the system of capitalist production." In other words, these scholars saw class struggle as completely immanent to class formation. In another formulation, Nick Dyer-Witheford suggests that "[i]nsofar as workers, rather than being organized by capital, struggle against it, they constitute *the working* class" (1999, p. 66). Jodi Dean (2012, p. 72) proposes a similar understanding: "The proletarian is not just the worker; the proletarian is the worker radicalized, the worker politicized."

An Argentine collective of students, researchers, and professors engaged with grass-roots social movements[18] captures this conflict evocatively in their account of an inquiry into the power relations characterizing a call centre in Rosario. Echoing Deborah Cameron's description of "top-down talk" (2008), the *Cátedra Experimental* (2007a, p. 133) researchers found that the communication between call centre employees and customers on the other end of the phone produced a form of linguistic interaction that is "linked to the economic interests of the firm," where "each word is emitted at high speed, mechanically," and "[f]ailure to achieve the stated objective will mean firing or immediate sanctions."

The second kind of communication encountered by the collective operated both within and beyond the logic of the firm, however. Developed among workers, this horizontal form of sociality is a "subjective operation capable of constructing a terrain of encounter, affect, and common endeavors on the basis of the workplace instability, control, and fragmentation." Whereas the production of standardized, abstract communication among employees and customers "provokes intense ill-feeling, general isolation, and links to a sinister logic of the firm," the communication that extends horizontally among workers is, in the estimation of the Argentine collective, a "tool for collective construction" (*Cátedra Experimental sobre Producción de Subjetividad*, 2007a, p. 135). It is what members of the German labour activist group Call Center Offensive describe as "communication without management and telephones" (as cited in Kolinko, 2002, section 6.3.c., para. 10).

This opposition between employers and employees has manifested in varying intensities, in different locations, and at different times, to be sure. In countless call centres, the subterranean stream alluded to by Braverman never surfaces, remaining invisible to researchers, labour organizers, and management. Regardless of whether this conflictuality becomes overt or stays below the surface, I argue it is a constitutive, ever-present feature of twenty-first-century call centres. If the working class is being reconstituted

---

[18] The *Cátedra Experimental sobre Producción de Subjetividad*, The Experimental Chair on the Production of Subjectivity, or, more recently, the Experimental University (2007b, para. 1). For a discussion of the worker inquiry carried out by the Cátedra Experimental into call centre labour in Rosario, see Chap. 2.

in these workspaces, it is also reconstituting itself in the process. The relationship between these two interlinked but opposed tendencies provides this book's entry point in describing the social relations characterizing this highly communicative form of labour.

The Structure of the Book

The book is divided into seven chapters. Chapter 2 positions the call centre within the emergence of communicative capitalism. Connecting the explosion of these workspaces to what I describe as the growing communicativity of firms across the economy, the chapter assesses the two main scholarly traditions in the analysis of a new workforce. While liberal-democratic and management scholars of "knowledge work" have produced apologetic portraits of engaged call centre workers in friction-free informational workplaces, Marxist labour process scholars have tended to serve up the dispiriting image of a subjugated workforce in return. I conclude the chapter by proposing an alternate approach to call centre labour, drawing upon theories of resistance to constituted forms of power—especially in the workplace. The theoretical tendency of post-*operaismo* that has established itself in the period since Tronti's influential text offers a useful tradition of inquiry in this respect and makes an important contribution to this book's perspective. Approaching this new workforce from the perspective of resistance, I argue, requires engagement with a literature that has mostly been ignored in academic studies of call centre work: the writings of call centre workers, labour activists, and union organizers in the sector. This book owes a great deal to the insightful inquiries into call centre work produced in Europe, Latin America, and South Asia in the context of labour/scholar/activist collectives such as Colectivo Situaciones, Cátedra Experimental sobre Producción de Subjetividad, Kolinko, Gruppo d'Inchiesta sulla Precarietà e il Comune, and Gurgaon Workers News. A method that traverses workplace composition and struggles, I argue, is best situated to outline the often-scathing view of the global call centre industry that has developed from the perspective of its employees.

Chapter 3 explores the rich terrain that is opened up to an approach to call centre labour that begins with resistance by surveying the many manifestations of workplace conflict surfacing within global call centres today. The chapter provides a composite portrait of labour's insubordination in the call centre, beginning from the least perceptible manifestations of disengagement and progressing towards more overt instances of labour conflict. From the refusal of work to traditional union drives, from cross-border organizing to innovative forms of sabotage through to flexible strikes, the chapter argues that labour resistance and collective organization have indelibly marked the call centre's early history. This compendium of the call centre workforce's arts of resistance offers a sense of the tremendously innovative ways in which the process of class formation unfolding in these workspaces has been met with recalcitrance, refusal, and occasionally outright rebellion by its subjects. Through the chapter I uphold the utility of informal kinds of refusal such as quitting, slacking, and emotional detachment among the workforce, suggesting that these can and have become the foundation for more coordinated, formal, and threatening varieties of labour organization in the call centre.

Chapter 4 explores the formation of the call centre workforce, its entry into the workplaces of communicative capitalism, and its encounter with the established yet struggling trade union movement. The twin backdrops for this account of how language was put to work in call centres during the 1990s and 2000s are Atlantic Canada and Ireland, regions divided by an ocean but united in their status as signature cases of state-sponsored informational development. In both regions a highly educated, multilingual workforce was introduced to working with a headset in the call centres that proliferated through newly wired urban centres. By zeroing in on the case of Aliant call centre workers in the province of New Brunswick, I relate how the lively intelligences and communicative capacities of this new workforce were compressed and reformatted into what I call *abstract communication*. Braverman's vision of the degradation of mental labour became the lived experience of employees in the customer relations departments of the Atlantic Canadian wireless sector, where management's subjection of workers to routinization, increasingly intrusive forms of monitoring, and threats of labour outsourcing eventually produced outbreaks of workplace unrest and labour organizing through incumbent trade unions. The cases in this chapter are not auspicious ones for the collective organization of the cybertariat, however, illustrating how even in-house, unionized call centre workers remain vulnerable to regional and global outsourcing strategies of their employers (Doellgast, 2012). This weakness appears to derive at least in part from the defensive organizing postures adopted by the trade unions representing these workers, raising the question of whether the established union movement in its present form is an adequate vehicle for the collective organization of the cybertariat.

Tracking the flow of outsourced work across borders and into the growing basin of precarious, non-unionized, and low-wage employment, Chap. 5 looks at how the cybertariat is confronting communicative capitalism's formidable powers of mobility. The chapter's analysis of the relationship between the globalization of customer relations and the transnationalization of worker resistance opens with an overview of the trends shaping the transnational portion of the call centre industry, or what I refer to as *global call centre capital*. The "Calling for Change" campaign launched in 2008 by the upstart New Zealand union Unite in cooperation with the Australian National Union of Workers is a particularly compelling example of how capital flight can generate collective organization and conflicts in its wake. Crossing the Tasman Sea to pursue call centres outsourced from Australia, the campaign utilized a medley of tactics including brand tarnishing, picketing, wildcat, and even hunger strikes. The organizing arising at the other end of the outsourcing from Australia is especially significant, I argue, as its protagonists come from sectors of New Zealand's workforce that are well outside those traditionally represented by the country's labour movement, including women, teenagers, migrant workers, and indigenous populations. As such the case not only offers insights into the feminization and racialization of the cybertariat but also into its potential to animate a labour transnationalism that can produce a counter-force to the mobility of global capital's most communicative sectors.

Chapter 6 pushes our attention beyond the margins of the established labour movement by recounting a case of call centre worker self-organization. Generated independently of, and mostly in opposition to, the consolidated trade union movement in Italy, the Collettivo Precari Atesia, a shop-floor collective formed in Europe's largest call centre in Rome, is an example of an organizational form developed within the widely noted crisis of the established labour movement. During the first half of the 2000s, Atesia represented the extreme edge of insecure employment in the sector, with over 4000 operators at the company working on a seemingly endless series of freelance contracts. While subjected to a form of masked permanent employment, workers were denied benefits, the right to unionize or to strike, paid holidays, sick days, or maternity leave. During this time, representatives for the three major Italian unions signed collective agreements on their behalf, deals that enshrined the insecure contractual status and woefully inadequate labour conditions of workers at the call centre. The Collettivo was formed in 2005, and over the next two years workers at Atesia employed digital sabotage, a series of "flexible" strikes, and a variety of escalating tactics in a bid to regularize their employment status. Like the Association of Call Centre Workers in Turkey, the activities of the Collettivo are an example of the labour conflict and organization that can occur outside established trade unionism, a strain of collective organization of which Italy has a rich tradition. Reflecting upon the intersection between autonomous forms of labour organization and call centre work, the chapter closes with a discussion of the achievements and limitations of the Collettivo's labour organizing at Atesia and within the Italian context.

Chapter 7 reflects on the significance of the cases explored for the theorization of call centre labour, the practice of call centre organizing, and the envisioning of call centre alternatives. Through a discussion of these cases, I argue that the rise of the cybertariat is part of the reformatting of class within the growing communicativity of capitalism, and that this mutation is both contested and open-ended in its development. Here I suggest that the distinctive traits of the call centre labour force are produced out of the *real subsumption of immaterial labour*, a process through which firms have revolutionized their quotidian, interpersonal communication with consumers. I adopt immaterial labour as a counter-concept to that of "knowledge work" developed in the latter half of the twentieth century by liberal-democratic scholars.[19] The chapter suggests that theories of immaterial labour can help us understand the rise of the global call centre workforce, but also that an investigation of labour struggles in call centres offers an equally important opportunity to intervene within and refine contemporary discussions of immaterial labour. The striking persistence of the logic of the factory within and across a range of jobs that sustain the network media industries, I maintain, underscores how these elements are much more than simply residual features of a bygone regime of accumulation, but rather a vital component of the contemporary composition of labour in capitalism's most communicative sectors. Situating call centre labour within this broader scenario, I move on to offer some strategic advice to organizers, highlighting three emergent axes in the composition of call centre work that affect and could propel the organization of workers in the sector—*feminization, precarity, and mobility.*

The book concludes by envisaging call centre alternatives. Here I critique "high-commitment" or "high-involvement" models of work organization that have been discussed by industrial relations and management scholars as a feel-good, profit-friendly option for mitigating the routinized and disciplinary forms of Taylorist management marking the call centre labour process. Against such models and their implicit acceptance that the only way we might organize communicative labour is from above, through the market, and via the wage relation, I suggest that one of the tasks of radical critique and labour activism is to imagine different and more liberatory alternatives to the organization of call centre work. This scenario of "unmaking" of the global call centre workforce as it is presently constituted would include the development of call centres that are subtracted from the market, with socially progressive applications (including health care, welfare, and rebuilding the demos), and that are organized and controlled democratically by those who work within them. There are many examples of socially progressive applications of the call centre, as

---

[19] The work of Vincent Mosco and Catherine McKercher (2008) remains a significant exception to this tradition in that while retaining the terms "knowledge work" and "information society" it also sees labour relations as conflictual, characterized by capital on one side and labour on the other.

well as both historical and contemporary examples of workers running the phone lines without bosses, whether through collectives, cooperatives, or during labour occupations. Acknowledging these examples, circulating them, and discussing how they could be adapted and re-proposed should the opportunity arise (and thanks to the volatility of global call centres these opportunities most certainly do from time to time), I argue, should become part of a broader discussion around how to transform a form of work that overwhelmingly produces low wages, unfulfilling jobs, and unstable employment.

"If It Is a Living Thing, Then It Will Grow"

This book responds to dominant discourse within analyses of the labour that sustains capitalism's most communicative sectors. One of the main themes of such discourse is that the rise of informational work and workplaces heralds a decline of labour as a conflictual force within the "information" or "knowledge" society. In support of this position liberal scholars, pundits, and captains of industry point to the great difficulties established trade unions have faced in seeking to adapt to wired workplaces at a time when union density rates are dropping, public attitudes towards labour organizations seem to be hardening, and even workers—especially in capitalism's most connected sectors—often appear to feel that trade unions are a retrograde and undesirable presence at work. Sociologist Manuel Castells expressed this position succinctly when he mused that, amid transition to what he calls the network society, the labour movement seems "historically superseded" (1997, p. 360).

For exponents of this position the union movement's current crisis is often explained by the alleged blurring of boundaries between employers and workers in the newly humane, knowledge-intensive workplace. An exemplary articulation of this point was offered by *The Economist* (2001, p. 16), when it claimed (just before the dotcom collapse incinerated the dreams of thousands of workers) that since "the means of production is knowledge, which is owned by knowledge workers and is highly portable," the contemporary workplace is one where "knowledge workers provide 'capital' just as much as does the provider of money. The two are dependent on each other. This makes the knowledge worker an equal—an associate or a partner."

With workers reduced to the status of "human capital" in management literature, economic theory and the mainstream media, lines of class division have become subject to a concerted effort of erasure in the high-tech workplace. As we shall see, even within some of the more critically oriented studies of call centre work labour scholars speak of how the subjectivities of the digital workforce have been brought into the fold of managerial culture and rendered compliant through informal workplace cultures, workforce "participation," and "teamwork."[20] This analysis undoubtedly comforts captains of communicative industry such as Jeff Bezos, who has stated that at Amazon they "don't believe in unions, because everybody is an owner" (as cited in Ross, 2004b, p. 204). Such discourse—one which tirelessly announces the end of labour exploitation, conflict, and the very conditions of possibility for collective organization—is described by the French economists Gerard Duménil and Dominic Lévy as the "everyone's a capitalist" story, and it lies at the very heart of neoliberalism's imaginary (2004, p. 16).[21]

Contrary to this position, the cases described in this book suggest that the conditions for workplace conflict and collective organization are not melting away simply because established trade unions are facing a potentially terminal crisis. Expanding on this point, I argue that to see the established trade union and the highly codified variant of labour relations handed down to us from Fordism as the ultimate horizon of collective organization for the cybertariat is a mistake that plays into the discourse just described. The error is replicated within studies of call centres when scholars discuss established trade unionism as if it exhausted all

---

[20] See the discussion of labour process research on the call centre in Chap. 2.
[21] As the labour activists associated with Kolinko and Gurgaon Workers suggested in 2012, these narratives "formed part of the general propaganda proclaiming the 'end of the working class', which has prevailed since the 1980s—while at the same time concentrating and 'proletarianising' large sections of previously 'white collar' workers under one roof and subjecting them to a Taylorised 'factory mode' of production. Instead of individualising neoliberal subjects, call centres simply extended the industrial system into the office world and collectivised a section of the working class, such as bank clerks or administrators, who previously saw themselves as 'educated employees'. As a labour intensive and mobile industry, call centres quickly combined labour in different parts of the globe" (para. 1).

possibilities for organized resistance on the part of workers. To the contrary, as the pages that follow amply relate, a wide variety of forms of resistance and collective organization are being enacted in these workplaces, including conventional trade union activity, trade union renewal driven from below, innovations in labour struggles developed at the margins of the labour movement, and even forms of collective organization forged by workers operating outside of the established trade union movement altogether.[22]

The point of this book is not to draw lines of conflict where none exist, or much less to locate a labouring subject that—like the male industrial worker of twentieth-century fame—can shoulder the revolutionary hopes of radical scholars. As I suggest in the conclusion, call centre workers are just one part of a vast workforce that has been summoned via the wage in order to service capital's intensifying communicative requirements, and labour conflicts have been set off in many, if not most, of these sectors. However, as labour scholars Julie Guard, Mercedes Steedman, and Jorge García-Orgales (2007) have pointed out in the Canadian context, the call centre is nonetheless a vital testing ground for labour movements and their ability to adapt and reorganize within a communicative economy. In the widespread disenchantment with hyper-Taylorized work and in the experimentation with new forms of collective organization, we may find the contours of a twenty-first-century labour movement, one that moves with great ease both within and beyond the high-tech workplaces of communicative capitalism. Such a movement, as this book details, is sorely needed. "If it is a living thing," as Tronti (2005, p. 11) pointed out almost five decades ago in a very different context, "then it will grow."

---

[22] One might add here that when established trade unions sign contracts enshrining insecure employment against the wishes of the workers they represent, or neglect their responsibility to organize unorganized workers, or support punishing austerity programs (all examples encountered in the research undertaken for this book), then the history of past experiences "serves us so that we may liberate ourselves from them" (Tronti, 2005, p. 11).

References

Bell, D. (1973). *The coming of post-industrial society: A venture in social forecasting*. New York, NY: Basic Books.
Bologna, S. (2014, December 15). Workerism beyond Fordism: On the lineage of Italian workerism. *Viewpoint Magazine*. Retrieved from https://viewpointmag.com/2014/12/15/workerism-beyond-fordism-on-the-lineage-of-italian-workerism/
Braverman, H. (1974). *Labor and monopoly capital: The degradation of work in the twentieth century*. New York: Monthly Review Press.
Brophy, E., & de Peuter, G. (2015). Communicative capitalism and the smartphone cybertariat. In A. Herman, J. Hadlaw, & T. Swiss (Eds.), *Theories of the mobile internet: Materialities and imaginaries* (pp. 60–84). New York, NY: Routledge.
Burawoy, M. (1979). *Manufacturing consent: Changes in the labor process under monopoly capitalism*. Chicago, IL: University of Chicago Press.
Burgess, J., & Connell, J. (Eds.). (2006). *Developments in the call centre industry: Analysis, changes and challenges*. New York, NY: Routledge.
Cameron, D. (2008). Talk from the top down. *Language & Communication, 28* (2), 143–155.
Castells, M. (1996). *The rise of the network society*. Cambridge, MA: Blackwell Publishers.
Castells, M. (1997). *The power of identity*. Malden, MA: Blackwell.
Cátedra Experimental sobre Producción de Subjetividad. (2007a). Call centre: The art of virtual control. *ephemera: theory and politics in organization, 7*(1), 133–138.
Cátedra Experimental sobre Producción de Subjetividad. (2007b). *From knowledge of self-management to the self-management of knowledge*. Retrieved from http://eipcp.net/transversal/0707/catedraexperimental/en
Cuccomarino, C., & Pezzulli, F. M. (2012, December 13). Tra mirafiori e Bangalore: L'inchiesta politica nei call center calabresi. *Il Manifesto*, pp. 8–9.
Cugusi, C. (2005). *Call center: Gli schiavi elettronici della New Economy*. Genoa, Italy: Fratelli Frilli Editori.
Dean, J. (2009). *Democracy and other neoliberal fantasies: Communicative capitalism and left politics*. Durham, NC: Duke University Press.
Dean, J. (2010). *Blog theory: Feedback and capture in the circuits of drive*. Cambridge, MA: Polity.
Dean, J. (2012). *The communist horizon*. London, UK: Verso Books.

Deery, S., & Kinnie, N. (2004). *Call centres and human resource management: A cross-national perspective*. Houndmills, UK/New York, NY: Palgrave Macmillan.
Doellgast, V. (2012). *Disintegrating democracy at work: Labor unions and the future of good jobs in the service economy*. Ithaca, NY: ILR Press.
Doucet, L. (2007, November 14). Upwardly mobile Afghanistan. *BBC News*.
Drucker, P. (1996). *Landmarks of tomorrow: A report on the new 'post-modern' world*. New Brunswick, NJ: Transaction Publishers.
Drucker, P. (2006). Knowledge workers need a new type of organization. *The Economist*, *378*, 9.
Duménil, G., & Lévy, D. (2004). *Capital resurgent: Roots of the neoliberal revolution*. Cambridge, MA: Harvard University Press.
Dyer-Witheford, N. (1999). *Cyber-Marx: Cycles and circuits of struggle in high-technology capitalism*. Urbana, IL: University of Illinois Press.
Edwards, R. (1979). *Contested terrain: The transformation of the workplace in the twentieth century*. New York, NY: Basic Books.
Florida, R. L. (2002). *The rise of the creative class: And how it's transforming work, leisure, community and everyday life*. New York, NY: Basic Books.
Fumagalli, A. (2007). *Bioeconomia e Capitalismo Cognitivo: Verso un Nuovo Paradigma di Accumulazione*. Rome, Italy: Carocci.
Gates, B., Myhrvold, N., & Rinearson, P. (1996). *The road ahead*. New York, NY: Penguin.
Gill, R. (2002). Cool, creative and egalitarian? Exploring gender in project-based new media work in Europe. *Information, Communication & Society*, *5*(1), 70–89.
Guard, J., Steedman, M., & García-Orgales, J. (2007). Organizing the electronic sweatshop: Rank-and-file participation in Canada's steel union. *Labor: Studies in Working-Class History of the Americas*, *4*(3), 9–31.
Gülsen, E. (2015). Resistance against the new working practices in the service sector in Turkey. In U. Schuerkens (Ed.), *Global management, local resistances: Theoretical discussion and empirical case studies* (pp. 135–148). New York, NY: Routledge.
Gurgaon Workers News. (2012). *GurgaonWorkersNews no.9/52*. Retrieved from https://gurgaonworkersnews.wordpress.com/gurgaonworkersnews-no-952/
Hastings, T. (2011). *A job worth doing? Reinterpreting control, resistance and everyday forms of coping with call centre work in Glasgow* (Unpublished PhD). University of Glasgow, Glasgow, UK.

Head, S. (2003). *The new ruthless economy: Work and power in the digital age*. Oxford, UK: Oxford University Press.

Hochschild, A. R. (2004). *The managed heart: Commercialization of human feeling*. Berkeley, CA: University of California Press.

Holman, D., Batt, R. & Holtgrewe, U. (2007). *The global call centre report: International perspectives on management and employment*. Retrieved from http://www.ilr.cornell.edu.proxy.lib.sfu.ca/globalcallcenter/upload/GCC-Intl-REpt-US-Version.pdf

Huws, U. (2003). Who's waiting? The contestation of time. In U. Huws (Ed.), *The making of a cybertariat: Virtual work in a real world* (pp. 177–186). New York, NY: Monthly Review Press.

Huws, U., & Paul, J. (2002). *How can we help? Good practice in call-centre employment*. Retrieved from http://www-it.fmi.uni-sofia.bg/TOSCA/pub/leaflet/Tosca_Book_text.pdf;

Kolinko. (2002). *Hotlines: Call centre, inquiry, communism*. Retrieved from http://www.nadir.org/nadir/initiativ/kolinko/lebuk/e_lebuk.htm

Lloyd, A. (2013). *Labour markets and identity on the post-industrial assembly line*. Burlington, VT: Ashgate.

Marazzi, C. (1999). *l posto dei calzini: La svolta linguistica dell'economia e i suoi effetti sulla politica*. Turin, Italy: Bollati Borlinghieri.

Marx, K. (1990). *Capital: Volume 1*. London, UK: Penguin.

McNally, D. (2011). *Global slump: The economics and politics of crisis and resistance*. Winnipeg, MB: Fernwood.

Moody, K. (1999). *Bell Canada outsources operator jobs to U.S. firm*. Retrieved from http://www.labornotes.org/1999/02/bell-canada-outsources-operator-jobs-us-firm

Mosco, V., & McKercher, C. (2008). *The laboring of communication: Will knowledge workers of the world unite?* Lanham, MD: Lexington Books.

Qiu, J. L. (2010). Network labour and non-elite knowledge workers in China. *Work Organisation, Labour & Globalisation, 4*(2), 80–95.

Roggero, G. (2011). *The production of living knowledge: Crisis of the university and transformation of labour in Europe and North America* [Produzione del sapere vivo.] (E. Brophy, Trans.). Philadelphia, PA: Temple University Press.

Ross, A. (2004a). *Low pay, high profile: The global push for fair labor*. New York, NY: New Press.

Ross, A. (2004b). *No-collar: The humane workplace and its hidden costs*. Philadelphia, PA: Temple University Press.

Schiller, D. (1999). *Digital capitalism: Networking the global market system*. Cambridge, MA: MIT Press.
Schiller, D. (2007). *How to think about information*. Urbana, IL: University of Illinois Press.
Scott, J. (1990). *Domination and the arts of resistance: Hidden transcripts*. New Haven, CT: Yale University Press.
Scott, J. (2012). *Two cheers for anarchism: Six easy pieces on autonomy, dignity, and meaningful work and play*. Princeton, NJ: Princeton University Press.
Standing, G. (2011). *The precariat: The new dangerous class*. London, UK: Bloomsbury Academic.
Stevens, A. (2014). *Call centers and the global division of labor: A political economy of post-industrial employment and union organizing*. New York, NY: Routledge/Taylor & Francis Group.
Taylor, P., & Bain, P. (1999). 'An assembly line in the head': Work and employee relations in the call centre. *Industrial Relations Journal, 30*(2), 101–117.
The Economist. (2001). Will the corporation survive? *The Economist, 360*, 16.
The Economist. (2016). Call centres: The end of the line. *The Economist, 418 (8975)*, 54–55.
Tronti, M. (2005). *Operai e capitale*. Rome, Italy: DeriveApprodi.
Vercellone, C. (2007). From formal subsumption to general intellect: Elements for a Marxist reading of the theory of cognitive capitalism. *Historical Materialism, 15*(1), 13–36.
Virno, P. (2001). Lavoro e linguaggio. In U. Fadini & A. Zanini (Eds.), *Lessico Postfordista: Dizionario delle Idee e della Mutazione* (pp. 181–185). Milan, Italy: Feltrinelli.
Virno, P. (2003). *A grammar of the multitude: For an analysis of contemporary forms of life*. Cambridge, MA: Semiotext(e).
Winseck, D. (2011). The political economies of media and the transformation of the global media industries. In D. Winseck & D. Y. Jin (Eds.), *The political economies of media* (pp. 3–48). London, UK: Bloomsbury Academic.

2

Communicative Capitalism and Call Centre Labour

This chapter connects the striking expansion of call centres to the emergence of communicative capitalism, a nascent political-economic order described by the American political theorist Jodi Dean. Dean uses the concept of communicative capitalism to reference the process by which economic relations have increasingly come to incorporate, depend upon, and be legitimated through the spread of "communicative access and opportunity" (Dean, 2009, p. 17). I argue that the global proliferation of call centre employment over the last quarter century illuminates the kind of communicative labour that is required in order to sustain the formation Dean describes.

While business and management-friendly scholars have sought to depict call centre agents as professionalized "knowledge workers" brought into being at the intersection of markets and information technology, labour process theories have responded by detailing the subordination and exploitation of call centre labour. In opposition to the former tradition of scholarship and building upon the latter, this book describes the making of an informational underclass within call centres as a contested and open-ended

© The Author(s) 2017
E. Brophy, *Language Put to Work*, Dynamics of Virtual Work,
DOI 10.1057/978-1-349-95244-1_2

process in which language, communication, and affect are put to work for the production of profit. To prepare the ground for my survey of the resistance and conflicts arising within this process of language put to work, I review these two traditions of scholarly research on call centres and conclude the chapter by proposing an alternate approach that begins from the resistant practices and perspectives of those employed in these workspaces.

* * *

Jodi Dean has described the fusion between the discourse of democracy and the practice of communication at the heart of capitalism's emergent symbolic order (2009, 2010, 2012). Within this consolidating imaginary, Dean underscores how the values of "access, inclusion, discussion and participation" (2009, p. 23) have progressively become merged with ideas of free markets, corporate actors, and commodified communication. Whether it is through burgeoning social media platforms, endless blogroll, or proliferating wireless networks, offering us the possibility to express ourselves and get in touch via digital media has become a key plank of neoliberalism's promise. Contrary to the late twentieth-century hopes nurtured by media theorists on the left, however, the diffusion of communication technology in daily life has done little to halt the growth of economic disparity and a lot to expand market relationships and their attendant inequities. Never mind whether or not our tweets or status updates ever reach their mark, register, or provoke a response from those in power, Dean suggests—what counts is that we have been given the opportunity to send them. Among the effects of communicative capitalism, Dean argues, are growing economic dispossession, a restriction of meaningful political discourse, and the disempowerment of progressive social movements. Expressing the concept in under 140 characters, we could say that more communication produces more inequality, not less.

While Dean's concept targets the ideology supporting the inequities of neoliberalism, I use communicative capitalism somewhat more literally and in two specific senses. The first is as shorthand to reference the economy's most communicative sectors, including the cultural industries, advertising/public relations, new media, telecommunications, and video games. Taken together, these sectors have been described by Dan Schiller and other political economists of communication as a "new and expansionary pole of growth" (2007, p. xiv) for capitalism as a whole (see Almiron, 2010; Dyer-Witheford & de Peuter, 2009; Mirrlees, 2013; Mosco, 2004, 2014; Schiller, 1999, 2007; Wasko, Murdock, & Sousa, 2011; Winseck, 2011). The rise of Amazon, Apple, and Google as some of the most valuable companies in the economic firmament, the searing expansion of mobile communication technology, the attention garnered by the contributions to gross domestic product (GDP) of the "creative industries," and the steep rise in profits harvested from rents on myriad forms of intellectual property all signal the growing influence of what the Canadian political economist Dwayne Winseck terms the "network media industries".[1]

The rising significance of this economic sector is not the only way capitalism has become more communicative however. The second and more important sense in which I use Dean's concept is to reference the increasing *communicativity* of companies across the entire economy.[2] My use of the term "communicativity" here signals the growing imperative for companies to remain in direct, one-to-one communication with their lifeblood—consumers. The concept of communicative capitalism can in this way be usefully deployed to reference the remarkable extension of "communicative access and opportunity" to billions of consumers for whom regular, mediated contact with the corporations in their lives has become a routine feature of day-to-day existence, a part of what media theorist Franco Berardi describes as the "regular and inescapable patterns of interaction" (2012, p. 15) that characterize life in a communicative economy. Just as important, for companies "information about consumers is essential for the operation of the high velocity markets enabled by the internet" (Gandy, 2011, p. 441; see also Schiller, 2007).[3]

---

[1] In one estimate, Winseck suggests the network media industries make up around 6.5% of global gross domestic product (GDP) and have almost doubled in size between 1998 and 2010 (2011, p. 11). Were one to add business process outsourcing, advertising, business to customer communication, and electronics production, this figure would be expanded even further.

[2] As Chakravartty and Schiller (2011, p. 672, emphasis added) point out, "digital capitalism coalesced, therefore, not as a sectoral or communications-centric phenomenon but *as an inclusive, economy-wide project*."

[3] As Dean puts it, "communication has become a primary means for capitalist expropriation and exploitation" (2014, p. 4).

The call centre plays a vital role in this scenario. As corporations restructured in pursuit of greater flexibility and responsiveness to volatile market conditions in the 1980s, large firms increasingly encouraged the development of a permanent flow of informational exchange between themselves and consumers.[4] Propelled by the privatization and restructuring of public utilities during the same period, the growing trend of companies establishing more efficient channels for customer contact was led by some of the sectors that would define the post-Fordist reformatting of capitalism, including finance, travel, and telecommunications.[5] Seizing upon declining telecommunications costs and simultaneous advances in computing, these companies began to develop, at the centre of this growing informational exchange with customers, the model of organizing a workspace we now know as the call centre.[6]

Since the 1990s, call centres have proliferated in tandem with the growing communicativity of capital. According to one estimate, by 1998 approximately two-thirds of all customer interactions were occurring through call centres (Barker, 1998). For most large companies today, there is the expectation that consumers will be offered the opportunity to get or keep in touch, customize their deal, get help using the product, check the status of their account, report failures, offer feedback, threaten

---

[4] This restructuring, as David McNally points out, occurred in the context of the defeat of established trade unions across the developed world: "As union resistance was pulverized, employers had carte blanche to reorganize work processes, introduce new technologies, downsize workforces, and speed up production in the quest for higher profits" (2011, p. 46).

[5] Ellis and Taylor (2006) offer an insightful study of the emergence of the call centre form in the United Kingdom. Also see Knights and McCabe (1998) for discussion of the process leading to the formation of a call centre by a British bank. As one report on the call centre sector summarizes, call centres live in a dependent relationship on what a recent report calls "key downstream industries" (Sherman, 2013, p. 5)—telecommunications, software, information technology, banking, insurance, and travel.

[6] A decrease in the costs of fixed-line telecommunication during the 1980s in the United States, itself brought about by the breakup of incumbent monopoly telecommunications provider AT&T, was also key to the industry's formation (see Doellgast, 2012; Schiller, 1999). As Vaughan Ellis and Phil Taylor (2006) have observed, more historical research remains to be done in detailing the political and economic processes that have shaped the remarkable rise of these workspaces. Perhaps the most obvious forerunner of the call centre were the operator services that developed within telephone companies, but the secretarial and clerical work that expanded within firms during the nineteenth and twentieth centuries were also fed into the call centre form.

to break their contract, and so on.[7] By 2007, American call centres alone received 43 billion calls in a 12-month stretch (Yellin, 2009, p. 105). In activities as diverse as providing tech support, proffering scams, promoting political candidates, surveying consumption patterns, dispensing health advice, pitching new products, or haranguing us to pay back our debts, call centres have become a vital apparatus for mediating the relationship between the institutions and the subjects of communicative capitalism in what some have called a "paradigmatic shift in the ordering of the customer inter-face across the entire economy" (Bain, Taylor, Watson, Mulvey, & Gall, 2002, p. 184). Through millions of transactions a day, call centres knit together relations between institutions and consumers across the information relays of the global economy. Total global spending on call centres in 2008 amounted to $34 billion (Zenith Optimedia, as cited in Yellin, 2009, p. 177), and the value of the rapidly consolidating global call centre market has been forecast by one study to reach $337 billion (US) by 2018.[8]

Call centres are, therefore, a vital product of communicative capitalism that both reflect the political-economic formation and enable its quotidian reproduction. As part of what Ursula Huws (2009) calls a new "interface" between corporations and the rest of us, call centres stand in for the promises of accessibility, responsiveness, and personalized attention that it would otherwise be much more expensive for companies to make. Little matter if that interface is infamous for being impersonal, exasperating, or simply designed to extract something from us, while offering little or nothing in return—a clear example of how under neoliberalism, as Dean

---

[7] The call centre is only one of several means by which corporations have increased their communicative interaction with and tracking of consumers. Online ordering of goods and services, spaces provided for customer comments on the web, and social media strategies are other examples, as is the practice of consumer surveillance. These modes of corporate-customer communication often overlap and intermingle. The move towards greater accommodation of consumer demands (including attention to niche markets, personalized service, greater responsiveness to customers, etc.) of which the call centre is a key component can be seen as part of an adaptive response by capitalism towards greater flexibility and responsiveness in the face of the accumulation crisis it faced during the late 1960s and 1970s (see Boltanski & Chiapello, 2005; Harvey, 1990).

[8] See Chap. 6 for an overview of the global call centre sector. A more recent report on the American call centre sector pointed to the growing power of large players in the industry when it suggested that "Despite 87.1% of companies employing less than 100 people, the majority of employees are located in large call centers. In 2012, an estimated 571 enterprises have more than 100 employees, with nearly half the companies employing more than 500 people" (Sherman, 2013, p. 21).

puts it, communication "produces its own negation" (2012, p. 127).[9] The tremendous growth of connectivity granted to the "diversity, multiplicity, and the agency of consumers" (Dean, 2009, p. 9) over the past two decades means the resulting ceaseless flow of communication must be organized and compressed so as to ensure it costs businesses as little as possible. The birth of the call centre during the last decades of the twentieth century represents capital's dominant response to this necessity, its rationalization of these functions, and its hidden abode of communicative production.

Discussion of the relationship between call centres and this more communicative variant of capitalism, however, like Dean's concept itself, risks overlooking the workforce that fuels these customer relations factories.[10] Communicative capitalism requires communicative labour, and for millions of people across the planet the experience of the call centre is much more immediate than fielding the infamous survey calls around dinner time, or being routed across the planet to find out why the printer doesn't work. As front-line info-service workers, these employees are the key actors in a digital workplace that combines language, emotion and communicative abilities, software-driven scripts, consumer information databases, automated call distribution systems, and sophisticated surveillance software, all seamlessly integrated so as to fulfil the company's promise behind those two words to be found on every company website: "contact us." Next we turn to academic analysis of call centre labour.

Competing Perspectives on Call Centre Work

As the customer relations industry exploded during the 1990s, two scholarly perspectives offered divergent assessments of the condition and experience of call centre work. Played out on the discursive terrain of social-scientific investigations of the call centre, their debate bears more

---

[9] In this corporate-consumer "communication without communicability" (Dean, 2012, p. 127), even the complaining customer represents "a huge opportunity for more business" (Pearson & Zehr, 2011, p. 203).

[10] See Chap. 1 for some figures regarding call centre employment in select countries.

than a passing resemblance to that which took place between Harry Braverman and his liberal-democratic adversaries in the 1970s.

The first perspective, coming predominantly from the academic disciplines of business, management, and occupational psychology, repurposed Daniel Bell's post-industrial narrative of increasing technological rationalization and declining class conflict in order to offer an optimistic portrait of call centre employment as "knowledge work."[11] Knitting Bell's post-industrial theory of the workplace onto the emergent conditions of call centre employment, these researchers delivered an appraisal of the call centre that minimized its similarities to the Fordist factory. The image of front-line call centre employment that surfaces in these studies is of a fairly rewarding job, marked by some autonomy, relatively high levels of employee satisfaction, and a workforce that largely identifies with management's objectives (see Donati, 1999; Dormann & Zijlstra, 2004; Frenkel, Tam, Korczynski, & Shire, 1998; Frenkel, Korczynski, Shire, & Tam, 1999; Korczynski, 2002; Pentland, 1995). The best example of this analysis is *On the Front Line: Organization of Work in the Information Economy*, which features repeated images of smiling call centre workers on the cover and introduces its analysis with a respectful discussion of Daniel Bell's theory of post-industrial society (Frenkel et al., 1999).

A recurring theme for these authors is that employee subjectivity in call centres is "semi-professionalized" rather than working class, with the obvious implication that the potential for labour strife is significantly diminished (Russell, 2008, p. 201). The high levels of worker identification with the goals of management, for these authors, are closely connected to employee satisfaction with the rewarding nature of the "knowledge work" performed in call centres.[12] In their aforementioned

---

[11] As suggested in Chap. 1, the adoption of the term "knowledge work" to describe call centre labour is not a politically neutral decision. According to knowledge worker theory—the genealogy of which can be traced from management guru Peter Drucker (who claimed to have coined the term—see Drucker, 1996), to the economist Fritz Machlup (1962), through Daniel Bell's (1973) Weberian sociology—the knowledge worker enjoyed a workplace where hierarchy was being flattened, participatory processes incorporated, and labour strife gradually eliminated.

[12] Marek Korczynski finds that call centre workers have "quite high levels of satisfaction" (2002, p. 256 or 95). David Holman (2004, p. 239) measures the "well-being" and "job satisfaction" among customer service agents working for a British bank and suggests that "call centre work compares favourably to shop floor manufacturing and clerical work with regard to wellbeing." In

international study on new forms of service work organization, Frenkel et al. report that call centre workers mostly have "expanded levels of discretion," and conclude this type of labour is similar to knowledge work (1999, p. 69).[13] In its message that the general tendency within info-service work is that of the "empowered, enriched worker coming to life," (Frenkel et al., 1998, p. 976) the image of labour relations offered by this tradition of research dovetails comfortably with the call centre industry's own descriptions of the labour conditions it provides.[14]

It is certainly true (as we shall see) that some call centre jobs are more rewarding, offer more autonomy, or feature more lenient managerial styles than others, and there is no question that call centre work can be a step up from many alternatives,[15] but scholarship seeking to connect the impressive growth of call centre employment to the broader fable of knowledge was, in the end, untenable.[16] Among those opposing this narrative of empowered call centre workers through the late 1990s were Harry Braverman's intellectual heirs. Led by the sociological work of Phil Taylor and Peter Bain, the labour process perspective has produced an extensive set of studies of the manner in which force and consent are combined so as

---

their analysis of technical support work in a Bangalore call centre, Premilla D'Cruz and Ernesto Noronha (2007, p. 57) point out that the job has created "a sense of self-esteem" for these young professionals, and that "overall satisfaction was high."

[13] This optimistic assessment repeats that of an earlier essay, in which the authors suggest "work tasks are less routine and more challenging" and "workers' discretion has been enlarged." Elsewhere in the same essay the authors maintain that "like professionals, call centre employees must be knowledgeable and flexible" in order to perform their duties (Frenkel et al., 1998, p. 961).

[14] This is perhaps not surprising when one considers that research undertaken in Frenkel et al.'s book (1999) was funded by Andersen Consulting, which (even after the Enron accounting scandal and its subsequent rebranding as Accenture) employs call centre workers in Europe, Asia, and North America.

[15] Call centre scholars devoted increasing attention during the 2000s to the project of distinguishing between different varieties of management styles in call centres, arguing that these differences need to be taken into account when discussing these workspaces (see Batt & Moynihan, 2002; Houlihan, 2002). Be this as it may, one of the most significant features of call centres globally is their striking similarity—not differences—across tremendously diverse contexts. As Anthony Lloyd puts it: "once inside the call centre, you could be anywhere in the world." (2013, p. 35).

[16] Not surprisingly, some of the leading exponents of this optimistic perspective have backed away from their more optimistic conclusions of the 1990s (see Russell, 2008). Frenkel (2005, p. 357 and 369), for example, states that most service work is "located at the lower range of the skills, creativity and knowledge continuum [and is] indecent in the sense that it is often poorly rewarded and provides little intrinsic satisfaction."

to maintain control over—and ensure the steady exploitation of—call centre workers' communicative capacities. While varied in their styles and emphases, the conclusions on call centres offered by labour process researchers have ultimately echoed the warnings of activist playwright Barbara Garson, who suggested at the end of the 1980s that a combination of twentieth-century technology and nineteenth-century scientific management was turning "the office of the future into the factory of the past" (1988). The four recurrent features of call centre work that surface in these studies are the routinization, intensification, surveillance, and subjective shaping of labour.

Telephone-answering automatons. Labour process scholars have seen call centre work not as a humane departure from, but instead as the latest, digital update of the Taylorist separation of conception and execution that shaped the factory floor (Bain et al., 2002; Head, 2004; Huws, 2003, 2009; Koskina, 2006; Taylor & Bain, 1999, 2008; Thompson, Warhurst, & Callaghan, 2001). Just as Braverman found the work of clerks, secretaries, and service workers to be degraded in the firms of his era, the inheritors of his approach have described in great detail how the dominant tendency across call centres is not employee autonomy or rewarding work but rather the managerial effort to diminish or even eliminate them.[17] The labour process in call centres, these authors have shown, is often engineered so as to break up the operator's communication into small, pre-programmed fragments, or "structure the very speech of workers into a series of predictable, regulated and routinised queries and responses" (Taylor & Bain, 1999, p. 109) in an attempt to both simplify their linguistic performance and achieve greater control over their actions.[18] For workers, labour process

---

[17] In the words of one employee working at the call centre of a formerly public utility in Scotland interviewed by Taylor, Baldry, Bain and Ellis, "I have yet to encounter any evidence that management at policy level regard their staff as anything other than telephone-answering automatons who must not be allowed any flexibility or latitude" (as cited in Taylor, Baldry, Bain, & Ellis, 2003, p. 448).

[18] While Frenkel et al. drew their optimistic conclusions in the late 1990s, evidence from the field led Taylor, Bain and other researchers to conclude that "routinization, repetitiveness and a general absence of employee control" were the dominant features of call centre work organization in the UK industry they examined (Taylor, Mulvey, Hyman, & Bain, 2002, p. 136). This conclusion was confirmed in America by the findings of journalist Simon Head, who, after paying close attention to the marketing of software to call centre owners in the pages of specialized trade publications,

researchers have suggested, the scientific management of their communicative labour has produced jobs of virtually unmatched psychic drudgery.
The day that I actually collapsed. Beyond the enforcement of degraded forms of communication, labour process scholars have found that the "mass production" model of organizing work in call centres is reminiscent of the Fordist assembly line in another respect: the constant push to increase the pace of work. Management's search for ever-greater levels of communicative production translates into rigid performance targets for call centre workers, and critical research into the industry brims with stories of work rhythms approaching the psychic breaking point and harsh cultures of enforcement (see Callaghan & Thompson, 2001; Head, 2004; Lavin, 2006; Stevens & Lavin, 2007; Taylor & Bain, 1999; van den Broek, 2004; van den Broek, Barnes, & Townsend, 2008).[19] The stressful

---

demonstrated how the very same technology that could be used to enhance the decision-making ability of call centre workers is instead shaped so that it acts as a tool of labour control, enforcing an increasingly present digital script dictating what service representatives should say to customers during their interactions.

[19] When the headphones are on, intensification takes the form of lowering the average time operators must take on each call for inbound workers (known as "average talk time," or ATT) or increasing the number of sales operators must make (or surveys carried out, etc.) for outbound workers. Here information technology, far from making life easier for workers, plays a key role in extracting this productivity. For inbound contact centre operations (those that field calls from customers) the automatic call distribution (ACD) software stacks customers in virtual queues where they wait as operators scramble to deal with them in as little time as possible. For outbound workers (those making calls to customers) automated dialling systems serve up call after call to the recipients of sales pitches, survey requests, etc. The time between the "wrap-up" time at the end of one call when workers enter the relevant data and the arrival of the next call can be as low as one or two seconds. The unrelenting pressure to perform in the face of what Taylor and Bain describe as the "constant stream of customers" (as cited in Callaghan & Thompson, 2001, p. 18) that characterizes the work is captured by the British journalist Simon Head (2004) when he describes workers in the American call centre heartlands of Arizona and New Mexico struggling to keep up with ATT targets of 1 minute and 30 seconds per call. At the Australian call centre Stellar, Diane van den Broek (2002) noted that customer service representatives were expected to dispatch calls in 18.9 seconds. Buchanan and Koch-Schulte (2000, p. 32) gathered an alarming set of accounts from front-line call centre workers in Canada regarding the effects of work speed-up. Two testimonies from workers who had breakdowns on the job stand out: "Paul: *But this was really bad and I started crying, and they asked me if I was all right, and I said "No." They said that they would try and find some work for me in quality control, reviewing tapes of transactions ... After about a month, they said I could come back to work on the phones or I could resign from the company ... With our wonderful new U.I. [Unemployment Insurance] regulations, if you resign, you can't collect a dime. So I was stuck. I went back, I lasted less than a week ... What happened then? I was under a doctor's care for a while for anxiety and depression. They had me on some medication ... It happened at work ... the stress was really getting to me. A couple of times, they sent me home early because I was just not coping. Each time, it got*

and sometimes humiliating ways this productivity is achieved range from the commonplace tactic of the public display of individual workers' performances on a digital board to reports of employers forcing workers to raise flags of a specified colour when they want to go to the toilet (Datta, as cited in Taylor & Bain, 2008). Failure to meet performance targets means coaching, disciplining, and ultimately dismissal, often on a three-strikes-and-you're-out model.[20] This combination of unsustainable work rhythms and inflexibility to the demands of worker's lives outside of work is so common in call centres that management scholars have given it a name: the "sacrificial HR strategy" is one in which "high levels of stress and emotional burnout of the front-line staff, accompanied by high turnover" are "tolerated, if not encouraged" (Wallace et al., 2000, p. 175). Not surprisingly, and as we shall see next, employment turnover levels in call centres are strikingly high.[21]

They measure everything. While the goal of extracting as much labour as possible from workers is a constant feature of capitalist labour relations, the call centre presents managerial innovations that may go beyond what even Braverman could have foreseen. Communicative productivity in call centres is enabled by management's scrupulous digital surveillance of the workforce, an aspect of the job that among others has captured the attention of critical researchers (Bain & Taylor, 2000; Buchanan & Koch-Schulte, 2000; Fernie & Metcalf, 1998; Taylor & Bain, 1999). Virtually

---

worse.'" *"Phyllis: The day that I actually collapsed it was just . . . you could just . . . any agent in there could tell you. Management knew that they should have cut the lines down. They should have slowed the records down."*

[20] In just one example of the overriding aim to intensify work, George Callaghan and Paul Thompson found that, in their study of "Telebank," a Scottish financial services call centre operation, "management deliberately choose a technology that has been designed to limit worker autonomy and are conscious of the power of the call queue in maximizing production pace" (2001, p. 20). See also Head (2004), Rose (2002), Taylor et al. (2003), and Wallace, Eagleson, and Waldersee (2000).

[21] Such strategies naturally have damaging effects on workers. In an early study aiming to document the health effects of call centre labour, Taylor et al. (2003) found that work intensification in a Scottish call centre was the most frequently reported source of health issues such as stress, mental fatigue, and physical tiredness by workers. The productivity imperative extends into the private lives of call centre workers as well. Head (2004) documents stories of workers in the American Sunbelt being refused time off or given demerits for surgeries, medical check-ups, family emergencies, and injuries acquired on the job.

every dimension of call centre labour is subject to monitoring. In their study of an Ontario call centre company, Canadian scholars Andrew Stevens and David Lavin (2007, p. 48) suggest that the goal of this surveillance is to get as close as possible to the complete mapping of a worker's time while on shift, with a view to logging "strict adherence to break-times, punctual arrival and departure from work, attendance, average call handle time, percent of time entering customer details in accounts, the amount of idle time, and the number of calls taken in a particular span of time." Such surveillance is pursued so zealously by management that call centres have become notorious for the practice of measuring workers right down to the time taken to go to the bathroom each day.[22]

They want you to be involved.[23] The relationship between management's organization of the labour process and the inner, emotional, and subjective life of front-line call centre workers has also been the focus of labour process research and critique (Callaghan & Thompson, 2002; Sewell, 1998; van den Broek, 2004). Here scholars have explored the ways managerial control over workers is secured in more insidious ways than routinization, intensification, or surveillance on the shop floor. The most common example is the practice of organizing call centre workers into "teams," a move management literature has celebrated as a move towards democratization in the workplace. Critical call centre researchers have illuminated the deeply ambivalent nature of "teamwork," seeing it as little more than a strategy aimed at inciting workers to police their own productivity and that of their colleagues. This technique, which Diane van den Broek calls "teams without teamwork," and Bain and Taylor refer to as "team Taylorism" (2000, p. 10), for Graham Sewell operates as a "powerful horizontal disciplinary force" (1998, p. 420) in which "teams are taking on the responsibility for rationalizing and intensifying their own work activities, i.e., they are working

---

[22] The words of one customer service representative interviewed by George Callaghan and Paul Thompson (2001, p. 22) in a UK call centre capture what it is like to labour under such intense electronic scrutiny: "They measure everything. I just saw someone getting picked up for having two toilet breaks, it's a ludicrous situation. If you disappear to the toilet, say you take an average six minutes a day, you get pulled for it. She just got pulled for 2 × 2.5 minutes... We get our stats the next day for the night before and they can tell you everything you've done and how long you've been logged on. Everything is measured."
[23] Cited in Knights and McCabe (2003, p. 1611).

'smarter' to work harder" (p. 401). As a result of this and other methods, Sewell (p. 399) notes that the frontier of control separating employers and workers on the shop floor has blurred in the call centre. These efforts to implicate the customer service agent in her own subordination through the selection and moulding of obedient workforce subjectivities has been the departure point of a prominent offshoot of labour process theory seeking to incorporate post-structuralist philosophy, in particular that of Michel Foucault (see Alferoff & Knights, 2000; Ball & Wilson, 2000; Ball, 2005; Fleming & Spicer, 2004; Fleming, 2009; Fleming & Sturdy, 2011; Knights & Willmott, 1989; Knights & McCabe, 1998, 2003).

In short, labour process theorists have maintained that for call centre employees, the digital workplace has turned out less like Daniel Bell's dream than Harry Braverman's nightmare. And their perspective is shared by at least one US call centre company CEO who has been quoted as claiming that the workspaces

> have become the sweatshops of the modern era. The industry is plagued with high turnover, with under-trained, under-motivated and unenthusiastic staff, most of whom are casuals with no long-term commitment to their jobs. (as cited in Fleming & Sturdy, 2011, p. 192)

Given the overwhelming evidence of disciplinary and exploitative labour relations in call centres, discussions among academic researchers soon touched upon worker resistance. The notorious first shot in this debate was fired by British researchers Sue Fernie and David Metcalf, who—drawing on the well-worn metaphor employed by Foucault in *Discipline and Punish*—went so far as to suggest that call centres were the contemporary, digital realization of the panopticon, an unsettling plan for the perfect prison constructed upon the search for total surveillance (see Fernie & Metcalf, 1998; Foucault, 1995). By announcing the arrival of the electronic panopticon, Fernie and Metcalf maintained that management's domination over labour was complete, and the possibilities for employee resistance against the perfect convergence of a routinized labour process and ubiquitous digital surveillance had dropped off to zero.

Fernie and Metcalf's paper struck a nerve within the academic community and even resonated beyond it, briefly becoming the subject of media attention in the United Kingdom. In their withering response,

Peter Bain and Phil Taylor made the basic point that call centre workers are not the inert victims of predatory labour control but possessors of agency and thus capable of resisting the call centre's organization from above (Bain & Taylor, 2000). Other scholars agreed, and in the decade following its publication Fernie and Metcalf's essay and its "Foucaultian" approach was routinely dispatched at the top of many an analysis of the call centre as simplistic, hyperbolic, and mistaken.[24]

Despite its overstated conclusions, however, Fernie and Metcalf's paper had the merit of illuminating the extent to which critical investigations of the call centre, in their desire to rebut the optimistic portrayals of knowledge work, had paid significantly more attention to how workers are organized by management than to how they organize for themselves. If knowledge worker theories were disingenuous in their portraits of happy call centre workers in rewarding informational workplaces, labour process critiques had tended—like Braverman—to serve up the dispiriting image of a subjugated workforce in return.[25]

Worker Inquiry: Seeing the Call Centre from Below

> Labour is not a thing. It is a perspective. (Qiu, 2012, p. 186)

This book proposes a view of call centres which foregrounds the conflicts and collective organization of the workforce that labours within them. The point of departure for this approach is described by a very different

---

[24] For example, see Callaghan and Thompson (2001, p. 14) who identify a dividing line in discussions about call centres between "purveyors of a Foucaultian perspective" and a "more traditional labour process approach."

[25] As late as 2005, Keith Townsend noted "the general notion of employee resistance in call centres is an area of research that has a limited, if growing, body of research" (2005, p. 48). Moreover, the legacy of these assumptions continues—Anthony Lloyd (2013, p. 90), for example, has recently suggested in an otherwise compelling study that "call centres appear devoid of institutional resistance." One must agree with Vincent Mosco and David Lavin when they suggest that "valuable as this research has been, it has treated labour as a largely passive category to be shaped by the dynamics of capitalism and has obscured how labour makes itself, at work and in its organizations" (2008, p. 148).

Michel Foucault than the caricatured theorist of domination one routinely encounters in call centre studies and labour process theory. In his 1982 essay "The Subject and Power," the French philosopher considers a different way of developing knowledge regarding power relations. This approach, he suggests,

> consists of using ... resistance as a chemical catalyst so as to bring to light power relations, locate their position, and find out their point of application and the methods used. Rather than analysing power from the point of view of its internal rationality, it consists of analysing power relations through the antagonism of strategies. (p. 780)

Foucault's passage offers a useful sketch of my approach to the analysis of labour relations in call centres. In proposing this "methodology from below" (Wittel, 2004, p. 27), I draw from the work of traditions that have privileged the study of resistance in their analysis of social processes and power relations. Prominent among these traditions is autonomist Marxism, a perspective forged since the 1950s by several generations of theorists and militants from Italy.[26]

Like labour process scholars, autonomists see relations between labour and capital as inescapably exploitative and conflictual. Differently from Braverman's heirs, however, autonomists begin their analysis of this relationship with labour's resistance and search for autonomy, a force that they maintain anticipates and provokes capitalist restructuring.[27] Mario Tronti's provocative claim in the landmark autonomist text *Operai e Capitale* that there is "no class without class struggle" conveys the priority autonomist scholars have accorded to investigating labour through the periodic

---

[26] Autonomist Marxist analysis is a heterogeneous tradition which has become prominent in the Anglophone world since the publication of Michael Hardt and Antonio Negri's *Empire* (2000), but has since its earliest days in post-war Italy mingled with a variety of radical currents, including American labour sociology, French post-structuralism and Regulation School political economy, radical feminism, and critical communication scholarship, to become an increasingly international perspective with an associated and evolving set of political tendencies. See Wright (2002), Cleaver (2000), Ryan (1982), and Dyer-Witheford (1999) for overviews.

[27] As Michael Hardt and Antonio Negri suggest, "[e]ven though common use of the term might suggest the opposite—that resistance is a response or reaction—resistance is primary with respect to power" (2004, p. 64).

tendency of workers to take flight from, mitigate, frustrate, confound, subvert, and sometimes overturn the subordinated relations to which they are subject (Tronti, 2005). These forms of resistance, as Foucault's quote suggests, can be used as an entry point, not to avoid an analysis of domination, but rather to outline it from the perspective of the workers whose refusals bring the fundamental antagonism between labour and capital into focus.[28]

Autonomists have devoted their efforts to exploring the potentialities residing in labour's side of the communicative capitalist coin described by Jodi Dean. Echoing her insights, Michael Hardt and Antonio Negri note the contemporary economy integrates "ever more centrally communicative networks, intellectual and cultural circuits, the production of images and affects, and so forth" (2009, p. 286). Within this epochal shift, communication has become more crucial than ever to the production process at large, and autonomist scholars have tracked the corresponding transformation in labour's composition. Of special interest to these scholars has been the growing significance of what Hardt, Negri, and others have called "immaterial labour," or labour "that produces immaterial products, such as information, knowledges, ideas, images, relationships, and affects" (Hardt and Negri, 2004, p. 65). Immaterial labour describes a growing variety of forms of work in the networked media industries and beyond. For post-workerist theorists like philosopher Paolo Virno and economist Christian Marazzi, such labour puts language, culture, and communication "to work" with great intensity, producing "communication by means of communication."[29] Call centre work is a paradigmatic example of the kinds of employment the concept of immaterial labour seeks to describe.

Adopting the autonomist concept of immaterial labour implies an approach to the investigation of call centre work along the lines of that

---

[28] As Maurizio Lazzarato puts it, "we must not take labor, whatever it may be, as our starting point but always the refusal of work" (2015). Franco Berardi (2013, para. 26) recently summed up the distinctive feature of the autonomist approach: "I have asked myself in what sense we can call ourselves workerists, and my answer is: only in the sense of the method, not in terms of our contents. . . .if I refer to method then I am completely in agreement with Tronti as far as what I would call the *precession of the subjective*, on the fact therefore that the subjective comes first and the structure comes afterward" [Translation by author].

[29] See Marazzi (1999) and Virno (2001, 2003).

advocated by Foucault in *"The Subject and Power."* Autonomists may agree with knowledge worker theorists that work has changed as capitalism has become more communicative, but they also point out that the extraction of value from the production of intangible products like culture and communication is by no means a friction-free matter.[30] Recent analyses of the labour that fuels the networked media industries at the heart of communicative capitalism have fruitfully explored these frictions (Cohen, 2012; de Peuter, 2014; Dyer-Witheford, 1999; Mattoni, 2012; Mosco & McKercher, 2008; Qiu, 2010). If video-game workers sabotage, film workers agitate, and freelancers organize, the concept of immaterial labour asks us to seek out these moments of conflict, to direct our inquiry towards those instances when the communicative worker becomes resistant and unmanageable, to explore what Negri and others refer to as the "self-valourization" of labour.[31]

The concept of immaterial labour does not come without its problems or controversies, but the style of inquiry it is associated with is especially relevant to this book as the approach has notable precedents among call centre labour activists, trade unionists, and worker collectives internationally.[32] These studies, in generating what Foucault would have called "counter-knowledges" of the call centre, have been inspired by the *worker inquiry*, an autonomist method that traces its roots back to Karl Marx.[33]

---

[30] This approach belies a characterization of autonomist scholars by Robert Wilkie (2011, p. 81), who suggests that they are not interested in "property ownership, production, and exploitation." To the contrary, these are central concerns for the tradition.

[31] As Negri (2005, p. 137) states, "from resistance to appropriation, from reappropriation to self-organization ... In short this is a journey through the various figures of self-valorization."

[32] See Chap. 7 for a more extensive discussion of immaterial labour in relation to call centre work.

[33] In 1880, Marx was asked by the *Revue Socialiste* to investigate the labour conditions of French workers, and the result was a document containing 101 questions that was to be distributed through workplaces across the country. In his preface to these questions, Marx proposes the collective production of knowledge from below as a means to confront these conditions: "In the hope that maybe we shall induce a republican government to follow the example of the monarchical government of England by likewise organizing a far reaching investigation into facts and crimes of capitalist exploitation, we shall attempt to initiate an inquiry of this kind with those poor resources which are at our disposal. We hope to meet in this work with the support of all workers in town and country who understand that they alone can describe with full knowledge the misfortunes from which they suffer and that only they, and not saviors sent by providence, can energetically apply the healing remedies for the social ills which they are prey. We also rely upon socialists of all schools who, being wishful for social reform, must wish for an *exact* and *positive* knowledge of the conditions

Flowing from their emphasis on resistance, this methodology from below has been succinctly captured by Sergio Bologna (2014):

> ... workerism never claimed to be able to "teach" workers the life of revolt or revolution. On the contrary, the workerist practice of "coresearch" meant simply that militants must "learn" from the workers and listen to them, but always maintaining the role of intellectuals, who were able to transmit the tools of thought and analysis which could be useful to the worker who intended to undertake a collective journey of liberation.

An early application of the worker inquiry to call centres came in 1999, when members of the labour collective Kolinko took jobs in German call centres in order to better understand worker subjectivities and the potential for collective organization in this swelling sector. In their introduction to *Hotlines*, the 2002 text that summarized their findings, Kolinko explained their research was intended "for everyone who wants to understand what the reality of exploitation looks like in call centres, how people ... do their work and rebel against it" (2002, section 1, para. 3).

In an extensive report, *Hotlines* gathers accounts of the collective's experiences at over ten call centres "in which we sweated" (Kolinko, 2002, section 1, para. 2), reports by workers in other countries, and press coverage of these workspaces. The book's defining feature is its rich collection of anecdotes highlighting the unequal and conflictual relations between labour and management, accounts which taken together transmit a seething view of the call centre from the perspective of its workforce. Descriptions of arbitrary dismissals of workers share space with reports of labour strikes enacted through established telecommunication worker unions, accounts of mobilization by workers through rank-and-file unions are gathered alongside stories of affective disengagement by those working over a headset, and sketches of quotidian sabotage and slacking by workers mingle with political-economic analyses of the call centre's role and

---

in which the working class—the class to whom the future belongs—works and moves" (para. 2). The worker inquiry has experienced a resurgence among feminist, student and labour movements in Europe and Latin America under a variety of names such as co-research, militant inquiry, and others. See Figiel, Shukaitis and Walker (2014), *Viewpoint Magazine* (2013) and Foucault (2003), particularly Lectures 1 and 2 on the genealogy.

development. Tying all of this material together is the search for a new, insurgent unionism in what Kolinko calls "the sweatshops of the New Economy" (2002, section 2, para. 6).

The collective was not alone in seeing the call centre as an ideal testing ground for the development of new forms of labour solidarity and collective organization. During the course of their study, Kolinko came into contact with activists from Berlin who were engaged in a similar project of inquiry. Calling themselves the Call Center Offensive (CCO) (an ironic reference to a state initiative promoting the growth of call centres), this parallel project was described on a leaflet distributed to workers:

> Some of the people who make up the Call Center Offensive work in call centres themselves. We try to support agents in their struggles against work or for the improvement of their working and payment conditions, through publicity or legal aid, for example. At the same time we want to set up a framework in which the experiences of such struggles and working conditions can be reflected collectively. (as cited in Kolinko, 2002, section 6.3.c., para. 3)

From their first meetings, organizers from the CCO encouraged counter-mobilization and horizontal communication among workers, or, as they put it, "communication without management and telephones" (as cited in Kolinko, 2002, section 6.3.c., para. 10). In documenting experiences such as that of the CCO and others, *Hotlines* offers a vivid account of the labour discontent simmering within the process of call centre class formation. This labour discontent, as we shall see, is the common element within a gathering and transnational counter-perspective of the call centre developing from below.

Beginning in 2005–2006, the worker inquiry was also carried out by some Kolinko members and local labour activists among call centre workers in the business process outsourcing sector in Gurgaon, on the industrial outskirts of Delhi, India. Similar inquiries were launched during the following decade as call centres multiplied. On the other side of the planet, in Rosario, Argentina, in collaboration with local trade unionists, a group of students and lecturers began to investigate the forms of discipline, subjectivity, and resistance produced when language was put to work in the call centre of a company called Apex. Described as a "collaborative project of militant research," (2007a, p. 134) the *Cátedra Experimental sobre Producción de Subjetividad* (Experimental Chair on the Production of Subjectivity) outlined what they saw as the "art of virtual control" (p. 133) enacted in the call centre, including the daily subordination of communication to Taylorist rhythms and the hyper-turnover characterizing employment conditions. Significantly, they also documented the building of union power among the depoliticized, youthful, and feminized workforce (Cátedra Experimental sobre Producción de Subjetividad, 2007b).

Argentina was also the site of another inquiry, this time a collaboration between the militant-scholar collective Colectivo Situaciones and Buenos Aires workers employed in call centres outsourced to by transnationals such as Spain's Telefónica. The resulting book, *¿Quién Habla?* (Who's Speaking?), collects sophisticated theorizations of the call centre, firsthand worker accounts of experiences within them, and candid reflections on the attempts by workers in the city to organize across call centre companies between 2004 and 2008 (Colectivo Situaciones, 2006). In an uncanny echo of Kolinko's project, the authors point out that "their challenge was to think through these new labour conditions, the type of unease that motivates many to rebel, but also the fears and the tools with which the company responds to organization and protest" (Colectivo Situaciones, p. 39). *¿Quién Habla?* brings the Colectivo's project of producing knowledge on the borders between scholarly research and collective political action into one of the fastest growing workspaces of our age.[34]

More recently, the worker inquiry has been applied to call centres by a collective of Italian workers and labour activists in the southern Italian province of Calabria, where over 10,000 people work through a headset in an industry flourishing thanks to its location in a region where (even by

---

[34] While on the one hand the Argentine collective has been highly critical of the empiricism and pretences of objectivity they see as characterizing academic research, on the other they take aim at the position within activist movements "which prescribes that there is no room for thought within a struggle, only room for agitation, mobilization" (Colectivo Situaciones, 2006, p. 18). See also Colectivo Situaciones (2003, 2009, 2011).

Italian standards) labour costs are low.[35] In collaboration with rank-and-file union activists, the authors of a series of bulletins and newspaper articles on the topic have outlined in great detail the "absurdity of the precarious conditions" working in what they (notably) call the Calabrian "Mirafiori" (a reference to Fiat's largest and oldest factory in Turin). Describing themselves as a "research group on precarity and the common," these activists have applied autonomist concepts (including immaterial labour) to the conditions they encounter in the call centre sector, generating analyses which successfully transmit the neither entirely pacified nor utterly subordinated subjectivity of the informational underclass labouring within it. The collective's ongoing inquiry is inspired, in their words, by the conviction that "social transformation can occur through the construction of a precarious point of view" one which, they maintain, "cannot but be born out of conflicts" (Gruppo d'inchiesta sulla precarietà e il comune, 2013, para. 8).

Jamie Woodcock's inquiry at a call centre in London, England, has added itself to and enriched this tradition. An important aim of this research, for Woodcock, "was to uncover the possibilities for resistance and organization" (2013, para. 38) that within the job he investigated. While he details the emotional labour and exploitative conditions encountered in selling life insurance to union members, the author also explains how he used his experience to launch a labour organizing effort at the company. Personal connections with colleagues soon turned into organizing opportunities:

> One of the trainees who started at the same time as me passed me a hand-drawn cartoon of the consultant, with a speech bubble saying "you'll lose your job son!" This was the beginning of more serious discussions about how we could organize in the workplace. He said he did not care whether he lost his job, and suggested that we could meet some other people in a pub after work. (para. 41)

The overview of worker inquiries offered here is not exhaustive, but it gives a sense of how this new workspace has been investigated from

---

[35] 650 euros is an average monthly salary for full-time work, although such employment conditions are rare (Cuccomarino & Pezzulli, 2012, p. 8).

below by networks of workers, labour activists, trade unionists, and academic allies. While business and management scholars have pursued empiricist, survey-heavy, and management-sanctioned studies of call centre work, the worker inquiries described here offer an energetic counter-narrative to such accommodating takes. Producing a view of the call centre as a site for class formation and conflict, these studies are an exemplary case of the orientation towards knowledge production advocated by the overlooked Foucault of the mid-1970s.

Inspired by these budding analyses of call centre work, this book draws on discussions with labour activists, trade unionists, and call centre workers that have animated moments of collective counter-organization along the digital assembly lines in Italy, Canada, New Zealand, and Ireland. In documenting these experiences, my aim is to offer a study of the "arts of resistance" (Scott, 1990) developed by the workforce in global call centres, and through this a portrait of class formation in communicative capitalism. To set the stage for these inquiries, we now turn to an overview of labour resistance and collective organization in call centres.

References

Alferoff, C., & Knights, D. (2000). Quality time and the beautiful call. *Are regimented forms of work organisation inevitable? Call centres and the chances for an innovative organisation of service work in Europe*, University of Duisburg-Essen, Germany.

Almiron, N. (2010). *Journalism in crisis: Corporate media and financialization*. Cresskill, NJ: Hampton Press.

Bain, P., & Taylor, P. (2000). Entrapped by the 'electronic panopticon'? Worker resistance in the call centre. *New Technology, Work, and Employment, 15*(1), 2–18.

Bain, P., Taylor, P., Watson, A., Mulvey, G., & Gall, G. (2002). Taylorism, targets and the pursuit of quantity and quality by call centre management. *New Technology, Work and Employment, 17*(3), 170–185.

Ball, K. (2005). Organization, surveillance and the body: Towards a politics of resistance. *Organization, 12*(1), 89–108.

Ball, K., & Wilson, D. (2000). Power, control and computer-based performance monitoring: Repertoires, resistance and subjectivities. *Organization Studies, 21*(3), 539–565.

Barker, G. (1998, February 24). Factories of the future. *The age.*

Batt, R., & Moynihan, L. (2002). The viability of alternative call centre production models. *Human Resource Management Journal, 12*(4), 14–14.

Bell, D. (1973). *The coming of post-industrial society: A venture in social forecasting.* New York, NY: Basic Books.

Berardi, F. (2012). *The uprising: On poetry and finance.* Los Angeles, CA: Semiotext(e).

Berardi, F. (2013). L'autonomia dell'intelletto generale: Ecco il problema. *Commonware: General Intellect in Formazione.* Retrieved from: http://www.commonware.org/index.php/neetwork/45-autonomia-intelletto-generale

Bologna, S. (2014, December 15). Workerism beyond Fordism: On the lineage of Italian workerism. *Viewpoint Magazine.* Retrieved from https://viewpointmag.com/2014/12/15/workerism-beyond-fordism-on-the-lineage-of-italian-workerism/

Boltanski, L., & Chiapello, E. (2005). *The new spirit of capitalism.* New York, NY: Verso.

Brophy, E. (2010). The subterranean stream: Communicative capitalism and call centre labour. *ephemera: theory and politics in organization, 10*(4), 470–483.

Buchanan, R., & Koch-Schulte, S. (2000). *Gender on the line: Technology, restructuring and the reorganization of work in the call centre industry.* Ottawa, ON: Status of Women Canada.

Callaghan, G., & Thompson, P. (2001). Edwards revisited: Technical control and call centres. *Economic and Industrial Democracy, 22*(1), 13–37.

Callaghan, G., & Thompson, P. (2002). We recruit attitude: The selection and shaping of routine call centre labour. *Journal of Management Studies, 39*(2), 233–254.

Cátedra Experimental sobre Producción de Subjetividad. (2007a). Call centre: The art of virtual control. *ephemera: theory and politics in organization, 7*(1), 133–138.

Cátedra Experimental sobre Producción de Subjetividad. (2007b). *From knowledge of self-management to the self-management of knowledge.* Retrieved from http://eipcp.net/transversal/0707/catedraexperimental/en

Chakravartty, P., & Schiller, D. (2011). Global financial crisis: Neoliberal newspeak and digital capitalism in crisis. *International Journal of Communication, 4*(23), 670–692.

Cleaver, H. (2000). *Reading Capital politically*. Edinburgh, UK: AK Press.
Cohen, N. (2012). Cultural work as a site of struggle: Freelancers and exploitation. *tripleC (Cognition, Communication, Co-Operation): Open Access Journal for a Global Sustainable Information Society, 10*(2), 141–155.
Colectivo Situaciones. (2003). *Causes and happenstance: Dilemmas of Argentina's new social protagonism*. Retrieved from http://www.nodo50.org/colectivosituaciones/borradores_04_eng.htm
Colectivo Situaciones. (2006) *¿Quién habla? Lucha contra la esclavitud del alma en los call centers*. Buenos Aires, Argentina: Tinta Limón Ediciones.
Colectivo Situaciones. (2009). *Genocide in the neighborhood* [Genocida en el barrio: Mesa de escrache popular] (B. Whitener, D. Borzutzky, & F. Fuentes, Trans.). Oakland, CA/Philadelphia, Pennsylvania: ChainLinks.
Colectivo Situaciones. (2011). *19 & 20: Notes for a new social protagonism*. Retrieved from http://www.minorcompositions.info/?cat=27
Cuccomarino, C., & Pezzulli, F. M. (2012, December 13). Tra mirafiori e Bangalore: L'inchiesta politica nei call center calabresi. *Il Manifesto*, pp. 8–9.
D'Cruz, P., & Noronha, E. (2007). Technical call centres: Beyond "electronic sweatshops" and "assembly lines in the head". *Global Business Review, 8*(1), 53–67.
de Peuter, G. (2014). Confronting precarity in the Warhol economy: Notes from New York City. *Journal of Cultural Economy, 7*(1), 31.
Dean, J. (2009). *Democracy and other neoliberal fantasies: Communicative capitalism and left politics*. Durham, NC: Duke University Press.
Dean, J. (2010). *Blog theory: Feedback and capture in the circuits of drive*. Cambridge, MA: Polity.
Dean, J. (2012). *The communist horizon*. London, UK: Verso Books.
Dean, J. (2014, November). Communicative capitalism and class struggle. *Spheres, Journal of Digital Cultures*. Retrieved from http://spheres-journal.org/communicative-capitalism-and-class-struggle/
Doellgast, V. (2012). *Disintegrating democracy at work: Labor unions and the future of good jobs in the service economy*. Ithaca, NY: ILR Press.
Donati, E. (1999). I call center.' una nuova opportunità di business e di lavoro nell'economia della conoscenza. *Office Automation, 3*, 2–8.
Dormann, C., & Zijlstra, F. (2004). *Call centre work: Smile by wire*. Special Issue of the European Journal of Work and Organisational Psychology. London, UK: Routledge.
Drucker, P. (1996). *Landmarks of tomorrow: A report on the new 'post-modern' world*. New Brunswick, NJ: Transaction Publishers.

Dyer-Witheford, N. (1999). *Cyber-Marx: Cycles and circuits of struggle in high-technology capitalism*. Urbana, IL: University of Illinois Press.

Dyer-Witheford, N., & de Peuter, G. (2009). *Games of empire: Global capitalism and video games*. Minneapolis, MN: University of Minnesota Press.

Ellis, V., & Taylor, P. (2006). 'You don't know what you've got till it's gone:' Re-contextualising the origins, development and impact of the call centre. *New Technology, Work and Employment, 21*(2), 107–122.

Fernie, S., & Metcalf, D. (1998). *(Not) hanging on the telephone: Payment systems in the new sweatshops* London, UK: London School of Economics and Political Science.

Figiel, J., Shukaitis, S., & Walker, A. (2014). The politics of workers' inquiry. *ephemera: theory & politics in organization, 14*(3), 307–314.

Fleming, P. (2009). *Authenticity and the cultural politics of work: New forms of informal control*. Oxford, UK: Oxford University Press.

Fleming, P., & Spicer, A. (2004). 'You can checkout anytime, but you can never leave': Spatial boundaries in a high commitment organization. *Human Relations, 57*(1), 75–94.

Fleming, P., & Sturdy, A. (2011). 'Being yourself' in the electronic sweatshop: New forms of normative control. *Human Relations, 64*(2), 177–200.

Foucault, M. (1995). *Discipline and punish: The birth of the prison* [Surveiller et punir.]. New York, NY: Vintage Books.

Foucault, M. (2003). *Society must be defended: Lectures at the Collège de France, 1975–1976*. New York, NY: Picador.

Frenkel, S. (2005). Service workers in search for decent work. In S. Ackroyd (Ed.), *The Oxford handbook of work and organization* (pp. 356–375). Oxford, UK: Oxford University Press.

Frenkel, S., Korczynski, M., Shire, K., & Tam, M. (1999). *On the front line: Organization of work in the information economy*. Ithaca, NY: Cornell University Press.

Frenkel, S., Tam, M., Korczynski, M., & Shire, K. (1998). Beyond bureaucracy? Work organisation in call centres. *International Journal of Human Resource Management, 9*(6), 957–979.

Gandy, O. (2011). The political economy of personal information. In J. Wasko, G. Murdock, & H. Sousa (Eds.), *The handbook of political economy of communications* (pp. 436–457). Malden, MA/Chichester, SXW: Wiley-Blackwell.

Garson, B. (1988). *The electronic sweatshop: How computers are transforming the office of the future into the factory of the past*. New York, NY: Simon & Schuster.

Gruppo d'inchiesta sulla precarietà e il comune. (2013). *Boll Center n. 1: Bollettino d'inchiesta sui call center calabresi.* Retrieved from http://www.sudcomune.it/site/index.php/9-inchiesta/17-bollettino-n-1

Hardt, M., & Negri, A. (2000). *Empire.* Cambridge, MA: Harvard University Press.

Hardt, M., & Negri, A. (2004). *Multitude: War and democracy in the age of empire.* New York, NY: Penguin Press.

Hardt, M., & Negri, A. (2009). *Commonwealth.* Cambridge, MA: Belknap Press of Harvard University Press.

Harvey, D. (1990). *The condition of postmodernity: An enquiry into the origins of cultural change.* Cambridge: Blackwell.

Head, S. (2004, January 2). Victims of the white-collar assembly line: ONT Edition. *Toronto Star.*

Holman, D. (2004). Employee well-being in call centres. In S. Deery & N. Kinnie (Eds.), *Call centres and human resource management* (pp. 223–244). Basingstoke, UK: Palgrave.

Houlihan, M. (2002). Tensions and variations in call centre management strategies. *Human Resource Management Journal, 12*(4), 67–67.

Huws, U. (2003). Who's waiting? The contestation of time. In U. Huws (Ed.), *The making of a cybertariat: Virtual work in a real world* (pp. 177–186). New York, NY: Monthly Review Press.

Huws, U. (2009). Working at the interface: Call-centre labour in a global economy. *Work Organisation, Labour & Globalisation, 3*(1), 1–8.

Knights, D., & McCabe, D. (1998). 'What happens when the phone goes wild?' Staff, stress and spaces for escape in a BPR telephone banking work regime. *Journal of Management Studies, 35*(2), 163–194.

Knights, D., & McCabe, D. (2003). Governing through teamwork: Reconstituting subjectivity in a call centre. *Journal of Management Studies, 40*(7), 1587–1619.

Knights, D., & Willmott, H. (1989). Power and subjectivity at work: From degradation to subjugation in social relations. *Sociology, 23*(4), 535–558.

Kolinko. (2002). *Hotlines: Call centre, inquiry, communism.* Retrieved from http://www.nadir.org/nadir/initiativ/kolinko/lebuk/e_lebuk.htm

Korczynski, M. (2002). *Human resource management in service work.* New York, NY: Palgrave.

Koskina, A. (2006). How 'taylorised' is call centre work? The sphere of customer-practice in Greece. In J. Connell & J. Burgess (Eds.), *Developments in the call centre industry: Analysis, changes, and challenges* (pp. 170–188). London, UK: Routledge.

Lavin, D. O. (2006). *Call centres in the "new economy:" A Canadian case study* (M.A. thesis). Queen's University, Kingston, ON.

Lazzarato, M. (2015). *Governing by debt* (J. D. Jordan, Trans.). Los Angeles, CA: Semiotext(e).

Lloyd, A. (2013). *Labour markets and identity on the post-industrial assembly line.* Burlington, VT: Ashgate.

Machlup, F. (1962). *The production and distribution of knowledge in the United States.* Princeton, NJ: Princeton University Press.

Marazzi, C. (1999). *I posto dei calzini: La svolta linguistica dell'economia e i suoi effetti sulla politica.* Turin, Italy: Bollati Borlinghieri.

Mattoni, A. (2012). *Media practices and protest politics: How precarious workers mobilise.* Burlington, VT: Ashgate.

McNally, D. (2011). *Global slump: The economics and politics of crisis and resistance.* Winnipeg, MB: Fernwood.

Mirrlees, T. (2013). *Global entertainment media: Between cultural imperialism and cultural globalization.* New York, NY: Routledge.

Mosco, V. (2004). *The digital sublime: Myth, power, and cyberspace.* Cambridge, MA: MIT Press.

Mosco, V. (2014). *To the cloud: Big data in a turbulent world.* Boulder, CO: Paradigm Publishers.

Mosco, V., & Lavin, D. O. (2008). The laboring of international communication. In D. Thussu (Ed.), *Internationalizing media studies* (pp. 148–162). New York, NY: Routledge.

Mosco, V., & McKercher, C. (2008). *The laboring of communication: Will knowledge workers of the world unite?* Lanham, MD: Lexington Books.

Negri, A. (2005). *Books for burning: Between civil war and democracy in 1970s Italy* [Libri del rogo.]. New York, NY: Verso.

Pearson, B., & Zehr, D. (2011). *Pre-commerce: How companies and customers are transforming business together.* San Francisco, CA: Jossey-Bass.

Pentland, B. (1995). Information systems and organizational learning: The social epistemology of organizational knowledge systems. *Accounting, Management and Information Technologies, 5*(1), 1–21.

Qiu, J. L. (2010). Network labour and non-elite knowledge workers in China. *Work Organisation, Labour & Globalisation, 4*(2), 80–95.

Qiu, J. L. (2012). Network labor: Beyond the shadow of Foxconn. In L. Hjorth, J. Burgess, & I. Richardson (Eds.), *Studying mobile media: Cultural technologies, mobile communication, and the iPhone* (pp. 173–189). London, UK: Routledge.

Rose, E. (2002). The labour process and union commitment within a banking services call centre. *Journal of Industrial Relations, 44*(1), 40–61.

Russell, B. (2008). Call centres: A decade of research. *International Journal of Management Reviews, 10*(3), 195–219.

Ryan, M. (1982). *Marxism and deconstruction: A critical articulation.* Baltimore, MD: Johns Hopkins University Press.

Schiller, D. (1999). *Digital capitalism: Networking the global market system.* Cambridge, MA: MIT Press.

Schiller, D. (2007). *How to think about information.* Urbana, IL: University of Illinois Press.

Scott, J. (1990). *Domination and the arts of resistance: Hidden transcripts.* New Haven, CT: Yale University Press.

Sewell, G. (1998). The discipline of teams: The control of team-based industrial work through electronic and peer surveillance. *Administrative Science Quarterly, 43*(2), 397–428.

Sherman, A. (2013) *Telemarketing & Call Centers in the US.* IBISWorld Industry Report 56142.

Stevens, A., & Lavin, D. O. (2007). Stealing time: The temporal regulation of labor in neoliberal and post-Fordist work regimes. *Democratic Communiqué, 22*(2), 40–61.

Taylor, P., & Bain, P. (1999). 'An assembly line in the head': Work and employee relations in the call centre. *Industrial Relations Journal, 30*(2), 101–117.

Taylor, P., & Bain, P. (2008). United by a common language? Trade union responses in the UK and India to call centre offshoring. *Antipode, 40*(1), 131–154.

Taylor, P., Baldry, C., Bain, P., & Ellis, V. (2003). A unique working environment: Health, sickness and absence management in UK call centres. *Work, Employment & Society, 17*(3), 435–458.

Taylor, P., Mulvey, G., Hyman, J., & Bain, P. (2002). Work organization, control and the experience of work in call centres. *Work, Employment & Society, 16*(1), 133–150.

Thompson, P., Warhurst, C., & Callaghan, G. (2001). Ignorant theory and knowledgeable workers: Interrogating the connections between knowledge, skills and services. *Journal of Management Studies, 38*(7), 923–942.

Townsend, K. (2005). Electronic surveillance and cohesive teams: Room for resistance in an Australian call centre? *New Technology, Work and Employment, 20*(1), 47–59.

Tronti, M. (2005). *Operai e capitale*. Rome, Italy: DeriveApprodi.
van den Broek, D. (2002). Monitoring and surveillance in call centres: Some responses from Australian workers. *Labour & Industry, 12*(3), 43–58.
van den Broek, D. (2004). Globalising call centre capital: Gender, culture and work identity. *Labour & Industry: A Journal of the Social and Economic Relations of Work, 14*(3), 59–75.
van den Broek, D., Barnes, A., & Townsend, K. (2008). 'Teaming up': Teams and team sharing in call centres. *The Journal of Industrial Relations, 50*(2), 257–269.
Viewpoint Magazine. (2013, September 30). Issue 3: Workers' inquiry. *Viewpoint Magazine, 3*. Retrieved from https://viewpointmag.com/2013/09/30/issue-3-workers-inquiry/
Virno, P. (2001). Lavoro e linguaggio. In U. Fadini & A. Zanini (Eds.), *Lessico Postfordista: Dizionario delle Idee e della Mutazione* (pp. 181–185). Milan, Italy: Feltrinelli.
Virno, P. (2003). *A grammar of the multitude: For an analysis of contemporary forms of life*. Cambridge, MA: Semiotext(e).
Wallace, C. M., Eagleson, G., & Waldersee, R. (2000). The sacrificial HR strategy in call centers. *International Journal of Service Industry Management, 11*(2), 174–184.
Wasko, J., Murdock, G., & Sousa, H. (2011). *The handbook of political economy of communications*. Malden, MA: Wiley-Blackwell.
Wilkie, R. (2011). *The digital condition: Class and culture in the information network*. New York, NY: Fordham University Press.
Winseck, D. (2011). The political economies of media and the transformation of the global media industries. In D. Winseck & D. Y. Jin (Eds.), *The political economies of media* (pp. 3–48). London, UK: Bloomsbury Academic.
Wittel, A. (2004). Culture, labour and subjectivity: For a political economy from below. *Capital & Class, 28*(3), 11–30.
Woodcock, J. (2013, September 25). Smile down the phone: An attempt at a worker inquiry in a call centre. *Viewpoint Magazine*, (3). Retrieved from https://viewpointmag.com/2013/09/25/smile-down-the-phone-an-attempt-at-a-workers-inquiry-in-a-call-center/
Wright, S. (2002). *Storming heaven: Class composition and struggle in Italian autonomist Marxism*. London, UK: Pluto Press.
Yellin, E. (2009). *Your call is (not that) important to us: Customer service and what it reveals about our world and our lives*. New York, NY: Free Press.

3

Labour's Resistance in the Call Centre

> We also had our ways of defending ourselves, of organizing ourselves, of being able to handle it.
> (Colectivo Situaciones, 2006, p. 40)

Reflecting on his time at "Call Direct," a Middlesbrough, UK call centre at which he carried out a six-month covert ethnography, Anthony Lloyd (2013) expresses scepticism as to the potential for labour resistance among this new workforce. Collective organization by workers seemed like an unlikely prospect when it was difficult to even form friendly relationships amid the temporariness and upheaval marking the firm: "[t]here appeared to be an underlying feeling of not wanting to try too hard with new co-workers because we would likely be moved around again soon and end up on different shifts" (p. 66). As a result of this impermanence, Lloyd suggests, workplace relations were "superficial and instrumental; useful for passing the time but without any deeper meaning or sacrifice from the individual" (p. 66). "Short, shallow conversations aimed at passing the time," he says, "were the best we could manage" (p. 65). Even when employees at Call Direct appeared to be on the verge of rebellion after work teams were restructured and schedules changed unilaterally,

© The Author(s) 2017
E. Brophy, *Language Put to Work*, Dynamics of Virtual Work,
DOI 10.1057/978-1-349-95244-1_3

resistance fizzled out quickly. One of Lloyd's colleagues, Ollie, vented his anger at the company by being belligerent with a customer on the phone, hanging up, and taking an unsanctioned "comfort break." Despite this misconduct, for Lloyd, the event points to how resistance in the call centre has been "reduced to acts of disobedience that in no way affect the work process, the management strategy, or the company" (p. 76).

Lloyd's ethnographic account of Call Direct is valuable (Brophy, 2015), but the distinction he proposes between acts of mere "disobedience" such as Ollie's and forms of rebellion that qualify as genuine resistance limits our analysis of the power relations taking shape within call centres. This chapter surveys the many different forms labour antagonism in the call centre can take, from individualized and subterranean rebellion to collective moments of organization and sabotage. This spectrum of resistant behaviours, I suggest, constitutes the vernacular of a counter-perspective that has surfaced among the call centre workforce since its inception—a perspective that has signalled, contested, and even disrupted the process of class formation taking place in call centres.

Scholars of resistance have argued for the utility of paying attention to the broad range of ways antagonism to power can be expressed, in the workplace as elsewhere. First-generation *operaisti* such as Raniero Panzieri and Romano Alquati were sensitive not only to the standard channels of labour conflict (the union, the party), or to its most intense manifestations (strikes, demonstrations, occupations), but also and perhaps especially to the seemingly innocuous undercurrents of dissatisfaction, disavowal, and disengagement which might become breeding grounds for escalating forms of insubordination.[1] Similarly, in his study of systemic power relations such as slavery, serfdom, and caste systems, the anthropologist James C. Scott explores the wide range of practices by which those in subordinate positions have historically sought to thwart the material appropriation of their labour, production, and property, including

---

[1] This sensibility allowed workerists to anticipate a ferocious, decade-long wave of labour militancy, one that was led by the very workers that had been written off by the Italian Communist Party and the major trade unions as overly materialistic or even apolitical (see Roggero, 2011, pp. 135–142; Wright, 2002). A key theme running through Alquati's ground-breaking research at Fiat in 1961, for example, was the pre-eminence of a new working class that was "disillusioned with the company, but also indifferent to left-wing unions and parties" (Pizzolato, 2013, para. 6).

poaching, foot-dragging, pilfering, dissimulation, and flight.[2] Guided by such examples, this chapter provides a composite portrait of labour resistance in the call centre, beginning from the least perceptible manifestations of disengagement and progressing towards more overt instances of labour conflict. While not comprehensive, this overview offers a sense of the many ways in which the process of class formation unfolding in these workspaces has been met with recalcitrance, refusal, and rebellion by its subjects. The findings presented here are therefore valuable in and of themselves as a kind of compendium of resistance in a digital workspace that is generally associated with labour's powerlessness rather than its agency. More broadly, however, these examples of insubordination are gathered because when taken together they suggest that an approach to the call centre which begins with resistance will find fertile ground upon which to inquire.

Flight "If you work a year in the call centre then you're a veteran" (as cited in *Cátedra Experimental sobre Producción de Subjetividad*, 2007b, p. 134). This caustic quote attributed to a worker in Rosario, Argentina, points to a defining feature of call centre employment—its extraordinarily high rates of "churn," or employee turnover. Churn rates offer an initial, statistical glimpse of the most prevalent method by which the workforce has refused the conditions marking call centres—by simply leaving. The figures are striking: according to the first global study of these workspaces authored by David Holman, Rosemary Batt, and Ursula Holtgrewe, call centres haemorrhage a fifth of their employees per year on average, but in some countries, and particularly in the outsourced sector where labour conditions are harsher, the rates of flight are higher. In outsourced call centres in Ireland and the United States, for example, turnover was estimated at over a third of the workforce per year (Holman,

---

[2] As James C. Scott notes, "social science is, in general then, focused resolutely on the official or formal relations between the powerful and weak. This is the case even for much of the study of conflict, as we shall see, when that conflict has become highly institutionalized" (Scott, 1990, p. 13). Andrew Ross points out what might be missed by focusing on these formal relations: "A good deal of creativity on the job is devoted to employee resistance, in the form of slowdowns, sabotage, pilfering, and other petty acts that enable workers to win back from their employers some control over their time and effort" (Ross, 2009, pp. 48–49).

Batt, & Holtgrewe, 2007, p. 40). The attrition rate for workers within the Australian industry is 40% for full-time staff and 44% for part-time workers (Kidman, 2010). Taylor and Bain (2008, p. 39) suggest that in India official figures report turnover of 30–40%, but the real rate has been estimated at 65–75%, and even exceeding 100% at some companies. Notably, across 20 countries participating in the global research project, a full third of the workforce was only in their first year on the job (Holman et al., 2007, p. ix). Call centres produce a great deal of employment but not many long-term employees.

An American call centre manager describes this steady pattern of employee exit from the call centre as the result of a new, young, and fickle workforce: "these kids just come in to make some money, and are out the door next week" (as cited in Doellgast, 2012, p. 3). The sociologist Shehzad Nadeem likewise points to a kind of mercenary subjectivity developing among call centre workers in India, where "the fluidity of the labour market has allowed employees to move horizontally from company to company in search of the best compensation package" (Nadeem, 2011, p. 98). This mercenary approach by "mobile and unfaithful labor subjects," as the autonomist scholar Gigi Roggero has noted of workers across knowledge and communication-based sectors, is also a product of the volatility and flexibility capital itself has imposed on the workforce (Roggero, 2011, p. 100). Flight from work is one of the most basic and common forms of resistance to problematic labour conditions, a time-tested tool in the "infrapolitics" of waged labour that would seem perfectly suited to conditions of post-Fordist labour flexibility (Scott, 1990, p. 183).[3] Seen from this perspective, the arrestingly high levels of turnover suggest that flight presents an unfaithful workforce with the simplest possible solution to problematic labour conditions encountered in call centres.

---

[3] Notable treatments of this phenomenon include Marx's (1990, p. 932) discussion of workers' flight from "the manufacturing of wage labourers in the colonies" that propelled the American frontier, or Peter Linebaugh and Marcus Rediker's discussion of pirating as a manifestation of worker's escape from the burgeoning commercial and military naval sectors of the British maritime state through the seventeenth and eighteenth centuries (2000, pp. 143–173).

3 Labour's Resistance in the Call Centre 63

That a 2008 Italian film narrating the story of two university graduates reluctantly working in the industry was entitled *Fuga dal Call Center* [Escape from the Call Centre] (Rizzo, 2008) is therefore not a coincidence: accounts of contempt for the job and a resultant desire to flee it are ubiquitous. The Gruppo d'Inchiesta sulla Precarietà e il Comune, a Calabrian collective of call centre workers, reports that among the ex-call centre employees they interviewed, most were thankful for having made a choice to quit the job:

> Despite the economic difficulties and the forced recourse to so-called family welfare, they still say they are convinced: we live far better today, we have economic problems but we are better within ourselves, before we didn't realize it but our lives were far worse, it had become a vicious cycle in which we were trapped, we were only one step away from a breakdown. (Pezzulli, 2013, para. 7)

Labour process researcher Kate Mulholland's revealing article on the informal means of resistance deployed by employees in an Northern Irish call centre describes the rampant disaffection she found there as a direct cause of the 8% monthly turnover afflicting the workplace. Quitting your job at the call centre, Mulholland notes, was only one element of what she describes as a "widespread pattern of work rejection" (Mulholland, 2004, p. 720) on the shop floor. One employee cited by Mulholland offers some insight into the sentiments of countless thousands exiting the revolving doors of call centres around the world:

> It was a struggle for me to get to the end of the week, I got very stressed and would crash out. Just being away from the place was great, then you walk in on Monday and it starts all over again. I couldn't cope with this see-saw life and left. (2004, p. 720)

As Nadeem's reflection on worker disengagement from the goals of their employers indicates, this aversion to the job is not limited to the relatively privileged workers of the global North. Feminist scholar Kiran Mirchandani (2004, p. 368) discovered in her research with workers in India that despite having gone through a long series of tests to gain such employment they were "unanimously unconvinced by the arguments about the quality of call centre jobs." By October of 2007 a *Time Magazine* article on the growing troubles of the outsourced industry in India confirmed this view and quoted a student at a college in New Delhi as saying: "Earlier it was considered cool to work at a call centre ... That died out quite quickly" (Thanawala, 2007, para. 5). The piece went on to suggest that interviewees felt "it is no longer worthwhile going through sleepless nights serving customers halfway around the world. They have better job opportunities in other fields. The work is tiring and stressful and offers few career advancement opportunities" (para. 2). Nadeem confirms the utility of flight in the Indian context when he suggests that escape from the call centre may, "somewhat perversely," be "good for workers' health" in an otherwise unsustainable environment of high stress, disrupted circadian rhythms, strained familial relations, and routine racist abuse (Nadeem, 2011, p. 89).

The degree to which this continual making and unmaking of the call centre labour force is a product of employers' power over workers, or of the latter's agency, varies depending on the context of course. And, as we shall see next, there are important counter-examples of stable employment in call centres—notably, in unionized ones. Yet the constant, centrifugal movement of workers out the doors and away from call centres worldwide points to a palpable and far-reaching affective detachment among the workforce. If, along with labour process scholars Peter Fleming and Graham Sewell, we wish to expand our view of labour resistance so as to include "forms of opposition that are more inconspicuous, subjective, subtle and unorganized" (Fleming & Sewell, 2002, p. 859),[4] then the uninterrupted pattern of worker flight from the call centre constitutes a

---

[4] This call is echoed by Thomas Hastings (2011, pp. 23–24) in his thesis on power and resistance in call centre work in Scotland. At a time when union membership is on the decline globally, Hastings observes, organized collective action provides only a partial picture of labour agency. As such he suggests that "more nuanced expressions of labour agency" (p. 9) would pay attention not only to overt acts of rebellion but to the coping strategies of call centre workers which may not even be directed toward anything more threatening than day-to-day survival.

telling sign of labour's refusal of this new workspace. In fact, as E.P. Thompson (1966, p. 78) suggested in another context, it may be one of those facts of history that is so big it is easily overlooked.

Moreover, worker flight is a strategy which has consequences for employers and even for workers who stay in the job. Scholars and industry observers have regularly noted the hit to the bottom line taken by employers forced to train new workers, and there is evidence that the prevalence of worker churn has been an important factor in recent moves by management to implement "softer and less coercive techniques" (Hastings, 2011, p. 156) to keep workers on the job.[5] The rise of managerial strategies encouraging workers to "be themselves" in their work that have been highlighted by Fleming and Sturdy (2011) can be read in this light.[6] What's more, in some areas there are even signs that the practice of worker flight may have determined the course of industrial development in the outsourced call centre sector. Carrillo Rowe, Perez, and Malhotra (2013, p. 186) suggest that the Indian call centre industry, despite attempts to install agreements not to poach each other's workers, has been "relatively unsuccessful at containing agents' mobility," and, even more interestingly, have suggested that the difficulties in keeping workers put has made "consolidation a necessity" in the sector. In this way, we can see how the most seemingly mundane and individualized form of worker disengagement, when repeated thousands or even hundreds of thousands of times, produces a much larger and more threatening pattern which can create great difficulties for employers and to which they are forced to respond.

---

[5] Hastings (2011, p. 156) suggests that each of the call centres he surveyed "demonstrated a waning reliance on targets as a means of governing the labour process ... In doing so, management recognised that softer and less coercive techniques of control were vital to reducing monotony, stress, and turnover." Another account of the Indian sector observes that "[a]n annual attrition rate of 30% struts about like a prima donna. The attrition is forcing BPO companies to pay more. Wages have risen so quickly in India that it's not much cheaper in comparison to Canada as an offshoring location." (*The Telegraph*, as cited in Friends of Kolinko & Gurgaon Workers News, 2012, para. 28).

[6] And, perhaps predictably, the gloss began to wear off this "high-involvement" model of management fairly quickly: "Indeed, for some employees, this identity-orientated detraction from control was experienced more as an attempt at mystification, inspiring its own variants of resistance" (Fleming & Sturdy, 2011, p. 194).

Detachment, Slacking, and Sabotage Exit from the digital assembly lines is only the first and most basic form of labour resistance available to those working for a wage over a headset. Whether by choice or necessity, millions remain in call centre employment despite misgivings they may have about the job. Among those who stay there are ample signs of what sociologists Peter Taylor and Phil Bain described as "a deep undercurrent of distrust of management motives" in the call centre (2003, p. 1497). Flowing below the organizational surface of this new workspace, this undercurrent of detachment carries with it a range of techniques for slowing the pace of work so as to create and protect what David Knights and Darren McCabe call the "autonomous form" (1998, p. 170) of the workforce.

Techniques for slacking and sabotage are more likely to develop in an environment of worker detachment from management's objectives. An early example of such conditions is found in an account that memorably conveys the disaffection reigning within the walls of a San Francisco call centre:

> The customer is transferred to me. "Are you a supervisor?" he demands instantly. Since the beginning of the month, everyone in the call centre has been transformed into a supervisor. Brian sleeping at his desk is now a supervisor. Ian with purple hair gelled into points is a supervisor. Ron who begged not to be made a supervisor is a supervisor. I am hoping next month, whoever decided to make us all supervisors will make us CEOs. "Yes, I am a supervisor." "At last," he sighs. I feel sorry for him: he thinks he's reached someone in authority. (East Bay Express, as cited in Kolinko, 2002, section 6.e)

Such lack of dedication to the job, or what Arlie Hochschild (2004) observed as detachment from the rigours of what she called emotional labour, carries obvious risks of lost profits for call centre operations. Management's answer to this problem has been the establishment of elaborate surveillance systems in order to monitor the productivity of front-line agents and avoid what Simon Head calls "the unauthorized, the disruptive, and the dysfunctional" (2014, p. 23). This digital assemblage for the purposes of surveillance supports the employer's goal of reducing to a minimum what is increasingly being articulated as the perpetration of "time theft," a term which, according to Canadian sociologist David Lavin, "has come to include everything from loafing, reading on the job, unnecessarily arguing with customers, non-work related conversations and interactions with co-workers, faking illness and taking a sick day, to going to the washroom too often during a shift" (2006, p. 164). The mobilization of such cutting-edge surveillance technologies alongside discourses of "time theft" underscores the degree to which call centre management, as a general rule, lacks faith in its workforce. The feeling, as it turns out, is often both mutual and entirely justified.

Despite the formidable apparatus for labour surveillance directed against call centre workers, the techniques employees have developed to slow down or turn back the pace of work range from elementary forms of hacking to twenty-first-century variants of industrial sabotage. As Kiran Mirchandani points out, "technology is not only a tool of managerial control but can also be manipulated for the workers' benefit, especially when workers have four-year degrees in programming and engineering as some customer service agents do" (2012, p. 93). In his thesis on the coping strategies employed by call centre workers in Scotland, Thomas Hastings notes that while listening in to calls at the "Sales-Com" call centre he "sometimes heard long periods of silence whereby the dialler had failed to queue a subsequent call" (2011, p. 165). Where language has been put to work, remaining silent amounts to a withdrawal of labour—as the Cátedra Experimental collective says, "Inside Apex, silence is a synonym for health" (2007b, p. 135)—and examples of intentionally and surreptitiously withheld communicative production are common in the call centre sector. A typical case was described in Australia, where van den Broek, Barnes, and Townsend (2008) reported workers pressing the "transfer" button a split second before customers hung up the phone at the end of the call, a tactic allowing employees an extra two or three extra minutes before the next call while it appeared to supervisors that they were still in conversation. In Kingston, Ontario, workers called their variant of this technique the "double wrap," a "delicate game" that David Lavin (2006, p. 173) characterizes as a reappropriation of time by workers. The Colectivo Situaciones also reports this technique being used in Argentina: in ¿Quién Habla? the collective of activist-scholars suggests that "one of the ways of escaping calls is to log out, to leave the system and stop receiving calls: these are, in a non-metaphorical sense, simulations of strikes" (2006, p. 38).[7] These forms of disorderly and profit-threatening behaviour by workers often amount to only dispersed and individualized expressions of labour resistance to be sure, yet as researchers have found in some of the most revealing case studies of call centre labour, such tactics can also sync up within more broadly based strategies of work refusal.[8]

Kate Mulholland, for example, has described a range of informal strategies through which workers "collude, collaborate and co-operate" (2004, p. 710) in order to collectively resist, avoid, or frustrate the worst parts of their job. At the Belfast call centre Mulholland examined, things had gotten so bad that an antagonistic culture had developed among workers where activities such as cheating, work avoidance, and phoning in sick were all seen as reasonable responses to the conditions. Knights and McCabe (1998) report cases of call centre workers pretending to answer the phone by donning headphones and mouthing words in simulated conversation. Such informal acts, aimed as they are at reclaiming stretches of time from the notoriously punishing rhythms of the call centre, certainly have "an adverse and immediate impact on profitability" as Mulholland and others have pointed out, but they can also become a breeding ground for more organized forms of resistance (Knights & McCabe, 1998, p. 713).

Other ploys by workers fall further into the realms of sabotage and pilfering. Kolinko reports examples of "making the machinery crash when the work stress has reached its limit. Ctrl-Alt-Del . . . and you have a three-minutes-break extra while the PC is rebooting" (2002, section 6.2.a). Kiran Mirchandani describes the *talla*, a hoax solution offered by Indian call centre workers when customers are irate and unmanageable (2012, p. 93). Call centre workers at Convergys in India reportedly created fake favourable ratings online so as to generate performance bonuses for

---

[7] My thanks to Paula Velázquez Lanzmaier for the translation of this passage.
[8] In addition to the accounts from workers that are available from sources such as worker inquiries and online forums, my account in this section is indebted to the studies carried out by van den Broek, Barnes, and Townsend; Mulholland; and Taylor and Bain, which are cited here.

themselves.[9] Mulholland describes the practice of "slammin'," whereby workers at the call centre she investigated manipulated data so as to record more sales than they had actually made and thereby increase their bonus (2004, p. 713). According to another account (AES, 2013, post #5), in Scotland, resentment against disciplinary management by a group of pension call handlers resulted in a decision to deliberately target the company's profits. Call centre agents conspired to put calls from financial advisors or other institutions ("which caused us stress") on hold and then used the time to search through files for unclaimed pensions and try to track down the pensioner in question so that the pension could be claimed. According to the anonymous poster in a Libcom forum dedicated to a discussion of call centre work:

> I witnessed this method being used for long over a year until I had my final conflict with the managers. Workmates I spoke to years afterwards said that this method was still used occasionally. We cost Scottish Widows millions of pounds—SW bosses are selfish bastards—We hit them where it hurt! (AES, 2013, post #5)

Given the risks faced by workers employing such techniques, as well as management's interest in banishing them from the culture of their workplaces, evidence of slacking, pilfering, and sabotage in call centres is invariably anecdotal. As a result, more accurate knowledge regarding the relative frequency with which these activities are deployed across regional contexts is simply not available. This notwithstanding, the accounts found in academic case studies, worker inquiries, and online forums, in addition to the fairly brazen cases documented later on in this book, testify as to the important, even critical role such behaviours can play in the build-up and intensification of labour resistance in call centres.

Teaming Up If telling the boss exactly what you think, quitting, or finding small ways to mitigate the relentless pace of work can all be

---

[9] The technical savvy required for their scam was even underscored by the ex-CEO of competitor Wipro, who was cited as saying "... it's possible if one has a strong understanding of technology. If these kids could manage that, then they are wasting their talents in a BPO" (Steven, 2010, para. 3).

rewarding for workers in the short run, it is also true that in isolation these behaviours do little to challenge management's structural power in the call centre. Some research has provided compelling glimpses of the ways in which workforce dissatisfaction and disavowal can promote the creation of both formal and informal horizontal bonds designed to resist management's productivity push from above. In Turkey, Esin Gülsen documents how workers in a Burger King call centre, knowing that management was picking on employees who fielded the least number of calls, decided to equalize the number of calls taken by each member, warning workers whose productivity was rising (2015, p. 145). In another example, van den Broek, Barnes, and Townsend described Australian workers "teaming up" not to increase productivity, but to challenge managerial directives and improve their labour conditions (2008, p. 257). The researchers recount how a team of 13 customer service reps signed a petition registering their opposition to excessive monitoring and "relentless conditions of work"—thus transforming the "team" structure designed to intensify their workload into an informal vehicle through which to strike back against work intensification (2008, p. 264).[10] Peter Taylor and Phil Bain's study at Excell describes how collective humour by workers, including the public ridiculing of authoritarian team leaders and managers, fed a "vigorous counterculture" that eventually forced the reversal of a colleague's dismissal and led to an overwhelming vote for union recognition across the company's three call centres (2003, p. 1487).

Such research provides clear examples of how management's quest for technological control and work intensification begets the worker cynicism and revulsion fleetingly evoked by Harry Braverman (1974, p. 104) in *Labor and Monopoly Capitalism*. As the Excell case evidences, cultures of workplace disobedience and the informal bonds that are developed from below by workers can also become the basis for formal relationships with organized labour. Call centre workers are engaged in a range of

---

[10] This case demonstrates how management's adoption of workplace democracy discourse clearly carries the risk that workers might begin to take it seriously. In this instance, the manager urged them to recast their complaints individually, and (in an irony not missed by the researchers) despite the impressive degree of cooperation they had displayed, dealt workers low marks in the "teamwork" category of their performance appraisal.

relationships with trade unions, whether through already-existing unions or organizing drives to form new ones. While scholars such as Bob Russell (2008) have suggested that unionism is "embryonic" in the call centre, they have also regularly pointed to the dearth of academic study of union organizing. Over the last ten years, however, research on trade unionism in the call centre has grown and the findings might surprise those who imagine this communicative workspace to be union-free territory.

Notably, Holman, Batt, and Holtgrewe's (2007) global study found that close to half of the workplaces they examined were already covered by some form of collective representation (collective bargaining, works councils, or both), generally as the legacy of collective agreements covering the industries the call centres operated "downstream" from.[11] This is the case at Canada Post, for example, where call centre workers belong to (and took part in a strike organized by) the Public Service Alliance of Canada (Rynor, 2008). In the North America (as the next chapter recounts) call centre workers employed by continental oligopolies such as Sprint, Verizon, Telus, and Bell are often part of "convergent" unions such as the Communication Workers of America, the Telecommunications Workers Union, and Unifor (previously the Communications, Energy and Paperworkers Union of Canada) (Brophy, 2009; Mosco & McKercher, 2006). In some countries, particularly ones with higher levels of collective representation, established unions have successfully incorporated outsourced call centres into industry-wide collective agreements as the GPA (*Gewerkschaft der Privatangestellten*) union has done in Austria (Holst, 2008). The prevailing image of call centres as union-free environments, while not altogether inaccurate, may therefore owe more to ideology than it does to reality, proposing management's favoured scenario as if it were an accomplished state of affairs. Not surprisingly, the presence of a union tends to bring with it less surveillance, higher pay, and lower turnover.

When workers are not already represented by a union they can often form one, and academic research has begun to examine the labour organizing taking place along the digital assembly lines. Research in this area offers further examples of the overlap between labour activism and

---

[11] It should be noted that the sampling method used in this study was non-random.

academic inquiry. Al Rainnie and Gail Drummond (2006) describe a labour organizer's experience leading a successful unionizing campaign at an Australian call centre in the Latrobe Valley, east of Melbourne. In Canada, Julie Guard, Mercedes Steedman, and Jorge García Orgales (2007), and then Andrew Stevens (2014) documented the United Steelworkers Union's initially successful call centre organizing campaign in the mining town of Sudbury, Ontario. Andrew Stevens and David Lavin (2007) depict the bitter (yet ultimately unsuccessful) struggle to organize a call centre in southern Ontario, and writer and journalist Andrew Bibby (2000) was one of the first to catalogue organizing efforts at financial call centres in Australia, Germany, Austria, the Netherlands, and the United Kingdom. As Chap. 5 of this book recounts, the formation of unions also appears to be pursuing some employers to the locations where they had relocated precisely in order to escape collective organization and higher wages, be it to the outsourced sector domestically or internationally. A promising example of the latter that has received some attention is the Union for IT Enabled Services Professionals (UNITES) organization in India, formed under the aegis of the international umbrella labour organization Union Network International (UNI) in 2005 and now acting as an organized presence in six cities with 6000–7000 members (Stevens & Mosco, 2010; Taylor & Bain, 2006).

At least a couple of call centre-specific unions have also been developed. In South Africa, the National Contact Centre Union was formed in 2009 with the goal of organizing workers in the country's burgeoning business process outsourcing (BPO) industry. In Turkey, Esin Gülsen (2015, p. 142) has written about the formation of the Association of Call Center Workers in 2008, an organization with the stated purpose of questioning "the capitalist discourse on work" and whose action against the Garanti Bank management was discussed at the beginning of this book. It is unclear how active these incipient unions have been in recent times, but however embryonic the unionism driving these examples may be, securing a collective agreement or even the threat of collective organizing can make real differences for workers as far as labour conditions and job security are concerned.

Striking When conditions become intolerable, call centre employees across the world have also taken part in work stoppages and other forms of direct action to address their conditions. In Mexico, 1700 call centre workers at Tecmarketing, which provides support for the telecommunications giant Telmex (owned by the world's richest man, Carlos Slim) organized the first strike since the company's privatization in February of 2008, achieving a 4.4% pay raise (Reuters News, 2008a). The following month, in Finland, some 1200 Union of Salaried Employees call centre workers at telecom operator Elisa's subcontractor Teleperformance voted to strike after they were barred from the sectoral agreement for telecommunications workers (Reuters News, 2008b). In Durban, South Africa, Communication Workers' Union (CWU) call centre workers at Telkom struck in August 2009, achieving a 7.5% salary increase (Moodley, 2009). In Nigeria, workers at Airtel Telecommunication shut down two of the company's major call centres in Lagos and Abuja and declared indefinite strike in 2011 in order to protest management strategies and the threat of layoffs (Ahiuma-Young, 2011). In Ghana, workers answering calls for Vodafone went on an indefinite "sit-down strike" against their outsourced employer (the South African company Teletec) to negotiate better working conditions and pay ("For about two years no salary increment, nothing. We are like slaves," one anonymous worker was quoted as saying). In 2008, city council call centre workers in Ipswich City, Australia, rallied and struck against a proposed "shared services" model which aimed to bring a privately listed Australian outsourcing company, UCMS, into the provision of public services (Gardiner, 2008). In Uruguay, call centre workers called for and organized a 24-hour national strike of both public and private sector workers, adopting "we don't want a sector of impoverished youth" as its rallying cry and demanding better salaries, more time between calls and regular breaks on shift (Cámara de Telecomunicaciones del Uruguay, 2010; Zecca, 2010).

Job action by call centre workers has been spontaneous as well, such as in 2009 when United Services Union call centre workers at New South Wales electricity retailers wildcatted after the state government failed to guarantee their jobs in its decision to privatize the utility (*Daily Telegraph*, 2009). Against the backdrop of the 2001 Argentine financial crisis, 1500 call centre workers attended a FOETRA meeting (the Argentine union of telco employees) to reject the restructuring plan proposed by the telecommunication companies, which included a 10% salary cut, a decrease of overtime hours and a reprogramming of work shifts. Workers ended up occupying two Telefónica de Argentina buildings in the process (Fernández, 2015). The Colectivo Situaciones (2006) also reports on occupations of call centres and strikes featuring the coordinated refusal of calls in Buenos Aires, Argentina. The *Hotlines* book contains a worker's report of a wildcat strike at the Blu call centre in Florence, Italy, in response to news the company was being sold and some of its workers let go:

> When they told us on the 13th [of February] that no contract would be prolonged it was a shock. Not just for the 24 workers who were affected that day, but for all the others with the same kind of contracts. When the news kicked in, everybody stopped phoning immediately. Most of the managers kept out of sight that day. Some of the team leaders were also affected themselves. The ones that remained were more or less passive. Some angry discussions started. The people felt betrayed. They thought of themselves as the 'good agents', the experienced ones, some of them have already been promoted ... and now this. Especially the people sacked that day that had personal relationships with the management, originating from the time when the call centre was opened and there were only a few people working there. The discussions lasted for some hours. The calls for the private customer hotline were re-routed to the second Blu call centre, located in Palermo. Probably resulting in an over-flow there. The situation in the commercial customer hotline became more and more critical. Because these calls could not be re-routed—and because the commercial customers are much more important, of course—the managers tried to get the people back on the lines. The people refused and heavy disputes surged up again. (as cited in Kolinko, 2002, section 6.2.c)

As we shall see in Chap. 6, labour struggles in Italian call centres have been especially intense at their peaks. Customer service representatives employed at Omnia engaged in an ongoing series of actions against the company, including strikes, demonstrations outside its Turin headquarters, and the kidnapping of the company's managing director in Milan, who was forced to reply to workers' questions regarding late wages and the use of temporary contracts (ANSA, 2009). In 2010, workers occupied the Turin call centre in response to the threat of company closure, and a year later, workers from a number of different call centres took part in a general strike marching behind a banner that declared "CALL CENTER IN LOTTA" [call centres in struggle] (Voce Proletaria, 2011, para. 2).[12] The march ended with an open assembly of workers ("the only form of contact we actually like") in front of another call centre company, Comdata.

It is impossible to offer an exhaustive overview of labour's insubordination in the call centre here, but it would be remiss not to finish with a more specific mention of the organizing that has occurred around the outsourcing of work, a permanent source of managerial discipline and thus a pivotal labour issue in call centres around the world. A good example of how strife arises from the potential for outsourcing comes from Thames Water in the United Kingdom, a privatized utility providing water to people in London owned by the Australian corporate banking and investment company Macquarie. In fall of 2008, Thames announced it was raising water rates for 13.5 million customers by 3% above inflation for five years, allowing it to reap half-year profits of £23.2 million UK (Morning Star Online, 2009). At the same time, management at Thames told 282 unionized call centre workers that their jobs would be outsourced to India if they did not agree to "family unfriendly" changes in working hours, provoking calls for a strike ballot through the GMB union (*Daily Mail*, 2009). Workers in this case accepted the changes and signed a new contract, but the company never abandoned its plans to outsource its customer service labour, and signed a contract with Wipro in 2016 (United News of India, 2016).

Similar stories of labour strife over outsourcing can be found in news coverage from a range of different countries. Workers at South African Airlines in the South African Transport and Allied Workers Union (SATAWU) pursued action in 2008, threatening to strike over the airline's plan to outsource 250 call centre jobs to Dimension Data and ultimately causing the company to back off (Modimoeng, 2008). In

---

[12] See also Parola (2010).

September of the same year, employees of the transnational company Teletech took to the streets of Palmerston North, New Zealand, to protest the outsourcing of their Yellow Pages inquiry assistance jobs to the Philippines (Duff, 2008). In 2011, activists from the Taiwan Labour Front and other labour groups protested the National Communications Commission (NCC) in Taipei against outsourcing of call centre work to China by telecoms companies such as Far-EasTone Telecommunications (Shan, 2011).

Bain and Taylor have dissected the battles arising around outsourcing at five companies in the United Kingdom, concluding that strike action was the most likely to get companies to make concessions and that there was promise in the UNI's transnational approach to organizing (Bain & Taylor, 2008). Aiming to promote international cooperation and exchange between workers at risk of being outsourced and those in areas to which jobs are being shipped, UNI developed its *Offshoring Charter* in 2006 as one of the opening acts in a set of labour struggles that have clearly become international in scope.

"The Only Form of Contact We Actually Like"

The connective promise of communicative capitalism is neatly captured in those two little words on a company's website that consumers must click upon to get a response: "contact us." Thus far this book has shown how behind those two words there lies the rise of a multibillion-dollar customer relations industry, the expansion of a paradigmatic new workspace, and the formation of a transnational and highly communicative workforce.

As Jodi Dean (2012, p. 77) notes, the job of this new informational underclass is to "smile, care, communicate, and be friendly." A call centre company's pitch to prospective clients reveals the corporate fantasy of this workforce, depicted as a caring, always-on employee working around the clock so as to enable the promises of permanent customer connectivity:

> Imagine having a receptionist who doesn't take lunch breaks, never has a sick day and doesn't require health benefits! Yes, it's possible. Telelink

provides a live receptionist to answer your calls 24/7, 365 days a year. Allow us to answer all of your calls, so you can concentrate on the other important aspects of your business, or have us take your after-hours and weekend calls so you have peace of mind knowing your customers are still being taken care of. (Telelink Call Centre, n.d.)

While disarmingly candid in its offer of a diligent and tireless labour force that is prepared to work for less, the offer fails to mention the inherent unpredictability of the labour power upon which this promise depends. This chapter has surveyed the ways in which the subjects enabling capital's growing communicativity can be disinclined, disloyal, unproductive, refractory, defiant, vengeful, conspiratorial, and even destructive in their refusal of the optimistic image of the always-on call centre worker outlined earlier. These behaviours, I suggest, offer the basis for a distinctive analysis of call centre labour, one which details an emergent counter-subjectivity that is signalling, contesting, and even disrupting the process of class formation taking place in these workspaces. Far from the well-adapted call centre knowledge worker depicted by the more accommodating, business-friendly literatures, these workers are quitting, slacking, and organizing in order to improve their often regrettable conditions of work and life. Their practices of resistance, as well as the knowledges, literatures, and cultures being cultivated around them, are the vernacular of a gathering counter-perspective from below, one that is developing within and against the process of language put to work in call centres.

This counter-perspective has been circulated and developed thanks to a kind of communication that, rather than being imposed by management through software-dictated scripts, extends horizontally among workers. This form of communication is described by the *Cátedra Experimental sobre Producción de Subjetividad* (2007a, p. 135) as a "tool for collective instruction," or what members of the German labour activist group Call Center Offensive termed "communication without management and telephones" (as cited in Kolinko, 2002, section 6.3.c., para. 10). When call centre workers in Turin ended their aforementioned march with a general assembly, they likewise vindicated the oppositional nature of this self-organized communication by describing it as "the only form of contact we actually like" (Voce Proletaria, 2011, para. 2). What this book explores is therefore a gathering counter-perspective on call centres, as well as the kinds of communicative practices and forms of resistance through which it has been circulated.

It is important to note that the instances of detachment, conflict, and counter-organization I have collected in this chapter, impressive as they might sound when listed in succession, are likely to be only exceptional cases among an otherwise relatively subdued global workforce. A method beginning with resistance such as the one I adopt in this book, critics might point out, does run the risk of seeing the birth of a digital labour movement in what are actually relatively rare and disconnected instances of collective action. My goal has not been to make the case that resistance is the key tendency in call centres, a move that would only replicate the exaggerated nature of the claims made by Fernie and Metcalf (1998), only this time in the service of a diametrically opposed reading of the power relations in these workspaces. It is important to note at the outset, therefore, that the cases recounted here and in the chapters that follow are only a sample, we cannot know how large, of the antagonisms—dormant or manifest—generated by the contemporary process of class formation taking hold in call centres. My intention is not to inflate their significance beyond the scope of what they can meaningfully tell us about the process of proletarianization in communicative capitalism.

Nevertheless, when considered together these cases and others are sufficient to argue that the production of an informational underclass in call centres is, at a minimum, a contested and open-ended process. An approach that privileges the resistance generated within this process begins with a very different set of questions than the one that motivated the project described by Michael Burawoy in his classic text, *Manufacturing Consent*. Where Burawoy asked why workers worked as hard as they did, the inquiries gathered in this book begin by asking: Why are workers resisting? What kinds of workers are organizing? What tactics are they using? What are the challenges they are facing? What are the allied groups and organizations they are connecting with in these struggles? What organizations are they forming? What is the outcome of their efforts?

In order to better understand the counter-perspective on call centre labour I have sketched out here, as well as the forms of practice through which it has been articulated, the chapters that follow explore three cases of labour resistance and collective organization in greater depth, gathering examples ranging from strikes by established trade unions to autonomous rank-and-file organizing by shop-floor collectives. Chapters 4, 5, and 6 draw on field work completed in New Zealand, Italy, Ireland, and Atlantic Canada between 2006 and 2012, research that produced over 60 interviews with call centre workers, labour activists, union organizers, and industry observers. Cases were chosen according to the form of collective organization adopted (established trade unionism, rank-and-file trade unionism, and worker self-organization, respectively), the industry served by the call centres (mostly telecommunications, but also consumer research), and the degree of conflict achieved by the struggles (strikes and other direct manifestations of antagonistic collective organization such as demonstrations, direct action, media campaigns, and legal cases). Through a discussion of these events, I offer a portrait of this emblematic form of immaterial labour that foregrounds the resistant, antagonistic, and always at least potentially autonomous capacities residing in the informational underclass.

References

AES. (2013, October 4). *Are you stealing from your boss?* Retrieved from https://libcom.org/forums/oceania/are-you-stealing-your-boss-04102013

Ahiuma-Young, V. (2011). *Nigeria: Aggrieved workers shut down Airtel's call centre*. Retrieved from http://allafrica.com/stories/201110040014.html

ANSA. (2009, April 3). Omnia network late with wages, protest in Turin. Accessed via Factiva database: https://global.factiva.com/

Bain, P., & Taylor, P. (2008). No passage to India? Initial responses of UK trade unions to call centre outsourcing. *Industrial Relations Journal, 39*(1), 5–23.

Bibby, A. (2000). *Organising in financial call centres: A report for the UNI*. Retrieved from http://www.andrewbibby.com/pdf/fin-callcent-e.pdf

Braverman, H. (1974). *Labor and monopoly capital: The degradation of work in the twentieth century*. New York: Monthly Review Press.

Brophy, E. (2009). Resisting call centre work: The Aliant strike and convergent unionism in Canada. *Work Organisation, Labour & Globalisation, 3*(1), 80–99.

Brophy, E. (2015). Revisiting the digital assembly line: New perspectives on call centre work. *Labour/Le Travail, 75*, 211–230.
Cámara de Telecomunicaciones del Uruguay. (2010). *Call center pierden competitividad y piden normas laborales flexibles.* Retrieved from http://www.telecomunicaciones.org.uy/web/index.php?option=com_content&task=view&id=285&Itemid=74
Carrillo Rowe, A., Perez, K., & Malhotra, S. (2013). *Answer the call: Virtual migration in Indian call centers.* Minneapolis, MN: University of Minnesota Press.
Cátedra Experimental sobre Producción de Subjetividad. (2007a). Call centre: The art of virtual control. *ephemera: theory and politics in organization, 7*(1), 133–138.
Cátedra Experimental sobre Producción de Subjetividad. (2007b). *From knowledge of self-management to the self-management of knowledge.* Retrieved from http://eipcp.net/transversal/0707/catedraexperimental/en
Colectivo Situaciones. (2006) *¿Quién habla? Lucha contra la esclavitud del alma en los call centers.* Buenos Aires, Argentina: Tinta Limón Ediciones.
Daily Mail. (2009, March 5). Thames battles union over "sacking threat". *Daily Mail*, p. 73.
Daily Telegraph. (2009, July 18). Power plug pulled. *Daily Telegraph*, p. 16.
Dean, J. (2012). *The communist horizon.* London, UK: Verso Books.
Doellgast, V. (2012). *Disintegrating democracy at work: Labor unions and the future of good jobs in the service economy.* Ithaca, NY: ILR Press.
Duff, M. (2008, September). Teletech 018 staff are hopping mad. *Manawatu Standard.*
Fernández, R. (2015). *Terror center: Flexibilidad laboral en los call center.* Retrieved from http://razonyrevolucion.org/terror-center-flexibilidad-laboral-en-los-call-center/
Fernie, S., & Metcalf, D. (1998). *(Not) hanging on the telephone: Payment systems in the new sweatshops* London, UK: London School of Economics and Political Science.
Fleming, P., & Sewell, G. (2002). Looking for the good soldier, Svejk: Alternative modalities of resistance in the contemporary workplace. *Sociology, 36*(4), 857–873.
Fleming, P., & Sturdy, A. (2011). 'Being yourself' in the electronic sweatshop: New forms of normative control. *Human Relations, 64*(2), 177–200.
Gardiner, Y. (2008, December 4). Workers will rally at park, strike today. *The Queensland Times*, p. 7.

Guard, J., Steedman, M., & García-Orgales, J. (2007). Organizing the electronic sweatshop: Rank-and-file participation in Canada's steel union. *Labor: Studies in Working-Class History of the Americas, 4*(3), 9–31.

Gülsen, E. (2015). Resistance against the new working practices in the service sector in Turkey. In U. Schuerkens (Ed.), *Global management, local resistances: Theoretical discussion and empirical case studies* (pp. 135–148). New York, NY: Routledge.

Gurgaon Workers News. (2012). *GurgaonWorkersNews no.9/52*. Retrieved from https://gurgaonworkersnews.wordpress.com/gurgaonworkersnews-no-952/

Hastings, T. (2011). *A job worth doing? Reinterpreting control, resistance and everyday forms of coping with call centre work in Glasgow* (Unpublished PhD). University of Glasgow, Glasgow, UK.

Head, S. (2014). *Mindless: Why smarter machines are making dumber humans*. New York, NY: Basic Books.

Hochschild, A. R. (2004). *The managed heart: Commercialization of human feeling*. Berkeley, CA: University of California Press.

Holman, D., Batt, R. & Holtgrewe, U. (2007). *The global call centre report: International perspectives on management and employment*. Retrieved from http://www.ilr.cornell.edu.proxy.lib.sfu.ca/globalcallcenter/upload/GCC-Intl-REpt-US-Version.pdf

Holst, H. (2008). The political economy of trade union strategies in Austria and Germany: The case of call centres. *European Journal of Industrial Relations, 14*(25), 25–45.

Kidman, A. (2010). *10 reasons call centre work is so painful*. Retrieved from http://www.lifehacker.com.au/2010/09/10-reasons-call-centre-work-is-so-painful/

Knights, D., & McCabe, D. (1998). 'What happens when the phone goes wild?' Staff, stress and spaces for escape in a BPR telephone banking work regime. *Journal of Management Studies, 35*(2), 163–194.

Kolinko. (2002). *Hotlines: Call centre, inquiry, communism*. Retrieved from http://www.nadir.org/nadir/initiativ/kolinko/lebuk/e_lebuk.htm

Lavin, D. O. (2006). *Call centres in the "new economy:" A Canadian case study* (M.A. thesis). Queen's University, Kingston, ON.

Linebaugh, P., & Rediker, M. B. (2000). *The many-headed hydra: Sailors, slaves, commoners, and the hidden history of the revolutionary Atlantic*. Boston, MA: Beacon Press.

Lloyd, A. (2013). *Labour markets and identity on the post-industrial assembly line*. Burlington, VT: Ashgate.

Marx, K. (1990). *Capital: Volume 1*. London, UK: Penguin.

Mirchandani, K. (2004). Practices of global capital: Gaps, cracks and ironies in transnational call centres in India. *Global Networks, 4*(4), 355–374.

Mirchandani, K. (2012). *Phone clones: Authenticity work in the transnational service economy*. Ithaca, NY: ILR Press.

Modimoeng, K. (2008, November 27). Airline faces strike action. *Sowetan*, p. 21.

Moodley, J. (2009, August 3). Telkom strike puts us on hold. *Daily News*.

Morning Star Online. (2009, February 18). Thames water staff vote on massive cull. *Morning Star Online*.

Mosco, V., & McKercher, C. (2006). Convergence bites back: Labour struggles in the Canadian telecommunications industry. *Canadian Journal of Communication, 31*(3), 733–751.

Mulholland, K. (2004). Workplace resistance in an Irish call centre: Slammin', scammin', smokin' an' leavin'. *Work, Employment and Society, 18*(4), 709–724.

Nadeem, S. (2011). *Dead ringers: How outsourcing is changing the way Indians understand themselves*. Princeton, NJ: Princeton University Press.

Parola, S. (2010). *Omnia, blitz del commissario: 'Fuori tutti, lasciate le chiavi'*. Retrieved from http://torino.repubblica.it/cronaca/2010/10/01/news/omnia_service_occupata-7612737/

Pezzulli, F. M. (2013, July 4). La solitudine del telefonista. *Il Manifesto*.

Pizzolato, N. (2013). The American worker and the *forze nuove*: Turin and Detroit at the twilight of Fordism. *Viewpoint Magazine*, (3).

Rainnie, A., & Drummond, G. (2006). Community unionism in a regional call centre: The organiser's perspective. In J. Burgess & J. Connell (Eds.), *Developments in the call centre industry: An overview* (pp. 136–151). New York, NY: Routledge.

Reuters News. (2008a, February 20). Strike ends at Mexico's Telmex call center unit. *Reuters News*.

Reuters News. (2008b, March 3). Union plans strike at Elisa customer service. *Reuters News*.

Rizzo, F. (2008). *Fuga dal call center*.

Roggero, G. (2011). *The production of living knowledge: Crisis of the university and transformation of labour in Europe and North America* [Produzione del sapere vivo.] (E. Brophy, Trans.). Philadelphia, PA: Temple University Press.

Ross, A. (2009). *Nice work if you can get it: Life and labor in precarious times*. New York, NY: New York University Press.

Russell, B. (2008). Unions in the information economy: Info-service work and organizing in Australian call centres. *Journal of Industrial Relations, 50*(2), 285–303.

Rynor, B. (2008, November 17). Postal workers launch strike action. *Canwest News Service.*

Scott, J. (1990). *Domination and the arts of resistance: Hidden transcripts.* New Haven, CT: Yale University Press.

Shan, S. (2011). Call center outsourcing panned. Retrieved from http://www.taipeitimes.com/News/taiwan/archives/2011/07/27/2003509251

Steven. (2010, February 16). *Techy wage increase attempt at Convergys in Gurgaon.* Retrieved from http://libcom.org/library/techy-wage-increase-attempt-convergys-gurgaon

Stevens, A. (2014). *Call centers and the global division of labor: A political economy of post-industrial employment and union organizing.* New York, NY: Routledge/Taylor & Francis Group.

Stevens, A., & Lavin, D. O. (2007). Stealing time: The temporal regulation of labor in neoliberal and post-Fordist work regimes. *Democratic Communique, 22*(2), 40–61.

Stevens, A., & Mosco, V. (2010). Prospects for trade unions and labour organisations in India's IT and ITES industries. *Work Organisation, Labour & Globalisation, 4*(2), 39–59.

Taylor, P., & Bain, P. (2003). 'Subterranean worksick blues:' Humour as subversion in two call centres. *Organizational Studies, 24*(9), 1487–1509.

Taylor, P., & Bain, P. (2006). Work organisation and employee relations in Indian call centres. In J. Burgess & J. Connell (Eds.), *Developments in the call centre industry: Analysis, changes and challenges* (pp. 36–57). New York, NY: Routledge.

Taylor, P., & Bain, P. (2008). United by a common language? Trade union responses in the UK and India to call centre offshoring. *Antipode, 40*(1), 131–154.

Telelink Call Centre. (n.d.). *Answering services.* Retrieved from http://telelinkcallcentre.com/services/answering-services/

Thanawala, S. (2007, October 16). India's call-center jobs go begging. *Time Magazine.*

Thompson, E. P. (1966). *The making of the English working class.* New York, NY: Vintage Books.

United News of India. (2016). *Thames water picks up Wipro for customer service and billing needs*. Retrieved from https://www.highbeam.com/doc/1P3-4044868881.html

van den Broek, D., Barnes, A., & Townsend, K. (2008). 'Teaming up': Teams and team sharing in call centres. *The Journal of Industrial Relations, 50*(2), 257–269.

Voce Proletaria. (2011). *Lavoratori dei call center Uniti a Torino*. Retrieved from http://blog.libero.it/VoceProletaria/10198680.html

Wright, S. (2002). *Storming heaven: Class composition and struggle in Italian autonomist Marxism*. London, UK: Pluto Press.

Zecca, E. (2010). *Histórico paro de trabajadores de call centers*. Retrieved from http://www.180.com.uy/articulo/14602_Historico-paro-de-trabajadores-de-call-centers

4

The Making of the Call Centre Cybertariat

In April 2006 I travelled to Moncton in the Atlantic Canadian province of New Brunswick, a region known for its booming call centre sector and the economic development strategy that has been constructed around these workplaces. Labour relations in New Brunswick call centres had mostly been quiet in the decade or so since this economic strategy had been enacted, but workers at the newly merged telecommunications firm Aliant had just been through an acrimonious five-month strike, the first significant labour conflict in Canadian telecommunications since a firestorm of privatization, convergence, and restructuring had remade the industry after deregulation in the 1990s. The confrontation at Aliant included workers from the provinces of Nova Scotia, Newfoundland, and Prince Edward Island, but what drew me to Moncton was that many of the New Brunswick workers who had participated in this strike were new to trade unionism, and many of these in turn were employed in Aliant's call centres.

The interviews with Aliant call centre workers illuminated a set of developments that had brought these employees to be sitting across a

© The Author(s) 2017
E. Brophy, *Language Put to Work*, Dynamics of Virtual Work,
DOI 10.1057/978-1-349-95244-1_4

table from me at the Communications, Energy and Paperworkers Union of Canada (CEP) offices in Moncton—processes that had determined the formation of a sizeable and highly educated call centre workforce in New Brunswick.[1] Foremost among these shifts were the deregulation of Canadian telecommunications (Shniad, 2007; Winseck, 1998), the informational development strategy adopted by the Province of New Brunswick (Buchanan, 2002; Good & McFarland, 2005; McFarland, 2000, 2009), the global trend towards the restructuring and Taylorization (or "call centreification") of customer service (Huws, 2009), and the move towards "convergence" through mergers by Canadian trade unions (Mosco & McKercher, 2008).

Many if not most of these developments were also in evidence three years later, in 2009, when I visited Ireland in order to understand the formation of the Irish call centre workforce. The cases were strikingly similar: Ireland had also taken an "informational" path towards economic development (Breathnach, 1998; Grimes, 2003), had become a key destination for outsourced call centres (Breathnach, 2000; Jobs et al., 2007), and featured an established union—the Communication Workers' Union (CWU)—vying to represent workers in this exploding form of employment.[2] In both of these regions, I was especially interested in the points of contact between call centre workers and the trade unions that had pre-existed the arrival and expansion of call centres. What relationship, if any, was developing in these two regions between a new workforce forged to service the economy's growing communicative needs and the established but struggling labour movement?

Drawing on field research conducted on these visits to Ireland and Atlantic Canada, this chapter describes the formation of the call centre workforce, its entry into the workplaces of communicative capitalism, and

---

[1] The research in the portion of this chapter that discusses Atlantic Canada draws on 14 interviews conducted with Aliant call centre workers and CEP members in Moncton. These workers had all been present at the telecommunications company when it was NBTel and had experienced the merger that would turn it into Aliant, unionization through the CEP, the ongoing restructuring at the company subsequent to the merger, and the 2004 strike. In 2013, the CEP merged with the Canadian Auto Workers (CAW) union to form Unifor.

[2] In Ireland, I conducted 13 interviews with call centre workers, trade unionists, and labour activists in the sector.

its participation in the trade union movement. In what follows, I relate these processes primarily through the lens of the Atlantic Canadian experience and the Aliant strike, but my account weaves in a discussion of the process of informational development and the related formation of the call centre workforce in Ireland. Where possible, I note the multiple points of connection that exist between these two regional experiences and reports of workers' encounters with call centre employment coming from other countries.

I use this evidence to make a foundational point for the rest of the book, arguing that the Atlantic Canadian and Irish histories reveal a close connection between the pursuits of informational development on the one hand and the proletarianization of immaterial labour on the other. As David McNally (1993, p. 31) suggests, "just as proletarianization is key to creating a fully capitalist market, so that market, once created, will continually reproduce proletarianization—and on a growing scale." This dynamic was precisely what I found in Ireland and New Brunswick. The proletarianization of immaterial labour described in this chapter is a process marked by declining traditional forms of employment, expanding education levels, and the putting to work of the population's communicative competencies in call centres. As a result of these shifts, by the year 2000 one out of every fifteen working New Brunswickers was employed in a call centre, and in Ireland one out of every three new jobs in the decade that followed was a call centre position. Adopting a concept from the labour researcher Ursula Huws (2003), I describe these regional processes of class formation as the making of a cybertariat.

The research conducted for this chapter broadly confirms Harry Braverman's arguments regarding the degradation of what he called "mental labour" through the rationalizing and restructuring of the labour process. The last act in the production of a call centre workforce is a project of structuring the way workers communicate while on the job. Once he or she is inside the call centre, the worker's capacity to communicate through language is subject to a process of standardization and quantification, rendering the interaction he or she produces with customers more amenable to measurement and therefore to the production of value. The ultimate aim of this managerial project that seeks to shape language from above is the production of what I call *abstract communication*—an adaptation of the Italian theorist Gigi Roggero's (2011) insightful discussion of abstract knowledge, itself a riff on Karl Marx's (1990) category of abstract labour.

However, as the Aliant strike demonstrated, the process of abstraction through which the making of a call centre workforce and its communicative labour is ultimately realized is an uncertain and contradictory one. While on the one hand the pre-existing linguistic, affective, and relational capacities of workforces are cultivated through the educational system and then fed into the process of communicative production in call centres, on the other hand those very same capacities are systematically structured, disciplined, and regularly denied expression within that production process. In other words, and as the testimony of Aliant employees illustrated so clearly, call centre workers are brought into the workspace because of their communicative abilities, but those capacities then tend to be systematically suppressed in the interest of generating predictable, undifferentiated, and measurable customer communication. This structuring of the communicative labour process has serious implications for call centre workers—the most urgent being that it facilitates the transferability of their work. This chapter explores and theorizes these foundational tensions at the heart of language put to work, and in doing so considers the primary organizational vehicle through which workers' resistance is channelled today: trade union organizations and the established labour movement.

Informational Development

Histories of Moncton, New Brunswick, recount that the city received its name due to a clerical error. Named after Robert Monckton, the British military commander who captured nearby Fort Beauséjour in 1755 and subsequently oversaw the deportation of the Francophone Acadians, at the moment of its incorporation in 1855 a clerical worker fixed its name with the current mistaken spelling.

If this act by an unknown ancestor of today's call centre workers named Moncton, its contemporary skyline recalls the more recent history of immaterial labour and of how it has fuelled the restructuring of the city and the province. Rising much higher than any of Moncton's church spires, a 127-metre concrete microwave communications tower dominates the horizon from its downtown location. Built in 1971 for NBTel (the former monopoly telecommunications provider for the province), it was renamed the Aliant Tower after the merger of four Maritime telecommunications companies in 1999.[3] During the five-month strike in 2004, with the front entrance of the Aliant building adjacent to the tower surrounded by picketers, company management had a hole ripped through the brick wall at the back to create an entrance for the managers and replacement workers brought in to carry out the tasks of the strikers. The patch where that door has been filled in with newer bricks was still visible when I visited two years later, a scar from labour conflict that played itself out in Moncton and across the Maritimes.

In New Brunswick, the immediate historical context for the strike was the "New Economic Strategy" enacted during the 1990s by Frank McKenna's Liberal government, a restructuring project that transformed the composition of labour and capital in the province. As critical scholars Joan McFarland, Tom Good, and Ruth Buchanan have documented in their research on call centres in New Brunswick province (Buchanan, 2002; Good & McFarland, 2005; McFarland, 2000), the strategy bore all the hallmarks of the neoliberal economic development playbook, including tax incentives for the private sector, removal of social assistance support for workers, and the reshaping of education for the goals of business.

Crucially, the New Economic Strategy was directed towards *informational development*, or a recalibration of the province's economy away from its traditional but waning forms of employment (on the fish-packing line, at the railway yards, and in forestry) and towards informational industries—especially the emergent call centre sector. Rather than resource extraction or the production of physical commodities, the development strategy was based upon what Cristina Morini and Andrea Fumagalli (2010, p. 239) describe as "productive activity that is

---

[3] The companies involved in the merger were NBTel (New Brunswick), Island Telecom Inc. (Prince Edward Island), Maritime Telegraph and Telephone Company (Nova Scotia), and NewTel Enterprises Limited (Newfoundland and Labrador). In early 2000, Bell Canada Enterprises increased its controlling interest in the new firm to 42% (Rideout, 2003, p. 119), and by 2004 its stake had risen to 53% (Wong, 2004).

tendentially immaterial, based on the exploitation of learning and networking economies." Informational development in New Brunswick was initiated as a collaborative venture between the provincial government and NBTel.[4] The latter invested heavily in fibre optic and digital switching technologies during the 1990s, developing an advanced telecommunications infrastructure that offered potentially seamless integration between the headquarters of major American and Canadian companies and their New Brunswick operations (UNCTAD, 2004, p. 197). By 1999, NBTel was offering to cover virtually all of the costs associated with telecommunications hardware and software, as well as its maintenance and regular upgrade, for companies that were considering relocating their call centre operations to New Brunswick (Good & McFarland, 2005, p. 104).

If NBTel offered companies the cutting-edge technology, the provincial government took care of providing the workforce and financial incentives (Balka, 2002; Buchanan & Koch-Schulte, 2000; McFarland, 2000). Among the appealing features of the New Brunswick "business climate" touted by McKenna's government to prospective buyers was one of the lowest unionization rates and highest unemployment levels in Canada.[5] The provincial government even advertised the weakness of its labour movement in the promotional literature. As the New Brunswick Department of Economic Development and Tourism website proclaimed in 1999:

> The industry that reflects call centre activities the most is the communications industry and [in that industry] New Brunswick has the lowest rate of unionization in Canada ... NBTel is the only telephone company in Canada with non-unionized clerical employees ... There has never been

---

[4] Joan McFarland (2000, p. 8) suggests the original impetus for the call centre development strategy can be traced to a single government employee who had been hired away from NBTel.

[5] Richardson, Belt, and Marshall (2000) have argued that call centres are often deliberately located in areas with a large surplus supply of wage labour. As McKenna promoted his political economic strategy for the province, a full 12% of the active labour force (roughly 40,000 people) was officially unemployed, a figure that did not even include part-time or casual workers seeking full-time work (Good & McFarland, 2005, p. 99). Julie Guard (2003) found that while pay varies according to the type of call centre and whether or not the call centre is unionized, the lowest annual average salary for customer service representatives in Canada was in the Atlantic provinces, at CDN$23,370.

an industry attempt to unionize [call centres in the province]. (as cited in Good & McFarland, 2005, p. 111)

In addition to its high unemployment and low unionization, New Brunswick's workforce is bilingual and highly educated. Critical to the development of a suitable workforce for call centres was the expansion and reproduction of this regional reservoir of mass intellectuality, a responsibility taken on by the provincial government. During the 1990s, educational initiatives were enacted towards the development of computer literacy (which became mandatory for high school graduates), and both public and private institutions offered call centre training programs which developed in students the affective and relational skills required for customer service (UNCTAD, 2004, p. 197). By 2002, Ruth Buchanan noted the high levels of education existing among the New Brunswick call centre workforce, suggesting that most had had at least some post-secondary education, including two-year degrees from newly minted community college courses in "teleservice" (p. 53).[6] By 2005 (Good & McFarland, 2005, p. 106), 70% of call centre workers in the province had completed post-secondary education.[7]

Along with a state-of-the-art infrastructure and an obedient workforce, McKenna's government also promised billions in forgivable loans to lure call centre operations to New Brunswick. Companies were enticed, and

---

[6] The high level of education among call centre workforces is a feature we will encounter repeatedly during the course of this book. It was recently confirmed in the UK setting, where one in three call centre workers in the UK now has a degree, according to a 2010 survey by recruitment firm Hays in conjunction with Top 50 Call Centres for Customer Service (as cited in Snowdon, 2010).

[7] These figures were higher than the Canadian average at the time. A 2004 report by the Canadian Customer Contact Centre Industry (CCCI) noted that nearly half of customer service representatives in Canadian inbound call centres, and just over one in four workers in outbound call centres, had achieved a post-secondary diploma or degree (as cited in Schatz & Johnson, 2007). As a whole, the education levels of workers employed in call centres is therefore notable, especially when one considers the fact that many of those employed in these workspaces may not have a degree yet but are still students enrolled in university and therefore on the way to obtaining one. Ursula Huws (2014, p. 41) situates the development of this mass intellectuality within a broader, global project to serve the needs of employers: "There is convincing evidence that we have now entered a phase in global capitalism in which, just like the need for universal literacy in the nineteenth century, there is now a universal need for new generic attitudes and abilities. And, just as in the 19th century, state agencies have leaped to the assistance of employers to provide them. Only this time it isn't within national borders, or competing empires, but on a global scale."

by one count at least 35 call centres were established in the province between 1991 and 1996 (Jaimet, 2006). By the late 1990s call centre employment in the province had tripled, and in 2001 it was estimated that there were 15,000 call centre jobs in New Brunswick, accounting for 1 employee out of every 15 in the province's private sector (as cited in McFarland, 2009, p. 29). Moncton accounted for around half of the total employment: by 2002 there were 43 call centres employing an estimated 6000 workers in the city (Warson, 2002).

Across the Atlantic, Ireland's path of state-led informational development mirrored that of the province of New Brunswick in almost every respect. Ireland invested heavily and upgraded its telecommunications infrastructure in the 1980s (Burnham, 2003), offered a low corporate tax rate and other incentives for transnational corporations, and boasted a "low-cost, high-calibre, flexible bilingual" labour pool to select from (Breathnach, 2000, p. 481). Ireland's Industrial Development Agency (IDA—the state agency responsible for promoting foreign direct investment) introduced a call centre program in 1992, positioning the country as the European hub for American companies seeking to outsource their back office operations.[8] During this time, as in New Brunswick, the IDA and Telecom Eireann (the national telecommunications provider) established

> joint marketing programs, focused on the United States, to point out to investors the happy coincidence of a young, literate, English-speaking (in many cases multilingual), technically trained labor force in a low-tax environment with a technically advanced and relatively inexpensive telecommunications infrastructure—a place where many multinational firms already were established comfortably. (Burnham, 2003, p. 554)

Ireland also embarked on a process of reform and expansion for the post-secondary education sector, one intended to suit the needs of transnational (especially American) business. Regional technical colleges

---

[8] Ireland's wooing of foreign multinationals in the emergent informational sector has a longer history that cannot be addressed here. Suffice it to note that, by 1985, IBM, Lotus, and Microsoft had established development centres for software and data processing in the country (Burnham, 2003, p. 541), which was also a destination for electronics manufacturing (see Lüthje, Hürtgen, Pawliki, & Sproll, 2013).

(RTCs) were expanded and two new universities were constructed during this time, with the IDA described as a "powerful force" in "persuading the RTCs to emphasize programs in electrical engineering and information technology" (Burnham, 2003, p. 283).

The formation of a call centre workforce in both regions and the marketing of its abilities internationally are examples of what linguistic anthropologist Monica Heller (2003, p. 474) has described as the commodification of language, a process that "renders language amenable to redefinition as a measurable skill, as opposed to a talent, or an inalienable characteristic of group member."[9] As a vital resource for the broader project of informational development, the linguistic capacities of the workforces in both regions were a key selling point for call centre operations looking to relocate. In New Brunswick (as a legacy of the Acadians who trickled back into New Brunswick after their 1755 expulsion), almost half of call centre workers in the province speak both English and French, a factor that makes the workforce attractive for companies who need to manage their interaction with a bilingual customer base. In Ireland, proficiency in two languages for citizens became a stated goal of educational policy during this period.[10] Reflecting the European orientation of the country's call centres, over half (55%) of workers spoke a language other than English at work, and of these workers just under one-half were foreign nationals (Breathnach, 2000). Inward migration addressed the linguistic requirements of foreign multinationals in Ireland, producing, in some call centres, a veritable Tower of Babel where migrant labour from across the European Union populated the different national departments oriented towards the company's operations in corresponding European countries.[11]

---

[9] Heller continues, speaking of the Canadian context: "What we are seeing then, in francophone Canada, is a shift from understanding language as being primarily a marker of ethnonational identity, to understanding language as being a marketable commodity on its own, distinct from identity" (2003, p. 474).

[10] As Breathnach notes (2000, p. 481), three-quarters of call centre companies reported the availability of language skills as either the first or second most important reason for relocating.

[11] An Italian worker employed in a bank's Dublin call centre described it to me this way: "In the call centre, there are, let me just think ... There are Italians, the Italian department, Italian marketing, the Greek department, the French department, and I missing one ... another department, so four different markets" (Irish worker 1, personal communication, July 24, 2009).

During the 1990s, Ireland and New Brunswick's projects of state-led informational development and the associated formation of future call centre workforces were therefore running on parallel tracks. In Atlantic Canada, however, the corporate entity that had been so essential to unleashing this process in New Brunswick would be entirely transformed as a result of deregulation in the Canadian telecommunications industry. The 1999 merger of four companies in Atlantic Canada produced the third-largest telco in the country and the largest in the region, worth CDN$3 billion and employing 9000 workers (Aliant, 1999).

The business plan for newly convergent telecom companies such as Aliant involved compensating for revenue lost from their former status as long distance monopolies by offering services such as wireless, Internet access, and satellite television—all of which bolstered the need for a workforce dedicated to customer service. Thanks to the loosening of service requirements by the Canadian Radio-Television and Telecommunications Commission, however, corporate re-engineers at telecommunication companies across North America went to work restructuring their workforces, and, in the process, advanced a sustained attack on their incumbent unions (Niemeijer, 2004; Shniad, 2005, 2007). Aliant was no exception: after the merger it closed operator service operations in Nova Scotia, Newfoundland, and Prince Edward Island, centralized significant parts of its other operations, downsized its workforce by several hundred employees and transferred a major part of its network surveillance operations and buildings real estate management to its parent company, Bell Canada.

For Aliant, the most significant impediment to this restructuring was its union. The organization representing Aliant employees had pursued its own "convergent" growth strategy since the 1990s, merging with two other unions to create the CEP in the early part of that decade.[12] Union convergence was supported by the Canada Industrial Relations Board (CIRB), which closely followed the state of labour relations at Aliant in the aftermath of the merger. Prior to the amalgamation, the Atlantic

---

[12] The CEP's "communication" portion was born in the early 1970s when the Canadian contingent of the Communications Workers of America opted for secession from its US-based parent (McKercher, 2002).

4 The Making of the Call Centre Cybertariat 95

companies contained nine bargaining units: the CEP represented craft, clerical, and operator units in Newfoundland and Labrador at NewTel (Local 410) and Prince Edward Island at IslandTel (Local 401) but only craft and operator bargaining units in New Brunswick at NBTel (Local 506). In Nova Scotia, the historically more militant Atlantic Communications and Technical Workers Union (ACTWU) represented employees in all three occupations and boasted the best collective agreement. As noted, the New Brunswick workers were the only non-unionized clerical or call centre employees of these four companies prior to the Aliant merger.[13]

On the heels of the merger in March 2000, the CEP began its third campaign to organize clerical workers in New Brunswick. After a card-signing meeting with the majority of the workers, the CEP applied to the CIRB for certification in August 2000. Aliant sought a review of the bargaining unit structure that same year, requesting the consolidation of the different bargaining units in an application to the CIRB. The existing units agreed to the merger, and by order of the CIRB in 2001 a single bargaining unit, representing all of Aliant's unionized workers, was formed. The bargaining agent for the new entity was to be the Council of Atlantic Telecommunication Unions (CATU), formed through an agreement between the CEP and the ACTWU. The CIRB thus granted

---

[13] Why these workers were not unionized previous to the Aliant merger is unclear. The CEP had tried to unionize them at least twice previously in the 1990s, without success. As one worker describes it: "We were presented with it, and we were asked to join the union throughout my career at least twice before we actually did. [...] And we voted on it, and voted against it because whatever [the other unionized clerical/call centre workers in other provinces] had, we also got. Without paying the union dues or anything like that. I mean in terms of money and hours of work [...]. As far as protection and stuff like that, we didn't have what they had, but we didn't feel the need to have it, at that point in time" (Aliant worker 1, personal communication, April 6, 2006). Workers I interviewed often cited a lack of trust towards trade unions or a relatively good relationship with management as reasons for the lack of unionization. Whether the suspiciousness of unions arose from personal experience or not, it was often related alongside descriptions of trade unions as overly bureaucratic or as inclined to focus on the pettier aspects of the labour-management relationship. Others pointed to what they suggested was New Brunswick's lack of an established labour history, or to the strong work ethic of its inhabitants. One worker's comments are typical: "[Our tradition of trade unionism] is lacking compared to the other provinces. Especially in Moncton, because it's more of a service city, not an industry [city]. If you go up north, where the economy runs on paper mills and other wood products, they're all unionized right, so union[s] [are] a lot stronger in the northern economy" (Aliant worker 2, personal communication, April 6, 2006).

Aliant its wish, yet in its decision the Board *also* ordered the inclusion in the new bargaining unit (now some 4300 workers strong) of the nearly 800 clerical employees in New Brunswick. Perhaps sensing that the newly unionized call centre workers could be an important signal to other workers on the province's digital assembly lines, CEP Atlantic region vice president Max Michaud marked the decision by suggesting these were "among the first-ever call centre workers to join a union in Canada" and that the CEP hoped their unionization would "open the door for others who desperately need the protection of a union" (Communications, Energy and Paperworkers Union of Canada, 2001). In February 2002, the arbitrator produced an interim collective agreement until a new agreement could be reached.

Callcentreification at Aliant: The Production of Abstract Communication

After the workforce has been formed and the businesses lured, the last act of the communicative production process investigated in this book takes place inside the call centre and over a headset. Since the 1990s, call centres have become a distinct and dominant model for the reorganization from above of customer service, remaking the communicative work of employees in a range of industries. This restructuring has often involved companies outsourcing their customer contact operations, either entirely or in part, to the outsourced call centre businesses that have arisen to form a sizable and dynamic sector of communicative capitalism. Where customer relations operations have remained in-house, the labour processes of front-line workers have also been transformed so as to converge with those of outsourced call centres. Ursula Huws refers to this process as "callcentreification" (2009), and researchers of this new workspace have detailed its signal features, including the imposition and intensification of routinization, surveillance, and quantitative measurement upon tele-workforces in sectors such as banking, health, and telecommunications.[14] This section of the chapter describes the experience of this transformation as related by Aliant workers in New Brunswick, outlining the contest for control between labour and management that characterized this restructuring of the labour process. At stake, I argue, was ultimately the job security of this in-house, unionized call centre workforce.

The process of transforming the communicative labour process of customer service workers, at Aliant and elsewhere, towards the rationalized, mass-production model that tends to mark outsourced call centres, I suggest, is an effort directed towards the production of what we could call *abstract communication*. Abstract communication is interpersonal communication that is generic, instrumental, impersonal, predictable, quantifiable, and therefore amenable to the extraction of value.[15]

I use the concept of abstract communication to reference the continuities and the differences between factory and call centre. The term registers the similarities between the process of extracting value from linguistic interactions in call centres and the factory-centred process of valourization described by Karl Marx (1990) in his nineteenth-century discussion of *abstract labour*. By that term, Marx denoted the difference between specific, concrete forms of labour (tailoring, weaving, etc.) and their reduction to "labour in general," or the "expenditure of human labour-power in the abstract" (p. 308). Speaking with the factory and the production of tangible commodities in mind, Marx argued that capital's

---

[14] See also Pia Bramming, Ole Sørensen, and Peter Hasle (2009), and Pupo and Noack (2009). For a summary of labour process analysis of the taylorization of call centre work, see Chap. 2. As Huws (2009) suggests, "numerous case studies have documented the colonization of other professions by this mass-production model of organizing communicative work, as the labour process of health care, civil service, bank and other workers becomes subject to 'callcentreification.'"

[15] The concept of abstract communication is indebted to the work of Gigi Roggero (2011, p. 95), who, in his discussion of the university's transformation within post-Fordism, develops the concept to describe how "[l]iving knowledge is reduced to abstract knowledge, so as to be captured and valorized. Paraphrasing Marx, we could say that abstract knowledge corresponds to the indifference toward every specific form of labor: it is knowledge in general, knowledge *sans phrase*."

objective in organizing production is the reduction of living labour to abstract labour, or labour that is an undifferentiated, measurable, and predictable input in the production of surplus value.[16]

The ultimate goal of the call centre labour process, I suggest, is strikingly similar across such a wide range of contexts in that it tends towards the reduction of specific or concrete forms of communication to ones that are generic, homogeneous, and measurable.[17] This "subsumption of language" (Berardi, 2013, p. 18) aims to freeze the complexity, unpredictability, and potency of human communication, reducing it to the shallow and highly instrumental variety produced in call centres. The production of abstract communication in call centres involves what the sociologist A. Aneesh (2015, p. 238) describes as "a recalibration of sociocultural particularity to systemic requirements of the global market society."[18]

As this section of the chapter demonstrates however, the production of communicative interaction or linguistic performances in call centres also differs qualitatively from that of mass-produced, tangible objects in factories. The structuring of the communicative labour of call centre workers according to the mass-production model documented by critical researchers may be more financially efficient for business, but it also

---

[16] The Regulation School economist Michel Aglietta defines abstract labour as "a social relation that transforms the products of labour into equivalent categories, known as commodities, in a homogeneous space in which a measure known as value can be applied" (1979, p. 39).

[17] As the research of Taylor and Bain (2001) and Callaghan and Thompson (2001) has shown, recognizing that there is some diversity within call centre, labour processes "should not lead to the conclusion that call centres are equally distributed between 'quality' and 'quantity' operations" (Taylor & Bain, 2003, p. 1492). Quantification and measure have been at the heart of managerial strategy in call centre settings precisely because "[t]he capitalist economy involves the victory of quantity over quality; all qualitatively different things must be reduced to quantitative units of the same thing (measured in money)" (McNally, 2011, p. 71). This does not mean that quality, or affective connection, is unimportant in call centre communication, however, as we shall see below.

[18] Vincent Mosco observes the power of the commodification process to transform communication: "commodification processes at work in the society as a whole penetrate communication processes and institutions, so improvements and contradictions in the societal commodification process influence communication as a social practice" (2009, p. 130). In this sense, the production of abstract communication in call centres occurs when communication begins to take on the features of commercial exchange. As described by David Graeber (2011, p. 103): "What marks commercial exchange is that it's impersonal: who it is that is selling something to us, or buying something from us, should in principle be entirely irrelevant."

4 The Making of the Call Centre Cybertariat

generates a set of problems and tensions as a result of the labour process that is imposed. One of the most obvious examples is that the mass production of customer communication runs up against the limits of workers' psychic and emotional endurance, producing burnout and employee flight. Another problem is that the production of customer communication may seem easy to measure in quantitative terms, yet key features of that communication, as we shall see, elude measure in crucial ways. Workers are told to smile down the phone, but a smile cannot be measured in the same way that the length of a conversation can. Many accounts of call centre work argue that successful communication with customers happens despite the scripted conversations rather than because of them. And, crucially, workers have also resisted this alienation from their own capacity to communicate. Like abstract labour, therefore, the production of abstract communication is, from management's perspective at least, an ideal—but it is never a given. The process by which value is extracted from communication in call centres is a perennially contradictory and contested one.

At Aliant, the imposition of "callcentreification" unleashed major changes on the working routines of customer service employees after the merger. In an era of heightened competition and ever more complex product offerings, telecommunications companies increasingly need employees who can interact with customers over the phone in both an efficient and productive manner.[19] These workers must know and tell customers about the packages on offer, negotiate with them to stay on as customers, or sell them more expensive services than they already have. The customer service role goes beyond sales, however. Once customers are signed up, a whole host of technical difficulties can arise, and another group of workers acts as the front-line solvers of such problems, helping the customers keep the services running and, if possible, avoiding the expense to the company of a trip to the location in question. Should a trip

---

[19] Marcela Miozzo and Matías Ramírez (2003, p. 65) note the expanding need for customer service work in their discussion of the United Kingdom telecommunications sector: "by diversifying the range of services that they are able to provide with new technologies, firms have increased 'front-end' employment to meet data traffic in areas such as sales, solutions, helpdesk, product development, design, media and marketing."

by an outside worker for repairs or to install service be necessary, call centre workers schedule the visit.

In the putting-to-work of communication over the phone at Aliant, the communicative and linguistic abilities gained *outside* the company are the raw ingredients of the labour process within it, whether these derive from the public education system, the service sector at large, or a simple aptitude for dealing with people. Discussions with workers in Moncton confirmed the extent to which the hires at NBTel and, subsequently, Aliant were drawn from the reservoir of educated, bilingual workers in the province. By the early 2000s, the majority of clerical/call centre employees at the company had some kind of post-secondary degree. Underscoring this fact, one worker recalled how on his first day at NBTel he "saw a lot of faces that I recognized from university. [...They had] different backgrounds, lots of backgrounds: commerce, arts, science, engineering..." (Roy, personal communication, April 5, 2006).[20]

Alongside the competencies gained in the post-secondary education system, workers also stressed how interaction with customers required a pre-existing set of linguistic, communicative, and affective abilities. When asked what management expected of their interaction with callers, employees tended to mention the affective demands of their job: "They want me to build a relationship with a customer, definitely" (Aliant worker 2, personal communication, April 6, 2006). This dimension of the work was stressed to Donovan Richard from the get-go: "I got to Aliant, [and] they said, 'we can train for computers, but not for customer service'" (personal communication, April 4, 2006).

Language and local cultural knowledge were a key part of creating an affective bond when employees spoke to customers from their province. As Philippe Roy noted,

> I get a lot of calls from the French communities also, and I know pretty much all the different areas, so I can relate to customers a lot... sometimes

---

[20] Research suggested a strikingly similar composition of the call centre labour force in Ireland as far as its high levels of education were concerned. Consider the description offered of his colleagues by an Italian call centre worker interviewed in Dublin: "For example, they are from different backgrounds. People, which have degrees, have different, really different degrees: law, political science, or whatever, philosophy, different people" (Irish worker 1, personal communication, July 24, 2009).

they have different dialects from different areas, and you can recognize what region they're from, and right away you can empathize with them. (personal communication, April 5, 2006)

This putting to work of language in Aliant call centres extended, as Sandy Brideau (personal communication, April 6, 2006) relayed, to knowledge of *chiac*, the regional dialect constructed out of a mixture between French vernacular and English:

> Some people mix their French and English, and if you're only French or only English you're not able to understand that type of language. You need to be able to switch from French to English rapidly, because a lot of people do that.

The observations by Aliant workers are confirmed in the recent accounts of call centre work emerging from inquiries carried out in Italy. Since these workspaces are oriented towards the production of communicative rather than physical commodities, Carlo Cuccomarino and Francesco Maria Pezzulli (2012) have noted that the labour of customer service over a phone requires abilities that are "acquired through life experiences and socialization, not in the workplace." What is put to work in call centres are the *social* qualities of labour: the speaking of a language, the ability to communicate in the vernacular, to name a place known to both participants in the conversation, to make a regionally specific joke. As Cristina Morini and Andrea Fumagalli (2010, p. 243) observe:

> ... the call center operator, connected through a phone to the customer, attempts to establish a relationship of loyalty by means of a response that is as appropriate as possible. In doing so, she activates in her working performance not only what she learned during her professional education, but also her relational intelligence—developed since her childhood—her innate relational attitudes, her faculty of language, her interests and social contacts. To this list we must add "physical" components, such as a persuasive tone of the voice and a positive attitude during the phone call. This amount of "subjectivity" and "affectivity" is clearly present in the relation with the customer, but is not represented in the operator's wage.

What the employer appropriates and puts to work in the call centre then, at least initially, is the capacity to make common that lies at the foundation of human communication.[21]

While specific linguistic and communicative capacities gained outside of the workplace were clearly put to work at NBTel, the labour process of customer service workers would be profoundly affected by the firm's restructuring, however. These transformations combined to unleash the process of "callcentreification" on the work of teleservice employees in the wake of the merger. Within this upheaval, the relational and linguistic capacities described earlier were submitted to the labour routinization, intensification, and surveillance for which call centres have become notorious.

The inauguration of this shift in the customer service labour process clearly manifests in the literature produced out of the merger and was confirmed in the accounts offered by employees. In union publications, press releases, CIRB decisions, or public quotes from representatives of Aliant, the workers I interviewed were most often defined as "clerical" workers. This label differentiated them from "operator" services (who, despite the automation affecting their jobs, still carry out a contemporary iteration of the roles they have played since the emergence of telephony) and "craft" or "outside" workers, who make repairs and install new services at homes and businesses. Soon after the merger, a looming transformation of the "clerical" labour process was signalled by the fact that these employees were increasingly referred to as "call centre" workers by management. Significantly, by the time I interviewed the workers in 2006, many of them were calling themselves by that appellation.

After the merger, workers described how the complex skill set described above was pushed closer to its limits by management in an attempt to extract greater amounts of communicative labour in Aliant's call centres. Even as employees were expected to develop productive relationships with the customer and find solutions to their problems, virtually all of the

---

[21] This appropriation of labour's communicative capacities in call centres is a feature that Michael Hardt and Antonio Negri (2009, p. 267) see operating across the broader economy, where "knowledge that is widespread across society—mass intellectuality—is becoming a central productive force." Christian Fuchs echoes this position when he suggests that "the production process of knowledge is a social, common process, but knowledge is appropriated by capital" (2010, p. 187).

workers interviewed suggested that since the merger Aliant had subjected their work to a different set of logics and rhythms—ones that were much closer to those of outsourced call centres in the province. Sandy Brideau (personal communication, April 6, 2006) traced the transformation of their labour process back through its appearance in management discourse, suggesting that prior to 2001 management referred to their labour as "help desk" work. As he pointed out,

> [there is] a big difference between help desk and call-centre ... And then, three years after, they sent an email [and] for the first time it says "... the call centre working hours." So we said, "what happened with [the] help desk?" "Ahhh [they said] ... by the way, no, we're a call centre."

Underscoring how callcentreification is part and parcel of the ever-resurfacing contest for control between workers and management, Brideau also noted that the term "call centre" entered managerial lexicon "shortly after we signed our union card" (personal communication, April 6, 2006). Indeed, as they began to implement these changes, Aliant management could not have been unaware of the well-entrenched methods of disciplining call centre labour—as well as the lack of unionization and much lower wages—marking the outsourced call centre sector in New Brunswick. After all, several outsourced call centre companies—operating "just down the road" in the words of one worker—were already a part of Aliant's corporate family. Following the merger, the new company had transferred a portion of its technical support operations to xwave, a non-unionized subsidiary of Bell Aliant offering call centre services. xwave's newest Moncton location consolidated three different call centres, employed 850 workers, and was opened in 2001 in a ceremony attended by New Brunswick Premier Bernard Lord. In launching xwave, Aliant was utilizing the strategy adopted by American telecommunications firms, which had opened up non-unionized subsidiaries as a destination for outsourced customer contact work (see Doellgast, 2012).

At Aliant, the transition from help desk to call centre was therefore much more than a matter of semantics for the workers—it was a set of changes that harboured a very serious threat of job transfer. For most of the customer service positions, this shift implemented labour processes uniting them with their non-unionized colleagues across the province in a most unwelcome form of convergence: software-driven scripts, intensified electronic monitoring, and disciplining based on performance. Philippe Roy (personal communication, April 5, 2006) observed that since the merger his work was "very structured: call flows, you know, productivity and sales quotas and everything. It is very call-centre structured now, more than it was before." As he suggested, "... if the performance isn't there, they notice fairly quickly." More monitoring of performance meant greater surveillance, a practice Aliant workers unanimously disliked. Keenan Richard described it as like having "an extra pair of eyes behind you all the time" (personal communication, April 4, 2006). The reformatting of their labour process was an unsettling reminder that customer service jobs could be outsourced, as so many noted, "at the flick of a switch."

Aliant employees were quick to identify the move towards a more structured, measured, and surveillance-heavy labour process, at the expense of quality, as typical of the work rhythms faced by their non-unionized counterparts across New Brunswick. Workers at Aliant in Moncton had friends and relatives employed in the outsourced call centre sector, and so they were more than familiar with the labour conditions at these workplaces. Karen Buckley, who offered tech support at Aliant, described the impact of this work on those close to her:

> The call centre industry is getting a bad name because of the stress level that is added to the individual who's working that particular job. The expectation that one person is going to extrapolate that kind of quality from interacting with a person on the telephone [in such a short period of time] ... it's unreasonable, it's unbelievable, and it's landed so many people in stress leaves from work that the unemployment office actually has a way to deal with them. You know that there's an issue when you go to unemployment and tell them that you're out on stress leave, and they'll send you back to school to re-educate you to do something else, provided you never ever, ever, ever, go back to call centre industry. Because my daughter took it. Yeah, they'll pay her [Employment Insurance] for the whole time she's in school provided she never goes back to a call centre. She

was working at ClientLogic. And she was their top salesman for two consecutive months prior to leaving on stress! And they were still hounding her because her calls weren't less than 12 minutes. She was their number one salesperson. (Buckley, personal communication, April 6, 2006)

Of special significance to this story is that ClientLogic, an American multinational call centre business, had taken over xwave's contract to offer outsourced tech support for the Canadian telecommunications firm Bell Canada's Sympatico Internet service. As Aliant was a key piece of the Bell corporate empire, knowing the labour conditions endured by her daughter and other ClientLogic call centre workers gave Karen Buckley a reliable insight into what her own job could turn into, were it outsourced. Other sources confirm the disciplinarity of the working conditions at ClientLogic. The hundreds of posts by workers there and at other companies in an online forum discussion thread titled "ClientLogic Employment Issues" offer a rich and candid set of insights into the distressing labour conditions at the company, as well as workers' responses to them. The initial anonymous post, made in 2005 by someone who identifies as a ClientLogic employee, is worth quoting at length here:

> I'm posting this because I want to know what customers think about the possibility of ClientLogic employees walking off the job. There are a few employees from ClientLogic, myself included that are seeking a union to represent us. If a union vote does come, and pass, it's almost guaranteed we will strike. We aren't upset with Bell customers, or Bell Canada itself, but with our own management who has simply taken everything of value away from us since they took over from Xwave. I really want to know if Bell customers would be supportive of a strike if one were to happen.
>
> In recent weeks, there have been several changes to procedures and rules that have simply pushed us to the edge. I would simply like to list a few of the complaints against our company, to get it off my chest and also, to let you, the customer, know just how poorly we are being treated. Our management has eliminated sick time. As of September we will no longer be paid for taking time off ill. Our previous years' vacation time was not paid out on February first, like we were promised; instead, it was pushed back to April

and we were forced to take the time off. Management has seen fit to disallow us from browsing the internet between calls or even when we are on a break. There have been multiple firings of agents for very poor reasons (caught browsing while on break, etc.). The internal hiring policy that was once in place had been removed, and many of our ops managers and coaches have no idea what a computer looks like. We are no longer allowed to read a book or play cards when we are not taking calls. Our schedules are usually 2–3 days in advance, our days off rarely are in a row or the same week to week. Bilingual agents receive no extra money for their talents. Raises are non-existent, even when moving to a better role within the centre like Tier 2. Unlike all other Bell centres, we receive no commission or any incentive to sell. We are told to meet our sales targets or be fired.

Most employees have had enough, ever since ClientLogic took over things have gone severely downhill. We will be actively seeking a union in the upcoming months and quite simply, if we get one. I'd expect a strike.[22] (sp00n, 2005)

The ensuing discussion in the forum displays the broad spectrum of employee responses to disciplinary working conditions in call centres, ranging from some who accuse the original poster of being lazy, to others who suggest a skills upgrade so the poster can get a better job at another call centre, to those who concur that unionizing and striking would be a good idea. While such action does not seem to have occurred at ClientLogic, the testimony from this worker and many others employed by this company and other outsourced call centre operations in this forum vividly illustrates the tendency for labour conditions in the outsourced sector to be more routinized, regimented, and intense than those of in-house operations. In short, conditions there are much more clearly and consciously dedicated to the production of abstract communication as a commodity for sale on the market.

---

[22] The original post, in English, includes spelling and grammatical mistakes throughout, and most of those have been removed here. These errors may be due to the fact that the worker is francophone, or (given the risks involved in denouncing labour conditions at their company) that they did not wish to be identified through their writing.

4 The Making of the Call Centre Cybertariat

When asked about the nature of the work in outsourced New Brunswick call centres, Aliant employee Dina Gallant-Vautour's description evoked a highly disciplinary production of abstract communication:

> It's vicious, because people are ... under a lot of stress. Because you have to work under certain conditions where you're constantly being watched and listened to. And if you don't cut it, you're out. And if you don't say exactly what they want you to say you're out. You're getting paid—not in our call centre, obviously, because we're unionized, but in other call centres—not minimum wage, but not a lot much more. (personal communication, April 5, 2006)

Aliant employees were, therefore, well aware of the threat they faced from outsourcing, and that the routinization of their labour process was the first step towards it.

Their testimony confirms the accounts of workers and scholars from other contexts of the transformation of the customer service labour process towards the mass-production call centre model. Mark Malone, who worked at a British Telecom's in-house call centre in Belfast during the 1990s (and credits the experience with pushing to become politically involved), offered a valuable perspective on this shift during an interview in Dublin. He described the restructuring of his communicative labour in language that has significant parallels to the testimony shared by call centre workers across the Atlantic:

> But there was definitely a momentum towards a sort of a much more professionalized, stats-oriented, sort of method of management, I guess .... There wasn't [much monitoring of performance] at the start. There wasn't a tremendous amount of monitoring at all. And it actually seemed to be that, I don't know whether it was 1994, 1995, 1996 or whatever ... When the monitoring performance seemed to come as rule, it was with new ways of actually being able to do it, you know ... Thinking back, it actually seemed to make sense not to have all this stuff at the start and kind of build up a bit of workforce first and then sort of bringing in this stuff slowly. (Malone, personal communication, July 21, 2009)

In a penetrating analysis of his daily routine at an outsourced Italian call centre where the mass-production model is firmly established, Paolo Greco notes that "[managerial] control of the call flow is the equivalent to the control of available time, of the rendering productive of workers' downtime as moments of possible and hoped for valourisation" (2011, section 4, para. 2). Greco describes how this regime, in a workplace where the average time of an interaction over the phone is just 210 seconds, filtered down into the culture of his workplace: "[t]ime is the object of obsession in every discussion between colleagues, and features in every warning that comes from the team leader."[23]

The process through which abstract communication is produced in call centres does not necessarily produce more *effective* communication however, nor is it always straightforward in practice. As the labour activist collective Kolinko put it in their *Hotlines* inquiry, "... here we are not dealing with nuts and bolts that have to fit an industrial norm, it's about damned words that they want to come out of your lips" (2002, section 6.1.e, para. 5). At Aliant, employees felt that the upshot of the managerial effort to restructure workers' communicative labour was often a *decreased* capacity to affectively connect with and adequately assist the customer. In fact, this finding is reported so often in studies of call centres that it can be classified as a central contradiction in the call centre labour process. While the scripting of customer service work "facilitates control of information," Kiran Mirchandani (2012, p. 87) notes in the Indian context, "it is also acknowledged to interfere with opportunities to build rapport between workers and customers."[24] The abstraction of communication in call centres, in emptying linguistic interaction of anything but the most instrumental content, runs the constant risk of hampering its effectiveness in the process.

---

[23] This reduction of communication to a process that can be measured in quantitative terms would hardly have come as a surprise to Harry Braverman, who argued in the early 1970s that "[a]s flows subject to mathematical rules, clerical processes can be checked at various points by mathematical controls" (1974, p. 217).

[24] For example, Mirchandani (2012, p. 57) describes the way in which genuine contact between American customers and Indian call centre workers is thwarted because the latter, forced through extensive language training to present (or abstract) themselves as fictional Americans, must engage in "locational masking", and therefore sidestep ice-breaking questions from customers on the conflict over Kashmir, or how the weather is in Bangalore.

The persistent accounts of this foundational tension, in which the channelling of labour's capacity to communicate risks killing the very utility of that communication, are striking and deserve a closer look as they reveal some of the limits of the valourization process within call centres. From their experiences working at call centres in Calabria, the *Gruppo d'Inchiesta* note how "often it is precisely the [managerial] obsession with speed that generates serious problems for the customer on the other end of the phone" (Gruppo d'inchiesta sulla precarietà e il comune, 2013, p. 4). In their early research on Taylorism, Bain, Taylor, Watson, Mulvey, and Gall (2002, p. 172) observed that the attempt to mitigate this contradiction by balancing the quantity and quality of calls presented a "perennial challenge" for management. In his account of working at an outsourced call centre in Middlesbrough, England, Anthony Lloyd (2013, p. 82) captures the confusion created in workers when what is required of them in order to communicate effectively with customers exceeds what is actually permitted within their labour process: "[i]ndividual characteristics had no place on the call centre floor but, crucially, we were expected to be employed on calls where our personality and emotional labour were put to work." From Argentina, the Colectivo Situaciones echoes the experience of this paradoxical condition:

> The situation is contradictory: call center transactions (communication with others and with the computer) are limited and controlled, at the same time that those who execute them are permanently ordered to "exceed the limits." What limits?! Those of mental fatigue, when you feel burnt out and you can't take it anymore. (2006, p. 30)

This foundational tension, as Maeve Houlihan points out, is driven by "a central and inescapable problem with the scripting and codifying approach, ... that it neglects the basic organic nature of human communication and interaction" (2001, p. 213).[25] Cuccomarino and Pezzulli (2012,

---

[25] In their study of subject formation among the Indian call centre workforce, Carrillo-Rowe et al. (2013, p. 178) also find this process at work when they note that the enforced projection of fictional American identities "isolates and insulates the agents' bodily and affective inhabitance from their immediate surroundings."

para. 4) go as far as to maintain that this tension points to the ultimate impossibility of the Taylorist project as applied to communication:

> Notwithstanding managerial attempts to regiment the conduct of operators with predefined scripts in the handling of calls . . . the work of a call centre employee is not capable of being standardized, because it pertains to the biology of the subject, to her feelings and her capacity for rationalization, to the versatility and reactivity she is able to express, to the knowledge she is able to functionalize and communicate.

We will return to this foundational tension in the concluding chapter, but in the meantime these accounts allow us to make the basic point that the quest to reduce the worker's capacity for communication to a dependable input for valourization within the call centre labour process is at the very least a fraught endeavour, and on numerous fronts. For companies like Aliant, "callcentreification" is also a preliminary step towards outsourcing in-house customer relations functions, a process which transforms this communicative labour from a cost for the home company to a source of profit for the outsourced call centre sector. The outsourcing of call centre work thereby brings the process by which language is put to work to its logical conclusion: commodifying said communication and turning customer contact into a source of surplus value. Within that process of abstraction, communication is deprived of its specificity through the imposition of linguistic scripts, digital surveillance, and quantitative measure. The worker's experience of this process of abstraction is powerfully summed up by Lloyd: "[a]s individual workers, we were stripped of all unique characteristics and dealt with as an abstraction, a formless, characterless object" (2013, p. 81).

At the same time, however, the immaterial production such as that which occurs in call centres, as Morini and Fumagalli (2010, p. 248) put it, "rejects a quantitative measure."[26] Not only do call centre workers

---

[26] As media scholar Nicholas Garnham has observed (adopting the perspective of management), "white-collar labour time is inherently difficult to assess and to price" (2011, p. 56). In the analysis of the production of value in call centres we are reminded of Gigi Roggero's point that the need to reduce "living knowledge to abstract knowledge, or the possibility of measuring it, forces capital to impose completely artificial units of time" (2011, p. 25).

4 The Making of the Call Centre Cybertariat   111

report feelings of intense frustration arising out of being unable to adequately assist customers, but, as we shall see in the next section, the processes associated with "callcentreification" have become a flashpoint for labour resistance. The project of creating abstract communication in call centres is by no means an irresistible or irreversible one.[27] Even as their labour processes converged with those of their non-unionized colleagues down the street, Aliant employees retained an ability to resist such pressures when they got in the way of carrying out their responsibilities. For several interviewees, personal standards of professionalism and human decency simply superseded management's demands, and (doubtless bolstered by the fact that there is a union behind them) they described their decision to take matters into their own hands:

> ... with the Quality Care they want you to talk on average X amount of minutes on each call, but to me numbers aren't as important. I do very well on certain things where I know, but there are certain things that they're going to ask and I know I won't do as well as they want me to do, but I still take the time anyways. [...] I don't think they can fire me for taking the time to help the customer, so I just take the time! (Aliant worker 2, personal communication, April 6, 2006)

---

[27] In Ireland, I interviewed several workers who had brought in the Communications Workers' Union to their in-house call centre (for a transnational wireless company) who described how they had managed to push back against management in the process: "Well, they definitely know there is a union there now. ... For a long time they kept it under wraps, because people were joining every other day and we kept it all quiet. And it worked well that way. And then things started to happen and we were caught in union hands, if you like, and quoting our rights when things weren't going our way or when things were bad. We were quoting what our rights were. And we were told in no uncertain terms that 'there was no union in the house and that we couldn't have one.' And we told them 'yes we can. It is our statutory right to be a union member if we want to be.' And they said 'no, no, no, there is no union here.' And eventually we told them one day 'yes there is and there is a lot of members.' They kind of backed off a bit that way, because they knew then that we were seeking advice. It happened. We were restructuring and they were being bought over. There were a lot of things happening that were nasty at that time. ... They know kind of the union there now and actually we have had open union meetings and they send their little spies to the meetings, quite obvious. ... We knew who they were. We knew who our members were and who the little spies that were appearing who they were. They know that there is a union there now. It was very hard with the technical department that was being broken up." (Irish worker 2, personal communication, August 5, 2009).

Beyond resisting such changes to their labour process, it should be noted that the rationalization evident in the work of some call centre workers was also not present across the board at Aliant. Within some forms of clerical labour such as tech support, expertise still resided with workers rather than being embedded in software scripts as it was at xwave. When asked whether she had more knowledge of her job than her supervisors, Buckley (personal communication, April 6, 2006) replied "Yeah! Far more! They remind me of a group of people playing with toy soldiers. All the little plastic men are lined up, but they don't have a clue what's going on in any of their heads." Donovan Richard experienced this as well: ". . . probably because our group is a little bit more experienced, we've been there a long time . . . the supervisors we have now don't really know what we do" (personal communication, April 4, 2006).

We will explore the resistance shortly, but for the meantime, it is important to note that the transition towards a more regimented work routine for customer service workers, the imposition of scripts, surveillance and measure on the labour process, and the resulting risk of outsourcing were some of the central tensions around which the contest for control between Aliant management and call centre workers was playing out. As workers suspected, the changes to their labour process were warnings of the approach the newly merged company would take to its unionized employees. By 2003, management was determined to break the convergent union it had created in its wake and restructure the labour process as it saw fit. The strike that followed saw call centre workers enact their collective resistance to this process through the established trade union movement.

The Aliant Strike

The 2004 Aliant strike occurred amid a wave of labour confrontation in the Canadian telecommunications sector. As the strife broke out in Atlantic Canada, trade unions and convergent telecommunications companies across the country were paying close attention since the issues on the table appeared to be remarkably similar in several situations. In Ontario and Quebec, 7500 CEP technicians were in contract talks with

Bell Canada, with similar issues (outsourcing, pensions, and wages) coming up as key. On the west coast, the Telecommunications Workers Union and Telus were in the middle of a four-year dispute. Thousands of TWU members had been without a contract for years, and eyes were turned to Atlantic Canada to assess what might happen when push came to shove.

The 2004 conflict was a test of the soundness of the CEP's organizational decisions in a rapidly changing economic landscape. In an age of outsourcing, success for it and CATU would primarily mean maintaining the kind of job security for Aliant employees that telecommunication workers had achieved under the "permeable Fordist" (Rideout, 2003, p. 30) regime established in the post-World War II period. On the other side of the divide, management was absolutely focused on "cutting costs by reducing workforces, eliminating restrictive contract language, and reducing benefits" (Niemeijer, 2004, p. 6).

By December 1, 2003, when Aliant workers across Atlantic Canada voted by a 92.5% margin to give their negotiating committee the authority to call a strike, the company and CATU had been squaring off for three years and Aliant workers had been without a contract for almost two. Changes in the labour process described earlier had continued during that time. Aliant remained unwilling to offer CATU what it wanted on pensions and outsourcing, and negotiations broke down. In March 2004, CEP negotiators secured a new strike mandate following Aliant's offer.

As the conflict approached, Aliant management played up its ability to circumvent strike action via a combination of automation and managers carrying out the jobs of striking workers. "We've got pretty good systems, a good network," suggested the company's public affairs manager Brenda Reid, "we don't expect if there is a work stoppage that it will have any major impact on the network itself" (as cited in Macphee, 2004). The company was training over 1800 of its managers to fill in for call centre workers in the case of a strike.

For its part, the CEP's strategy became clear: while it would not be able to shut down Aliant's networks entirely, it might cause enough of a slowdown to routine maintenance, repair, and support functions to jeopardize the influx of new customers, diverting them towards competitors and thereby putting a squeeze on Aliant's profits. Considering the size of Aliant's operations, even the maintenance of routine operations in call centres would put enormous pressure on Aliant's managers, who would have to "keep the lights on," as CEP President Brian Payne suggested (as cited in Canadian Press, 2004), for an estimated 2 million residential customers and 80,000 businesses across Atlantic Canada.

On April 23, pickets went up across four provinces. In Moncton, the newly unionized workers were facing the unknown: "90% of the people [...] going out the door had no idea what a strike was, they'd never gone on strike before" (S. Brideau, personal communication, April 6, 2006). While the conflict was mostly played out within the framework imposed by the Canadian Labour Code, it produced a great deal of friction across the Maritimes. In a tactic that would feature prominently in the looming Telus strike on the west coast, Aliant employed private security guards to monitor and intimidate the striking workers:

> We did get harassed quite a bit by the security guards. Several tactics, fear tactics, were used and stuff like that. So it was kind of rough, you know, they showed us our home address on a piece of paper, just to rub it in that we know where you live. They delivered letters at my home about conduct and stuff, they were saying I was harassing people and all that which, you know, is kind of scary ... (Aliant worker 3, personal communication, April 6, 2006)

Tension was also high between strikers and managers, who belonged to the same union but were in different bargaining units, meaning that the latter crossed picket lines to carry out the former's work. Assault charges were laid against picketers in several locations as the hustle and bustle of strike activity took on an analogous life in the courts (Bouzane, 2004). Aliant and CATU ended up in the Newfoundland Supreme Court in July after a riot squad was called to the St. John's Aliant headquarters three days earlier to watch over about 200 striking workers who were holding up management trying to enter the building (Bouzane, 2004).

Confirming the strategic importance of outsourced subsidiaries, Aliant used non-management workers from xwave to do the work normally done

4 The Making of the Call Centre Cybertariat 115

by striking workers. Since customer service work was being outsourced and installations and repairs continued across the city of Moncton, strikers also used roaming pickets: "people got in cars and looked for vans to picket. And then there was the xwave parking lot, because they were doing our job" Karen Buckley recalls (personal communication, April 6, 2006).

Instances of worker sabotage surfaced through the spring and summer. In May an Aliant automated systems building in Holyrood, Newfoundland, suffered fire and smoke damage to its exterior and an Aliant vehicle had its tires slashed (Bouzane, 2004). In June primary and backup cables in the Aliant network were severed, disrupting telephone, cellular and Internet services for 250,000 customers in Newfoundland. The same tactic was employed that month on the east coast of Nova Scotia (Bradbury Bennett, 2004a). By late July police were reported to have investigated at least 25 acts of vandalism and sabotage (CBC News, 2004a).

As the strike hit the two-month mark the parties met to resume negotiations, but these exploratory talks between ended after two days (Cronk & MacDonald, 2004). With strike pay offering little more than CDN$200 per week (Bradbury Bennett, 2004b), pressure grew on both strikers and the union coffers.[28] At roughly the same time, the TWU contributed CDN$1 million to the Halifax-based Atlantic Communication and Technical Workers' Union, an early sign that there were financial difficulties at the Nova Scotian organization.

When Bell Canada technicians in Ontario and Quebec accepted a contract their bargaining committee had advised them to reject in mid-August (one which fell short of CATU's own bargaining objectives), it was likely an indication that they did not see things proceeding well in Atlantic Canada. Workers in Ontario and Quebec agreed to a contract that allowed outsourcing and agreed to Bell Canada's pension plan demands. Their defeat provoked a special member update from CATU's bargaining team urging strikers at Aliant not to be discouraged by what had happened elsewhere (Cronk & MacDonald, 2004).

---

[28] At the end of July national treasurer Andre Foucault stated that the CEP had spent roughly CDN$3 million on the local union's strike fund (Bradbury Bennett, 2004a).

By mid-summer the strike was also cutting into Aliant's bottom line. The company's second quarter financial results at the end of July revealed the strike had cost it somewhere in the region of CDN$21 million, with a drop of CDN$9 million in revenues and a CDN$12 million increase in costs (CBC News, 2004b). Considering it was relieved of the burden of paying its unionized workers, these figures suggest Aliant was prepared to pay a hefty price for unfettered control of its labour process. In August, with the strike closing in on its fifth month, provincial Labour Minister Joe Fontana announced that a federal mediator would try to resolve the dispute. The parties met with Elizabeth MacPherson in Halifax on August 30, and four days later it was announced that a tentative agreement had been reached.

Not all was peaceful within the CATU alliance however. As its workers were reviewing the tentative deal, friction was developing between the CEP and the ACTWU. The Nova Scotia ACTWU members were far from happy with the Aliant offer, especially the outsourcing contract language and how long it would take them to reach wage parity with Aliant workers doing the same work in other provinces. As the ratification of the agreement by union members was pending, the CEP withdrew its support for the 1800 Nova Scotia workers through its strike fund. "The CEP has really kicked us while we are down, our union brothers" one ACTWU member lamented, "in my opinion, they are trying to force a yes vote" (as cited in *Halifax Chronicle-Herald*, 2004, para. 3–7). With the ACTWU on the rocks financially, Nova Scotia workers were facing no strike pay if they rejected the tentative deal. While some Nova Scotians may have felt the offer was the best they could get from the company, the sentiment of betrayal appears to have been widespread. "It was [a] real blow," suggested Nova Scotia dispatcher Joan Ross, "my own personal feeling is I think we should be contacting the Auto Workers and Teamsters, and saying: 'we're here, take us.' And leave the CEP in the dust" (as cited in McLaughlin, 2004). CEP Local 410 president Tom Retieffe added his voice to the chorus: "The contracting-out language that we enjoyed for years in Newfoundland has been completely left out of the collective agreement and all we have now is basically a no-layoff clause ..." (as cited in Bradbury Bennett, 2004b). While unionized workers at Aliant had gained protection through a series of measures against layoffs, or "workforce reduction" as it is referred to in the collective agreement

(Aliant & Council of Atlantic Telecommunications Unions, 2004), they could still be shifted around to other positions so long as they were unionized ones. In addition, once a unionized worker left or retired from their position, they did not have to be replaced with another unionized worker.

The five-month strike came to an end when workers at Aliant accepted the contract offer with a lacklustre 76% "Yes" vote. The last act of the strike was the disappearance of the ACTWU, which in January of the following year opted to merge with the CEP due to financial difficulties. The strike that began with corporate convergence thus ended with another round of trade union convergence. Aliant's revenues for the year of the strike were more than CDN$2 billion, with reported profits of CDN$137 million (Communications, Energy and Paperworkers Union of Canada, 2005).

With employees back to work across the four provinces, Aliant resumed its restructuring. In September, the company announced the closure of a walk-in phone centre in St. John's (Vaccaro, 2004). In November 2005, it announced it would outsource 129 permanent call centre jobs (including technical support for dial-up Internet, high-speed Internet, telephone repair, and mobility repair) and drop around 100 temporary employees from the payroll (Tutton, 2005). The positions were shipped from call centres in St. John's, Halifax, and Moncton to the non-unionized ICT Group, whose two call centres in Miramichi already provided the helpdesk service for a portion of Aliant's dial-up Internet customers.

The company's strategy of outsourcing its call centre support work where possible and retaining its call centre sales work in-house, as one employee illustrated, translated into regular upheaval for many of the call centre workers in Moncton as portions of the labour process were spun off to other companies:

> I was doing the technical support at first for the dialup portion of it, then they got me into high-speed, and then the company decided to move their dialup to a contractor. So we lost the dialup part that we were doing, and we were doing high speed up until now and now they outsourced the high speed as well. So all of the technical side has been outsourced. And they're

keeping the unionized force for service. (Aliant Worker 2, personal communication, April 6, 2006)

By the time of my visit in 2006, Aliant's outsourcing was proceeding on multiple fronts:

> Technical support is mostly done by ICT, and I know they have a centre in Miramichi. They have another one in Moncton, and they might have one in St. John I'm not sure. There's also Minacs, I'm not sure how you pronounce that—they're starting to take a lot of the billing enquiries and repairs. And there's also another company that's taking operator assistance, Nordia or something like that. They're based in Quebec. They're the same one that handles Bell operator services. (A. Boudreau, personal communication, April 4, 2006)

For the call centre workers at Aliant, the ongoing experimentation meant permanent uncertainty: "[Management's] always telling us, 'you know, you guys can always be moved around to other trouble resolution groups'" said Donovan Richard (personal communication, April 4, 2006). Ferdinand Leblanc summed up the ambivalence of their unionized job security: "you have a job, but not necessarily the job that you want to have" (personal communication, April 3, 2006). For those who remained in technical support, like Donovan Richard, work had been further intensified as portions of it were outsourced: "same workload, just less people."

The rapid pace of change in the structuring of the labour process accompanied changes occurring at the corporate level. In March 2006, the company announced further restructuring in the formation of Bell Aliant. This entailed Bell Canada Enterprises (BCE) taking over Atlantic Canada's wireless operations, with Bell Aliant now being responsible for the traditional wireline operations in Ontario and Quebec, a move that boosted employment numbers to 10,000. According to CEP Atlantic region vice president Ervan Cronk, Bell was "hiving off the growth part of the company," leaving the more imperilled parts to Bell Aliant and its unionized employees (as cited in Tutton, 2006). This restructuring would continue the trend of union attrition at Aliant. As one telecommunications analyst suggested, "[t]hey're going to fracture the company and move employees around. Clearly some of the unionized employees will change unions, seniority is going to be affected and over time there will be attrition" (as cited in Tutton, 2006).

Bell Aliant's strategy towards its union in the wake of the strike was fairly clear. While for the moment Aliant was forced to keep on unionized positions by offering workers employment elsewhere in the company when their job was outsourced, over the long-term management aimed to reduce the union's presence through retirements and people leaving their jobs. Donovan Richard captured the disquieting feeling this outsourcing strategy produced: "So you see, our department got smaller, and they don't replace people, they just let it go smaller and go smaller until at one point there won't be anybody left" (personal communication, April 4, 2006).

One of the last questions I asked the interviewees was how secure they felt their positions to be. While responses were not unanimous on this point, most employees felt like Aliant Worker 6, who suggested her job was "not secure at all." Despite their collective agreement, she said, "Anybody can fall" (personal communication, April 6, 2006). By 2010, when the collective agreement was renewed for a second time after the strike without any major changes, Bell Aliant employed about 1100 people at call centres in Halifax, Charlottetown, Moncton, Saint John, and Mount Pearl.[29] Those workers are now represented by Unifor, Canada's largest private sector union that was produced by a merger between the CEP and the Canadian Auto Workers (CAW) in 2012.

The Cybertariat and Convergent Unionism

This chapter has shown how the making of a call centre cybertariat in Atlantic Canada and Ireland was premised upon expanding educational levels among the workforce, the forging of an informational development

---

[29] The collective agreement was extended in 2007 amid the general uncertainty of the drawn-out ownership bid (the largest takeover bid in Canadian history) for Aliant's parent company BCE on the part of a consortium of investors led by the Ontario Teachers' Pension Plan. The bid fell through in late 2008.

strategy by the state and the private sector, and, as a last act, the putting to work of language and communication within these workspaces. Discussions with participants in the Aliant strike illuminated these broader political and economic transformations, as well as how the tendency towards the intensification of routinization, surveillance, and measurement of info-service work is a constitutive tension marking the relations between labour and management in call centres.

By using the accounts of participants in the strike as a window into the call centre labour process, this chapter has described how the putting to work of language in NBTel/Aliant's call centres was characterized by two stages. In the first, communicative and educational capacities workers had gained outside of the workplace were allowed more autonomy within the labour process at NBTel. In the wake of the Aliant merger and subsequent restructuring, these discursive capacities were channelled into the more regimented and depersonalized model characterizing the mass production of customer communication in outsourced call centres. In a shift from what Phil Taylor and Peter Bain (2001) have described as managerial strategies focusing on "quality" towards ones based on "quantity," the communicative capacities of workers were subjected to a process of "callcentreification," within which communication is stripped of its complexity in an attempt to turn it into a generic and regimented input for the labour process.[30] As this chapter has further illustrated, the tensions inherent in this transition are by no means unique to call centres in New Brunswick. The contradiction between management's drive to produce what I have called abstract communication and labour's refusal of this process is constitutive of call centre work, and surfaces in worker accounts of the labour process from Argentina to India, from Canada to the United Kingdom—indeed in any setting where call centres have been established.

---

[30] I refer to this process as the real subsumption of immaterial labour in Chap. 7. Speaking of customer service work at British Telecom, Miozzo and Ramírez describe a similar process of abstraction: "It is apparent that [British Telecom] has designed and customised ICT, on the one hand, to exploit the complementary features associated with achieving higher productivity and better customer service (quicker response times, etc.) but, on the other hand, to drive down skill levels of operators and enforce economies of time and control, which allow the efficient provision of a high volume of standardised low cost services" (2003, p. 70).

4 The Making of the Call Centre Cybertariat

My goal here has not been to suggest that call centre work is the same everywhere. There is global diversity in terms of its labour conditions, ranging from unionized and well-remunerated positions in the public service to the precarious, low paying, highly routinized, and more intensely stressful work commonly found within the outsourced call centre sector. This chapter has shown how customer contact work in the telecommunications sector has seen a slide from the former to the latter over the last 20 years, as incumbent telecommunications monopolies have been privatized, outsourced their production processes to non-unionized companies, or spun off their call centre operations into entirely new ventures. As these companies have seen their need to interact with the customer increase due to competition and the nature and range of products they offer, they have also acted to decrease their dependence on the well-remunerated, unionized portion of their workforces.

In fact, as the German labour collective Kolinko reported in their pioneering call centre inquiry, the process of abstraction Ursula Huws refers to as "callcentreification" found particularly fertile ground in the telecommunications sector during the 1990s and early 2000s:

> At Telecom Italia, British Telecom, Verizon, Deutsche Telekom and other trusts that emerged from the former state-run telephone companies there has been a restructuring for years. Many administrative and service task were and still are being organised after the "call center model." We witnessed a taylorisation of work, a dequalification of the employees, an extension of shift work, outsourcing of whole company departments... The fact that in some of the call centres in this sector the resistance seems to be bigger than in other sectors has to do with a certain tradition of struggles and union organisations there—at least in countries like Italy, Britain and the USA. (2002, section 6.2.c)

If call centres impose punishing labour conditions it is because they are, quite literally, a form of punishment: far from facilitating the liberation of "knowledge workers," these workspaces, as Kolinko puts it, "were and are an attack on the refusal of many office workers to accept a deterioration of their conditions" (2002, section 6.1). The workforces I came into contact with in Ireland and New Brunswick during the 2000s were forged out of this project to restructure the immaterial labour upon which companies such as Bell Aliant increasingly depend.

Established trade unions such as the CEP have been the major line of defence for workers in call centres. The case of the 2004 Aliant strike is one where the emergent jobs of communicative capitalism and the institutionally enshrined forms of collective action forged within Fordism overlapped. Aliant workers across the Maritimes are heirs to the kind of company-level collective bargaining process that was typical of Canada's post-World War II Fordist telecommunications regime but is increasingly being overtaken by the political-economic restructuring described above. While the established labour movement remains the key vehicle for collective action in this new workspace, the disintegration of the Fordist telecommunications regime has created profound challenges for trade unions in this sector, as it has elsewhere.

Crucially, the visit to Moncton revealed how management's restructuring of the customer service labour process towards that of an outsourced call centre model was part and parcel of transferring work to some of those very same call centres in the region. The reengineering of the labour process had a double purpose: it was employed as a disciplinary tool against unionized call centre workers, spreading fear through the constant threat of job loss and thereby securing greater flexibility in the labour process, but it also devalued the labour of customer service workers to the point where the outsourced companies arising to fulfil these customer contact functions stood to profit significantly once it was subcontracted. The Aliant strike is an instructive case because through it we can clearly see the process by which customer contact has been transformed from being an in-house cost of doing business into a source of profit for the companies that arose to form the global call centre sector (our focus in the next chapter). The unionized call centre workers labouring for the North American continental oligopolies like Sprint, Telus, and Aliant will continue to face serious challenges in the years to come as a result of the pervasive outsourcing threat. As the recent Verizon strike in the United States underscores (Maass & Sustar, 2016), workers that are already organized will have to fight these pressures through their incumbent unions simply in order to maintain the jobs and benefits they have.

Trade union consolidation, or convergence, has been the most prominent response adopted by established trade unions in order to confront this changing scenario. When the CEP merged with the Canadian Auto Workers (CAW) in 2013 to form Unifor, the new union became

Canada's largest in the private sector, representing more than 300,000 workers. The experience of the Aliant strike will no doubt be an important one for the new union to draw upon—especially its 27,000 workers in the telecommunications sector. Having a bigger union confront a bigger employer produced advantages, including a larger strike fund and a more coherent bargaining position. In addition, contract language was achieved limiting the outsourcing of work, meaning that unionized Aliant workers maintained a degree of labour security. Despite these wins however, Aliant call centre employees remained subject to the steady erosion of their positions and continual upheaval in their jobs. Most important, the CEP clearly had a weakened bargaining position because it had no presence in the regional outsourced call centre industry, which, as we have seen, offers an ample basin of bilingual labour for electronically transferred work. My discussions with both rank-and-file union members and senior figures in the CEP suggested their focus was squarely on defending already unionized workers, with little more than vague commitments offered to organize the outsourced call centre sector.

Meanwhile, since the strike Bell Aliant's restructuring has continued almost unabated. In 2009 it announced it would close 11 call centres in Atlantic Canada by the following year and consolidate operations in its five largest call centres (CBC News, 2009). In 2012 the company announced plans to close three of the five remaining Atlantic call centres, employing a total of 1100 workers. In parallel to companies like Bell Aliant gutting their in-house operations, as Andrew Stevens notes, "the Canadian call centre industry has witnessed tremendous expansion over the last decade" (2014, p. 60). With over 14,000 call centres employing over half a million full- and part-time staff, or 3.4% of the total Canadian workforce (Stevens, 2014, p. 59), call centres need to be the object of a concerted organizing effort by the country's labour movement. Unifor's stated commitment to organizing precarious workers is encouraging, because as long as call centre workers in the outsourced sector are not organized, unionized employees such as those at Aliant will remain vulnerable to outsourcing. The recent Communications Workers of America (CWA) strike against Verizon offers some hope in this regard, since while the union struggled early on to organize call centre subcontractors that handle outsourced telecommunications work (Doellgast,

2012, p. 44), according to the terms of the most recent contract the firm reportedly agreed to make 1500 new hires, and most of these will be workers at outsourced call centres (Maass & Sustar, 2016). Next, we turn to labour organizing the outsourced and transnational call centre sector.

Interviews Cited

Aliant worker 1, Moncton, April 6th, 2006.
Aliant worker 2. Moncton, April 6th, 2006.
Aliant worker 3. Moncton, April 3rd, 2006.
Aliant worker 6. Moncton, April 6th, 2006.
Brideau, Sandy. Moncton. April 6th, 2006.
Buckley, Karen. Moncton, April 6th, 2006.
Irish worker 1. Dublin, July 24th, 2009.
Irish worker 2. Dublin, August 5th, 2009.
Leblanc, Ferdinand. Moncton, April 3rd, 2006.
Malone, Mark. Dublin, July 21st, 2009.
Richard, Donovan. Moncton, April 4th, 2006.
Richard, Keenan. Moncton, April, 4th, 2006.
Roy, Philippe. Moncton, April 5th, 2006.

References

Aglietta, M. (1979). *A theory of capitalist regulation: The US experience*. London, UK: Verso.
Aliant. (1999, May 31). Atlantic business combination complete: Aliant launched; enters TSE as CDN$3B growth company. *Canada NewsWire*. Accessed via Factiva database: https://global.factiva.com/
Aliant, & Council of Atlantic Telecommunications Unions. (2004, September). *Collective agreement*.
Aneesh, A. (2015). Emerging scripts of global speech. *Sociological Theory, 33*(3), 234.
Bain, P., Taylor, P., Watson, A., Mulvey, G., & Gall, G. (2002). Taylorism, targets and the pursuit of quantity and quality by call centre management. *New Technology, Work and Employment, 17*(3), 170–185.

Balka, E. (2002). The invisibility of the everyday: New technology and women's work. In *Sex and money: Feminism and the political economy in the media* (pp. 60–74). Minneapolis: University of Minnesota Press.

Berardi, F. (2013). L'autonomia dell'intelletto generale: Ecco il problema. *Commonware: General Intellect in Formazione.* Accessed at: http://www.commonware.org/index.php/neetwork/45-autonomia-intelletto-generale

Bouzane, B. (2004, July 30). Union brings it home: Pickets set up at manager's houses. *St. John's Telegram*, p. A4.

Bradbury Bennett, T. (2004a, June 11). Police seek list from Aliant: Want to know who has knowledge to bring service down. *St. John's Telegram*, p. B7.

Bradbury Bennett, T. (2004b, July 21). Strikes draining food bank. *St. John's Telegram*, p. A1.

Bramming, P., Sørensen, O. H., & Hasle, P. (2009). In spite of everything: Professionalism as mass customised bureaucratic production in a Danish government call centre. *Work Organisation, Labour & Globalisation, 3*(1), 114–130.

Braverman, H. (1974). *Labor and monopoly capital: The degradation of work in the twentieth century.* New York: Monthly Review Press.

Breathnach, P. (1998). Exploring the "celtic tiger" phenomenon: Causes and consequences of Ireland's economic miracle. *European Urban and Regional Studies, 5*(4), 305–316.

Breathnach, P. (2000). Globalisation, information technology and the emergence of niche transnational cities: The growth of the call centre sector in Dublin. *Geoforum, 31*(4), 477–485.

Brophy, E. (2009). Resisting call centre work: The Aliant strike and convergent unionism in Canada. *Work Organisation, Labour & Globalisation, 3*(1), 80–99.

Buchanan, R. (2002). Lives on the line: Low-wage work in the teleservice economy. In F. Munger (Ed.), *Laboring below the line: The new ethnography of poverty, low-wage work, and survival in the global economy* (pp. 45–72). New York, NY: Russell Sage Foundation.

Buchanan, R., & Koch-Schulte, S. (2000). *Gender on the line: Technology, restructuring and the reorganization of work in the call centre industry.* Ottawa, ON: Status of Women Canada.

Burnham, J. (2003). Why Ireland boomed. *The Independent Review, 8*(4), 537–556.

Callaghan, G., & Thompson, P. (2001). Edwards revisited: Technical control and call centres. *Economic and Industrial Democracy, 22*(1), 13–37.

Canadian Press. (2004, May 4). Union leader predicts Aliant managers will tire as strike drags on. *Canadian Press.* Accessed via Factiva database: https://global.factiva.com/

Carrillo Rowe, A., Perez, K., & Malhotra, S. (2013). *Answer the call: Virtual migration in Indian call centers*. Minneapolis, MN: University of Minnesota Press.
CBC News. (2004a, July 6). Aliant using outside workers: Strikers. *Canadian Broadcasting Corporation*. http://www.cbc.ca/story/canada/national/2004/07/06/Aliant_040706.html
CBC News. (2004b, July 30). Strike has cost CDN$21M: Aliant. *Canadian Broadcasting Corporation*. Accessed at: http://www.cbc.ca/news/business/strike-has-cost-21m-aliant-1.495490
CBC News. (2009, October 16). Bell Aliant to close 11 call centres. *Canadian Broadcasting Corporation*. Accessed at: http://www.cbc.ca/news/canada/nova-scotia/bell-aliant-to-close-11-call-centres-1.838216
Colectivo Situaciones. (2006) *¿Quién habla? Lucha contra la esclavitud del alma en los call centers*. Buenos Aires, Argentina: Tinta Limón Ediciones.
Communications, Energy and Paperworkers Union of Canada. (2001, September 27). Aliant Inc: Call-centre workers among 800 newly-unionized phone workers. *Market News Publishing Via COMTEX*.
Communications, Energy and Paperworkers Union of Canada. (2005, September 27). Phone customers should be rebated for poor service – CEP Canada. *NewsWire*.
Cronk, E., & MacDonald, D. (2004, July 16). *Council of Atlantic Telecommunication Unions info update: Bell contract offer & CIRB hearing*. Retrieved from http://www.cep.ca/reg_atlantic/files/aliant/040716_e.html
Cuccomarino, C., & Pezzulli, F. M. (2012, December 13). Tra mirafiori e Bangalore: L'inchiesta politica nei call center calabresi. *Il Manifesto*, pp. 8–9.
Doellgast, V. (2012). *Disintegrating democracy at work: Labor unions and the future of good jobs in the service economy*. Ithaca, NY: ILR Press.
Fuchs, C. (2010). Labor in informational capitalism and on the internet. *The Information Society, 26*(3), 179–196.
Garnham, N. (2011). The political economy of communication revisited. In J. Wasko, G. Murdock, & H. Sousa (Eds.), *The handbook of political economy of communications* (pp. 41–61). Malden, MA: Wiley-Blackwell.
Good, T., & McFarland, J. (2005). Call centres: A new solution to an old problem? In J. Sacouman & H. Veltmeyer (Eds.), *From the net to the Net: Atlantic Canada in the global economy* (pp. 99–114). Aurora, ON: Garamond Press.
Graeber, D. (2011). *Debt: The first 5,000 years*. New York, NY: Melville House.
Greco, P. (2011, May 27). *Analisi di un call center*. Retrieved from http://www.uninomade.org/analisi-di-un-call-center

Grimes, S. (2003). Ireland's emerging information economy: Recent trends and future prospects. *Regional Studies, 37*(1), 3–14.

Gruppo d'inchiesta sulla precarietà e il comune. (2013). *Boll Center n. 2: Bollettino d'inchiesta sui call center calabresi*. Retrieved from http://www.sudcomune.it/site/images/ALLEGATI/inchiesta/Bollettino_inchiesta_call_center_n._2.pdf

Guard, J. (2003). *Manitoba's call centre explosion: A preliminary overview*. Toronto, ON: United Steelworkers Canada.

Halifax Chronicle-Herald. (2004, September 9). Many striking Aliant workers to lose some strike pay, employee says. *Halifax Chronicle-Herald*.

Hardt, M., & Negri, A. (2009). *Commonwealth*. Cambridge, MA: Belknap Press of Harvard University Press.

Heller, M. (2003). Globalization, the new economy, and the commodification of language and identity. *Journal of Sociolinguistics, 7*(4), 473–492.

Houlihan, M. (2001). Managing to manage? Stories from the call centre floor. *Journal of European Industrial Training, 25*(2), 208–220.

Huws, U. (2003). Who's waiting? The contestation of time. In U. Huws (Ed.), *The making of a cybertariat: Virtual work in a real world* (pp. 177–186). New York, NY: Monthly Review Press.

Huws, U. (2009). Working at the interface: Call-centre labour in a global economy. *Work Organisation, Labour & Globalisation, 3*(1), 1–8.

Huws, U. (2014). *Labor in the global digital economy: The cybertariat comes of age*. New York, NY: Monthly Review Press.

Jaimet, K. (2006, June 9). The plot to enslave New Brunswick: Did the former premier make a secret pact or was the Bilderberg just a place 'to meet interesting people'. *Ottawa Citizen*.

Jobs, C., Burris, D., & Butler, D. (2007). The social and economic impact of the call center industry in Ireland. *International Journal of Social Economics, 34*(4), 276–289.

Kolinko. (2002). *Hotlines: Call centre, inquiry, communism*. Retrieved from http://www.nadir.org/nadir/initiativ/kolinko/lebuk/e_lebuk.htm

Lloyd, A. (2013). *Labour markets and identity on the post-industrial assembly line*. Burlington, VT: Ashgate.

Lüthje, B., Hürtgen, S., Pawliki, P., & Sproll, M. (2013). *From Silicon Valley to Shenzen: Global production and work in the IT industry*. Toronto, ON: Rowman & Littlefield.

Maass, A., & Sustar, L. (2016). *Why they won: The Verizon workers' campaign for union democracy set the stage for a successful strike*. Retrieved from https://www.jacobinmag.com/2016/06/verizon-strike-contract-deal-cwa-ibew-union-pickets/

Macphee, N. (2004, April 13). Aliant workers could strike by Friday. *St. John's Telegram.*

Marx, K. (1990). *Capital: Volume 1.* London, UK: Penguin.

McFarland, J. (2000). 1-800 New Brunswick: Economic development strategies, firm restructuring and the local production of global services. In J. Jenson & B. Sousa Santos (Eds.), *Globalising institutions: Case studies in social regulation and innovation* (pp. 53–79). Hampshire, UK: Ashgagate.

McFarland, J. (2009). Telling the story of globalization, neoliberalism and the call centre industry in New Brunswick. *Socialist Studies: The Journal of the Society for Socialist Studies, 5*(1), 24–50.

McKercher, C. (2002). *Newsworkers unite: Labor, convergence, and North American newspapers.* Lanham, MA: Rowman and Littlefield.

McLaughlin, P. (2004, September 11). Aliant workers vote on deal. *Halifax Daily News*, p. 11.

McNally, D. (1993). *Against the market: Political economy, market socialism and the Marxist critique.* London, UK: Verso.

McNally, D. (2011). *Global slump: The economics and politics of crisis and resistance.* Winnipeg, MB: Fernwood.

Miozzo, M., & Ramírez, M. (2003). Services innovation and the transformation of work: The case of UK telecommunications. *New Technology, Work and Employment, 18*(1), 62–79.

Mirchandani, K. (2012). *Phone clones: Authenticity work in the transnational service economy.* Ithaca, NY: ILR Press.

Morini, C., & Fumagalli, A. (2010). Life put to work: Towards a life theory of value. *ephemera: theory & politics in organization, 10*(3/4), 234–252.

Mosco, V. (2009). *The political economy of communication* (2nd ed.). London, UK: Sage.

Mosco, V., & McKercher, C. (2008). *The laboring of communication: Will knowledge workers of the world unite?* Lanham, MD: Lexington Books.

Niemeijer, M. (2004, August 6). Unions slow to develop new strategies: Canadian telecom industry rocked by deregulation, competition, mergers, technology. *Labor Notes*, p. 305.

Pupo, N., & Noack, A. (2009). Standardising public service: The experiences of call-centre workers in the Canadian federal government. *Work Organisation, Labour & Globalisation, 3*(1), 100–113.

Richardson, R., Belt, V., & Marshall, N. (2000). Taking calls to Newcastle: The regional implications of the growth in call centers. *Regional Studies, 34*(4), 357.

Rideout, V. (2003). *Continentalizing Canadian telecommunications: The politics of regulatory reform.* Kingston, ON: McGill-Queen's University Press.

Roggero, G. (2011). *The production of living knowledge: Crisis of the university and transformation of labour in Europe and North America* [Produzione del sapere vivo.] (E. Brophy, Trans.). Philadelphia, PA: Temple University Press.

Schatz, L., & Johnson, L. (2007). Smart city north: Economic and labour force impacts of call centres in Sudbury, Ontario. *Work Organisation, Labour & Globalisation, 1*(2), 116–130.

Shniad, S. (2005, January 6). Lessons from the TWU-Telus dispute. *Labor Notes*. Retrieved from http://labornotes.org/node/26

Shniad, S. (2007). Neo-liberalism and its impact in the telecommunications industry: One trade unionist's perspective. In C. McKercher & V. Mosco (Eds.), *Knowledge workers in the information society* (pp. 299–310). Lanham, MD: Lexington Books.

Snowdon, G. (2010, September 22). Call centres benefit from rise in graduate applicants. *The Guardian*.

sp00n. (2005, May 22). ClientLogic employment issues. Retrieved from http://www.dslreports.com/forum/r13467423-Clientlogic-employment-issues

Stevens, A. (2014). *Call centers and the global division of labor: A political economy of post-industrial employment and union organizing*. New York, NY: Routledge/Taylor & Francis Group.

Taylor, P., & Bain, P. (2001). Trade unions, workers' rights and the frontier of control in UK call centres. *Economic and Industrial Democracy, 22*(1), 39–66.

Taylor, P., & Bain, P. (2003). 'Subterranean worksick blues:' Humour as subversion in two call centres. *Organizational Studies, 24*(9), 1487–1509.

Tutton, M. (2005, November 16). Aliant outsources 129 jobs, slashes 100 temp positions. *Halifax Daily News*, p. 13.

Tutton, M. (2006, March 8). Shakeup won't mean job cuts, CEO says. *St. John's Telegram*.

United Nations Conference on Trade and Development. (2004). *World investment report: The shift towards services*. United Nations Conference on Trade and Development, Switzerland.

Vaccaro, A. (2004, September 22). Aliant workers wary. *St. John's Telegram*, p. D1.

Warson, A. (2002, July 30). Moncton's core gets urban facelift: City's fortunes have been reversed by new businesses, prompting building. *Globe and Mail*.

Winseck, D. (1998). *Reconvergence: A political economy of telecommunications in Canada*. Cresskill, NJ: Hampton Press.

Wong, T. (2004, July 31). Strike could hit Bell this week: Technicians give union mandate to set up picket lines. *Toronto Star*.

5

The Migration of Struggle

Capital moves, looking for profitable conditions, trying to escape the contradiction of workers' collective aspirations and resistance within profit production. In its flight it re-establishes the contradictions on a higher and wider social level. Call centres are no exception to that rule. (Friends of Kolinko & Gurgaon Workers News, 2012, para. 28)

In July 2008, Godfrey Moase walked onto the floor of the TNS call centre in Auckland, New Zealand. Employees there were carrying out the same kind of tele-survey work that until recently he had performed himself in Australia, where he had got a job with TNS in 2004. As an employee of the company, Moase joined the National Union of Workers (NUW), which at the time represented around 3000 Australian call centre workers at TNS and other market research companies. His employment at the company came to an end in 2006 however. Moase and his colleagues were informed their jobs were being shipped to New Zealand, where they would be performed for less than half the hourly pay rate they were getting.

While stories of labour outsourcing are typical of call centre work, what happened in the wake of this particular case was remarkable.[1] Two years after he was laid off, Moase travelled across the Tasman Sea as part of a transnational call centre organizing campaign—*Calling for Change*—launched by the NUW in partnership with Unite, an upstart rank-and-file union based in New Zealand. After spending six hours talking to the New Zealanders working at his old company, Moase and fellow organizers walked away from the call centre having signed up 87 of 90 workers on shift to Unite.

This chapter turns its attention to the global flows of labour and resistance within the call centre sector. The previous chapter described how the imposition of the call centre labour process has been an integral component of employer efforts to undermine, fragment, and confound the forms of collective power achieved by office workers during the post-World War II era of Fordism. In the case of Aliant customer service workers, what became evident during the course of my research in New Brunswick was the close connection between the imposition of a more intensely rationalized labour process—what Ursula Huws (2009) has called "callcentreification"—and its logical extension, the corporate practice of outsourcing.[2] Labour arbitrage, as the Aliant strike confirmed, presented an ongoing and critical threat to unionized call centre workforces.

The process of outsourcing tele-service work was gathering steam by the time of my visit to New Brunswick, but it was not new. By the late 1990s, the German labour-activist collective Kolinko (2002) had

---

[1] Stories of outsourcing are omnipresent in discussions of call centre work. In one of the most poignant examples, staff from an Orange call centre in Britain were told in 2001 they could keep their jobs if they moved to the Philippines. The company, which cut 1200 jobs following its merger with T-Mobile to create Everything Everywhere, known as EE, told 40 night-shift workers at its Darlington call centre that they could take different and lower-paid jobs, or relocate 7000 miles to Manila. Staff claimed that the company gave them details of a "rice allowance" that they could claim as part of the transfer to IBM, Orange's outsourcing partner in the Philippines (Neate, 2011).

[2] As Huws (2014, p. 72) notes, "[t]hese standardization processes make it possible to use information and communication technologies more extensively, for instance by introducing standard reporting procedures that make it possible to compare performance over time or between different locations, by making it possible to pool knowledge in common databases or 'knowledge banks,' and by making it possible to overcome the limits of space and time."

identified outsourcing, as they saw it unfolding at Hewlett-Packard (HP) and other companies, as a defining feature of call centre work. At HP, the quantified and measurable "service level" offered by employees to customers became what the collective called "the holy measuring stick" for both in-house and outsourced call centres:

> They threaten the "internal" call workers ... with outsourcing the calls to external companies if the service level is not achieved. They do the same thing to the "external" workers announcing the possibility of using the service of other call centre companies. It's a shitty game. (Kolinko, 2002, section 6.1.d, para. 7)

Offshoring, a term I use in this chapter to reference the outsourcing of labour across borders to workers in another country, is just another expression of the employer's desire to make info-service labour replaceable, transportable, and docile.[3] In this chapter, I zero in on these processes by tracking what a subset of call centre scholars have taken to calling the *virtual migration* of labour—in this case from New Zealand to Australia. In the process, I try to expand the analysis of virtual migration by investigating both the flows of capital that set it in motion and the migration of struggles that can follow in its wake.

In what follows, I first situate virtual migration within a broader political-economic context by offering an overview of the transnational portion of the call centre sector—or what I call *global call centre capital*. Using the expansion and eventual assimilation of the market research firm Synovate as an exemplar of the transnationalism and consolidation marking this sector, I tell the story of how Australian call centre companies seized upon New Zealand's trailblazing application of neoliberalism during the 1980s and 1990s in order to set up shop in the country and take advantage of the cheap, well-educated, and articulate Kiwi workforce.

---

[3] Some companies establish their call centre operations in other countries yet retain operating control over them (the term *captive operation* is sometimes used to describe this arrangement). Other companies simply outsource the operations entirely to another company in another country. In the latter case, this outsourcing has given rise to the transnational outsourced call centre industry, explored in this chapter.

In this particular case, capital's desire to flee higher wages and a more organized workforce, as the Kolinko quote that opens this chapter predicts, encountered a different and more threatening set of conditions than expected. The neoliberal mode of regulation which made New Zealand such an attractive destination for TNS, Synovate, and others also allowed Unite's experimentation with an unorthodox and militant form of trade unionism, one which adopted the tactics fashioned within the global justice struggles of the 1990s and 2000s. These tactics were then directed against Synovate and nine other global call centre companies in a relatively rare transnational, rank-and-file attempt to organize outsourced communicative labour. In 2011 I travelled to New Zealand to meet the protagonists of the Calling for Change campaign and several other remarkably successful drives to organize low-paid workers in the service sector. These drives are notable in that they were organized for and by populations—young people, women, and indigenous workers—that have historically been on the fringes of the country's established union movement.

In its investigation of the Calling for Change campaign, this chapter not only shifts the focus from national to transnational dynamics of call centre struggle but also from the established trade unions that are a legacy of the Fordist period to more recent experiments at the margins of the union movement—ones that are seeking to renew collective organizing in response to the explosion of part-time and precarious work in the service sector. Through the analysis of Unite and its campaign to organize outsourced call centre workers, I highlight the contested nature of what call centre scholars have referred to as virtual migration. This process, once set in motion by capital, can become the vehicle for an unpredictable migration of struggles—from country to country, from workplace to workplace, and across different branches of the low-wage service sector—as it follows the ebbs and flows of an increasingly disposable workforce.

Virtual Migration and Global Call Centre Capital

The transnationalization of call centre work became notorious during the first decade of the twenty-first century thanks to the transfer of outsourced customer service work from the United States (and to a lesser extent, Britain) to India. This surge of offshoring provoked a number of scholarly efforts dedicated to investigating the labour dynamics entailed in this shift (Aneesh, 2006; Carrillo Rowe, Perez, & Malhotra, 2013; Mirchandani, 2012; Nadeem, 2011; Patel, 2010).[4] Among the more influential concepts developed within this set of perspectives is that of *virtual migration*, contributed by the sociologist Aneesh (2006) as part of an early investigation of offshored information technology enhanced services (ITES) work. Virtual migration, as Carrillo Rowe et al. (2013, p. 2) indicate in their adaptation of the concept, names the dynamic by which "in the call center industry the labour, not the body, is transported across national boundaries."

Scholars of the emergent global call centre workforce have shown how virtual migration, often enacted in circumstances where the identity and the location of the call centre worker must remain concealed, produces an unprecedented set of cultural and subjective dislocations among the labour forces submitted to it. The testimony offered by a Moroccan employee speaking to customers in France for the multinational call centre company Sitel transmits both the virtuality and the suppression of identity characterizing by this transnational labour process: "We have to change our first names and are forbidden from speaking Arabic in the

---

[4] While varied in terms of their focus, this set of perspectives could be described as deploying a postcolonial approach to the analysis of offshored call centre labour in India. In developing a perspective on call centre labour that is distinct from the debates of the late 1990s, these scholars have highlighted the profoundly ambivalent effects of offshored, affective labour on the new Indian workforce to whom it is shifted. Winifred Poster (2007) and Kiran Mirchandani (2012) have traced the way India's colonial history has determined not only the path of this informational work transfer, but the Indian labour force's subordinate role within the emergent transnational configuration of service work. Forced to serve American, British, or Canadian customers half a world away, Indian workers are subject to disrupted identities and circadian rhythms, routine racism, and intensely rationalized labour processes. Describing the Indian call centre workforce as "something of a white-collar proletariat," Shehzad Nadeem (2011, p. 4) argues that globalization "does not entail the loosening of temporal chains, but their reconfiguration: a combination both rigid and flexible that binds even as it liberates" (p. 101). For reviews of this approach, see Brophy (2014, 2015).

workplace. It is as if we left Morocco at 6 a.m. in the morning and spent the whole day on another planet" (David, 2008, para. 9) This virtual movement of workers across borders, post-colonial scholars of the call centre have noted, "reconfigures the parameters of migration" and produces "an emerging form of mediated transnational labour" (Carrillo Rowe et al., 2013, p. 70).

The research carried out by A. Aneesh (2006) and other scholars of Indian call centre labour has had the merit of transnationalizing the analysis of this profession, and the concept of virtual migration is valuable for how it conveys the novelties of the labour process unfolding in global call centres. Less explored by these scholars however has been the bigger picture within which such virtual migration occurs. What are the political and economic dynamics characterizing the transnational call centre sector? What are the firms driving these virtual migratory flows? Is the transfer of call centre work from the "developed" West to the "developing" rest, or from the economic "centre" to the "periphery," the dominant trend in this sector? These questions are key to understanding not only the context within which the virtual migration of communicative labour is in motion but also to grasping the potential for labour struggles to migrate along those same trajectories. In order to address the broader context of virtual migration, this section of the chapter describes the portion of the outsourced call centre sector that controls and shapes the globalization of call centre labour—a set of transnational companies which together I refer to as *global call centre capital*.

Chapter 2 described how call centres have become an integral component of communicative capitalism, or the increasing centrality of "communicative access and opportunity" (Dean, 2009, p. 17) to economic relations across the economy. The affirmation of communicative capitalism has had enormous consequences for the spatial distribution of labour. Tobias Kämpf and Andreas Boes (2007, p. 200) have summed up these changes by suggesting that as the global information networks capitalism relies upon have become "a new space of production for information work," they are bringing about nothing less than a "new stage in the internationalization of labour." The call centre is a paradigmatic example of this re-spatialization of labour.[5] These informational workspaces have been at the forefront of capital's efforts to overcome geographic barriers, a process which (as we saw in Chap. 4) has been nurtured by the ubiquity of information technology, the rationalization of communicative work, the popularity of the informational development paradigm with entrepreneurial states, and the growing availability of well-spoken educated labour workforces in urban centres across the world.

As a model for extracting communicative work from these labour forces, the call centre is immediately global in scope, having developed rapidly and been translated into a remarkably diverse range of settings with relative ease. In her research on contact centres in Colombia, the sociologist Anita Weiss (2007, p. 151) remarks on the striking similarities in the organization and operation of these workspaces from one region to the next, suggesting that it is "not just the technology, but also the organisational practices that are globally diffused."[6] Underscoring the strategic importance of customer service, consumer research and other forms of virtual interaction with the population, the Argentinean activist-scholar collective Colectivo Situaciones (2006, p. 31) describes the call centre as "a key piece in an economy that articulates decentralized processes with productive localizations scattered across the entire planet."

How did this transnationalization of the call centre come about? The picture we have is fragmentary, but it seems that a key driver of the process was the financial sector, which following the dotcom meltdown of 2000 demanded cost-cutting measures across a range of sectors associated with communicative capitalism, from telecommunications to IT equipment manufacturing (see Lüthje, Hürtgen, Pawliki, & Sproll, 2013; Schiller, 2007). As a part of this shift, "[w]hile consumers got used to ordering goods online and accessing support via call centers," Ursula Huws (2014, p. 21)

---

[5] The development of the global call centre industry is a classic example of the process Vincent Mosco (2009, p. 128) characterizes as *spatialization*, in which "communication technology overcome[s] the constraints of geographical space."

[6] Weiss (2007, p. 147) further illustrates the global parallels in labour processes and technologies: "Because there is a global dissemination of technology and software, Colombian call centres are organised according to the universal parameters found globally. In several companies we visited, the technology and software are purchased from transnational corporations like Avaya, and the databases and their maintenance are provided by Oracle or Microsoft."

relates, "managers began to be asked by their directors why they had not considered outsourcing as a solution to reducing their costs." With IT, financial services, and newly privatized telecom firms leading the move to disperse their customer contact workforces away from corporate headquarters, the offshoring of clerical, support, and sales functions soon became a prominent strategy to keep labour costs low and workers in line (Mosco & McKercher, 2008). If domestic outsourcing marked the rise of call centres in the 1990s, offshoring became pervasive during the 2000s.

Seizing upon this transnationally outsourced customer contact business was what the United Nations Conference on Trade and Development (UNCTAD, 2004) described as a "new breed of multinationals." At the top of the world market for outsourced call centre services stands a group of global players servicing the communicative needs of a broad range of industries.[7] Convergys, Sitel, Teletech, Sykes, and Accenture are among the leading American providers of call centre services, but the list also includes Wipro and Infosys from India, Teleperformance from France, and Grupo Atento from Spain—all companies with annual revenues exceeding a billion US dollars. These companies take customer contact responsibilities or fulfil shorter-term contracts for the world's biggest corporations, spreading portions of customer service labour across their global frontline workforces. Through their investments in fixed capital (call centre premises and technology) and labour, these sellers of industrialized consumer interaction are a critical force that determines transnational flows of virtual migration.

As an example of the size and reach of their operations, after its 2014 purchase of Aegis, Teleperformance has over 182,000 employees in 270 call centres scattered across 62 countries. After its 2007 merger with ClientLogic (whose driving call centre rhythms were discussed in the previous chapter), Teleperformance's competitor Sitel now provides its services to Fortune 500 companies such as T-Mobile, Verizon, Microsoft, Philips, Dell, and HP through 108 call centres employing over 61,000 workers on every continent except for Antarctica (Sitel, 2015). Customers who made an anxious call to Sony in order to find

---

[7] Some of these companies are themselves (as was the case with Aegis, before its 2014 sale to Teleperformance) components of larger, diversified conglomerates.

out whether their credit card information was stolen in its 2011 security breach might well have spoken to a Sitel employee on the other end of the line.

While some of these companies date back to the 1970s, their "internal global division of labour" (Huws, 2014, p. 56) is much more recent. Sykes, founded in 1977, set up its first contact centre in a developing country (the Philippines) in 1997. Once the process of transnationalization began, its pace intensified rapidly. Convergys set up its first developing world affiliate in 2000, but only three years later it had call centres in Argentina, Brazil, India, Indonesia, Mexico, the Philippines, South Korea, Singapore, Sri Lanka, Taiwan, and Thailand (UNCTAD, 2004, p. 158). Similarly, by 2004 EDS, Sykes, and Merchants were among the largest call centre employers in South Africa (UNCTAD, 2004), priming that country to become a global destination for offshored call centres in the following decade.

Virtual migration of call centre labour across borders is set in motion by significant transnational flows of investment. Through the 2000s, the growing heft of call centre multinationals began to surface in statistics tracking foreign direct investment (FDI) patterns across the globe. While the bulk of FDI investment has historically been in manufacturing, in the period immediately following the dotcom bust, the proportion of FDI investment in services began to grow significantly, causing UNCTAD (2004, p. xxiv) to suggest that "[w]hile the offshoring of services is still in its infancy, the tipping point may be approaching rapidly." By 2006, one in five (20%) of the 100 largest non-financial transnational corporations listed by UNCTAD was a company providing services compared with only 7% in 1997 (as cited in Huws, 2014, p. 130).

The flows of international call centre investment and the virtual migration of call centre labour it sets in motion are complex and in rapid evolution. While post-colonial scholars of the call centre have highlighted virtual migration from developed countries such as the United States and the United Kingdom towards developing nations such as India, emergent patterns within the global industry remind us that its changing division of labour defies simple unidirectional models (Mosco & Lavin, 2008).[8] To offer an early example, while the outsourcing of call centre work from the United States to India received the lion's share of popular and scholarly attention during the 2000s, the majority of offshore call centre investment at the turn of the twenty-first century actually went from developed countries to *other* developed countries, with Ireland, Canada, and the United Kingdom in the lead as far as destinations (UNCTAD, 2004).

To be sure, offshoring routes frequently retrace and reinscribe the centuries-old colonial passages of capital's expansion (Mirchandani, 2004). In the process, flows of capital investment in one direction, and of communicative labour in the other, circulate among regions of the planet that have historically determined cultural or linguistic connections, such as when an American company outsources to Canada or Ireland, a French company to Morocco, Mauritius, or Senegal, or a Spanish company to Colombia, Chile, or Mexico (see Weiss, 2007). For example, catering to a "diverse-shoring" market, Grupo Atento (sold in 2014 by Spanish telecom multinational Telefónica to US private equity firm Bain Capital for over a billion Euros) provides call centre services for companies operating across the Spanish-speaking world (Thomas, 2012). Atento has over 150,000 employees scattered through 15 countries, including the United States, Spain, and numerous Latin American states (Atento, 2015b). In 2014, Atento opened its third call centre in Guatemala, investing US$ 4.6 million in Guatemala City for a site employing 1200 people. Workers there should be careful: in 2006, at Atento de Puerto Rico 19 labour organizers were fired for union activities (UNI, as cited in Mosco & Lavin, 2008, p. 154). While the company is heavily indebted, Atento's 2014 revenue stood at nearly US$ 2.3 billion (Atento, 2015a).

If the flows of call centre offshoring are often path-dependent on the routes established during the history of colonial plunder, they also chart

---

[8] As Sandro Mezzadra (2010) and others (Lüthje et al., 2013) have observed, global flows of capital and labour increasingly challenge the analytical model of a "new international division of labour" (NIDL) theory developed during the 1970s, which centred around the construction of a model describing unidirectional flows of offshored labour from the "centre" to the "periphery" of capitalist globalization.

the emergent, multipolar networks of post-Fordism. As Western companies have begun to look beyond India for labour forces to exploit, so too have Indian companies, now global players in their own right. In the process, the colonial flows of global call centre investment are sometimes being reversed entirely. By 2009, when Tech Mahindra was considering a new BPO operation in the Philippines, the Indian company already had two overseas operations in Ireland and the UK (Stevens, 2014, p. 74). Tata Consultancy Services launched its first call centre in the Philippines in December 2010 (Fontanella-Khan & Landingin, 2010), and Indian companies such as Wipro and Tata employ thousands of call centre workers back in the United States, as wages in the subcontinent rise and America's cybertariat swells (Glader, 2011).

These new challengers to the US call centre companies are also proving to be intrepid pioneers in untapped call centre markets. In the summer of 2014, Aegis announced it had agreed to sell its US, Philippines, and Costa Rican centres to Teleperformance for over US$ 600 million as it reorients its focus towards the faster-growing Asia-Pacific by entering call centre markets in Japan and Korea. Here a company executive announced they would combine the virtual migration of labour with the more traditional kind by

> bringing small groups of native Japanese and Korean speakers and bas[ing] them in Malaysia for two-three year stints. That way we can offer clients native speakers, a mix of native and non-native speakers or just nonnative speakers, depending on what they want. We can still offer a cost benefit even with the native speakers working out of Malaysia. (Mendonca, 2014, para. 8)

As Andrew Stevens (2014, p. 4) notes then, "the economic terrain of offshoring and outsourcing is hardly one where the so-called peripheral economies have been the only recipients of value-added services and employment." Rather, the emerging picture suggests the transnational portion of the call centre sector increasingly displays features of a multipolar, financialized, and highly cosmopolitan industry, with a variety of regional hubs taking advantage of a growing series of options as far as potential labour pools to choose from.[9] Phil Taylor's description of the patterns characterizing global call centre capital corroborates this emergent picture of flexible multipolarity:

> What has happened over the last half-decade or so has been a change in which buyer companies if they are larger, or suppliers if they've got greater capability, have tended to locate different facilities and different services in different locations. The suite of global locations has grown. Now it could be that an organisation might offshore English-speaking voice services to India or the Philippines, but might at the same time seek to utilise Eastern Europe for IT solutions or perhaps Latin America for a Spanish-speaking voice capability. So what have emerged have been multi-locational strategies as the scale and complexity of offshoring and outsourcing have grown. (Outsource, 2012, para. 2)

It is important not to exaggerate the originality, degree, or effects of offshoring as it applies to call centres, a mistake that only bolsters the breathless discourse of industry analysts and state agencies. For example, despite its novelty the process of outsourcing customer contact work remains similar to the outsourcing of manufacturing in several ways. Like the outsourced manufacturers making clothing for big name brands such as the Gap, global call centre companies segregate frontline info-service workers from the rest of the employees at the home company, introducing a fundamental line of division and hierarchy through these global workforces. A call centre job that is outsourced tends to be much worse than one that is not, a logic that unites customer service provision over a headset with electronics assembly and any number of other manufacturing industries. In this sense, as Stevens (2014, p. 53) argues, the practice of call centre offshoring cannot be divorced from "the deterioration of employment standards and the growth of temporary and part-time work" more generally.

---

[9] As such, the global nature of call centres illuminates what geographers Jaime Peck and Adam Tickell (2002, p. 386) propose is one of the signal features of neoliberalism, a "regime of highly competitive interlocal relations" in which most local social settlements become "tendentially subject in one way or another to the disciplinary force of neoliberalized social relations."

Nor should the transnational dimension of the call centre industry be exaggerated. Relatively large domestic companies (like Atesia, discussed in the next chapter) are a significant part of the call centre ecosystem in many a national economy, and when business services are outsourced they are still far more likely to be outsourced domestically (Huws, 2003). The *Global Call Centre Project* study found that most contact centres they surveyed remained domestic in their orientation, with interactions between employees and customers on the other end of the phone occurring within the borders of the same nation-state (Batt, Holman, & Holtgrewe, 2009). Moreover, sensationalistic (and often xenophobic) predictions in the British and American media of widespread unemployment caused by call centre offshoring have simply not come to pass.[10] While some types of call centre work (especially the more routinized kinds) are inherently mobile, call centres themselves appear to have become a structural feature of economies in which increasing importance is accorded to consumer involvement, feedback, and participation.[11] Just as important, call centre capital is never exactly as footloose as it might like to be, encountering significant political barriers to its mobility—as we shall see.

These important qualifications notwithstanding, however, if the information-intensive capitalism that emerged in the 1970s is "based on a transnational organizational model" where "new nodes can be continuously added and removed" (Fuchs, 2010, p. 180), then the global call centre companies investigated in this chapter are a prime exemplar of this development. In pursuing their own "patterns of spatial and contractual disaggregation" (Huws, 2014, p. 96), these companies and their clients increasingly spread their labour forces across a shifting "global network of back offices" (p. 73). As call centres have been transformed from a necessary in-house expense for companies requiring regular

---

[10] For a critical treatment of these reports in the United States, see Mirchandani (2012) and Carrillo Rowe et al. (2013). It is important to note that many of the sectors (like call centres) where outsourcing is taking place are actually expanding (Huws, 2014, p. 44). Employment in the UK call centre industry, for example, grew at the same time as offshoring was picking up, and by 2013 jobs in US call centres were still being forecasted to expand, despite the offshoring phenomenon (Deloitte Consulting, 2013).
[11] For a discussion of the potential for automation of call centre labour, see Chap. 7.

communication with customers to becoming a "global industry in its own right" (Stevens, 2014, p. 56), there can be few doubts that this emergent sector has pioneered a new stage in the global division of immaterial labour. This process has reshaped workforces across the world and transformed the very way we think about work.[12] To see call centres from the perspective of labour is to see them from the vantage point of a workforce that is summoned, disciplined, and dismissed in the name of economic globalization. One cannot therefore understand the call centre without confronting its transnational dimension, one in which global call centre capital enjoys the freedom to traverse borders if it wishes, but labour is regularly denied this possibility—other than virtually, of course.

The "institutional" analysis of global call centre capital I have offered here is only one part of the story, however. The "new international class of cyberworkers" (Huws, 2014, p. 56) produced out of the call centre transnationalization process has not always acquiesced to the demands of employers. Workers can communicate and organize across borders as well, not just with customers, but transversally, with each other, in a process I have called *communication from below*. The second part of this chapter looks at how transnational call centre employers seeking to exploit a border to divide and weaken their workforces unwittingly created an opening for labour organizing. In what follows, I shift my focus from the strategies of global call centre capital to one of the more compelling and conflictual responses adopted by its workforce.

Synovate, "Free Market Unionism," and the Calling for Change Campaign

As we have seen, transnational call centre companies use outsourcing and offshoring to produce not only highly flexible forms of customer interaction but also what Michael Hardt and Antonio Negri (2004, p. xiii) describe as a "network of hierarchies and divisions" among their global

---

[12] Underscoring the observations made by scholars of Indian call centre work, Huws suggests that as this process has advanced, "the idea of work as something unbounded and 'virtual' began to take root" (Huws, 2013, p. 4).

workforces. A closer look at one of the firms organized by the Calling for Change campaign, the market research company Synovate, offers another example of just how transnational call centre operations can get. Synovate was formed in 2003 when Aegis (discussed earlier) consolidated all of its market research functions under one brand name. The resulting company, British owned, headquartered in Singapore, and operating in over 60 countries across 24 time zones on every continent, described itself as "truly borderless." Synovate catered to a niche in customer relations, providing consumer research for government, finance, telecommunications, and other sectors. As knowledge of consumers becomes increasingly strategic to the production process under post-Fordism, Synovate probed, gathered, packaged and sold this knowledge to business and the state, promising them the capacity to "communicate with consumers at the right moments and in the best way."

The labour that elicited, gathered, and distilled this public opinion was put in by the company's roughly 6000 employees, a portion of whom designed surveys that harnessed social scientific methodologies for corporate profit, but most of whom performed the monotonous labour of polling the public through the company's many and far-flung call centres. As a subunit of Aegis, Synovate was a slightly smaller-scale operation than the companies occupying the top tier of the global customer relations business, but the reach and revenues of the "biggest small research company in the world" (Synovate, 2007, para. 8)—US$ 816 million in 2010—were nonetheless significant. Highlighting the important role consolidation plays in shaping the call centre landscape (and, eventually, in sealing its own fate), Synovate used Australia as a beachhead for its 2005 regional touchdown, purchasing local firms in Perth and Adelaide. Two years later, it crossed the Tasman Sea to New Zealand, opening up shop in Wellington and taking ownership of an Auckland company, Research Solutions, with 45 full-time staff and a "field force" of over 200 interviewers.

Synovate's arrival in New Zealand took advantage of enticing local conditions. Almost 30 years after its trailblazing experience with neoliberal governance had begun, the country was open for business.[13] The market for call centre operations was especially friendly. While domestically oriented call centres were already well-established by the end of the 1990s (with an estimated 300 businesses employing 15,000 people), in order to lure global call centre capital like Synovate to its shores, the country launched the Call Centre Attraction Initiative (CCAI) through Trade NZ in 1999 (Larner, 2001, 2002).[14] With its relatively cheap, well-educated workforce and incentives for business, the country quickly became a popular destination for call centre investment flowing from Australia, and during the 2000s the industry grew considerably. By 2008 it was estimated that call centres employed approximately 27,000 people in New Zealand (Hendery, 2008), a figure which, given the rapid turnover and transient nature of work in the industry, illuminates only a portion of the much broader pool of workers the industry can draw from.

According to NUW organizer Godfrey Moase, the period following the introduction of the CCAI coincided with a noticeable spike in threats to outsource made by Australian employers at the bargaining table (personal communication, June 22, 2011). Thanks to Australia's centralized awards system regulating wages across most sectors of the economy and a relatively well-entrenched labour movement, average pay in the country has remained frustratingly high for employers.

For call centre owners hoping to route around the power of workers in Australia, New Zealand also offered an added bonus in the form of a decimated labour movement. Like their Australian counterparts, Kiwi trade unions had enjoyed the benefits of a Keynesian-style centralized bargaining system until the late 1970s, but first under a Labour government (1984–1990), and subsequently under the National Party

---

[13] Shortly after the company's arrival, the *Wall Street Journal* and Heritage Foundation Index, which ranks states according to their adherence to the market fundamentalist principles of Chicago School economics, announced that New Zealand was an impressive third in the world in economic "freedom," pointing out that it took only 12 days on average to start up a business there (The Heritage Foundation, 2015).

[14] In the only comparative academic study of the development of the call centre sector in New Brunswick and New Zealand that I am aware of, Wendy Larner outlines many of the similarities between these two cases and also the important differences. Above all, as Larner notes (2002, p. 142), "not only did New Zealand come relatively late to the idea of call centres as a development strategy, nearly a full decade after New Brunswick, also the strategy was enacted in a very different context."

(1990–1999), state assets were privatized, welfare cut to the bone, and labour law radically overhauled in favour of employers. Indeed, in few other countries across the world has the imposition of market rule been so successful in decomposing the established labour movement without resorting to the use of force, a historical trajectory that prompted New Zealand's *National Business Review* to compare the country's reforms of the 1980s to those carried out in Pinochet's Chile, only "without the gun" (as cited in Choudry, 2003, para. 6).

The 1991 Employment Contracts Act brought in by the National Party was a watershed moment in the country's labour relations landscape, doing away with the national award system, establishing an open-shop model of labour relations, enshrining flexible work arrangements, and individualizing contract negotiations. First under a Labour government and then under its National Party successors, union membership plummeted from 70% of the workforce in 1980 to just over 20% at the end of the late 2000s (Annis, 2009, para. 13).

If the trade union void created by neoliberal governance was a welcome one for transnational companies like Synovate, it also offered favourable conditions for the formation of Unite. The labour reforms did away with the "closed shop" and central bargaining system of worker representation and brought in open membership rules and what Unite organizer Mike Treen described as a "free market in unionism" (personal communication, May 10, 2011) that would eventually allow Unite to build up a presence in historically unorganized businesses and sectors. Founded in Wellington in response to the threat of American-style workfare policies during the waning years of the National Party government in 1998, Unite remained small and tied to that city until 2003, when labour activists Matt McCarten and Mike Treen repurposed the Auckland branch. As parliamentarians for the left-of-centre Alliance Party during the short-lived Labour-Alliance coalition government (1999–2001), McCarten and Treen had played a part in bringing the Employment Contracts Act to an end and replacing it with a piece of legislation that would also play a critical role in facilitating Unite's early development. The new Employment Relations Act did not reverse the neoliberal tide in labour relations, but it did allow unions legal right of access to workplaces for the purposes of recruiting workers.

In addition to seizing upon conditions that were favourable for a new union targeting unorganized sectors, Unite took advantage of what interviewees described as inertia on the part of established trade unions in New Zealand. While the period of Labour's rule coincided with economic recovery, lower unemployment, and more accommodating laws around labour organizing, McCarten suggests established unions failed to take advantage of these conditions in order to connect with a growing workforce on the front lines of the service industries:

> [Unions] have walked away from low-pay workers and the casualized work force, which is the new workforce. That's where young people go. They're low paid, migrant people, indigenous people, and youth, and those who come out of poverty tend to be in those industries. (M. McCarten, personal communication, May 11, 2011)

Picking precisely these casualized sectors, Unite began by targeting cinemas, hospitality, and fast food, quickly distinguishing itself for a militant approach, spectacular stunts, and rapid growth. The union's breakthrough was the 2005 *Supersize My Pay* campaign, which organized thousands of workers in Auckland's fast-food industry by targeting employees at McDonalds, Burger King, Starbucks, Pizza Hut, and KFC—all of which were run by a company called Restaurant Brands. The campaign to organize these companies bore the unorthodox mark of its organizers, recruited by Unite from different currents of the anti-globalization movements of the late 1990s.[15] This strategy provided the union with an energetic core of activists and a style of labour organizing that resonated with the teenagers filling the dead-end, hyper-Taylorized service jobs proliferating in New Zealand's economy. The Supersize campaign was built around the goals of bringing service workers a degree of control over otherwise arbitrary management scheduling, raising the minimum wage to NZ$ 12 and hour from $10.25, and, above all, abolishing the youth rates which had 16- and 17-year-olds working for $2 an hour less than minimum wage.

---

[15] As a critical account of the campaign describes, "some of the organizers were anarchists, some were Leninists, some were social democrats, and many were non-aligned" (Toby, 2007, para. 7).

The Supersize campaign utilized tactics that would characterize the union's approach in subsequent years, combining relatively militant industrial action with forms of brand sabotage pioneered by the anti-globalization movement. Unite set up pickets in front of high-traffic fast-food outlets at peak hours to embarrass employers who opposed the union, and organized "flash strikes" at targeted businesses.[16] By stopping work for only a few hours at a time the union could hurt the business at strategic periods while lowering the stakes for workers who joined in.[17] While participation in these strikes was hardly unanimous, press releases and savvy use of media amplified the effects and further tarnished the brands. The result was businesses on the back foot, and, by all accounts, an enthusiastic uptake of struggle by those young employees the established labour movement had overlooked.

Omar Hamed, who became involved with Supersize My Pay as a member of the high school group Radical Youth (which led a 2006 secondary school walkout and march of over a thousand high school students in Auckland against youth employment rates), describes the union's encounter with a generation bereft of trade union experience:

> My generation, and the generation even a couple of years older than me who were involved in the Supersize My Pay, we don't remember these unions, these old unions. So when someone says "do you want to join a union?," we go: "what's that"? And when someone says "it's about fighting for better pay and better conditions." We go "OK, we want to do it." So I think young people who don't have a bad experience with unions are more open, so you can renew, you can replenish the union movement for young people. And ... if you keep giving them a good experience of unionization, then that's important. You don't have to win, but you have to show them it's worth it, you know? (O. Hamed, personal communication, May 6, 2011)

---

[16] Matt McCarten captured the union's attitude towards high-profile picketing when he noted that "you see a picket as an industrial spat, I see it as marketing opportunity" (personal communication, May 11, 2011).

[17] Supersize My Pay was inaugurated with what the union believes was the world's first Starbucks strike, an action which began as a small protest by workers from a downtown outlet and turned into a city-wide action when Starbucks workers heard that managers would be brought in to cover the shifts of the striking workers. Its mechanics are described in detail, from a critical perspective, in Toby (2007).

For Unite organizer Joe Carolan, the union's approach to labour politics was succeeding precisely where the global justice movement's ritualistic summit protests had become stale and ineffective: "here was a campaign that was actually going *inside*, that was talking to the *workers* in these companies, not just smashing the windows in McDonald's" (personal communication, May 6, 2011). What organizers connected with inside these fast-food businesses was the emergent composition of precarious service employment, a who's who of populations established trade unions had ignored. Young people were not the only demographic that was over-represented in these jobs, which counted disproportionately high numbers of indigenous Maori and Pacific Islanders, women, and migrant workers from South and East Asia.

The Supersize campaign also brought Unite into contact with call centre workers. As former Unite organizer Simon Oosterman recalled (personal communication, May 6, 2011), the different fast-food companies used the same call centre for delivery orders, meaning that the tele-workspace, which primarily handled Pizza Hut deliveries, was identified as a choke point through which to apply pressure to Restaurant Brands as a whole. Nearly a hundred call centre workers joined the union and participated in the weekly Friday night lightning strikes during peak ordering hours. One of the employees recollected they went out so many times "it became a habit. The staff really got into it" (Unite member, personal communication, May 16, 2011)—to the point that Unite's leadership eventually asked employees to hold off striking during negotiations with the company. In 2006, with Restaurant Brands under intensifying pressure Unite signed collective agreements covering between 6000 and 7000 members across all of the group's businesses. Significantly, the employers also agreed to phase out youth rates, which were ultimately repealed by parliament through a private member's bill, giving the local labour movement its first success in decades and putting Unite on the map.

On the heels of Supersize My Pay, Godfrey Moase got in touch with Unite on behalf of the NUW to propose what would become the Calling for Change campaign. As call centre offshoring from Australia was picking up steam, the two unions decided to tackle the outsourced industry that was developing in New Zealand. Ten market research call centres were identified in Auckland—including Synovate—and Omar Hamed was hired to lead Unite's side of the organizing.[18]

Hamed and Moase began by drawing on the skills of Unite's existing unionized workers at the consumer research company Nielsen in a self-polling exercise that identified the issues that were likely to become key to the campaign's unionization drive at the outsourced call centres. Site visits were carried out to the call centres to sign up employees, and meetings organized with committees of workers from each of the targeted companies to strategize around generating a common set of demands across the call centres.

The complaints arising from workers were many. Employment at the companies was often on temporary contracts with erratic hours, with a great deal of the roughly 800 workers on minimum wage. Depending on how busy things were, some might work only a week out of four, or be let go just an hour into a shift. Pay raises were allocated arbitrarily, leading to situations where some who had been at a call centre for over a year were receiving less per hour than someone who had just been hired. Performance pay, when present, was negligible. Sick days or holiday pay were unheard of. And then there was the work itself, carried out, according to many workers, in subpar conditions, with inadequate or damaged keyboards and headphones at the workstations, a lack of sound proofing to mitigate the loudness of the environment, and disciplinary management techniques of the sort call centres have become known for.

Calling for Change incorporated these findings into the campaign by focusing on the need for collective agreements, greater control over erratic scheduling, paid breaks, wages of at least $15 per hour, and the right to permanent status after two years of employment. Recalling the industrial unionism of the Industrial Workers of the World, campaign literature called for "one big union agreement" across all of the companies (Unite Union, 2008b).

Significantly, organizers also seized upon the divisions and hierarchies created by the research firms in their harnessing of national borders to separate workers. Not only did tele-researchers at companies in

---

[18] In addition to Synovate, these included TNS, SurveyTalk, UMR, Phoenix, MarketPulse, OCIS, Colmar Brunton, DigiPoll, and Reid Research.

New Zealand often make less than half of what their Australian colleagues took home for the same work, but according to the campaign literature, some were even monitored from Sydney via a surveillance camera affixed to the call centre wall (Unite Union, 2008a). Calling for Change took aim at the call centre companies' brands, and their customers, through a series of protests designed to shame them in both New Zealand and Australia. While Unite organized workers at the Auckland branches, activists from the NUW picketed the offices of client companies in Australia.

Unite found that their message resonated with the diverse group of workers at these call centres, a significant number of whom, organizers discovered, had moved on from the fast-food industry, and some of whom had even been a part of the Supersize My Pay campaign. In the first four weeks organizers managed to recruit over 400 workers (G. Moase, personal communication, June 22, 2011). When companies obstructed organizers' visits to the site or refused to bargain for a collective agreement, Unite staged pickets and lightning strikes, stopping work at the call centres at crucial times and forcing the employer's hand. In just one of the many colourful moments produced out of the organizing campaign, at OCIS (one of the call centres) managers threatened to call the police on two teenaged Unite delegates after strikers downed headsets and headed to the lunchroom to eat pizza and play table tennis (Unite Union, 2009).

Workers also described forms of digital sabotage cropping up at several of the Auckland call centres around this time. As a means to put pressure on employers, at some call centres employees engaged in "slowpace" dialing, sent surveys back to clients with the word "Unite" typed dozens of times in a row in the space provided for the last answer, called into call centres and placed bogus orders during busy times, and even pried vital keys from keyboards rendering surveys difficult to fill in.

The campaign at Synovate was particularly nasty. According to an ex-employee, the composition of the workforce was predominantly made up of students, although with a significant presence of other groups with financial situations "ranging from needy to desperate," including a strong contingent of single mothers. Beyond the low pay, the employer's unilateral control over scheduling was a big issue for workers:

We were permanent part time, but in our contracts it did specify that we weren't able to refuse to work and there was no guarantee of them providing us work, so from our perspective it operated more as a casual contract because they were never obliged to supply us with work, but from their perspective we were also permanent, we could never refuse to work and had to apply for (that) and those kinds of things. (ex-Synovate employee, personal communication, May 11, 2011)[19]

According to New Zealand organizers, the British firm was the most hostile of the call centres, initially refusing them access to the site. As an ex-employee recalls, in the period immediately after the union drive began "we were constantly having briefings about how we were able to refuse the union should we choose not to sign up" (ex-Synovate employee, personal communication, May 11, 2011). Taking advantage of existing labour laws, Unite responded with a highly publicized "walk-in" to the Auckland site in April of 2009, a move that resulted in the arrival of the police.

When most of its employees went ahead and signed up with Unite, Synovate refused to bargain, and the local employee committee responded with a series of escalating actions. A "work slow" campaign was the first move, but when that garnered no response from management, employees adopted the lightning strikes that by that point were also being used at other call centres targeted by the campaign. As an ex-employee recalls, "we kept morale up by making a bit of a game out of it, so Thursday nights would be our strike night and [at] whatever stage we wanted to we'd walk out and go out to the pub across the road, have a few drinks, and text our friends in the call centre to make them jealous" (ex-Synovate employee, personal communication, May 11, 2011). Some employees even began a series of 24-hour hunger strikes as a way to further embarrass the company.

When management locked out workers after they turned down a raise offer of 20 cents an hour, Unite parked its bus at the call centre's back entrance during opening hours, effectively locking management inside (*The New Zealand Herald*, 2009). The next day, the union picketed the director's house for the Easter weekend. "We know which side Jesus

---

[19] Such contracts are more commonly known as "on-call" or "zero-hours" contracts.

would be on," Unite's press release declared. McCarten recalled the scene on the director's lawn:

> They locked the workers out and we fought back. We went to the director's home and we put pickets on their lawn and woke them up in the morning, "Good morning! Did you know your neighbour is screwing his workers?" The kids are crying inside and they come out and say "our children are crying." I said "yeah, what about the children whose parents have lost their jobs? You care about them?" No, so you don't mention that. It's good that the children of rich parents who exploit their workers learn at an early age that their parents are hypocrites, that's a *good* thing ... I say look, security guards were going around people's homes last night and issuing them letters saying they've lost their jobs, but *that's* alright. Kids open the door, [there's a] security guy with a uniform [who says] "hey there you lost your job, you're locked out." But *that's* OK, no? But waking them up in the morning at their wealthy homes, oh that's *outrageous* ... (personal communication, May 11, 2011)

As tensions peaked over the weekend, union campaigners deployed flying squads to picket Synovate customers—including insurance companies and the New Zealand Ministry of Social Development—in Auckland and Wellington. Meanwhile, NUW members picketed prominent Synovate NGO customers across the Tasman in Australia, urging them to contact the company and inquire about their labour practices. McCarten remembers the company's indignant response to Unite and the NUW's offensive:

> What happened is the company said "we're in 127 countries, and no one has ever taken industrial action against us." Which is interesting, you know, because it was all puzzles to them, like how this happened, we'd get away with this shit everywhere in the world so why should we have this problem in one little puny country? So they threatened to leave, and I say "I think you should leave. I think you should." (personal communication, May 11, 2011)

Five days later, Unite and Synovate settled on a contract, including prior warning on cancelled shifts, guaranteed minimum shifts of four hours, more flexible scheduling arrangements, and higher pay through increased bonuses.

The Calling for Change campaign ultimately produced collective agreements, wage increases and scheduling concessions at several of the targeted call centres. Among the campaign's more notable achievements, according to Moase (personal communication, June 22, 2011), was a significant decrease in the number of times that New Zealand was mentioned at bargaining tables in Australia. Four years after Synovate arrived in New Zealand, the company was sold by its parent, Aegis, to Ipsos, the French polling company, for NZ$ 987 million (StopPress, 2011).

The Global Division of Labour and Migration of Struggles

In their inquiry into the expanding call centre labour force in Buenos Aires, the Colectivo Situaciones (2006) theorized the borderless, liminal labour conditions of the offshored call centre worker: "At the same time as she is fixed in her chair" the Colectivo noted, the call centre worker "can serve customers in Miami or Puerto Rico as long as she doesn't say she does it from Buenos Aires or Mendoza" (p. 31). Moreover, as the group's inquiry revealed, while the employee speaks on behalf of one company, she is usually contracted by another. In these cases, her employer, the outsourced call centre, "acts as a ventriloquist, a clandestine mediator" as the worker labours "at the service of a brand" (p. 31). In this activity of representing a brand to its customers, while not working for (or at) the company that actually owns that brand, "the profitability of the parent company—that in whose name problems are resolved—never affects the wage of that far away offshore worker" (p. 31).

Far from being a simple side effect of the re-engineering of companies that began in the 1990s, the Colectivo concluded, the outsourced call centre is "a fundamental segment of a new global division of labour" (2006, p. 31). During the 1990s and 2000s, this global division of labour was developed by a new breed of outsourced call centre firms that provided the labour of customer service, interaction, and management for corporations across the broader economy. In the course of their transformation from being an increasingly necessary in-house cost for the parent company to a source of profit for the outsourced sector, call centres became a formidable industry in their own right. Here we have explored that industry's transnational dimension, surveying a set of companies I have described as *global call centre capital*. These companies have pioneered the flexible employment of their call centre workforces, expanding into new regions, transferring work between one country and another, and providing a wide and growing range of interactive options to prospective customers.

The flexible configuration of virtual customer interaction work across borders takes an increasingly wide variety of forms. Some companies transfer only part of their customer service work to outsourced call centre companies, keeping portions of it in-house. But the division of labour can be even more complex. To offer one example encountered in New Zealand, some of the call centre workers I interviewed worked at the Auckland site of an outsourced call centre company headquartered in Australia answering calls from Vodafone customers in New Zealand. During my time in the country, I also visited one of Vodafone's three *in-house* call centres, where Unite was building a presence. (Organizers told me this particular call centre was taking on some of the work that had previously been performed in Egypt but had been transferred to New Zealand when the unrest that brought down the Mubarak regime broke out in 2011.) In addition to Vodafone's division of call centre labour across borders and the boundaries separating in-house and outsourced operations, according to organizers the company also employed workers via local temp agencies, which offer one more option within a broad suite of potential labour arrangements to choose among (J. Minto, personal communication, May 11, 2011).

The process of virtual migration that scholars have identified in call centre work is decisively shaped by the activities of global call centre capital. These companies are a major force determining the process of class formation I have called language put to work. As we have seen, the flows of investment and the virtual migration of labour through these firms belie simple theories of the relationship between the economic

5 The Migration of Struggle 157

"centre" and "periphery," producing a terrain where "the colonial order of time and space becomes scrambled" (Carrillo Rowe et al., 2013, p. 39). The developments described in this chapter are part of what Ronaldo Munck (2008b, p. 222) has called the new "regional modalities" of capitalist development. As the case of research-based call centres in Australia and New Zealand suggests, communicative capitalism brings within itself fresh strata of educated, articulate workers as it alights in new settings, only to expel them when they are no longer necessary, or flee when their demands become unmanageable (Dyer-Witheford, 2015).

Virtual migration is also riven with the dynamics of power and contestation that are formative of global production networks. Call centre owners invest in new parts of the world not only to take advantage of new opportunities for profit but also in order to escape the collective power and expectations of workers. The tactical advantages flowing from the mobility of call centre capital was noted by Italian rank-and-file trade unionists as early as the late 1990s, when they observed the diminishing effectiveness of their strikes as the communicative work they performed was simply redirected to different companies. As a result, they concluded,

> [t]he logical consequence is to extend the strike to all call centres of a company in order to achieve some impact. And not just to the call centres of a single company, also the connected companies ... have to be included in the struggle. (Flmu-CUB, as cited in Kolinko, 2002, section 6.2.c)

The ability to organize across borders, not only national ones so that labour might organize itself "as internationally as capital" (Huws, 2012, p. 7) but also across those dividing the home company and the outsourced provider, have therefore become a critical concern for call centre workers and their organizations.

If the customer service industry's transnational scope allows employers to segment workforces and pit them against each other, straddling the world market can also have unpleasant consequences for call centre capital, creating "new circuits of cooperation and collaboration" that reach across borders (Hardt & Negri, 2004, p. xiii). Researchers have begun to document cases of transnational call centre organizing by established trade unions and global federations.[20] For many, the natural place to look for indications as to the challenges and opportunities facing transnational labour organizing in call centres has been India. Studies assessing collective organization by Indian call centre workers (D'Cruz & Noronha, 2006, 2013; Mosco & McKercher, 2008; Noronha & D'Cruz, 2009; Stevens & Mosco, 2010; Taylor & Bain, 2005) have described the fledgling status of such ventures, including UNI-Global (the international confederation of trade unions aiming to be a global voice for communication workers), the Union for IT Enabled Services Professionals (UNITES), and the Young Professionals Collective. Yet despite the importance of the Indian case to the project of labour internationalism, established trade unions in the country (like their counterparts in the countries from which the work is being sent) have thus far made little progress in the outsourced sector, offering what sociologist Shehzad Nadeem (2011, p. 207) describes as "modest organizing goals mixed with occasional agitation." India certainly remains a key test case for labour organizing in global call centres, but given the shifting and diverse flows of transnational call centre investment addressed in this chapter, it is important to look beyond it to other examples as well.

While smaller in scale and ambition, the NUW-Unite campaign is significant because it spotlights both an under-explored case of transnational labour transfer on the one hand and a highly militant and relatively successful response by workers on the other. The Calling for Change campaign is a compelling example of what Munck (2008a, p. 21) calls "local transnationalism," demonstrating how the same circuits created by call centre capital can become a path not only for the virtual migration of labour but for the migration of labour struggles. In this case, the migration of struggle is all the more significant because of the central role played within it by a new rank-and-file union, Unite, and its decision to "swim in the activist movements outside of it" (O. Hamed, personal communication, May 6, 2011).

---

[20] Vincent Mosco and David Lavin (2008, p. 150) have described the four types of international labour organization that have arisen to address capital's mobility and transnational scope, including international federations, global federations of unions, government or public federations, and "worker associations that may be rooted in one nation but are testing new forms of organizing and are partnering with unions and federations outside the nation."

5 The Migration of Struggle 159

Significantly, the union organizes across several different forms of migration, and the Calling for Change campaign drew upon and enabled the circulation of struggles along these same routes. The picketing of call centre company customers on both sides of the Tasman Sea, organized through the very same communication networks linking companies in Australia and New Zealand, is perhaps the clearest example of how virtual migration both preceded and was accompanied by the migration of labour struggles. Beyond strengthening the hand of Australian workers, for Unite the Calling for Change campaign consolidated its attention to call centre workers as an important segment of its membership, extending its presence to companies such as SKY-TV, Vodafone, and several outsourced customer relations providers. The union now represents close to a thousand call centre workers, and from a few hundred members at the end of the 1990s, it now counts somewhere around 7000 dues-paying members in total (Treen, 2014).[21]

Other instances of migration overlapped and intertwined with the virtual migration of call centre work confronted during the Calling for Change campaign. In Auckland I attended a Unite convention at which security guards, English as a second language instructors, theatre concession workers, fast-food employees, casino workers, and call centre operators met in order to go over organizing strategies, educate themselves on labour law, and compare notes as to the difficulties they faced keeping the membership involved. There I spoke to Arnold Fatu and Ross Asiata, indigenous Pacific Islanders who assisted Vodafone customers in New Zealand over the phone while being employed by the (previously mentioned) outsourced provider in Australia.[22] Arnold and Ross had led their colleagues, including indigenous Maori and migrant workers from South and East Asia, in a successful fight for better wages and working conditions through Unite. When workers at the call centre company struck, company representatives were flown in from the Australian head

---

[21] Given the rapidity of turnover in the industries they have organized and therefore in their membership base, it is quite possible, as several organizers have pointed out, that the union has actually signed up two or three times as many members since 2005.
[22] Occasionally, when customers on the other end of the phone were Pacific Islanders with little English, the call was transferred to Arnold or Ross so they could conduct the interaction.

office for a mediation session because, as one of the workers put it, "they knew we actually meant business" (A. Fatu & R. Asiata, personal communication, May 16, 2011). In this case, virtual migration across borders encountered and overlapped with physical migration.[23]

Finally, the Unite case is significant because of the migration of struggles from workplace to workplace in an overwhelmingly precarious service sector. The union's initial success in organizing fast-food workers brought it into closer contact with call centre workers at Restaurant Brands, and a number of the workers who ended up organizing in call centres had come out of the Supersize My Pay campaign. Moreover, as Joe Carolan noted, many of these low-wage workers making the jump from fast food to call centres were Pacific Islander and Maori workers who had "that tradition of the union with them" (personal communication, May 6, 2011). In this sense, the Supersize My Pay campaign can be seen as a precursor to the contemporary Fight for 15 movement of low-wage service workers in the United States.[24]

Unite continues to face significant challenges. For a union that organizes employees in some of the most precarious and marginal forms of service sector employment, even keeping track of how many dues-paying workers it represents, not to mention organizing a critical threshold of workers in the sector, is an extremely difficult task.[25] The pay gains and levels of security achieved for workers, in call centres and elsewhere,

---

[23] Omar Hamed recalled that during the Calling for Change campaign an Irish woman joined as a delegate for one of the companies and "organized the whole site basically." This case is notable because the woman had been in the political strikes in Ireland during the Troubles and according to Hamed "had this radical tradition of unionism," thus offering another example of the migration of struggle (personal communication, May 6, 2011).

[24] The Fight for 15 is a movement of North American service workers in childcare, home and health care, airport, gas station and, most visibly, fast-food workers, which has been striking for increased pay and union recognition in the workplace.

[25] McCarten placed turnover in the union at 66% a year, and believed 90% of members are part time or casual (personal communication, May 11, 2011). Joe Carolan offered a sense of how challenging it is to maintain a strong presence in the service industry, noting that in sectors like fast food "the churn is relentless," and "if we stop still for a couple of months, all our members would be gone" (personal communication, May 6, 2011).

remain modest.[26] The union has been accused by some of not being as innovative or member-driven as it might appear, and even of intervening in key moments to quash rank-and-file militancy in order to achieve collective agreements.[27] Finally, New Zealand offers its very own particular context and history, one that may be too laden with its own idiosyncrasies for the model to be relevant to other settings.[28]

These objections notwithstanding, the Calling for Change campaign offers a lively example of how global call centre capital can be confronted by those whose labour generates its profits. Just as important, the case demonstrates how the cybertariat can forge strategies that reassemble the fragmented and diverse workforces put to work within communicative capitalism to turn their "actual global productive cooperation" (Friends of Kolinko & Gurgaon Workers News, 2012) to different ends. An original ground zero of neoliberal economic policy, New Zealand and its call centre industry featured a daunting mix of precarious employment, "apolitical" subjectivities, workers fractured along racialized, gendered and post-colonial lines, and an absence of trade union culture. Union organizers, drawn from the ranks of the counter-globalization movement, combined brand tarnishing, spectacular stunts, and militant actions in

---

[26] As John Minto suggested, some of the pay gains barely meet inflation: "Well, the union contracts we have are relatively good. We've been able to, with the call centers we've been involved in for a while, over time you can build improvements into the contract. But the contracts are still quite modest in terms of what contracts would've been like 20years ago. But we've been able to make some significant gains. You know, one of our call centers we've got workers being paid a $20 meal allowance after 7 o'clock, so those sorts of things, (kind of in a way) we're trying to push that hard through other agencies, through other call centers, but we're not sure . . . we're still . . . those things would've been, 20 years ago, quite common, they're not common now. Look, it's minimum pay, minimum conditions, so generally we're able to push for . . . we're able to get some small improvements each year, aside from giving some sort of inflation-based pay increase" (personal communication, May 11, 2011).

[27] One critique of the Supersize campaign suggested Unite is only "partially a new organizational form" from the established unions it critiques. Where the union is innovative, this anarchist critique maintains, is in its "attempt to update old-school bureaucratic unionism for today's fragmented workplace" (Toby, 2007, para. 34).

[28] Some features of Unite's rapid growth are no doubt especially connected to the context of the union's emergence, including the economic climate at the time. As Mike Treen suggested, with strong economic growth, low unemployment, and entire sectors of the service industry run on minimum wage, it was an ideal moment to organize workers in these industries, who could move from job to job with less worry about engaging in union activity (personal communication, May 10, 2011).

their campaigns, and the tactics appear by all accounts to have resonated among the call centre workforces they organized. Given Unite's successes working within this kind of labour composition, the Calling for Change campaign also demonstrates that labour unions can return to doing the most important task they were designed for—organizing unorganized workers, including those who move from job to job amid intensifying labour precarity. In other words, the case offers an illustration of how labour recomposition involves "different strata of workers" with "fresh capacities of resistance and counterinitiative" (Dyer-Witheford, 1999, p. 66). In the next chapter we travel to Italy, to see how workers there have self-organized outside of (and even in opposition to) established trade unions at the extreme edge of precarious employment in the call centre sector.

Interviews Cited

Carolan, Joe. Auckland, New Zealand, May 6th, 2011.
ex-Synovate employee. Auckland, New Zealand, May 11th, 2011.
Fatu, Arnold, & Asiata, Ross. Auckland, New Zealand, May 16th, 2011.
Hamed, Omar. Auckland, New Zealand, May 6th, 2011.
McCarten, Matt. Auckland, New Zealand, May 11th, 2011.
Minto, John. Auckland, New Zealand, May 11th, 2011.
Moase, Godfrey. Auckland, New Zealand, June 22nd, 2011.
Oosterman, Simon. Auckland, New Zealand, May 6th, 2011.
Treen, Mike. Auckland, New Zealand, May 10th, 2011.
Unite member. Auckland, New Zealand, May 16th, 2011.

References

Aneesh, A. (2006). *Virtual migration: The programming of globalization*. Durham, NC: Duke University Press.
Annis, R. (2009). Unite union wins gains for vulnerable workers in New Zealand. *The Bullet*, (No. 216). Retrieved from http://www.socialistproject.ca/bullet/bullet216.html.

Atento. (2015a). *Atento reports fourth quarter and full year 2014 results* (press release). New York, NY.
Atento. (2015b). *Our locations*. Retrieved from http://www.atento.com/about-atento/our-locations/
Batt, R., Holman, D., & Holtgrewe, U. (2009). The globalization of service work: Comparative institutional perspectives on call centers. *Industrial and Labor Relations Review, 62*(4), 453–488.
Brophy, E. (2014). Phone clones: Authenticity work in the transnational service economy, by Kiran Mirchandani (review). *Canadian Ethnic Studies, 46*(1), 225–227.
Brophy, E. (2015). Revisiting the digital assembly line: New perspectives on call centre work. *Labour/Le Travail, 75*, 211–230.
Carrillo Rowe, A., Perez, K., & Malhotra, S. (2013). *Answer the call: Virtual migration in Indian call centers*. Minneapolis, MN: University of Minnesota Press.
Choudry, A. (2003). *New wave/old wave: Aotearoa New Zealand's colonial continuum*. Retrieved from http://www.voiceoftheturtle.org/show_printer.php?aid=328
Colectivo Situaciones. (2006) *¿Quién habla? Lucha contra la esclavitud del alma en los call centers*. Buenos Aires, Argentina: Tinta Limón Ediciones.
D'Cruz, P., & Noronha, E. (2006). Being professional: Organizational control in Indian call centers. *Social Science Computer Review, 24*(3), 342–361.
D'Cruz, P., & Noronha, E. (2013). Hope to despair: The experience of organizing Indian call centre employees. *The Indian Journal of Industrial Relations, 48*(3), 471–486.
David, N. (2008). *Spotlight interview with Laïla Nassimi (Morocco – CDT)*. Retrieved from http://www.ituc-csi.org/spotlight-interview-with-laila.html?lang=en
Dean, J. (2009). *Democracy and other neoliberal fantasies: Communicative capitalism and left politics*. Durham, NC: Duke University Press.
Deloitte Consulting. (2013). *2013 global contact centre: Survey results*. Retrieved from http://www2.deloitte.com/content/dam/Deloitte/us/Documents/process-and-operations/us-sdt-consulting-2013-global-contact-survey-051513.pdf
Dyer-Witheford, N. (1999). *Cyber-Marx: Cycles and circuits of struggle in high-technology capitalism*. Urbana, IL: University of Illinois Press.
Dyer-Witheford, N. (2015). *Cyber-proletariat: Global labour in the digital vortex*. London, UK: Pluto Press.

Fontanella-Khan, J., & Landingin, R. (2010, December 2). Tata unit joins call-centre rush to Philippines. *The Financial Times*.
Friends of Kolinko, & Gurgaon Workers News. (2012). *Burn-out in the global call centre*. Retrieved from http://www.metamute.org/editorial/articles/burn-out-global-call-centre
Fuchs, C. (2010). Labor in informational capitalism and on the internet. *The Information Society, 26*(3), 179–196.
Glader, P. (2011, May 20). As Indian companies grow in the U.S., outsourcing comes home. *The Washington Post*.
Gurgaon Workers News. (2012). *GurgaonWorkersNews no.9/52*. Retrieved from https://gurgaonworkersnews.wordpress.com/gurgaonworkersnews-no-952/
Hardt, M., & Negri, A. (2004). *Multitude: War and democracy in the age of empire*. New York, NY: Penguin Press.
Hendery, S. (2008, September 11). Firms plan more call centre outsourcing. *The New Zealand Herald*.
Huws, U. (2003). Who's waiting? The contestation of time. In U. Huws (Ed.), *The making of a cybertariat: Virtual work in a real world* (pp. 177–186). New York, NY: Monthly Review Press.
Huws, U. (2009). Working at the interface: Call-centre labour in a global economy. *Work Organisation, Labour & Globalisation, 3*(1), 1–8.
Huws, U. (2012). Bridges and barriers: Globalisation and the mobility of work and workers. *Work Organisation, Labour & Globalisation, 6*(2), 1–7.
Huws, U. (2013). Working online, living offline: Labour in the internet age. *Work Organisation, Labour & Globalisation, 7*(1), 1–11.
Huws, U. (2014). *Labor in the global digital economy: The cybertariat comes of age*. New York, NY: Monthly Review Press.
Kämpf, T., & Boes, A. (2007). The nexus of informatisation and internationalisation: A new stage in the internationalisation of labour. *Work Organisation, Labour & Globalisation, 1*(2), 193–208.
Kolinko. (2002). *Hotlines: Call centre, inquiry, communism*. Retrieved from http://www.nadir.org/nadir/initiativ/kolinko/lebuk/e_lebuk.htm
Larner, W. (2001). Governing globalisation: The New Zealand call centre attraction initiative. *Environment and Planning A, 33*(2), 297–312.
Larner, W. (2002). Calling capital: Call centre strategies in New Brunswick and New Zealand. *Global Networks, 2*(2), 133.
Lüthje, B., Hürtgen, S., Pawliki, P., & Sproll, M. (2013). *From Silicon Valley to Shenzen: Global production and work in the IT industry*. Toronto, ON: Rowman & Littlefield.

Mendonca, J. (2014). *Aegis plans to enter call centre markets in Japan and Korea.* Retrieved from http://articles.economictimes.indiatimes.com/2014-07-29/news/52186934_1_ceo-sandip-sen-indian-bpo-aegis

Mezzadra, S. (2010). Between centre and periphery. *Transit Labour: Circuits, Regions, Borders, 2,* 37–38.

Mirchandani, K. (2004). Practices of global capital: Gaps, cracks and ironies in transnational call centres in India. *Global Networks, 4*(4), 355–374.

Mirchandani, K. (2012). *Phone clones: Authenticity work in the transnational service economy.* Ithaca, NY: ILR Press.

Mosco, V. (2009). *The political economy of communication* (2nd ed.). London, UK: Sage.

Mosco, V., & Lavin, D. O. (2008). The laboring of international communication. In D. Thussu (Ed.), *Internationalizing media studies* (pp. 148–162). New York, NY: Routledge.

Mosco, V., & McKercher, C. (2008). *The laboring of communication: Will knowledge workers of the world unite?* Lanham, MD: Lexington Books.

Munck, R. (2008a). Globalisation and trade unions: Towards a multi-level strategy? *Work Organisation, Labour & Globalisation, 2*(1), 11–23.

Munck, R. (2008b). Globalisation, contestation and labor internationalism: A transformationalist perspective. In M. Taylor (Ed.), *Global economy contested: Power and conflict across the international division of labor* (pp. 220–238). New York, NY: Routledge.

Nadeem, S. (2011). *Dead ringers: How outsourcing is changing the way Indians understand themselves.* Princeton, NJ: Princeton University Press.

Neate, R. (2011, April 28). Orange tells call centre workers they can keep their jobs if they relocate to the Philippines. *The Telegraph.*

Noronha, E., & D'Cruz, P. (2009). Engaging the professional: Organising call centre agents in India. *Industrial Relations Journal, 40*(3), 215–234.

Outsource. (2012). *The future of rightshoring: Q&A with professor Philip Taylor, University of Strathclyde.* Retrieved from http://outsourcemag.com/qaa-professor-philip-taylor-university-of-strathclyde/

Patel, R. (2010). *Working the night shift: Women in India's call center industry.* Stanford, CA: Stanford University Press.

Peck, J., & Tickell, A. (2002). Neoliberalizing space: The free economy and the penal state. In N. Brenner & N. Theodore (Eds.), *Spaces of neoliberalism: Urban restructuring in North America and Western Europe* (pp. 33–57). Malden, MA: Blackwell.

Poster, W. R. (2007). Who's on the line? Indian call center agents pose as Americans for US-outsourced firms. *Industrial Relations, 46*(2), 271–304.

Schiller, D. (2007). *How to think about information*. Urbana, IL: University of Illinois Press.

Sitel. (2015). *Overview*. Retrieved from http://www.sitel.com/our-company/overview/

Stevens, A. (2014). *Call centers and the global division of labor: A political economy of post-industrial employment and union organizing*. New York, NY: Routledge/Taylor & Francis Group.

Stevens, A., & Mosco, V. (2010). Prospects for trade unions and labour organisations in India's IT and ITES industries. *Work Organisation, Labour & Globalisation, 4*(2), 39–59.

StopPress. (2011). *Synovate cuddles up to new global parent, changes unlikely for Kiwi outpost*. Retrieved from http://stoppress.co.nz/news/synovate-cuddles-up-to-new-global-parent-changes-unlikely-for-kiwi-outpost

Synovate. (2007). *Synovate expands footprint in Australia and New Zealand with Research Solutions deal* (press release). Retrieved from http://www.marketresearchworld.net/content/view/1700/74/

Taylor, P., & Bain, P. (2005). "India calling to the far away towns:" The call centre labour process and globalization. *Work, Employment & Society, 19*(2), 261–282.

The Heritage Foundation. (2015). *2015 Index of economic freedom*. Retrieved from http://www.heritage.org/index/ranking

The New Zealand Herald. (2009). *Locked out call-centre staff lock managers in*. Retrieved from http://www.nzherald.co.nz/nz/news/article.cfm?c_id=1&objectid=10566554

Thomas, D. (2012, October 12). Telefónica to sell Atento to Bain Capital. *The Financial Times*.

Toby. (2007). *Super-size my pay*. Retrieved from http://www.metamute.org/editorial/articles/super-size-my-pay

Treen, M. (2014). *A short history of the Unite union in New Zealand*. Retrieved from https://d3n8a8pro7vhmx.cloudfront.net/uniteunion/pages/21/attachments/original/1431924113/A_short_history_of_Unite_web2.pdf?1431924113

Unite Union. (2008a). *Auckland call centre workers strike* (press release). Retrieved from http://www.scoop.co.nz/stories/BU0812/S00203.htm

Unite Union. (2008b). *Calling for change: One big union agreement (campaign update #3)*. Retrieved from http://www.taikorea.co.nz/Unite/website_downloads/updateunionv3.pdf

Unite Union. (2009). *North shore call centre workers strike at OCIS* (press release). Retrieved from http://www.scoop.co.nz/stories/BU0903/S00141/north-shore-call-centre-workers-strike-at-ocis.htm

United Nations Conference on Trade and Development. (2004). *World investment report: The shift towards services*. United Nations Conference on Trade and Development, Switzerland.

Weiss, A. (2007). Global forces and national institutions: Call centre work in Colombia. *Work Organisation, Labour & Globalisation, 1*(2), 131–154.

6

The Organization of Autonomy

> The refusal of representation is deeply anchored in the new class composition. (Lazzarato, 2015, p. 22)

For hundreds, possibly thousands of Telecom Italia Mobile customers trying to contact the company in the mid-2000s, a routine communicative encounter with the customer service agent on the other end of the line suddenly became even more frustrating than usual—as the conversation approached the three-minute mark, the line would drop.

Most customers likely wrote off these aborted connections as yet another maddening encounter with the technologically mediated and utterly impersonal call centre form. Behind all those lines dropping, however, lay a bitterly contested story of language put to work in the call centre. It is a story of well-educated, mostly apolitical young workers thrown into deeply precarious and exploitative working conditions and forging surprisingly fierce forms of labour struggle in response. While call centre scholarship has tended to profile either informal and disorganized forms of labour resistance on the one hand—what Scott (1985) calls "everyday resistance"—or established and highly codified varieties of trade unionism on the other, the story of Atesia, the Roman call centre from which all those calls were dropped, offers a striking case of worker *self-organization*, or what I refer to in this chapter as autonomous labour organizing.[1]

In what follows, I share the results of research undertaken with the Collettivo Precari Atesia (CPA), a self-organized shop-floor collective that fought vigorously and with significant successes against their labour conditions at Atesia—at that point Europe's largest call centre. Between 2005 and 2007, working through a model of self-organization and regularly taking positions that were in outright conflict with Italy's three largest unions as well as with their bosses at Atesia, the Collettivo created the conditions for a national movement of call centre workers and forced a sweeping, albeit deeply flawed, legislative regularization of call centre employees across the country. Within this period, in addition to crafting forms of digital sabotage, the Collettivo launched a campaign of self-education on legal issues arising from their murky employment status, produced and circulated oppositional media, and brought Europe's largest call centre to a standstill over ten times with a series of flexible strikes.

The CPA's outsized organizational success, I argue, derived from their production and circulation of a powerful counter-perspective, one that signalled, contested, and disrupted the disempowering and individualizing discourses that had heretofore accompanied work at Atesia. To be sure, this collectively fashioned counter-subjectivity was produced at the

---

[1] Autonomous labour organizing is a long-standing tradition within the forms of collective organization historically adopted by workers. By self-organization I mean forms of labour organization that tend to be enacted outside the boundaries of established trade unionism, that work against the latter's hierarchies, and see themselves as both working for the improvement of their own immediate labour conditions and a part of social movements working for broader social change. This outlook on collective organization cuts across, and exists within, many forms collective organization by workers but was marginalized by the compromise between capital, the established labour movement, and the state that underwrote Fordism. I describe this form of labour organization as self-constituted and non-hierarchical in that those embracing it have tended to oppose the delegation of political representation, whether it is to established unions or political parties. This orientation towards collective organization has historically gone by many names, including anarcho-syndicalism, industrial unionism, council communism, or operaismo (see Azzellini & Ness, 2011; Rocker, 2004). Today's autonomous labour organizing continues to be initiated and pursued by workers independently of both employers and established unions, and expresses a critique not only of workplace exploitation but of exploitation and hierarchy more broadly (see Tait, 2005).

breaking point brought about by historical processes that long preceded the emergence of the call centre sector in Italy. This chapter uncovers these roots, describing the dissolution of the standard, full-time employment relationship and the expansion of precarious employment in the country from the 1970s, as well as the crisis of established trade union representation that was precipitated by this shift. At the intersection of these developments, and in conjunction with the explosion of call centre employment on the Italian peninsula, the CPA drew on the country's fertile tradition of autonomous labour organizing and opted for self-organization. In order to better understand this choice, we first turn to a discussion of subjectivity in the call centre.

Subjectivity and Counter-Subjectivity in the Call Centre

How does the new call centre workforce see its labour? To what extent does the communicative labour process that has been established within call centres shape the identities of employees? Does this workforce see itself as working class or as an upwardly mobile professional class? How does managerial discourse around call centre work secure the employee's investment in the goals of the firm? Such questions have constituted an ongoing line of analysis within academic investigations of the call centre since the 1990s.

Early research of call centre labour by management-friendly scholars theorized this form of employment as knowledge work and described the worker as a professionalized subject who, through emergent forms of "info-normative control," tended to be satisfied with his or her working conditions and largely identified with the goals of the employer (Frenkel, Tam, Korczynski, & Shire, 1998; Frenkel, Korczynski, Shire, & Tam, 1999; Kinnie, Hutchinson, & Purcell, 2000; Korczynski, 2002).[2] Labour process critiques have picked apart this image of the enthusiastic (or at

---

[2] For a more detailed discussion of this research, see Chap. 2.

least acquiescent) call centre worker, producing research that has highlighted how the organization of the labour process and the workplace culture promoted by management combine to produce worker detachment and subordination (Bain, Taylor, Watson, Mulvey, & Gall, 2002; Taylor & Bain, 1999; Thompson, Warhurst, & Callaghan, 2001). In their goal of expanding labour process analysis to investigate the inner dimension of workers that Harry Braverman had ignored, a number of these critical scholars turned to the analysis of subjectivity.

Michel Foucault (2000, p. 331) offered a description of subjectivity as shaped by material subordination ("being subject to someone else by control and dependence") and self-understanding ("being tied to his own identity by a conscience or self-knowledge"). Labour process researchers explored the interplay of these two dimensions in their efforts to explain how compliant and productive forms of worker identity are selected and moulded by call centre management through workplace rhythms, culture, and discourse.[3] Studies have highlighted management's recruitment of workers with a suitably productive "attitude" and the fostering of "specific personalities" (Callaghan & Thompson, 2002; van den Broek, 2004) appropriate to the communicative requirements of the firm. Critical researchers have also documented management's pursuit of control through fostering "fun" and informal workplace cultures (Fleming & Sturdy, 2011; van den Broek, 2004) and cultivating horizontal competition, surveillance, and control through "teamwork" (Sewell, 1998).

If management's strategies have been recognized consistently enough to develop a fairly detailed picture of how control is pursued from above across different call centre settings, the workforce's responses to these strategies are more diverse, ranging from passivity to disenchantment. Knights and Willmott (1999, pp. 19–20) found the employees they observed retreated from confrontation within the labour process to such an extent that they "willingly" turned themselves into "self-disciplined subjects" who "put in performances without management having to use up resources in distributing rewards and sanctions." Knights and McCabe

---

[3] In an early Foucaultian interpretation, subjectivity was understood by labour process researchers as the effect of "disciplinary mechanisms, techniques of surveillance and power/knowledge strategies" (Knights & Willmott, 1989, p. 554).

(2003, p. 1605) subsequently observed highly uneven responses from employees when the "disciplinary and normalizing" discourse of teamwork clashed with its "common sense appeal to autonomy and egalitarianism."

Despite the call centre cliché of management exhorting its workforce to display a "passion for service," however, workforce disenchantment in call centres is a constant. Anthony Lloyd (2013) offers one of the more recent confirmations of this scenario in a description of his six-month stint at an outsourced call centre in Middlesbrough. There he describes the "wider culture of agents who were generally apathetic to begin with" and their (almost assembly-line) passage "through a barrier towards a fatalism which results in them giving up any remaining loyalty or dedication to their work" (p. 40). Most employees, Lloyd suggests, neither saw work as "an important indicator of their identity" nor believed that the company cared about them (p. 122). In place of the coherent labour or class-based identities formed among workers during the Fordist era, Lloyd encountered their opposite: widespread work avoidance, a generalized ethos of working to live, and a regularized practice of blowing the week's wages on partying and consumer items on weekends. While these kinds of behaviours were certainly present under Fordism, what is important for the moment is that Lloyd's findings demonstrate the potential for forms of dis-identification with work to act, at least initially, as a coping mechanism, permitting employees to establish a space which enables them to continue to function in their job, detested as it may be (Fleming & Spicer, 2004).

The passage from disenchantment and the refusal of workplace interpellation to the production of collective forms of counter-subjectivity has featured less prominently in the academic literature. Kate Mulholland's (2004) memorable study of a Belfast call centre outlined the intense antagonism that developed from below towards managerial practices and manifested in work avoidance, theft, and exit—but not to a strengthening of the Communication Workers' Union's presence at the site. Taylor and Bain (2003) document the role of workplace humour as the basis for the development of a "vigorous counterculture" which undermined management and prepared the ground, in one of the two cases they investigated, for unionization. If the labour process is a struggle not only over the indeterminacy of labour but of knowledge (Sewell, 2005), then these case studies point to the crucial nature of worker identification with, or at least acceptance of, the firm's discourse, as well as how dangerous it can be for employers when workers turn their backs on the dominant interpretations of the power relations characterizing their jobs. For management, securing such acceptance in call centre settings is a necessary, challenging, and risky undertaking.

What is striking in these and other investigations of call centre subjectivity, however, is the degree to which, as Huws (2014, p. 40) observes in her studies of info-proletarianization, the "mix and match bundle" of affective, communicative, and linguistic skills required in the contemporary global, networked workplace don't add up to stable occupational identities.[4] The forms of disinvestment in evidence among the call centre workforce tend therefore to support the theory that a characteristic feature of the precariat's subjectivity is in fact the "*lack* of an occupational identity or narrative to give to life" (Standing, 2014, p. 22, emphasis added). Certainly, the case of the Collettivo Precari Atesia (2005a) explored below supports this view—from its very first days of organizing as a collective, the group described a "loss of social identity" as the main effect of precarious employment at Atesia. So where Foucault saw subjectivity as reflecting forms of attachment to an identity, the prevailing feature of call centre subjectivity seems to be its opposite—a widespread detachment from the job.

Given this subjective disengagement from work, we might then expect that those forced to toil for a wage in call centres would face real "difficulties in organization, in constructing clear narratives, and symbols" (Dean, 2014, p. 9). In other words, in the absence of the kind of coherent labour identities that were often developed among workers fortunate enough to enjoy the "standard employment relationship" (Vosko, 2005, p. 8) of Fordism (full-time, permanent, unionized, with benefits, etc.), how can a strong counter-subjectivity, one that is capable of challenging existing power relations within call centres, develop and circulate? An answer to this question, and a third approach to the question of call centre

---

[4] Huws notes that "[j]ust as occupational identities can be said to be both exclusionary and inclusive, they can also be said to be in a continuous process of construction and deconstruction" (2014, p. 31).

subjectivity, is offered by theorists of post-*operaismo*, a body of theory and tradition of activism known to Anglophone audiences as autonomist Marxism.[5] If call centre employment produces workforce ambivalence and a lack of identification with the job, another way to investigate the power relations within call centres is to explore "the production of subjectivity *through* resistance and struggle" (Hardt & Negri, 2009, p. 21, emphasis added). The premise underlying this approach is that the spark of conflict produces its own forms of identity.[6] As we shall see, the case of the CPA is one in which the different forms of interpellation within the workplace, including established trade unionism, were progressively countered by a collective and antagonistic subjectivity stitched together across innumerable acts of individual defiance. When these forms of refusal and associated critiques surfaced and combined, they produced a rapidly spreading counter-narrative of call centre work. Binding this new identity was the common experience of hyper-flexibility and the principle of self-organization that grew out of it.

Autonomous Labour Organizing, Precarization, and the Decline of Italian Unionism

Labour relations at Atesia were formed at the intersection of a set of processes that will be familiar to the many millions of call centre workers around the world, including the privatization of public telecommunications companies, the growth of mobile telephony and associated explosion of customer relations work, the increasing imposition of labour flexibility, and the erosion of the established union movement's ability to organize and represent the emergent workforce. Events at the company also developed as a result of Italy's idiosyncratic path out of Fordism, however, a story that we take up with the wave of unrest that shook the country to

---

[5] For a discussion of post-*operaismo*, see Chap. 1.
[6] This approach could draw on the writing of a different Foucault, a theorist attuned not only to forms of domination but to "an alternative production of subjectivity, which not only resists power, but also seeks autonomy from it" (Hardt & Negri, 2009, p. 56). This is the Foucault of the mid-1970s—one that does not figure in call centre studies.

its political, economic, and cultural foundations during the "Red Decade" of 1968–1977.

As Italy completed its transition from a largely agrarian society in the post-World War II period to one based on Fordist mass production at the end of the 1960s, labour struggles broke out among workers in virtually every economic sector. One element of these struggles in particular would surface in the revolt of the Atesia call centre workers decades later: a defining force within the *decennio rosso* was the heterogeneous and revolutionary political area that developed to the left of the Italian Communist Party (Partito Comunista Italiano, or PCI) and the country's established trade unions (Berardi, 1998; Castellano et al., 1996; Persichetti & Scalzone, 1999; Wright, 2002). The extraparliamentary left developed an insurgent critique of the constituted hierarchies and suppression of rank-and-file organization within the confederal trade unions that had dominated labour in the post-war period.[7] During the "Hot Autumn" of 1969 wildcat strikes crippled the country, forcing the confederal unions and the PCI to ride a wave of shop-floor militancy they could scarcely control. While not a majoritarian tendency, extraparliamentary groups like Lotta Continua and Potere Operaio, bolstered by students, established a significant presence among workers at companies in the Italian industrial north, especially at Fiat and in the petrochemical sector (Wright, 2002).

The Statuto dei Lavoratori (Worker Statute) of 1970 was passed in response to these struggles. This legislation, which would govern the relations between capital and labour for more than a quarter century thereafter, contained a series of concessions by the state in the face of the labour unrest, including freedom of association for all workers, protection against dismissal without just cause, and a new pension contribution system. The legislation cemented a typically Fordist contractual relationship by positioning the "subordinate" worker (the permanent, full-time employee, or "lavoratore subordinato") as the key actor within the Italian labour market. The defining characteristic of this worker,

---

[7] These are the Confederazione Generale Italiana del Lavoro (CGIL), the Confederazione Italiana Sindacati Lavoratori (Italian Confederation of Workers' Unions, or CISL) and the Unione Italiana del Lavoro (Union of Italian Workers, or UIL). The CGIL is the oldest and largest Italian union, which has existed since 1906. The CISL and the UIL both broke off from the confederation in the immediate post-war period in order to vindicate their Catholic and social-democratic/republican roots, respectively.

according to the Statuto, was that, not owning the tools of production, his labour produced profit for the company.

Like the 1935 Wagner Act in the United States, the Statuto also enshrined and protected the institutional role of the established trade unions in collective bargaining on behalf of Italian workers.[8] The legislation included a series of measures aimed at ensuring the CGIL, CISL, and UIL would remain the private sector's interlocutors in any labour negotiation. For their part, in 1972 the three unions signed a pact giving birth to the CGIL-CISL-UIL federation which, if not a return to the unity of the birth of the historic Confederazione Generale del Lavoro (General Confederation of Labour, or CGL) in 1906, consolidated a shared political direction for the "triplice." Unionization rates in Italy doubled between 1967 and 1977, from a quarter to a half of the workforce (Carrieri, 1995, p. 295; Ginsborg, 1990, p. 320). The external legitimacy afforded by the Statuto and the internal strength provided by the confederation combined to consolidate the hegemony of the confederal trade unions within the sphere of Italian labour relations for decades to come.[9]

The heyday of Italian trade unionism did not last long, however. As the economy restructured away from Fordism, established trade unions entered a period of crisis. Ominous generational trends in their base of support became difficult to ignore, with membership both aging and declining by the 1980s.[10] At the same time, a generation of activists forged in the 1970s began to form their own rank-and-file sectional trade unions as an organizational response to what they saw as the overly comfortable relationship that had developed between the confederal

---

[8] In Italy, companies have traditionally been subject to centralized collective bargaining via national agreements signed for specific sectors (such as metal-mechanics, petrochemical, telecommunications, etc.).

[9] In 1970–1971 the confederal unions also introduced changes that reached down to the lowest level of their structures, where the old system of internal commissions had been subject to harsh critique from the rank and file. First the CGIL, and subsequently CISL and UIL instituted a new system of worker representation known as the *consigli di fabbrica* (factory councils), which replaced the postwar system. According to this system, delegates for every shop or department in the workplace would now be elected by secret ballot of all workers, not just union members.

[10] Although they still boasted impressive membership numbers even by the standards of other European countries, by the 1980s the major unions were by most accounts "top-heavy and poorly oiled machines, with membership declining and ageing at the same time" (Ginsborg, 2001, p. 57). By 1990, the CGIL had 2 million pensioners out of a total of 5 million members (Ginsborg, 2001).

unions, employers, and the state. Among these, the Confederazione dei Comitati di Base (Cobas), which emerged in the public sector, challenged the confederals by organizing amid old and new sectors of the workforce, eschewing the professionalization of trade unionism, and employing direct action tactics such as occupations and wildcat strikes (Ghirardi & Murgia, 2013). Despite their hegemony within the Italian labour movement, the history of the confederal unions during the 1980s and 1990s is therefore one of deep disarray. As their material base of support eroded thanks to outsourcing and deindustrialization, they returned to squabbling among themselves. Rank-and-file critique became resurgent during what is referred to as the "stagione dei bulloni," or the "season of bolts," with which the trade union leaders were pelted by workers during public encounters in the first half of the 1990s.

In 1993 the confederal unions instituted the *rappresentanze sindacali unitarie* (unitary trade-union representatives, or RSU), a system of plant-level union representation that replaced the contested factory councils, which had been instituted in 1970–1971 and which were by the 1990s steadily losing their power to intervene in the struggle for control of the labour process. Since 1993 representatives on the RSUs have been elected directly by workers, but in a manner that has intensified rather than mitigated criticisms from the rank and file since this system of shop-floor representation means that even by gaining a majority of votes cast, Cobas and other rival unions cannot achieve a majority within the RSU at a given workplace.[11] Given the historically prominent role of centralized bargaining in Italy, the RSU's power is in any case quite limited: second-tier, or plant-level collective bargaining occurs between the owners on one side, and the RSU and the signatories of the national contract on the other, meaning that CGIL, CISL, and UIL de facto cannot be excluded from the bargaining table—at least by workers. Employers, on the other hand, can choose their counterpart, meaning they can exclude one of the unions from bargaining by signing a separate agreement if they wish.

---

[11] Under the current system, 33% of the votes are, a priori, allotted to and divided among the trade unions that sign national contracts for the sector (almost exclusively CGIL, CISL, and UIL), with the remaining two-thirds being freely voted in by workers.

While this has occurred only rarely for the big three unions, the practice regularly sidelines rank-and-file unions from collective bargaining.

A key reason for the decline of the major Italian trade unions has been the erosion, since the late 1970s, of subordinate work as the dominant contractual relationship and its substitution by a variety of less secure arrangements. As the economist Andrea Fumagalli (1997) has described it, this process has resulted in a constantly expanding "grey zone" of precarious employment for "parasubordinate" workers caught between full-time, permanent subordinate work on the one hand and freelance work (or "lavoro autonomo") on the other. What is more, these types of contracts are not bound by the national agreements hammered out by the confederal unions but instead allow compensation to be "freely" determined by workers and employers through negotiations in order to allow greater labour market flexibility. While in theory this individualized form of negotiation flows from the position of autonomy parasubordinate workers enjoy and their resulting ability to make their own price for providing a service, in practice, as we will see, it means these workers are effectively excluded from union representation.[12]

---

[12] Within the boundaries of subordinate work, contracts can be *a tempo indeterminato* (permanent) or *a tempo determinato* (meaning the worker is hired on full-time but for a specified period). By the 2000s a growing percentage of subordinate employment was of the latter variety. Moving from subordinate employment into the "grey zone" described by Fumagalli, a varying constellation of contractual relationships has been produced by reforms to Italian labour law between the 1980s and 2000s. The *partita iva* contractual relationship (whereby the employer pays the worker who is then responsible for paying his or her own taxes to the state) presents some important differences from subordinate forms of work, including the fact the employer cannot oblige the worker to work specific hours, and the assumption that it is the worker who owns the tools of production and that the employer pays them for the completion of a specific task—something like when a company pays a graphic designer to create a webpage on his or her laptop from home. By the mid-1990s, particularly in newer, less-regulated sectors with low union presence, but also in the public sector, the use of *collaborazione coordinata e continuativa* contracts (coordinated and continuing collaborative contract, or *co.co.co*) rose sharply. Differently from subordinate employment (where the employee's work schedule is determined by the needs of the employer), a *co.co.co* worker is only "coordinated" (a term which implies a milder form of command over his or her labour) and the relationship is "continuing" because (as opposed to the *partita iva* or the full freelance contract) it does not require a precise task to be performed within the duration of the contract. The short-lived centre-left government of Romano Prodi brought about the *rapporto interinale*, or temporary employment relationship, in 1997. Introduced as a part of the Pacchetto Treu (or Legge 196), the *rapporto interinale* enshrined third-party employment contracts through temporary employment agencies. Another expansion of the parasubordinate grey zone came in 2003, when Silvio Berlusconi's centre-right government passed the Legge 30. Also known as the Legge Biagi (after

Rise of the Call Centre Industry in Italy

As this succession of contractual relationships ate away at the subordinate employment relationship that once symbolized the composition of Italian labour, the 1990s also saw the rapid growth of call centres. Accounts of the sector's development in Italy underscore the privatization of state telecom monopoly SIP (now Telecom Italia), the rise of a private telecommunications sector (TOSCA D1 inventory report: Italy, 2002), and the dizzying take-up of mobile telephony as drivers in the process. According to one observer, the first large call centres emerged within major telecommunications and wireless companies such as Omnitel, Wind, TIM, Infostrada, and Telecom (Schuetz, 2010). By the latter part of the 2000s, this business had grown to the point that around 15 outsourced call centre businesses employing at least over 500 workers each won the biggest contracts and thereby dominated the expanding market (Farolfi, 2007). The spatial distribution of call centres has followed a pattern of agglomeration in and around the country's largest cities. By the mid-2000s, over half were in or close to Rome and Milan, where (repeating a trend we have seen elsewhere) there is an educated workforce and higher rates of unemployment. A third concentration of call centres can be found in the south of the country, where entrepreneurs can access state development subsidies (Gruppo d'inchiesta sulla precarietà e il comune, 2013).

As in other geographic regions, statistics charting this growth are scarce and need to be used with caution, but the figures that are available confirm the kinds of expansion we have already detailed in Ireland,

---

Marco Biagi, the economist assassinated by the Red Brigades in 2002, this legislation did away with *co.co.co* contracts in order to end their widespread fraudulent application, replacing them with the so-called *contratto a progetto* (per-project contract, or *co.co.pro*). As opposed to their progenitor, these contracts govern a one-time performance of a precisely defined job and require payment in one lump sum upon delivery. Similarly to the *co.co.co* contract, however, the worker is considered to be a professional, meaning compensation remains "freely" determined, national contracts do not apply, and union representation is excluded. As we shall see, this allowed a situation in call centres where workers can be paid by the phone call, by the length of a phone call, or by the number of sales made to a customer, all of which can be classified as a kind of digital piecework. In addition to not providing for vacation, maternity leave, or sick days, this type of contract can be terminated because of illness and pregnancy.

Atlantic Canada, and New Zealand. According to the research firm Datamonitor, the number of call centres in Italy almost doubled between 1997 and 1999 from 420 to 820, and employment within them expanded from 34,500 in 2000 to an estimated 53,000 in 2002 (TOSCA D1 inventory report: Italy, 2002). This growth continued through to the latter half of the 2000s, when estimates suggested that roughly 2000 call centres employed between 250,000 and 400,000 people (Cugusi, 2005, p. 50; Direttivo CGIL et al., 2006). A mid-2000s study carried out by the left-wing political party Rifondazione Comunista (in which anonymous questionnaires were distributed to thousands of call centre workers producing an overall sample of around 5000 responses) suggested that, in Atesia's home region of Lazio, employment in the sector more than doubled between 2000 and 2004, to just under 40,000 workers (Partito di Rifondazione Comunista, as cited in Cugusi, 2005, p. 57).

From the very beginning, as Carlo Cuccomarino (2013, para. 7) has noted, Italian call centres have been the scene of "precarity, of atypical labour contracts, of low and uncertain pay, or difficult work schedules." The population labouring in these conditions has predominantly been young, female, and well educated. *Il Manifesto* journalist Antonio Sciotto notes that current and recently graduated university students provide the ideal reservoir of the linguistic and affective capacities demanded by the call centre industry:

> These people are perfect for call centre companies, because they are in any case people who have studied, and therefore they are able to learn the ropes at a call centre quickly, they know how to be pleasant, they are articulate. So it's not like you're taking the peasant during the industrial revolution and throwing him in a factory where there isn't any need for him to speak ... [The call centre worker] has a capacity for relating to others. (Sciotto, personal communication, April 30, 2007)

While the communication factories are often seen as a steppingstone to a "real" job for younger workers, research into the demographics of the Italian labour force has increasingly belied its youthful image. The Rifondazione study found that while 45% of workers were under 29 years of age, the average age was 31. Moreover, the workforce as a whole appears to be aging. This appears to be confirmed in the most recent survey of Italian call centres to date (Fortunato & Palidda, 2012), where researchers found that only 37% of the over 1700 respondents were under 30 years of age, whereas over 40% were between 30 and 40, and just under a quarter were over 40.

The feminized composition of this workforce has remained a constant, however. As is true at Atesia, married women who add a day shift to their domestic work as a means to supplement the family income make up a sizeable slice of the Italian call centre workforce. The Rifondazione study offered early data concerning the gendered make-up of the Italian call centre, suggesting that 73% of their study respondents were women, and this figure was confirmed in the recent Fortunato and Palidda study (70%). The amount such employment can contribute to one's income is meagre, however. Four out of five call centre workers make less than a thousand euros a month (long considered to be the benchmark for a decent salary in Italy), and just over half made less than 800. Given the high cost of housing in cities like Milan and Rome, these constitute poverty wages for those who have no other sources of income to depend on.

As with call centres across the world, front-line worker salaries in Italy vary depending on whether one works in-house or for an outsourced operation. Wireless operators such as Vodafone and Telecom Italia Mobile (TIM) have portions of their call centre requirements carried out in-house, where workers are protected by nationally binding collective agreements with the confederal unions. A legacy of the wireline operator workforces pre-dating the expansion of the outsourced call centre industry in the mid-1990s, this in-house portion of call centre work is nonetheless at constant risk of being outsourced. One example is the Italian wireless company Wind, which during the mid-2000s had an in-house call centre in Milan employing around 270 people. In 2006 Weather Investments, a fund under the control of the Egyptian entrepreneur Naguib Sawiris, purchased the company. Sawiris expressed his concern over what he saw as its high labour costs, particularly at the in-house call centre portion of its operations. Call centre workers at Wind were employed on subordinate contracts governed by the national telecommunications sector collective agreement, working eight hours a day and making roughly 1000 euros a month after taxes. Wind then sold its centre to the call centre contractor Omnia. While the new Omnia workers maintained their previous contract by law, they were instantly more vulnerable to layoffs since the company worked on contract, and management could apply to lay off workers claiming the high labour costs jeopardized the chances of securing new contracts.[13] Even for in-house call centre workers, therefore, labour insecurity is only ever one market transaction away.

The remaining landscape of outsourced call centres features conditions ranging from the expanded "grey zone" of permanent insecurity to businesses operating in the shadows of the informal economy. As noted earlier, some of the companies with in-house operations also outsource portions of customer relations work to call centre businesses, and these companies have employed workers on all of the precarious contracts outlined previously. Estimates for the number of workers employed in this sub-sector vary, but in 2007 Umberto Costamagna, president of AssoContact (the industry association for outsourced call centres) and owner of Call&Call (which employs 1200 call centre workers across Italy), suggested that roughly 80,000 Italians work in outsourced centres. Of this figure, three quarters were on parasubordinate contracts and there was an even split between outbound and inbound workers (as cited in Sciotto, 2006b). There is disagreement on this figure however, since Claudio Cugusi (who also counts workers listed with temporary employment agencies but currently unemployed in his total figure of 400,000 call centre workers in Italy) has suggested that outsourced call centres are actually the dominant form of employment in the sector (2005, p. 23). A more recent study by Databank suggested roughly 80,000 workers were employed among the largest 200 outsourced call centre companies in the country in 2013 (as cited in Biondi, 2014), but this figure misses the many workers employed at smaller companies.

---

[13] These are referred to as *licenziamenti collettivi*, and in such situations Italian labour law dictates how these layoffs must happen. The company must agree with the union on the number of people to be let go and settle on the criteria by which these will be chosen, including length of service, age, how many dependents a person has, and so on, after which an agreement is signed. In these cases the state will often take on the costs of a worker's remaining pension contributions in order to ease the impact on the individual workers.

There are good reasons to suggest that higher employment estimates are warranted. Chief among these is the high number of call centre workers who are estimated to labour in the Italian informal economy, that is, call centre workers without a contract (Sciotto, personal communication, April 30, 2007). As Cugusi (2005, p. 44) pointed out by the mid-2000s, with the cost of information technology dropping so rapidly, 30,000 euros and a rented apartment are sufficient for the entry-level call centre entrepreneur to set up shop in any urban centre. In the shadowy ecosystem of subcontracting fractal parts of the customer management process, tiny companies employing less than ten workers in an apartment may receive a contract two or three tiers downstream for answering a large company's customer assistance calls. With no contract and no union representation, these invisible workers lie at the extreme end of precarious employment in the sector.

The Struggles at Atesia

> Our operators are, in fact, veritable Telephone Communication Professionals who speak the language of business and are motivated to manage the relationship with clients both competently and courteously. (Atesia, 2007)

By the mid-2000s Atesia was Italy's largest call centre. Employing around 4000 workers, it operated around the clock, seven days a week and 365 days a year, and was capable of processing 300,000 customer interactions a day (Atesia, 2007). The rapid growth of this call centre titan is underscored by its provenance: only a decade earlier the company was a relatively obscure part of the Italian public sector apparatus.

Atesia was founded in 1989 as a public company employing around 100 workers to conduct market research within STET (Società Torinese Esercizi Telefonici—the public telecommunications holding company that is the ancestor to Telecom Italia).[14] At the time, future centre-left

---

[14] STET was itself a part of the historical Instituto per la Ricostruzione Industriale, or IRI, a holding company for the Italian government that had been created in 1933 in order to respond to fallout from the Great Depression.

6 The Organization of Autonomy 185

Prime Minister Romano Prodi was head of IRI (the Italian public holding company of which STET was a part), but he would become a key player in the privatization of Italian public sector companies during the 1990s. One of the most important of these was Telecom Italia, founded in 1994 through the merger of several communications-related public sector companies (Iritel, Telespazio, Italcable, and Sirm) into the wireline operator SIP (Società Italiana per l'Esercizio Telefonico). Privatized in 1997 under the first Prodi government (1996–1998), the company was incorporated into STET, which took on the Telecom Italia name for the new telecommunications firm.

Amid this transfer of wealth to the private sector, Atesia began to expand its activities beyond simple market research functions and into the provision of outsourced call centre services. Its bread and butter were contracts from its parent company, Telecom. Atesia rapidly became an innovative site for the application of a variety of parasubordinate contracts. According to Cobas trade unionist and Telecom worker of 25 years Domenico Teramo, the contracts applied at Atesia became a template for the private call centres that sprouted "like mushrooms" in the 1990s (Teramo, personal communication, May 11, 2007). Atesia workers were test subjects for the series of flexible contracts described above, while the company would become the symbol of precarious employment in the Italian call centre industry.

In the early days of Atesia workers were put on *partita iva* contracts. According to this arrangement, employees rented a workstation at the call centre to pursue their "freelance" activities. The clients these operators answered the phones for (mainly Telecom Italia) were all Atesia's though, and employees' working schedules were determined by Atesia management. Nevertheless, through these contracts Atesia effectively hid the fact that it was employing people in a manner that was fully consistent with traditional, *subordinato* (full-time) work, using the fact that workers rented their tools as proof of their freelance status. Payment was made according to the *contatto utile* (effective contact), a threshold Atesia management determined on the basis of the length of the call (for inbound customer assistance) or the answers extracted from the customer in the case of outbound calling where a service was offered.

In this digital version of the piecework production that accompanied Italy's transformation towards Fordism in the 1950s and 1960s, management had a great deal of control over the labour process while the individual call centre operators had very little. On inbound calls, workers' pay per call rose up until the 2-minute and 40-second mark, when it hit a plateau of around one euro. This meant that a one-hour call was paid only one euro, and that a day's pay for workers when there were low volumes of incoming calls could be as low as 10 euros. Management, thanks to the technology it disposed of, could route calls towards certain workers and away from others, and assign workers to projects for better-paying clients,[15] meaning two workers making the same volume of calls could receive different levels of pay. Thus, Atesia management had a series of ways in which they could organize the workflow at the call centre and reward some workers or punish others. The call centre managers (or *assistenti di sala*)—whose main objective, as the CPA suggests, is "that of control"—were the key executors of this power, despite the fact that they themselves were on temp agency contracts (Collettivo Precari Atesia, 2005a).

Not surprisingly, Atesia drew the attention of the rank-and-file union Cobas during the 1990s. Workers had been answering the phones for the airline company Alitalia, and (foreshadowing the events of 10 years later) in 1996 SULTA (the Sindacato Unitario Lavoratori Transporto Aereo, or United Air Transport Workers' Trade Union) requested that the Work Inspectorate review the company to ascertain whether employees were actually performing subordinate work. In 1999 the inspectorate's report declared the contractual relationships at Atesia to be illegal. Just as important, it drew the confederal unions' attention to Atesia and their ongoing presence thereafter.[16]

---

[15] Most of Atesia's business was with Telecom Italia Mobile (TIM), whose customers the call centre workers interact with. TIM ranks its customers into "gold," "silver," or "copper" categories according to how much they spend. In an example of the striation of call centre workers across in-house and outsourced solutions, "gold" customers are taken care of by TIM's in-house workforce, but workers at Atesia are assigned to the "copper" customers.

[16] Faced with the transformed composition of Italian labour, the confederals have attempted to renew themselves. One example of this comes from the CGIL, which launched the Nuove Identità di Lavoro (New Identities at Work, or NIDIL) project in 1998 to "give a voice and representation to atypical workers" (NIDIL-CGIL, 2007). The NIDIL offers services and negotiates collective

6 The Organization of Autonomy 187

The arrival of the confederal unions inaugurated a paradoxical situation at Atesia that would last for years and set the stage for bitter conflict with the CPA. While the big three unions were by law unable to represent these "freelance" workers, the unions still bargained with the employer on the workers' behalf and even signed collective agreements for them beginning in 2000. Union representation at Atesia took the form of the RSAs brought in during the 1990s. Yet, because the vast majority of workers were on parasubordinate contracts, they were barred from voting for their union representatives, who were nominated by the confederals. The collective agreement of 2000 got rid of the *partita iva* contracts for Atesia employees, but it also sentenced their passage to *co.co.co.* contracts, cementing a slightly different contractual relationship, but a very familiar kind of precarity.

For new workers the pattern became having one's contract renewed once a month, then once every 3 months, then every 12 months. According to the contracts, workers were given swathes of time in which, as freelancers, they could in theory show up, work, and leave when they wanted. These work windows were scheduled for six hours a day, six days a week, although management could request an extension of up to four hours a day if there was a heavier volume of calls. While in theory employees had the right to work as little as one hour a day or refuse extra hours when they were requested, in practice management duly noted those who refused the extra work. Given the short span of their contracts, the disciplinary tool available to the company come renewal time was formidable. What was worse, according to the contract signed by the confederals in order to continue working at Atesia employees were also forced to sign an agreement waiving the right to seek compensation for past misclassification, a controversial tactic that would feature in the 2007 regularization of call centre workers across the country.

---

agreements for groups of workers on parasubordinate contracts in emerging professions. At Atesia, NIDIL, the Federazione Informazione Spettacolo e Telecomunicazioni (FISTeL), and Unione Italiana Lavoratori della Telecomunicazione (UILCOM) represented the confederals. FISTeL was born of the merger between the Federazione Informazione e Spettacolo (FIS) and the Sindacato Italiano Lavoratori Telecomunicazioni (SILT).

The agreement of 2000 was especially significant in that it paved the way for the confederal unions' involvement in the organizational restructuring that would result four years later in the splitting up and sale of a portion of Atesia. In 2004, Gruppo COS purchased 80.1% of the company, and the Atesia call centre became part of the biggest customer relations company in Italy. COS was a part of Almaviva, which employs 27,000 workers in Italy, has offices in Brazil, China, and Tunisia, and serves companies like Sky, Wind, Enel, Vodafone, and Mediaset, as well as the public sector through ministries and institutes like the Istituto Nazionale di Statistica (ISTAT, or the National Institute for Statistics) (Cuccomarino, 2013). Almaviva is also owned by Alberto Tripi, a prominent member of the Italian centre-left's base of support among the country's entrepreneurial class.

As a part of the sale, Telecom hived off the remaining 19.9% stake in Atesia to its own call centre, Telecontact. The agreement produced by CGIL-CISL-UIL and Telecom for the Telecontact centre and Atesia appeared to improve conditions for a small percentage of workers, who were now covered by national telecommunications sector agreements. From July 1, 2004, around 1200 Atesia employees answering Telecom customer service calls were transferred roughly 100 metres away to the Telecontact call centre building, where they became part of Telecom's in-house workforce. Of these, around 700 of the new Telecom employees were put on the least secure form of subordinate contracts, or *tempo determinato* contracts lasting 38 months. For the remaining 500 or so workers, the agreement included the application of several variants of "apprenticeship" contracts designed by the Legge Biagi.[17] Many of these contracts were applied to employees who had been working at Atesia for years, and in a familiar move the necessary prerequisite to accessing any contract for workers was to waive their rights to any benefits and back pay to which they may have been entitled due to previous misclassification.

---

[17] These workers were put on three types of contracts designed to allow an apprenticeship period for workers and facilitate their entry into the workforce: *contratti di apprendistato contrattuale*, *contratti di apprendistato professionalizzante* and *contratti d'inserimento*.

For the roughly 3000 employees left at Atesia the agreement decreed the continuation of precarious contracts, albeit under a different name. Atesia workers were now put on *co.co.pro* contracts, a measure made necessary by the labour market reforms introduced by the Legge 30, which had abolished *co.co.co* contracts. Basic features of the previous contracts remained however. Workers continued to not have paid holidays, sick days, or maternity leave, and the employer's pension contributions were minimal. For new mothers the rhythms were especially trying. Collettivo member Federica Ballarò recounted seeing many women forced to work during their eighth month of pregnancy for fear of losing their jobs, as well as new mothers leaving the workplace on breaks to breastfeed their babies.

For their part, the confederal unions claimed the 2004 agreement demonstrated the sector was being forced to phase out precarious employment contracts. Yet workers on both sides of the newly created divide criticized the agreement. As the Collettivo members observed in their interviews, if Atesia workers really were freelancers, then why had the confederals been striking bargains for them? And, if instead they were subordinate workers masked as freelance ones, then why were unions condemning them to these precarious contracts?

The first stirrings of unrest began at Telecontact. The combination of apprenticeship contracts being applied to experienced workers and enforced waiving of rights to back pay due to misclassification was too much for the new Telecontact workers to take and they struck for 15 days, organizing a permanent assembly in front of the company for the duration of the stoppage. They were supported in this action by Roman social movements that had been paying keen attention to Atesia almost since it had emerged. As CPA member Maurizio Testa suggests, these groups "had found in Atesia that symbol of precarity" they were looking for, and at long last it seemed like workers were fighting back (personal communication, May 8, 2007).[18]

---

[18] The Assemblea Coordinata e Continuativa Contro la Precarietà (Coordinated and Continuing Assembly Against Precarity, or ACCCP), which included the Ipò di Marino social centre and the Coordinamento dei Lavoratori di Roma Ovest (Coordinated Workers of Rome-West, or CLARO), brought together a number of activist groups (from neighbourhood collectives to social centres), and had tried to foment labour resistance at Atesia since 2001, to little effect.

The telecommunications section of the rank-and-file union Cobas was one of the groups that got involved in the strike. Many Cobas were Telecom workers themselves, and in the period following the 2001 G8 protests in Genoa they had flyered outside Atesia alongside militants from local occupied social centres and other social movement organizations in the hopes of creating a committee inside. For Cobas members at Telecom the relationship between their own labour conditions and those at Atesia could not have been clearer since, as Domenico Teramo points out, any outsourcing by a public sector company is "the other side of the coin of the precarization of stable workers" (personal communication, May 11, 2007). Teramo described Cobas' involvement as one of providing "material support" for the strike, while respecting the "autonomy and difference" of the groups organizing inside. Much to Cobas' disappointment however, the Atesia workers did not "take up that moment of conflict" and "at the time, when we showed up there, they weren't always receptive to the political signal, the direction we were trying to give them." At Telecontact, facing unemployment and uncertainty over when they would receive settlements from claims for retroactive benefits, most of the workers signed the waiver and went back to work.

Neither of the call centres would remain peaceful for long, however. On the Telecontact side, workers noticed that the form of managerial command had changed perceptibly in the passage between contractual relationships: the intensification of work became increasingly difficult for workers and there were many firings, both of which eventually contributed to the construction of a Cobas rank-and-file committee.

As far as their ex-colleagues at Atesia, the barriers to meaningful collective organization within the call centre were daunting. By the mid-2000s, management combined formidable organizational, technological, and contractual forms of control over the workforce. Collettivo member Alessandro Petricca offered a snapshot of the social isolation produced by the technologically mediated call centre labour process: "Everyone is there ... with headphones on, answering the customer, and so there isn't the kind of relationship between people that there might have been up until twenty, thirty years ago when work wasn't as fragmented. We're talking about post-Fordism" (personal communication, May 8, 2007).

The social isolation described by Petricca provided the perfect backdrop for the apolitical subjectivities prevalent within the call centre's workforce. Domenico Teramo suggests that Atesia's hiring among younger people entering the job market and married women looking to boost the family income was intended from the very beginning to produce a politically weak composition among the call centre workforce, of subjects who were "unused to rebellion." Despite Italy's rich history of trade unionism, only a handful of CPA members had any experience at all with political organizing upon entry into Atesia. Collettivo member Cecilia Benedetti's description of her own background was a common theme in interviews with members of the Collettivo: "Aside from the smaller experiences you would have in high school, like the self-management stuff... I was quite ignorant on a political level" (personal communication, May 8, 2007).[19]

The disinterest in labour politics was accompanied by a palpable detachment from the job. Benedetti, who had a degree in art history, pointed out that many of the younger workers used the paltry income earned at the call centre to support their dreams of achieving an unlikely career in another field (personal communication, May 8, 2007). This belief that workers were just passing through the industry suited management well given that it had no interest in giving the sense that the call centre offered the prospect of a career. CPA member Valerio Gentile (personal communication, May 8, 2007) offered a bleak description of the denial produced by the disjuncture between young people's life aspirations and the realities of employment at Atesia: "There's always the hope of trying to find something better, a bit like the heroin addict who says he'll quit when he feels like it."

Within this widespread disinvestment from the job, forms of work refusal and sabotage found fertile ground at Atesia. One opportunity for

---

[19] This quote reveals what is, in some respects, the uniqueness of the Italian situation. While occupation and self-management of schools and universities has been a tactic of the student left since the 1960s, it is not nearly participated in with the same collective fervour that characterized the first uprisings in these institutions during the 1970s, or even during a brief surge in the late 1980s/early 1990s during what was called the Pantera (Panther) movement. The presence of such tactics as a context is not negligible however, since such forms of struggle can act as a vital reference point when a labour situation ignites.

such soldiering was provided by the piece rate form of payment. On the TIM Business campaign, call centre operators were not paid at all for conversations on inbound calls clocking in at less than 20 seconds. Pay rates increased thereafter until they peaked for calls lasting from 2 minutes and 40 seconds to 3 minutes, after which they went down again. "Obviously at two minutes and forty-one seconds, for some reason, the call gets cut off," Federica Ballarò noted. "[Management] tried to make it impossible to hang up, but in reality, between ourselves we always figure out some kind of dodge. So it's currently still possible to do it" (personal communication, May 8, 2007).

By early 2005, for growing sections of the workforce detachment and refusal had turned into resentment and anger however. For many, their growing permanence among the precarious ranks of the call centre workforce became increasingly difficult to explain away as a steppingstone towards another career. In December 2004 the confederals agreed to prolong the existing labour agreement at Atesia until March 2005, and then extended it once more until September. In April the employer produced the spark that ignited the call centre by decreasing the rate paid to workers per call by five cents. It was only the latest of a series of unilateral cuts that had brought their compensation down from one euro per call to 90 cents, but the atmosphere on the night shift (when most of the Collettivo workers worked) became incandescent. Flyers appeared in the "Sala Break" (the space where employees spent their time between shifts) calling for action. After countless frustrations, a collective tipping point had been reached. As Mara Portolani suggests, "there was simply the need to say enough" (personal communication, May 8, 2007). For Teramo, workers had "in some way developed a consciousness of their working condition, of their own exploitation, and they felt the need to organize themselves" (personal communication, May 11, 2007).

The Collettivo may, as Rosanna Nastro jokes, have been "born over 5 cents," but organizing in a workplace like Atesia presented daunting challenges (personal communication, May 8, 2007). The call centre had thousands of employees divided into several shifts, and there was little socializing at work. Indeed, even though they had all worked at Atesia for years, most of those who would form the Collettivo had never met before they started to organize. There was therefore no pre-existing organization that brought them together, but rather a shared sense of outrage at the actions of management and the confederal unions. Benedetti (personal communication, May 8, 2007) found a protest flyer lying around the Sala Break announcing the Collettivo's first meeting and attended. The meetings quickly grew in size as what Nastro described as the "spontaneous aggregation" spread across the workstations at Atesia.

When asked to recount the formation of the collective, most members began by discussing the principle of self-organization, or as Nastro (personal communication, May 8, 2007) puts it the act of "doing things for ourselves without delegating to anybody." Moreover, as the group reached out to colleagues, Collettivo members decided to refrain from dictating a political line, in pointed contrast to the style of the confederal unions. By all accounts, there was not much need to goad their co-workers into action however, as frustration against both the employer and the unions had come to a head. In an ironic twist on the popular expression used to describe the trade unions in the Hot Autumn of 1969, Benedetti suggests the CPA merely "rode the wave" of the growing anger among Atesia workers (personal communication, May 8, 2007).

The Collettivo's autonomy may have been spontaneous, but as the title of this chapter suggests, it still had to be organized. The new group's first course of action was to get to the bottom of their contractual situation. The CPA members formed a working group and began compiling a dossier to both educate themselves and circulate knowledge on parasubordinate contracts and how they were being applied at Atesia. As Collettivo member Maurizio Testa puts it,

> we realized that nobody knew the Legge 30. The employers didn't know it, or pretended they didn't, the union didn't know it or similarly pretended not to know it, and we didn't know it. We were signing contracts without really knowing what they actually meant. (Personal communication, May 8, 2007)

The self-education project allowed the group to seize upon the contradictions of their contractual status. As Testa describes, "the moment we realized that our work was actually subordinate and we have a right to specific things, from that moment we behaved like we were subordinate workers in every way." This included holding public meetings, claiming the right to strike, demanding to vote for their union representatives, and seeking to bargain with the employer. Among the effects of the CPA's agitation was that the confederal unions began to appear more often at Atesia, holding public meetings and presenting the contracts they were about to sign to workers for approval.

One of the means by which the Collettivo spread its counter-perspective on their working conditions was a self-produced zine called *Sfront End*. The first issue published in May 2005 announces the formation of the collective and its first strike. Through 15 issues, the zine shared information on the company, the industry, and the law around parasubordinate contracts and also articulated a profoundly antagonistic vision of working in Italy's biggest call centre. *Sfront End* featured ferocious satire on the activities of managers and union leaders at the company. On the cover of the fifth issue, a union leader giving a speech to workers is depicted as having two testicles for a head, his arms guided from above by a puppeteer. Issue number ten considers whether it would be more cost-effective for Atesia management to put a slave to work in the call centre rather than to hire a misclassified freelancer (coming to the conclusion that it would not, since it does not involve paying for costs of subsistence). Not surprisingly, contributors were listed by a series of pen names to protect CPA members against dismissal. In addition to popping up around the call centre, *Sfront End* was available digitally on the Collettivo's website, adding itself to the many flyers, public letters, research reports, and submissions to work inspectors produced by the group.

The CPA organized its first strike on the heels of the pay decrease. Calling for a 24-hour work stoppage and a concurrent assembly in the square in front of the Atesia main entrance, the group voiced its demands to the company and the confederals in the face of what they called their "Far West" employment situation. They called for subordinate contracts, an immediate raise, benefits (including vacation, sick pay, severance and maternity leave), and repairs to the Atesia building (Collettivo Precari Atesia, 2005c).

The strike turned the flexibility imposed on workers back against the employer. Parasubordinate workers could not legally strike, yet if the overwhelming majority of Atesia workers were technically freelance then they could come to work whenever they liked in the six-hour shift allotted to them. The Collettivo ensured a coordinated claiming of this right to not work, crippling the call centre for 24 hours. The strike was followed by two more in June that enjoyed strong support and turned heads throughout the industry. The actions were arguably more effective than many of those organized according to the onerous bureaucratic process imposed on subordinate workers with a contract and clear union representation, given that in Italy the latter must ensure that the union sanctions the strike, respects windows in which the strike is permitted, and even applies for permission to the company.

Stung by the unexpected emergence of conflict within its workforce, Atesia management responded by announcing that CGIL, CISL, and UIL were the only interlocutors they would deal with in bargaining over contracts and working conditions. For the strike organizers and everyone else working at the company there was a publicly posted warning, couched in an appeal for the workforce's loyalty:

> The company hopes (...) that common sense will prevail, and appeals to the attachment workers have to their jobs, an attachment which up until this point workers at Atesia have demonstrated, in order to fight ... those who, by every means, even illicitly, work to divide, confuse, disorient, and thus gain, without any positive results, spaces of attention and legitimation which are not rightfully owed to them or deserved. (as cited in Collettivo Precari Atesia, 2005c)

The full scope of the Collettivo's challenge became clear the following day with the appearance of another warning, this time from the CGIL. The notice lashed out at strike organizers, describing them as

> forces bent upon inserting themselves within the social malaise, which at Atesia is strong, in order to affirm a voluntaristic and authoritarian notion of the management of trade union conflict, one which has inevitably produced defeat rather than victory for workers. (as cited in Collettivo Precari Atesia, 2005c)

From the first strike onwards, there was a rapid intensification of struggles as the Collettivo's organizing spread beyond Atesia. The group began to connect with workers and labour organizers at other call centres, and the language in their literature began to adopt autonomist hues. One flyer referred to the "process of recomposition occurring between various categories of workers," and suggested their struggle was worrying to both owners and "their" unions (Collettivo Precari Atesia et al., 2005). The confederals had called for a one-day strike on June 24, a move that was read as a bid to regain the initiative they had lost to the Collettivo. By mid-July, the latter was organizing regular demonstrations in front of Atesia and also held an assembly in front of the local municipal offices at Cinecittà. Beyond these forms of direct action, the CPA continued to pursue legal claims bolstered by their growing knowledge of parasubordinate contracts. Labour assessors from the region, province, and municipality were handed a dossier documenting the illegality of the contract situation at Atesia in June (Collettivo Precari Atesia, 2005d).

Meanwhile, with contracts for hundreds of workers set to expire at the end of September the temperature continued to rise at Atesia. In July the confederals posted a public notice claiming it was hearing rumours of *prezzolati* (mercenaries) among the CPA that were paid by management to derail the collective bargaining process. "In a democracy the union has the obligation to represent the will of the majority of workers," the notice suggested, "and not only that of a small, albeit noisy, minority" (NIDIL, FISTEL and CPO, & Delegazione Sindacale Unitaria, 2005). The union reiterated its plans for the path towards "stabilization for everybody" at the company.

The very same morning this notice was posted, however, roughly 800 people working on outbound calls found out their contracts would not be renewed. Rather than being extended as usual, workers were told to call a hotline in September, the month their contracts were due to expire, to find out if they would get a chance to work with the company again. The situation at Atesia degenerated through the course of the day, becoming tense and difficult to control. Alessandro Petricca was among those who found out they were losing their job: "There were real problems for the company's ability to manage the situation, which escalated. Inside the Atesia hall where calls are answered, people were getting up from their workstations, shouting, berating the managers..." (personal communication, May 8, 2007). Many of the Collettivo's members were among the list of the redundant. As harried managers oversaw the situation flanked by police officers who had been called in to Atesia, the CPA called a meeting to plan a response. It organized a picket at the entrance of the call centre, and that evening management fired four more of its members for obstructing the work of their colleagues and taking part in unauthorized assemblies (Collettivo Precari Atesia et al., 2005). The situation at Atesia had come to a head.

On September 15, the Collettivo struck Atesia again in response to the confederals' announcement of another agreement featuring *contratti d'inserimento* and *co.co.co* contracts. By this point, the concept of precarity and the discourse surrounding it had gained widespread currency on the Italian left, spreading beyond rank-and-file unions and social centres to become, as general elections approached, a key plank of the poll-leading centre-left coalition's platform. The CPA was suspicious of Prodi's coalition, suggesting in the first months of his government's tenure that social movements ought to see public institutions "not as a simple interlocutor or potential ally, but as a party with which to bargain—as one does with the boss—upon the basis of the real relations of force" (Collettivo Precari Atesia, 2005b). As 2005 turned into 2006, Atesia workers began to intensify their use of direct action, occupying the offices of various town councils, the Ministry of Labour, and the CGIL.

In April 2006, the confederal unions and Atesia reached yet another agreement including 170 subordinate contracts (for those who had been at Atesia for at least seven years) paid 650 euros a month gross for 25 hours a week. For other workers there was an array of parasubordinate contracts, and 900 layoffs were announced as a part of the deal. The CPA's response to the agreement was predictably bitter: "For 650 Euros a month a 'lucky' minority will always be at the company's disposal, and for the rest there is piecework, no rights, and layoffs." The group continued to demand permanent employment for all and at least 1000 euros a month with holidays, sick pay, and maternity leave (Collettivo Precari Atesia, 2006a). The contract took effect in May and ended up resulting in 400 layoffs, among which were most of the remaining members of the Collettivo.

As the summer of 2006 wore on, the struggles generated by the call centre workers at Atesia were by this point producing effects that were entirely out of proportion with respect to their modest beginnings. Most important, the situation was now becoming a problem for Romano Prodi's razor-thin majority. If Prodi had made vague promises during the election campaign that his government would address labour precarity in the country, the lower reaches of public bureaucracy were now threatening to act on their own to achieve this. In a repeat of the 1997 SULTA incident, the Work Inspectorate of Rome was preparing a report on its inspection of Atesia (requested months previous by the CPA), in which it would rule on the legality of the company's application of parasubordinate contracts. Placed in an uncomfortable position by the ongoing labour strife at Atesia and rumoured to be concerned over the outcome of the inspectorate's decision, the Prodi government's Minister for Labour, Cesare Damiano, was preparing a *circolare* (circular) for local labour inspectors that would determine the exact parameters of how parasubordinate contracts could be applied in call centres.[20]

Even if he did manage to beat the Roman Inspectorate to the punch by releasing the *circolare*, however, Minister Damiano had to tread delicately with this decision. On the one hand the centre-left was, nominally, the friend of labour and the repository of the confederal unions' hopes for a sympathetic ear in government. On the other, COS owner Alberto Tripi, who by that point employed 13,000 call centre workers in Italy (La Repubblica Online, 2006), was also very close to Margherita party leader and Vice Premier Francesco Rutelli, and thus a key figure in the centre-left coalition's base of support among the country's business class.

As if that were not enough, this was also the ministry's first intervention into the call centre industry, so the circular would inevitably be seized upon as representative of the centre-left coalition's strategy with respect to the controversial Legge Biagi. Lastly, in a situation that only neoliberalism could have created, the state itself was a major customer for the Italian call centre industry in general and COS in particular, and thus

---

[20] This is a *circolare applicativo* or a circular outlining how a particular law must be applied (in this case the Legge 30).

arguably had more than a simple passing interest in making sure capital's command over labour in the sector was assured.

Having been mostly ejected from Atesia, in the run up to these decisions the Collettivo members and their allies began to focus their attention on public institutions. In June they demonstrated in front of the Ministry of Labour as Damiano, trade union delegations, and call centre executives met to discuss the fate of the industry. Shortly thereafter the Ministry of Labour released its much-anticipated *circolare*, which, while it did not name any call centre in particular, was without a doubt made to measure for the events at Atesia. The *Circolare Damiano* was indeed an admirable bit of tightrope walking on the minister's part. It gave something to labour, decreeing that inbound call centre workers were to be regularized as permanent, subordinate workers since they had less control over their labour conditions than those working outbound campaigns. As far as outbound call centre workers were concerned, because they could, in theory, control their work to a greater extent, the gift to the call centre industry was that it could continue to hire workers on *co.co.pro* contracts.

In August the Work Inspectorate presented its report. If the *Circolare Damiano* had saved something for industry, the Ispettorato's report was a complete victory for Atesia workers. As a result of its inspection, it decreed that Atesia hire on *all* of its 3200 workers on subordinate contracts, as well as compensate the roughly 8000–10,000 workers that had passed through the company since 2001 due to their false classification as *co.co.pros* (Sciotto, 2006a).

The interventions by Minister Damiano and the Work Inspectorate of Rome occurred against a backdrop of growing labour unrest at call centres across Italy. In June, Snater (a national rank-and-file union for telecommunications, radio, and television workers) had called for strikes at the inbound Telecom call centres to protest the "nightmarish" work rhythms and intensified surveillance of workers. In September a national demonstration of call centre workers, organized by the CPA, was held in Rome. In December there was an unofficial work to rule campaign at a COS call centre in Palermo, where workers demanded collective bargaining rights, production quota prizes, passage from part to full-time contracts, and more flexible shifts for women with children. In a strategy that was reportedly costing the company 10,000 euros a day, call centre operators were staying on the phone as long as possible by being as helpful as they could with customers and creating digital queues that overloaded switchboards. Call centre agitation was also reported in the southern cities of Catania and Naples (Sciotto, 2006c).

The CPA also continued to pressure representatives of the confederal unions and the state. At an event in which Minister Damiano and the National Secretary of the CGIL Guglielmo Epifani were speaking, as Testa describes,

> we said to ourselves, let's intervene. And, when we say we're intervening, we mean we go there with thirty or forty people, we're blocking everything, and we're giving them our view on things, because if you don't have a voice that's what you have to do. (personal communication, May 8, 2007)

The action resulted in shoving matches between the CGIL's stewards, the CPA, and its allies.

By the fall of 2006, Gruppo COS decided to cut its losses and announced it would hire 4000 people at its various call centres permanently as long as the results of the inspection were annulled and the criteria regarding inbound and outbound workers decreed by the *Circolare Damiano* were adopted instead. In October, an agreement was signed between the confederal unions and companies in the call centre industry that called for the lesser evil from the perspective of employers, the application of the *Circolare Damiano* to the entire sector (Sciotto, 2006b). It must have been clear to Minister Damiano that such an agreement would not suffice to quell the unrest in the call centre sector, and that the state would have to step in more decisively. By late autumn, with the participation of the confederal unions, an agreement was being hammered out between the Ministry of Labour and the call centre sector regarding the back pay employers would be forced to offer to thousands of workers as a result of the inspectorate's ruling.

The plan, which was proposed and approved as a part of the government's 2007 budget (*Legge Finanziaria*), involved an unprecedented gift from the state to COS. Minister Damiano's legislation, like his position adopted in the circular, was once again creatively disingenuous in its approach to the sector's labour issues. It decreed the permanent hiring of parasubordinate inbound workers, but at the same time offered an enticement for Tripi and COS: Article 178 of the financial bill set aside roughly 300 million euros of public money, to be paid over two years, in order to offset the losses suffered by the company due to the inspectorate's decision. Damiano's solution also included a well-worn tactic. The financial law forgave COS' retroactive obligations towards individual workers if it hired them on permanently, via a waiver to be signed by each worker in exchange for a subordinate position. The much-fêted intervention by the minister required that the unions and COS' parent corporation, Gruppo Almaviva, reach an agreement for the call centres under Tripi's control. When they did, on December 12, Damiano called it "a success for unions and enterprise" (as cited in La Repubblica Online, 2006). The agreement stabilized inbound workers and those who did both inbound and outbound calling through a subordinate contract that was a part of the national contract for telecommunications workers. Beyond Atesia, according to the CGIL's figures the agreement stabilized 24,000 of the 300,000 workers employed in the call centre sector (as cited in Cuccomarino, 2013).

If this much was a positive development, there were less-publicized parts of the accord that were unfavourable to Atesia workers. For roughly 1000 outbound workers there would still be apprenticeship contracts. In addition, while inbound and mixed inbound/outbound workers would have stability at last, the company was not offering them full-time permanent work. The contracts offered by Atesia were part-time (20 hours a week), demanded 24 hours a day potential availability in scheduling, and paid 550 euros (gross) a month.

Many Atesia workers contested the accord. In a city like Rome, where students could pay 750 euros a month for a shared room in the university district, the salary was far from a living wage for call centre workers, who would also have to give up their past compensation in the process. In late December the CGIL held a vote on the contract among Atesia workers, who turned it down by a 60–40 margin (Collettivo Precari Atesia, 2006b). The confederal unions went ahead and signed the accord.

Counter-Subjectivity and the Organization of Autonomy at Atesia

The struggles at Atesia are significant in a number of respects. Most obviously because the extent of the measures bringing a portion of the precariously employed call centre workforce into more secure working arrangements was unprecedented, in Italy or elsewhere. In the wake of the financial law, the National Secretary of the CGIL's telecommunications sector Alessandro Genovesi described the measures applied to the call centre sector as "the broadest campaign of stabilization ever registered in a private sector in the last twenty years" (as cited in Farolfi, 2007). The stabilizations are especially worthy of note given the extreme forms of precarious employment workers were submitted to from the 1990s onward. By the time Atesia passed to Tripi in 2004, management at the biggest call centre in Italy enjoyed a command over the communicative labour in its customer relations factory that was bolstered by contractual, technological, and subjective forms of control. The challenges to enacting stable and powerful forms of recomposition among workers at the company were formidable. As Rosanna Nastro remembers, "[a]t the beginning, when we demanded job security, they called us crazy" (personal communication, May 8, 2007).

Despite the public celebrations of labour peace to come throughout the Italian call centre sector, however, 2007 was ushered in at Tripi's company with unannounced and unilateral changes to the workers' schedules. When four female employees suggested they could not meet the new demands made of them due to the fact that they had small children, they were let go on the spot. While the broader stabilization process has continued, with most inbound workers now on permanent contracts, from the perspective of some observers the pendulum has swung decisively back "from stable contracts to precarious ones" (Cuccomarino, 2013, para. 4) within the Italian call centre industry.

Surveying this scenario, it is tempting to suggest that the conflicts at Atesia merely resulted in fired workers and a slightly milder form of precarity. A more positive assessment would begin by underscoring that if the Italian state was forced to intervene at all, it is only due to the repeated outbreaks of unrest at Atesia between 2005 and 2007. In addition to the regulatory measures they provoked, the struggles at Atesia stand out for the self-organized form that they took and the degree of antagonism they generated. Collettivo member Christian Bosi signals the critical role played by self-organization when he suggests that "if today in Italy the legislation surrounding work has changed, it's not because of the CGIL, or CISL, or UIL—it's changed because of us" (personal communication, May 8, 2007). This section concludes by returning to the question of the production of call centre counter-subjectivity and connecting it to the autonomous organization of labour.

Call centre work is inherently communicative and relational in that it produces and reproduces relationships with consumers through language. When the communicative capacity of employees is put to work, its goal is the production of knowledge, the transmission of information, and the establishment or reproduction of relationships, forms of identification, and feelings of satisfaction on the part of consumers. In that sense, call centre work is directed towards a production of subjectivity which autonomists suggest is increasingly central to the contemporary generation of value (Hardt & Negri, 2009, p. 287). As Carrillo Rowe, Pérez, and Malhotra (2013, p. 4) note of their studies in the Indian context however, as a part of this process call centre work also involves a "performance of identity" that constitutes agents' subjectivities. Like the ventriloquist's dummy—to use the image proposed by the Colectivo Situaciones (2006, p. 31)—call centre workers are spoken through, even as they speak on behalf of a company. The communicative requirements of transnational corporations are paramount, dissolving consolidated forms of identity.

This enforced transformation of subjectivity and associated emotional performance on behalf of the company is well captured in the account of call centre work offered by Milanese activists associated with the Euro MayDay movement:

> And by magic, from five to midnight you become the cool McCenter lady, constantly connected by intercom with the world, courtesy in a human form, even though your life doesn't have a future; you, who puts the client before everything, however low your wages, you, a dragonfly among the

endless reeds of the urban network! Nymph of base wage plus commissions! (As cited in Ghirardi & Murgia, 2013, p. 188)

Like millions of call centre workers, employees at Atesia spoke on behalf of one company while being employed at another. However, in a workplace characterized by the extreme forms of precarious employment detailed above, management's lack of commitment to its workforce and an alienating labour process resulted in widespread refusal to identify with work. At Atesia we find none of the "postindustrial work ethic" that observers have identified in high tech or the creative industries "with its new emphasis on work as an avenue for personal development and meaning" (Weeks, 2011, p. 60). The case of the CPA, then, offers an example of the construction of a call centre counter-subjectivity out of an endemic *detachment* from the job and the firm. Young people saw themselves as "just passing through" the industry while they pursued their real passions elsewhere, and older women working part time were merely adding to the income of the family which was their real focus. Neither group seems to have had much by way of affective investment in their work.

What's more, the lack of identification extended to the unions seeking to represent workers at Atesia. This refusal to see unions as a vehicle for the advancement of their interests arose in an organic way, out of workers' exclusion from the decision-making process within the confederal unions. One anonymous Atesia worker (Fatur, 2006, p. 5) describes attending a union meeting to debate a proposed contract but being barred from voting on it because of their contractual status as freelancers: "The immediate sensation," the worker recounts, "was that of humiliation." Given stories such as this one it is not surprising then to hear labour scholars Sylvia Ghirardi and Anna Murgia (2013, p. 3) suggest that in Italy trade unions are having difficulties producing "social cohesion based on traditional identitarian mechanisms." Certainly, at Atesia the refusal of a workplace identity was accompanied by a refusal of established trade unionism.[21]

---

[21] Mattoni (2012, p. 41) refers to the Atesia case as being illustrative of the "difficult political relationship" between precariously employed workers and trade union confederations.

The passage from subjective detachment to the production of counter-subjectivity appears to have been swift. Just as important, it was formed in the heat of an outcry against management. Even among a workforce that was by most descriptions apolitical, once provoked by a pay decrease, what had previously been a simple refusal to identify with the job quickly turned into a process of collective identification. The basis for this was a collective recognition, constructed through the process of self-education around their contracts, that their employment status was fraudulent, and that the common denominator of their condition was to be found in the flexible employment conditions they were subject to. That the term "precarious" was a factor of aggregation is clear enough from the fact that it was included in the name of their organization. Once the construction of this counter-subjectivity was set in motion, hanging up on customers went from being an individualized act intended to maximize revenue and minimize work into a collective tool that was circulated widely as part of a broader contest with management.

While there is little question that the workplace remains a critical site of interpellation into a range of subjectivities (Brophy, Cohen, & de Peuter, 2016; Weeks, 2011), the Atesia case provides further evidence of the way in which forms of detachment and refusal along the digital assembly lines are risky for capital in that they can provide the critical seedbed for the development of counter-subjectivities. The danger of a sudden slide from hundreds of minor, individualized, and secret acts of defiance by workers to a more coordinated campaign of sabotage against an employer is inherent in the call centre, and perhaps especially so in one where employment relationships are highly unstable to begin with. Anecdotal proof of this unfaithfulness perennially lurking beneath the surface of social relations in the call centre is widespread, but it is captured well in Kiran Mirchandani's description of her research on call centre work in India, where she relates how one worker confessed that when engaged on a difficult call that could negatively impact one's scores, "it's kind of like better for you to hang it up" (2012, p. 93). At Atesia, it simply became an increasingly better idea to hang up, and this was despite union involvement rather than because of it. Refusal of work took on a new meaning, and counter-subjectivity was produced through struggle.

The case of the Collettivo demonstrates very clearly therefore that the models of engagement and traditions of established trade unionism are far from the ultimate horizon for collective organization by call centre workers. To the contrary, once a counter-subjectivity had begun to develop out of a shared experience of precarious employment, the autonomous labour organizing engaged in by the Collettivo seems to have been made to measure for the workforce at Atesia. There is some irony in the fact that workers who were classified for years as "freelance"—that is, ones who are theoretically autonomous, creative, and self-organizing—ended up adopting a form of organization in which they were autonomous (from unions), creative (in the forms of struggle they generated) and self-organized. Paradoxically, as Rosanna Nastro suggests, the Collettivo's strength was their inexperience, a lack of memory of struggle that was quickly filled with ideas for action (personal communication, May 8, 2007). Atesia workers in general and the Collettivo in particular were especially inventive in the coordination of digital sabotage and flexible strikes that harnessed the limits imposed by their post-Fordist contractual relationship.

The case of the Collettivo offers a number of elements that suggest prudence with respect to any attempts to generalize lessons from it. Italy's deep history of autonomous labour organizing acted as a reservoir which was accessible once the group decided on the kind of organizing it was interested in.[22] The highly contradictory and hierarchical approach to collective organization by the Italian confederal unions described in this case is not something one finds across the board, to be sure. Yet the organizational form adopted by the Collettivo was, importantly, an effect

---

[22] Italy has an extraordinarily rich tradition of self-organization and the refusal of political mediation in the form of political parties and trade unions, one that permeates activism, always resurfacing, perpetually being reinvented. In this way, there is what could be referred to as a deep and rich *memory of organization* that the CPA entered into a mutually constitutive relationship with during the course of its struggles at Atesia. There were rank-and-file unions like Cobas, the occupied and self-organized social centres, and local coalitions of activists to prove that the confederal trade unions were not the only way to organize struggle, to show workers the value of direct action tactics, and to demonstrate solidarity and mutual aid. All of these organizations and organizational forms emerged as a result of the Red Decade and constitute a collective memory that is constantly oriented towards radical change.

of their juridical *exclusion* from collective bargaining rights. When this exclusion combined with the entrenched nature of Italian corporate power and the confederals' opposition to this new political subject at the company, self-organization became one of the few practicable paths available to the members of the Collettivo. As Testa suggests when asked whether the struggle against the confederal unions was worth it: "I would have quite happily done without it. But it was unavoidable" (personal communication, May 8, 2007).

Once a decision to self-organize was made, however, the Collettivo demonstrated an impressive capacity to "capitalize on Atesia's contradictions and organize forms of struggle" (Teramo, personal communication, May 11, 2007). Key to this organization, I hope to have shown, is their exclusion—from working identities, employment stability, and meaningful union participation. If, along with Stuart Hall and many others, we agree with the idea that "the great social collectivities which used to stabilize our identities" have been, in our times, "deeply undermined by social and political developments" (as cited in Mosco, 2009, p. 150), then the Collettivo Precari Atesia is an example of the counter-subjectivities and struggles that can be born out of that destabilization.

Interviews Cited

Benedetti, Cecilia. Rome, May 8th, 2007.
Bosi, Christian. Rome, May 8th, 2007.
Gentile, Valerio. Rome, May 8th, 2007.
Nastro, Rosanna. Rome, May 8th, 2007.
Petricca, Alessandro. Rome, May 8th, 2007.
Portolani, Mara. Rome, May 8th, 2007.
Sciotto, Antonio. Rome, April 30th, 2007.
Teramo, Domenico. Rome, May 11th, 2007.
Testa, Maurizio. Rome, May 8th, 2007.

References

Atesia. (2007). *Chi siamo*. Retrieved from http://www.atesia.it/chisiamo/profilo.htm

Azzellini, D., & Ness, I. (2011). *Ours to master and to own*. Chicago, IL: Haymarket Books.

Bain, P., Taylor, P., Watson, A., Mulvey, G., & Gall, G. (2002). Taylorism, targets and the pursuit of quantity and quality by call centre management. *New Technology, Work and Employment, 17*(3), 170–185.

Berardi, F. (1998). *La nefasta utopia di potere operaio: Lavoro tecnica movimento nel laboratorio politico del sessantotto italiano*. Rome, Italy: Castelvecchi.

Biondi, A. (2014). *Call center, l'utile non è in linea*. Retrieved from http://www.confapimatera.it/wp-content/uploads/downloads/2014/11/sole-call-center.pdf

Brophy, E., Cohen, N., & de Peuter, G. (2016). Labor messaging: Practices of autonomous communication. In R. Maxwell (Ed.), *The Routledge companion to labor and media* (pp. 315–326). New York, NY: Routledge.

Callaghan, G., & Thompson, P. (2002). We recruit attitude: The selection and shaping of routine call centre labour. *Journal of Management Studies, 39*(2), 233–254.

Carrieri, M. (1995). Industrial relations and the labour movement. In S. Gundle & S. Parker (Eds.), *The new Italian republic: From the fall of the Berlin wall to Berlusconi* (pp. 294–310). London, UK: Routledge.

Carrillo Rowe, A., Perez, K, & Malhotra, S. (2013). *Answer the call: Virtual migration in Indian call centers*. Minneapolis, MN: University of Minnesota Press.

Castellano, L., Cavallina, A., Cortiana, G., Dalmaviva, M., Ferrari Bravo, L., Funaro, C.,... Virno, P. (1996). Do you remember revolution? In M. Hardt & P. Virno (Eds.), *Radical thought in Italy: A potential politics* (pp. 225–240). Minneapolis, MN: University of Minnesota Press.

Colectivo Situaciones. (2006) *¿Quién habla? Lucha contra la esclavitud del alma en los call centers*. Buenos Aires, Argentina: Tinta Limón Ediciones.

Collettivo Precari Atesia. (2005a). *Alcune notizie sulla sitazione dei lavoratori*. Retrieved from http://www.slaicobasmilano.org/precariatesia.htm

Collettivo Precari Atesia. (2005b). *Corteo cittadino contro la precarietà*. Retrieved from http://www.slaicobasmilano.org/precariatesia.htm

Collettivo Precari Atesia. (2005c). *Giusto per essere chiari*. Retrieved from http://www.slaicobasmilano.org/precariatesia.htm

Collettivo Precari Atesia. (2005d). *Resoconto assemblee in Atesia*. Retrieved from http://www.slaicobasmilano.org/precariatesia.htm
Collettivo Precari Atesia. (2006a). *Ennesima truffa di azienda e sindacati diciamo no!!! In francia l'hanno fatto...* Retrieved from http://www.slaicobasmilano.org/precariatesia.htm
Collettivo Precari Atesia. (2006b). *Le lavoratrici ed i lavoratori di Atesia respingono l'accordo-truffa voluto da padron tripi e firmato da CGIL-CISL-UIL*. Retrieved from http://www.slaicobasmilano.org/precariatesia.htm
Collettivo Precari Atesia, Collettivo contro la precarietà Telecontact center, RSU Cobas XCOS, Lavoratrici e lavoratori Unicab, Lavoratrici e lavoratori autorganizzati ACI Informatica, Lavoratrici e lavoratori Alicos,... Coordinamento lavoratrici e lavoratori Roma Ovest. (2005). *Mobilitazione contro la precarietà 22 giugno a Roma: Da Atesia a COS*. Retrieved from http://www.slaicobasmilano.org/precariatesia.htm
Cuccomarino, C. (2013). La parabola di una rivolta. Gli operatori dei call center Almaviva di Palermo. *Commonware: General Intellect in Formazione*, January 17, 2014.
Cugusi, C. (2005). *Call center: Gli schiavi elettronici della New Economy*. Genoa, Italy: Fratelli Frilli Editori.
Dean, J. (2014, November). Communicative capitalism and class struggle. *Spheres, Journal of Digital Cultures*. Retrieved from http://spheres-journal.org/communicative-capitalism-and-class-struggle/
Direttivo CGIL, e Lazio, R., Canti, D., Taormina, A., Turi, R., & Noce, O. D. (2006, April 29). Atesia: Accordo pessimo, referendum vero. *Il Manifesto*.
Farolfi, S. (2007, April 4). Call center, ride il telefono 16,000 de-precarizzati. *Il Manifesto*, p. 11.
Fatur. (2006). *Sindacato insindacabile*. Retrieved from precariatesia.altervista.org/Sfront_end/N_12.doc
Fleming, P., & Spicer, A. (2004). 'You can checkout anytime, but you can never leave': Spatial boundaries in a high commitment organization. *Human Relations, 57*(1), 75–94.
Fleming, P., & Sturdy, A. (2011). 'Being yourself' in the electronic sweatshop: New forms of normative control. *Human Relations, 64*(2), 177–200.
Fortunato, V., & Palidda, R. (2012). *Il call center in Italia: Lavoro e organizzazione tra retorica e realtà*. Roma, Italy: Carocci Editore.
Foucault, M. (2000). The subject and power. In J. Faubion (Ed.), *The essential works of Michel Foucault, 1954–1984: Volume 3 – Power* (pp. 326–348). London, UK: Penguin.

Frenkel, S., Korczynski, M., Shire, K., & Tam, M. (1999). *On the front line: Organization of work in the information economy.* Ithaca, NY: Cornell University Press.

Frenkel, S., Tam, M., Korczynski, M., & Shire, K. (1998). Beyond bureaucracy? Work organisation in call centres. *International Journal of Human Resource Management, 9*(6), 957–979.

Fumagalli, A. (1997). Aspetti dell'accumulazione flessibile in Italia. In S. Bologna & A. Fumagalli (Eds.), *Il lavoro autonomo di seconda generazione: Scenari del postfordismo in Italia* (pp. 133–170). Milan, Italy: Feltrinelli.

Ghirardi, S., & Murgia, A. (2013). Staging precariousness: The Serpica Naro catwalk during Milan fashion week. *Culture and Organization, 21*(2), 174–196.

Ginsborg, P. (1990). *A history of contemporary Italy: Society and politics, 1943–1988.* London, UK: Penguin.

Ginsborg, P. (2001). *Italy and its discontents: Family, civil society, state: 1980–2001.* London, UK: Penguin.

Gruppo d'inchiesta sulla precarietà e il comune. (2013). *Boll Center n. 1: Bollettino d'inchiesta sui call center calabresi.* Retrieved from http://www.sudcomune.it/site/index.php/9-inchiesta/17-bollettino-n-1

Hardt, M., & Negri, A. (2009). *Commonwealth.* Cambridge, MA: Belknap Press of Harvard University Press.

Huws, U. (2014). *Labor in the global digital economy: The cybertariat comes of age.* New York, NY: Monthly Review Press.

Kinnie, N., Hutchinson, S., & Purcell, J. (2000). 'Fun and surveillance': The paradox of high commitment management in call centres. *The International Journal of Human Resource Management, 11*(5), 967–985.

Knights, D., & McCabe, D. (2003). Governing through teamwork: Reconstituting subjectivity in a call centre. *Journal of Management Studies, 40*(7), 1587–1619.

Knights, D., & Willmott, H. (1989). Power and subjectivity at work: From degradation to subjugation in social relations. *Sociology, 23*(4), 535–558.

Knights, D., & Willmott, H. (1999). *Management lives: Power and identity in work organizations.* London, UK: Sage.

Korczynski, M. (2002). *Human resource management in service work.* New York, NY: Palgrave.

La Repubblica Online. (2006, December 13). Call center Atesia, raggiunto l'accordo: "Entro il 2007 assumeremo 6,500 precari". *La Repubblica Online.*

Lazzarato, M. (2015). *Governing by debt* (J. D. Jordan, Trans.). Los Angeles, CA: Semiotext(e).
Lloyd, A. (2013). *Labour markets and identity on the post-industrial assembly line.* Burlington, VT: Ashgate.
Mattoni, A. (2012). *Media practices and protest politics: How precarious workers mobilise.* Burlington, VT: Ashgate.
Mirchandani, K. (2012). *Phone clones: Authenticity work in the transnational service economy.* Ithaca, NY: ILR Press.
Mosco, V. (2009). *The political economy of communication* (2nd ed.). London, UK: Sage.
Mulholland, K. (2004). Workplace resistance in an Irish call centre: Slammin', scammin', smokin' an' leavin'. *Work, Employment and Society, 18*(4), 709–724.
NIDIL, FISTEL and CPO & Delegazione Sindacale Unitaria. (2005). *A tutti i lavoratori: Finiamola con le strumentalizzazioni.* Retrieved from http://www.slaicobasmilano.org/precariatesia.htm
NIDIL-CGIL. (2007). *Chi siamo.* Retrieved from http://www.eurofound.europa.eu/eiro/2006/06/questionnaires/it0606019q.html
Persichetti, P., & Scalzone, O. (1999). *Il nemico inconfessabile: Sovversione sociale, lotta armata e stato d'emergenza in Italia dagli anni settanta ad oggi.* Rome, Italy: Odradek Edizioni.
Rocker, R. (2004). *Anarcho-syndicalism: Theory and practice* (6th ed.). Edinburgh, Scotland/Oakland, CA: AK Press.
Schuetz, L. (2010). *Country's largest call centre company facing bankruptcy: Workers fight to save 10,000 jobs.* Retrieved from http://www.socialistworld.net/doc/3999
Sciotto, A. (2006a, August 3). Atesia, vanno assunti tutti: Le conclusioni dell'ispettorato sui 3.200 co.co.pro del call center romano. *Il Manifesto.*
Sciotto, A. (2006b, October 6). Call center, un nuovo accordo che frega i cocoprò. *Il Manifesto.*
Sciotto, A. (2006c, December 8). Cos, sciopero al contrario. *Il Manifesto.*
Scott, J. (1985). *Weapons of the weak: Everyday forms of peasant resistance.* New Haven, CT: Yale University Press.
Sewell, G. (1998). The discipline of teams: The control of team-based industrial work through electronic and peer surveillance. *Administrative Science Quarterly, 43*(2), 397–428.
Sewell, G. (2005). Nice work? Rethinking managerial control in an era of knowledge work. *Organization, 12*(5), 685–704.

Standing, G. (2014). *A precariat charter: From denizens to citizens.* London, UK: Bloomsbury.
Tait, V. (2005). *Poor workers' unions: Rebuilding labor from below.* Cambridge, MA: South End Press.
Taylor, P., & Bain, P. (1999). 'An assembly line in the head': Work and employee relations in the call centre. *Industrial Relations Journal, 30*(2), 101–117.
Taylor, P., & Bain, P. (2003). 'Subterranean worksick blues:' Humour as subversion in two call centres. *Organizational Studies, 24*(9), 1487–1509.
Thompson, P., Warhurst, C., & Callaghan, G. (2001). Ignorant theory and knowledgeable workers: Interrogating the connections between knowledge, skills and services. *Journal of Management Studies, 38*(7), 923–942.
TOSCA D1 Inventory report: Italy. (2002). Retrieved from www-it.fmi.uni-sofia.bg/TOSCA/pub/d1/Tosca_D1_IT_final.doc
van den Broek, D. (2004). Globalising call centre capital: Gender, culture and work identity. *Labour & Industry: A Journal of the Social and Economic Relations of Work, 14*(3), 59–75.
Vosko, L. (2005). Precarious employment: Towards an improved understanding of labour market insecurity. In L. Vosko (Ed.), *Precarious employment: Understanding labour market insecurity in Canada* (pp. 3–42). Montreal, QC: McGill-Queen's University Press.
Weeks, K. (2011). *The problem with work: Feminism, Marxism, antiwork politics, and postwork imaginaries.* Durham, NC/London, UK: Duke University Press.
Wright, S. (2002). *Storming heaven: Class composition and struggle in Italian autonomist Marxism.* London, UK: Pluto Press.

7

The Making and Unmaking of the Global Call Centre Workforce

This chapter reflects on the significance of the cases we have explored for the theorization of call centre labour, the practice of call centre organizing, and the envisioning of call centre alternatives. In what follows, I begin by considering the making of the global call centre workforce, or that contested process of class formation I have called, borrowing a concept from autonomist scholars, language put to work. Utilizing call centre conflicts on three continents as my guide, I then offer some observations regarding what this process of "making" has produced, identifying some of the key features marking the composition of the global call centre workforce.

In the last section of the chapter I change registers, moving from the descriptive to the prescriptive in order to describe the possible (and indeed advisable) *unmaking* of the global call centre workforce as it is presently constituted. Here I take managerial attempts to ameliorate call centre work (through "high-involvement" schemes) to task for simply proposing more humane forms of exploitation within an economy that remains marked by pointless and socially harmful forms of work. Instead, beginning from a discussion of work refusal I advance a perspective on call centre labour that imagines a more clearly divergent alternative to these workspaces as they are currently configured. This does not mean the capitalist fantasy of robots replacing workers (although, as we shall see, it could still involve robots replacing workers in some cases) but rather a call centre that is subtracted from the market, with socially progressive applications (including health care, welfare, and rebuilding the demos), that is organized and controlled democratically by those who work within it.

The Real Subsumption of Immaterial Labour in Call Centres

This section draws upon the arguments developed in the book so far in order to theorize the remarkable rise of the global call centre workforce and the linguistic labour it performs. In what follows, I use the concept of immaterial labour as a prism through which to describe the proletarianization generated by the expansion of call centres within the broader communicative turn of capitalism.[1] I suggest the distinctive traits of the call centre labour force are produced out of the *real subsumption of immaterial labour*, a process through which firms have revolutionized their quotidian, interpersonal communication with consumers. I adopt immaterial labour as a counter-concept to that of "knowledge work" developed in the latter half of the twentieth century by liberal-democratic scholars.[2] Unlike knowledge work, immaterial labour references a process of class formation, not professionalization, and emerges from a tradition of labour-allied, feminist, and anti-capitalist scholarship. I suggest that theories of immaterial labour can help us understand the rise of the global call centre workforce and also that an investigation of labour struggles in

---

[1] Dean (2012, p. 75) offers a useful definition of proletarianization as the process "through which capitalism produces, uses up, and discards the workers it needs." For a more comprehensive discussion of this process within capitalism's communicative turn, see Dyer-Witheford (2015).

[2] The work of Vincent Mosco and Catherine McKercher (2008) remains a significant exception to this liberal-democratic tradition in that while retaining the terms *knowledge work* and *information society* it also sees labour relations as divisive and conflictual, characterized by capital on one side and labour on the other.

call centres offers an equally important opportunity to intervene within and refine contemporary discussions of immaterial labour.

Bringing these two areas of inquiry into contact with each other highlights how communicative capitalism is the scene of new forms of exploitation, inequality, and social antagonism. As Jodi Dean (2012, p. 128) suggests, contemporary capitalism increasingly derives its productivity from the expropriation and exploitation of communicative processes. For Dean, communicative capitalism is "the materialization of ideals of inclusion and participation in information, entertainment and communication technologies in ways that capture resistance and intensify global capitalism" (2009, p. 2). I adopt Dean's concept of communicative capitalism to explain the growing *communicativity* of companies across the economy. This communicativity includes an increasingly obligatory "contactability" through which consumers are offered the possibility to get in touch, complain, check their accounts, or order new services as needed. Such promises of connectedness are expensive for companies to make however, and (as argued in Chap. 2) they demand a new kind of workforce in order to follow through on. The cases of New Brunswick and Ireland explored in Chap. 4 clearly illustrate how the communicative bargain offered to the post-Fordist consumer has translated into large-scale regional processes of informational development that have expanded technological infrastructure, restructured education systems, and transformed labour markets.[3] This retooling of economies for the purposes of producing mediated consumer interaction, a process that has occurred in highly diverse settings across the world, has as its ultimate goal the production of a specific kind of labour.

Call centre work can be seen as a paradigmatic example of immaterial labour, or labour which generates an intangible product, such as care, an emotion, communication, a conversation, or knowledge (see Dyer-Witheford & de Peuter, 2009; Hardt & Negri, 2000, 2004, 2009; Lazzarato, 1996). These forms of work were mentioned in passing by Karl Marx (1990, p. 1047) as "non-material production," or, more

---

[3] Huws discusses part of this project of informational development as an educational shift towards "more generic and fast-changing skills linked to the use of information and communication technologies" (2014, p. 48).

specifically, as labour generating a product which is inseparable from the act of production. This description underscores the immediately social and communicative dimension of activities such as a live musical performance, speech therapy, or sex work. Arlie Hochschild (2004, p. 6) pointed to the distinctive feature of such labour when she suggested that "[i]n processing people, the product is a state of mind." This labour of "processing people" draws upon a similarly intangible set of resources. Call centres, for example, certainly require a technological infrastructure for their operation (the fixed and tangible capital of telecom networks, computers, headphones, servers, monitors, etc.), but the vital ingredient for profits within these workspaces is labour which draws on linguistic ability, emotional intelligence, and cultural knowledge. What transpires in call centres, then, is what Christian Marazzi (1999) describes as a characteristic element of post-Fordist labour more broadly: the production of communication by means of communication.

It almost goes without saying that the many activities falling under the conceptual umbrella of immaterial labour are the basic stuff of society's quotidian production and reproduction of itself, including the rearing of children, caring for the elderly, and all forms of education. For this reason, Isabell Lorey (2015) describes these kinds of work as productive of "sociality."[4] These activities have of course traditionally been central to the working lives of women under capitalism, a relationship which feminist-autonomist authors explored through the course of their political struggles in the 1970s (G. Dalla Costa, 2008; M. Dalla Costa & James, 1972; Federici, 2012).[5] Immaterial labour can exist in the formal capitalist economy (a company offering tutoring services) or not (when a parent goes over their child's homework with them), as the case may be. Marx (1990, p. 1048) dismissed such forms of production as insignificant to

---

[4] As Isabell Lorey (2015, p. 75) puts it: "In this tendentially productless mode of production, no material things are manufactured in the classical sense, but socialities do emerge from them." The political theorist describes this work as "the form of labour that is currently becoming hegemonic, one that demands the whole person, is primarily based on communication, knowledge and affect, and becomes visible in a new way as virtuoso labour" (p. 5).

[5] The concept of immaterial labour owes a great (and regularly unacknowledged) debt to feminist discussions of reproductive labour in the home. See Dalla Costa (2008), Dalla Costa and James (1972), and Federici (2012).

capitalism in his day since their incidence in the formal economy was what he characterized as "peripheral," suggesting they weren't worthy of consideration in analyses of capitalism more broadly.[6]

While Marx's conclusion may have made sense in his era, it is unhelpful in ours. Today, these "peripheral phenomena" have become profoundly important to the formal economy. Forms of immaterial labour, from teaching to caring work to cleaning, not only have decisively entered the formal capitalist economy but have become defining features of it. This book has explored one aspect of this shift, describing how capitalism's growing need to at least appear to be responsive to consumers has contributed to the formation of outsourced call centres as a significant new economic sector which depends upon a vast global workforce for the production of its profits. Propelled by privatization, restructuring, and transnationalization, call centre employment involves immaterial labour that has been moved into the thick of waged value creation.

The expanding communicativity of firms across the economy explains *why* language was put to work in call centres on such a massive scale beginning in the 1990s, but it doesn't tell us much about *how* this incorporation of communication into the capitalist economy took place. Marx's discussion of the "formal" and "real" subsumption of labour by capital (1990, pp. 1019–1038) offers a useful way to confront the latter question, since these categories were developed to explain how different types of labour were absorbed by the capitalist economy during its initial expansion. The first phase of this integration, described by Marx as the "formal" subsumption of labour, is marked by the fact that even while existing labour processes are drawn into capital's valourization process, capital tends to leave the worker's labour process "as it finds it" (p. 1021). Marx uses, among others, the example of guild production under feudalism morphing into a shop of handicraft workers employed by a capitalist to

---

[6] "Here the capitalist mode of production occurs only on a limited scale and in the nature of the case it can operate only in certain areas. (I want *the doctor*, not his errand boy). For example, in teaching institutions, the teachers can be no more than wage labourers for the entrepreneur of the learning factory. Such peripheral phenomena can be ignored when considering capitalist production as a whole" (Marx, 1990, p. 1048). See Federici (2012) for an excellent discussion of the limits of Marx's analysis, especially regarding women's reproductive labour in the household.

illustrate this transformation. The labour process mostly stays the same, but the social relation changes significantly.

The next step described by Marx, and one that is more important for our purposes, is the shift towards what he calls a "specifically capitalist" mode of production (p. 1024). Here capital "not only transforms the situations of the various agents of production but actually *revolutionizes* their actual mode of labour and the real nature of the labour process as a whole" (p. 1021, emphasis in original). This describes the passage from the workshop to the factory, in what Marx calls the "real" subsumption of labour. This process involves the application of the division of labour, of technology, and science to the production process in the development of the "social productive powers" of labour. At the same time, for Marx this revolution decrees the definitive deterioration of working conditions, which he describes as characterized by "production in contradiction, and indifference, to the *producer*" (p. 1037, emphasis in original). This indifference to the producer's conditions is a recipe for industrial contestation and conflict.

The making of the global call centre workforce documented in this book has occurred within a passage towards the real subsumption of immaterial labour.[7] As we have seen, this process has propelled the transformation of secretarial, clerical, and other forms of customer service into call centre work.[8] The "callcentreification" (Huws, 2009) of established customer service labour processes represents the culmination

---

[7] I am not suggesting that our era is seeing the real subsumption of *all* forms of immaterial labour—my claim only extends as far as the subject of this book, call centre work. For example, Andrew Ross' discussion of the "industrialization of bohemia" (2004, p. 123) in high tech at the end of the 1990s or Tiziana Terranova's (2004) analysis of the free labour which drives the Internet could be seen as examples of the formal subsumption of communicative, cultural, and technological practices which previously existed largely outside of market relationships. I therefore use real subsumption to describe a process which is ongoing, rather than for the purposes of historical periodization. The Endnotes collective suggest that "[i]f subsumption cannot rigorously apply to historical periods per se, nor to anything beyond the immediate process of production, we must conclude that it is not ultimately a viable category for a periodisation of capitalist history" (2010, para. 47). While I agree with this statement, the collective's dismissal of the concept does not impair its utility for the analysis of the development of specific industries within particular phases of capitalist development. Moreover, as we shall see, the real subsumption of immaterial labour in call centres is part of a broader trend within media and communication industries.

[8] It also transforms sales work into outbound call centre work, although that has not been a key focus of the case studies explored in this book.

of what Harry Braverman documented so clearly in the early 1970s. It also draws on advances he did not live to see, including the application of digital technology for the purposes of surveillance and measurement, the exploitation of declining long distance costs brought about by the privatization and deregulation of telecommunications under neoliberalism, and the rise of global trade agreements. The results of this real subsumption of immaterial labour in call centres are the ones that were detailed by labour process critiques of the late 1990s.[9] The ultimate goal of putting language to work in and through a revolutionized labour process, as I have suggested, is the production of what we could call *abstract communication*, or interpersonal communication that is generic, impersonal, predictable, quantifiable, and therefore amenable to the extraction of value.

The broader reformatting of service work that occurred through the 1990s and 2000s repeated the "internal processes of standardization, fragmentation, and the introduction of a spatial division of labor" that were imposed upon manufacturing industries during the twentieth century (Huws, 2014, p. 95). As an integral part of this restructuring, the introduction of call centre operations constituted "a qualitative break with pre-existing forms of work organization" (Ellis & Taylor, 2006, p. 109). The rationalization of customer service work was primarily the result of companies pushing to liberate themselves from the unionized and/or decently remunerated in-house workforces that used to perform these communicative functions. Far from facilitating the liberation of knowledge workers described by business and management scholars, call centres, as Kolinko puts it, "were and are an attack on the refusal of many office workers to accept a deterioration of their conditions" (2002, section 6.1, para. 1). The companies that arose to provide those services have compressed and rationalized the immaterial labour of customer communication to such an extent that it bears only a dwindling resemblance to the kinds of work it descends from. Call centres are not entirely homogenous, but the work organization and labour processes fashioned within them are undoubtedly distinctive (Ellis & Taylor, 2006, p. 108). This distinctiveness clearly results from the kind of revolution from above that

---

[9] See Chap. 2.

Marx spoke of, occurring precisely in those kinds of occupations he dismissed as marginal and unimportant.

The process of class formation occurring in call centres highlights the growing importance of immaterial labour within capitalist economies globally. Call centres are key to companies across the economy, but they have also become a formidable sector in and of themselves.[10] The global call centre outsourcing market was recently estimated to be worth between $70 and $75 billion (US) (Skand Bhargava & Menzigian, 2015).[11] To give a sense of how this compares to other sectors in the network media industries, this is not far off of the size of the worldwide market for video games in 2014 ($81.5 billion [US]) and nearly double the size of total global box office revenues in 2015 ($38 billion) (McClintock, 2016). Where some critics suggest the concept of immaterial labour is used to "forecast that the economy based on the production of value will fade out of existence" (Amorim, 2014, p. 95), the research carried out on call centres across the world points to quite the opposite process being true—immaterial labour has clearly been integrated within communicative capitalism's production of surplus value. This process, as we have seen, has involved a massive devaluation of work which used to have a more elevated status when performed in-house. If our era offers outsized rewards to the creator of low-value, long-hours jobs (Mason, 2016), then the call centre sector is a paradigmatic example of a growth area within the digital economy, one that has incorporated the human capacity for sociality and put it to work in a distinctive way.

The mass production of customer communication in call centres clearly problematizes simple understandings of the rise of "knowledge work" or "creative labour" as paradigmatic, passionate, and rewarding forms of labour in the digital age. Yet an analysis of call centre work also tempers overstated claims regarding the special status of immaterial labour as a form of work that is not amenable to the kind of scientific management or

---

[10] Marx himself left the door open to the possibility that varieties of work that were inseparable from the act of production could one day become a dynamic sector of the capitalist economy in their own right when he suggested that "for the most part, work of this sort has scarcely reached the stage of being subsumed even formally under capital, and belongs essentially to a transitional stage" (1990, p. 1044).

[11] This figure does not include shared services or global in-house centres.

7 The Making and Unmaking of the Global Call Centre Workforce

disciplinary logics that characterized the Fordist assembly line. While theories of immaterial labour have tended to depict such work as pointing to an increasingly "post-Taylorist" (Lazzarato, 1996) scenario of autonomous work that "cannot be formalized" (Gorz, 2010, p. 8), call centre employment is a striking reminder of just how rationalized and directed immaterial labour can get.[12] Routinization, measure, and managerial command are flourishing in the call centre, a setting where, according to a more fitting observation by Lazzarato (1996, p. 135), "[o]ne *has* to express oneself, one *has* to speak, communicate, cooperate..." Call centre work offers us the most disturbing scenario possible for the famous "general intellect" described by Marx in the *Grundrisse* (1993, original 1858): one in which it is extracted by management, embedded in machines, and imposed through software.[13]

Moreover, call centre workers are only one segment of a vast labouring army of page scanners, warehouse sorters, commercial content moderators, retail employees, and data entry workers which testify to capitalism's ongoing need for highly rationalized forms of work, even in its most cutting-edge, communicative sectors. As such, embedded within communicative capitalism we can observe the logics of a departed regime of accumulation. Not only have these fragments of the Fordist regime become functional, but they are largely indispensable to the digital work environments of our time.[14] As the San Francisco-based collective Processed World predicted at the dawn of post-Fordism: "Offices of the future = More of the same" (Winks, 1981).

---

[12] Michael Hardt and Antonio Negri have also adopted this line of argument: "In general, the hegemony of immaterial labour tends to transform the organization of production from the linear relationships of the assembly line to the innumerable and indeterminate relationships of distributed networks... The central forms of productive cooperation are no longer created by the capitalist as part of the project to organize labour but rather emerge from the productive energies of labour itself" (Hardt & Negri, 2004, p. 113).

[13] In his notebooks for *Capital*, Marx predicted a stage when capitalist society's production and reproduction of itself would no longer depend primarily on physical labour, but on what he called the "general productive forces of the social brain" (1990, p. 694), or, more succinctly, the "general intellect."

[14] As Huws suggests, speaking of Fordism: "Although the death of this period is often proclaimed, we cannot be sure that elements of it will not continue to be or even necessary for capitalism in the future" (2014, p. 34).

The resurfacing of Fordist logics in the digital age is acknowledged repeatedly in the reports of call centre work offered by scholars and labour advocates. One of the earlier critical studies of the call centre suggested the form of managerial control it produces is *chimeric* (Sewell, 1998), a term that references the blending of older and newer forms of command in this workspace where the assembly line is digital, productivity is sought through encouraging workers to have "fun," and surveillance operates through competitive forms of "teamwork." Kiran Mirchandani (2012, p. 23) points to the hybrid nature of the call centre labour process when she notes that workers "are neither traditional blue-collar workers, even though they work in highly repetitive and controlled jobs, nor are they white collar workers engaged in creative knowledge production." In her vivid analysis of women working in offshored informational employment in Barbados, Carla Freeman (2000, p. 42) notes that informatics is "a new realm of work that occupies ambiguous place between traditional 'white'- and 'blue'- collar labour." This ambiguousness causes Jack Qiu (2010) to include call centre employees in the growing "grey-collar workforce" he has documented within China's long boom.

The process of class formation in call centres also reveals the extent to which the imposition of routinized communication from above is an inherently uncertain project, replete with potential contradictions and antagonisms.[15] On the one hand, as the Cátedra Experimental (2007, p. 137) collective found in Argentina, working in a call centre "obliges one to behave like a machine, with submission to a strict metric."[16] The form of worker subjectivity produced out of this condition is aptly described by the collective as "machinic."[17] What the Cátedra's investigation illustrates

---

[15] As Andreas Wittel suggests "... although labour is one of the key constituents for political economists, its contemporary uses suffer from a problematic reduction of labour to an abstract category, which brings about a neglect, and even an exclusion of its more concrete agency- and experience-related aspects" (2004, p. 18). To address this would "situate communication in light of the much-neglected, often-despised, and yet demonstrably resurgent side of the social relation that is capital" (Schiller, 2014, p. 364).

[16] See Mirchandani (2012, p. 31) for an insightful discussion of assessing workers' emotional skills, managing customer anxiety, and the need to judge which troubleshooting tips may generate feelings of incompetence and/or anger among customers.

[17] Such accounts, taken from one of the paradigmatic industries of the digital age, bear an uncanny resemblance to Antonio Gramsci's observation that what had become necessary to the rise of

7 The Making and Unmaking of the Global Call Centre Workforce 223

is how centre operations appropriate the communicative abilities of their workers, but then systematically stifle those capacities in the interest of generating predictable, undifferentiated, and measurable customer communication—in other words, communication that isn't communication. At the same time, in order for such labour to be genuinely productive, as the Cátedra collective further points out, "rather than not putting anything... one puts in intellectual, communicative, and affective capacities" (p. 137)—investments that were not strictly necessary on the assembly line.

As a result, one of the clearest and most constant tensions emerging from research on call centre work is that between the enforced "supremacy of the logic of automation over conversation" (Wolff, 2016, p. 138) on the one hand, and the requirement of affective input by workers on the other. The utterly contradictory nature of this situation means that often, as Simone Wolff finds in the Brazilian context, "dissimulation and tricks must be employed for the improvement of customer service" (pp. 138–139). Accounts of call centre workers being forced to route around the protocols imposed by management in order to actually service the often unpredictable needs of customers are a constant in the literature. Perversely, "this is the only moment when their work demands the kind of inventiveness that distinguishes them from machines" (p. 139).[18]

Here discussions of immaterial labour can make an important contribution to the analysis of such tensions in call centre work. Key to the

---

Fordism was "developing in the worker to the highest degree of automatic and mechanical attitudes, breaking up the old psycho-physical nexus of qualified professional work, which demands a certain active participation of intelligence, fantasy and initiative on the part of the worker, and reducing productive operations exclusively to the mechanical, physical aspect" (1971, p. 302).

[18] I encountered an extreme and humorous example of this otherwise pervasive dynamic in Ireland, where an ex-call centre worker related how he used his detection of management surveillance to know when it was safe to route around the nonsensical scripted interviews he was paid to conduct—until he got caught: "Then I found out how to, how to realize, you know, basically how to know if they are listening to the phone call or not. There would be a little light on the phone, like you know. Or it would say line 287. I didn't realize that before, but I found it out. So that was very welcome. So I used to do my own thing. Now I didn't make a joke out of the whole thing. I just skipped over the parts [of the interview] that I felt are ridiculous in terms asking the same questions repeatedly if the person has said 'no'. So I did that. Then I got caught, you know, not to my own knowledge. They took me aside and said: 'actually, we were listening in that time'. I didn't find out, I mean, I didn't realize. So a supervisor said: 'I am going to rip this up', because I got on with him, one of the guys" (Irish call centre worker, personal communication, July 15, 2009).

concept of immaterial labour has been the claim that those performing it create "an excess of sociability and subjectivity" (Tsianos & Papadopoulos, 2006). Another way to put this observation is to say that those engaged in forms of immaterial labour are never entirely governed by, or identical to, their working conditions. The capacities of call centre workers cannot be completely defined, contained, or captured by the labour process I have documented thus far. This is true of workers in any form of labour under capitalism of course, but to the degree that immaterial labour draws upon and produces sociality, theorists have suggested these emergent labouring subjectivities also tend to exceed the bounds set in their employment by capital (Hardt & Negri, 2009, p. 151).

Among the characteristics theorists ascribe to this "excessive" activity are that it is challenging to elicit, impossible to measure, and troublesome to appropriate with any predictability.[19] In call centres this surplus clearly corresponds to the cultural knowledge, communicative abilities and affect that workers put into and produce out of their interactions over the phone. When the pre-existing linguistic and relational capacities of workforces are fed into the process of communicative production in call centres, when employees are asked to "smile down the line" even as they read from a script, when the worker ignores a useless rule to serve a customer better, then it is this communicative surplus that is being appropriated.[20]

Some workers give this surplus communication freely to their employers, and many more deny it entirely. (We've all been "served" by an employee who is entirely unwilling to lift a finger to help us, or give us even a half-hearted emotional performance in the process.) But a key

---

[19] Hardt and Negri (2009, p. 152) suggest that this excess "does not produce value that can be captured by the individual capitalist," but only as externalities that can benefit capital as a whole (e.g., the rise in value of hip, bohemian neighbourhoods because of the cutting-edge cultures that constitute them). As we shall see, in the specific case of call centre work I disagree with this assessment, suggesting that while it may be difficult, it is not impossible by any stretch.

[20] The goal of capturing this excess in a predictable fashion explains the more recent managerial exhortation in some call centres to "just be yourself"—in other words, bring the *whole* of yourself into the communicative production process, feelings and all, body and soul. As Fleming and Sturdy (2011) point out, "this distraction (involving the 'authentic person') serves the double function of *capturing the sociality of workers* so that more 'authentic' emotional labour performances can be secured" (p. 189, emphasis added).

point made in discussions on immaterial labour is that this excess, when it is not channeled into economically productive activity, can spill over into labour resistance and antagonism. Much of the time it doesn't, of course. But in those moments when call centre workers have resisted their subjection in these high-technology workspaces an opposition between two kinds of communication soon becomes apparent: that which is structured coercively from above and that which is extended outward horizontally, among workers, from below. This communication from below is the clearest manifestation of the interpersonal and collective connections that are produced out of immaterial labour within, against, and beyond the call centre labour process.

One could further suggest (slightly adapting Wolff's point) that the production of this communication from below is actually *the most* creative act the call centre workforce engages in. Just as capital's command in the call centre is innovative, so too has been the refusal, resistance, and collective organization produced by labour. The blend of established and novel forms of conflict surfacing in this new workspace has adapted long-standing labour tactics such as the refusal of work, sabotage, and the strike, but in reinvented forms that are particular to this digital setting.[21] As a means to put pressure on employers, call centre workers in Auckland engaged in "slowpace" dialing, sent spoiled surveys back to clients with "Unite" typed dozens of times in a row in the space provided for the last answer, called into call centres and placed bogus orders during busy times, and even pried keys from keyboards rendering surveys difficult to fill in.[22] In Italy, workers in Palermo stayed on the phone as long as possible by being as helpful as they could with customers and creating digital queues that overloaded switchboards. The Collettivo Precari Atesia and Unite both used flexible strikes to counter the flexibility of their working conditions. Moreover, these forms of resistance have invariably seized upon many of the same communicative skills call centres exist to

---

[21] This is consistent with a broader trend of collective action among precarious workers, as Alice Mattoni observes in the Italian context: "Strikes, pickets and demonstrations continue to exist as means through which precarious workers express their claims at the public level. But they frequently assume different meanings and, also, change some of their traits." This means that the "repertoire of contention" of workers' movements were both "innovated and broadened" (2012, p. 48).

[22] For a discussion of the Unite union, see Chap. 5.

appropriate. Unite's campaign began by drawing on the research skills of workers at the consumer research company Nielsen in a self-polling exercise to identify the issues that were likely to become key to the unionization drive. Unite and the Collettivo Precari Atesia deftly utilized digital media to attack their employer's brands. Unite and the Australian National Union of Workers organized a transnational campaign among workers whose work has them virtually crossing borders every time they put on a headset.

It is difficult to say with much certainty what the impact of labour resistance has been on call centre companies. The sector as a whole is still healthy, and there has been no broad-based movement among call centre workers to organize the industry. But the organizational innovations coming from on high over the last decade give us some insight into how employers are confronting the risks inherent in managing their certainly reluctant, often unfaithful, and occasionally insubordinate call centre workforces. The first response has been an intensification of work. Pervasive within the call centre sector over the last decade has been a steady shift towards "contact centre" functions (incorporating additional communication channels like email and chat) and a more recent expansion towards what has been called "omni-channel" functionality, which allows customers to get in touch with a company via social media or mobile apps. This continual extension of "communicative access and opportunity" (Dean, 2009) for consumers that drives call centres sees companies vying to provide interaction through (and across) all of these channels—with a multitasking customer service agent always available on the other end. In some sectors, there has also been a more decisive move towards "digital enablement," or the downloading of service work to customers via apps and other platforms, which has the long-term effect of expanding the value that can be appropriated from the waged labour force by increasing their productivity.[23]

---

[23] The managerial shift in call centre environments towards encouraging "more traditionally non-work social competencies into the workplace" (Fleming & Sturdy, 2011, p. 178) can also be seen as part of the broader effort to secure managerial control. The "just be yourself" version of normative control by management that is detailed by Fleming and Sturdy seemingly aims to personalize customer service interaction, encouraging customer service agents to "have fun" when they're on the phone. Nonetheless, the authors (p. 189) point out that "the approach does not simply detract from, but actually reinforces, control."

7 The Making and Unmaking of the Global Call Centre Workforce

Perhaps more significantly, seizing on virtual call centre software and expanding broadband capacity, over the past decade call centre operations have continued to experiment with home-based customer contact work. This move allows companies to save on overhead but also to avert worker organization. Once again the Synovate case offers valuable insights.[24] After Unite's successful organizing drive and the company's subsequent purchase by Ipsos, the firm moved the bulk of its New Zealand market research jobs to home-based call centre work. Job ads announced the company's need for "casual home-based interviewers" (Ipsos, 2014). Unite organizer Omar Hamed pointed out the stakes of this labour process transformation within the industry:

> ... there's a move in market research online or to home based workers, right? You don't want a pool of workers sitting there that are union organizing and coming to work, put people out in their houses right? And this is the thing, technology is developing so that people can be sitting at home, doing home work, right? When people didn't have broadband internet connections in their home you couldn't do this. Now people can sit at home, and the broadband internet will put their answers into the company's machines, but the cost of running these big call centers, lighting, and leasing big buildings, and big computers ... goes away, hundreds of thousands of dollars that the company can save. And also, gets rid of all the unions. (personal communication, May 6, 2011)

If the shift towards call centres during the 1990s dissolved and reconstituted office labour across the world, here is a clear case of capital reorganizing its labour process as a response to political recomposition in the call centre. Such is the cut and thrust of the relationship between labour and capital, one that we have tracked in call centres, across borders, and now into workers' homes. While it is early to say whether the move towards virtual call centres is becoming a dominant trend (or whether it will be overtaken by automation), by using the conflictuality which triggered the restructuring as an entry point through which to investigate the social relations marking these workspaces we can clearly see how call

---

[24] For a discussion of the Synovate case, see Chap. 5.

centre work embodies neither the celebratory fantasy presented by knowledge worker theorists nor the largely accomplished domination of labour denounced by Harry Braverman's heirs. Carrying out research into these customer relations factories from the perspective of labour resistance offers the possibility of moving beyond a narrow focus on labour's sociological composition, or the objective characteristics of the labour process and the workforce within it. Utilizing the perspective of resistance allows us to see more clearly how the connective, creative capacities of immaterial labour can be submitted to the production of value by capital, or utilized to fight back against the labour conditions imposed in call centres, or even act as a trigger for employers to restructure and decompose worker organization. I end this chapter by discussing the subjectivation of call centre workers and the (possible and indeed advisable) unmaking of call centre work in its current form. Before this, I offer a few observations regarding the emergent make-up of the global call centre workforce and the lessons that we might draw from this composition for the purposes of expanding labour resistance and collective organization.

The Composition of Call Centre Labour: Feminization, Precarity, Mobility

If communicative capitalism produces an inordinately large number of what David Graeber (2013) calls "bullshit jobs," this book's gambit is that inquiring into the resistance such jobs generate from workers will offer insights as to how labour might regain the initiative from employers and thereby improve the lives of those who are forced to perform such work for a living. While the individual, covert and informal varieties of "everyday resistance" (Scott, 1985) that characterize employee responses to the call centre are critical and not to be underestimated, it will likely take something more to decisively overturn the disciplinary and exploitative conditions characterizing contemporary call centre work.[25] Driven by this rationale, the research project described in these pages has focussed on

---

[25] For a discussion of covert and informal resistance in the call centre, see Chap. 3.

moments of collective organization by workers where a significant degree of conflict and at least some success for workers was achieved. A retrospective study of these conflicts provides valuable insight into the "everyday" forms of resistance which preceded and prepared them. But overt struggles are also important in that they point to the future. As a rupture in the symbolic order marking normal power relations among employers and employees, such clashes offer us a view not only of how things are, but of how they could be.

Autonomist scholars have historically been oriented towards the creation of new forms of direct action, collective organization, and non-capitalist ways of living, a project grounded upon ongoing inquiry into the ever-changing "composition" of labour (Cleaver, 2000; Dyer-Witheford, 1999; Wright, 2002). Foregrounding the struggle between labour and capital in their analysis, autonomists have set out from the assumption that while it is continually decomposed by capital's attacks, labour emerges recomposed in a form that poses revived threats to capital's rule. The organization of work, and thus the expression, forms, and prospects of collective organization by workers, are constituted within a dynamic, ongoing, and mutual recomposition of labour and capital, a conflict autonomist historians have traced back through the formation of an industrial proletariat, the development of pirate communities, witch-hunts, and revolts against the enclosures.[26]

Autonomist interest in the composition of labour has contested the detached sociological analysis of social movements, advocating instead for the production of knowledge out of what Gigi Roggero (2011, p. 137) calls the "irreducible partiality of perspective." The project of understanding labour's composition through worker inquiry or co-research is therefore always directed towards uncovering "possibilities for resistance and organization," as Jamie Woodcock (2013) described the goals of his research at a UK call centre. There are several compelling reasons for applying a "compositional" form of analysis to call centres. Not only do these workspaces employ many millions of workers across the world and provide one of its fastest-growing forms of employment, but they are

---

[26] See Linebaugh and Rediker (2000), and Federici (2004).

emblematic of processes that have characterized the broader transformation of work in communicative capitalism. Call centres present a significant and transnational cross-section of the workforce, a new composition of labour, and a critical testing ground for labour's ability to adapt and reorganize in a digital economy (Guard, Steedman, & García-Orgales, 2007; Holst, 2008).

When considered alongside other research, the cases of labour conflict described in this book suggest three primary observations regarding the emergent composition of the global call centre workforce. As I note next, these qualities are important not only because they are consistent across the cases investigated in this book, but because they align with broader trends surfacing in the workforce. These observations are offered with some caution given the sheer size of the workforce and the diversity of the regions in which call centres have been established,[27] but the characteristics that are identified do tend to cut across remarkably different contexts.[28] Given these common traits, this section of the chapter makes the case that those seeking to organize among one of the fastest-growing jobs of the last few decades would do well to design campaigns tailored to a workforce that is *female, precarious, and mobile.*

---

[27] Workerist theorists were always, as Sergio Bologna has observed, attentive to the differences among sectors of the working class (2014), and it is certainly not my goal to efface these. Gurgaon Workers News (2012, para. 25), for example, underscore the fractured composition of call centre labour in India when they note that "[a]lthough the experiences of workers in English speaking call centers seem fairly homogeneous, the experiences and conditions in the wider sector are not. We see main lines of segmentation within the sector: between in-house call centers and outsourced processes; between English speaking international call centers and Hindi speaking domestic ones; between call centre agents and 'service workers' (cleaning, driving); between the call centre workers and the other industrial workers situated in the same industrial zones."

[28] Carrillo Rowe, Pérez, and Malhotra (2013, p. 148) reiterate the concern of post-colonial theorists about universalizing claims made by Western scholars regarding populations that are differentially included in processes of globalization. In what follows, I aim to take this concern seriously by eschewing broad and unjustified claims, or noting exceptions to them. At the same time, I feel it is important to make a distinction between the universalizing logic of capitalism and the political goal of establishing commonalities in labour's composition across different settings. While not losing view of the differentially situated power relations of subjects, to abandon a search for commonalities or affinities among different groups is to condemn oneself to a kind of political paralysis which only ensures that the universalizing logic of capital remains unchallenged. To put it differently, the common and the universal are not the same thing. My interest and focus are on the former, not the latter.

Female The inquiries at the heart of this book unmistakably point to the feminization of labour as a defining quality marking the composition of call centre work. In fact, it is impossible to think of call centre work outside of the gendered relations that constitute it. If the feminization of labour under post-Fordism is understood as a double process involving growing participation by women in the waged workforce and the expansion of the formal economy to include jobs that are female-associated (Morini, 2007), then call centres are one of the clearest examples of this trend. Most estimates put the info-service workforce at somewhere around 70% female (Holman, Batt, & Holtgrewe, 2007), and this trend is borne out in a striking variety of contexts. As Carrie Buchanan (2002, p. 52) noted in her early analysis of the populations contributing to the emergent Atlantic Canadian workforce, "the call centre has become a prime example of the growing category of feminized labour on the periphery: a majority of women perform the work, and those men who do it are often young, gay, or otherwise marginalized." Speaking from the Indian context, Carrillo Rowe, Pérez and Malhotra (2013, p. 119) also situate what they refer to as the "pink-collar, service-oriented labor" within the "larger trend of feminized global labour." Carla Freeman's analysis of informatics work in the Caribbean causes her to suggest that what emerges from her study is

> not strictly a proletarian figure, and certainly not a bourgeois one, but instead a blurry category of feminine worker who is created by corporate prescriptions and who chooses this realm of work much because of possibilities generated by its ambiguous position in the industrial/services hierarchy. (2000, p. 55)

While it is only a very small sample of a very large workforce, women clearly made up the majority of call centre workers in each case I investigated. Yet the feminization of labour is hardly an egalitarian process, as these workplaces provided a sharp reminder of the gendered power relations marking waged work more broadly. To give one example, at Aliant women made up most of the call centre workforce but the division of labour was segmented by gender, with men being over-represented in more highly prized jobs such as tech support. Research in Ireland, Italy,

Atlantic Canada, and New Zealand also all confirmed that as one moves up in the call centre hierarchy, floor managers are much more likely to be male.

The over-representation of women in the call centre sector in general and at its lowest levels in particular highlights the ambivalent condition women are faced with in their experience of call centre work. On the one hand, as Freeman (2000) noted in her early study of informatics work in Barbados, call centre work can give some women the sense that a new and more autonomous working identity is possible. On the other, call centre work vividly demonstrates how, as autonomist feminists warned in the 1970s, entry into the waged workforce hardly represents a panacea for women, but rather institutes and consolidates new forms of patriarchal and class relationships.[29] As a paradigmatic form of immaterial labour, call centre work draws on qualities traditionally associated with women's reproductive labour in the household, including caring work, emotional labour, and communicativity. The strong connection and overlap between waged work in call centres and reproductive labour in the household was most clearly demonstrated in Italy, where married women who add a day shift to their domestic work as a means to supplement the family income make up a sizeable slice of the call centre workforce. Moreover, despite their participation in waged work, women still perform the bulk of housework, making the prospect of career progression even more unlikely. In my own research, the contradiction between the working rhythms of the call centre and the productive and reproductive demands on women's lives were obvious in each of the settings I investigated, but they were most starkly demonstrated by the intensely precarious employment at Atesia, where there was no maternity leave or sick days and getting pregnant could mean losing your job. Moreover, the gains from the labour struggles were not shared equally in that instance: despite the successful battle fought by the Collettivo Precari Atesia and the stabilization agreement that was reached in the Italian call centre sector, company management soon ushered in unilateral

---

[29] See Federici (2012).

7 The Making and Unmaking of the Global Call Centre Workforce 233

changes to workers' schedules that were irreconcilable with the childcare obligations of four female workers and resulted in their dismissal.

Just as significantly, my research confirmed the disjuncture between the feminized composition of call centre labour and that of trade unions working in this field, since the mostly male trade union has not adapted to this transformation. In the cases I have described, women have taken leading roles within the organizing, but this has not translated into their entry into established trade union structures, which remain largely dominated by men.[30] The main exception to this was the Collettivo Precari Atesia, a shop-floor, self-organized union in which, there being no formal hierarchy, women participated on the same footing as men. The gendered composition of call centre labour should therefore be seen not only as a key reason to attune labour campaigns and organizing to women's issues but as an important opportunity to transform unions by feminizing them.[31]

Precarious When the Cátedra Experimental collective first connected with call centre employees in Rosario, Argentina, in order to carry out their inquiry, the workers told them about a rumour they had heard: the call centre was soon going to leave the city. As the Cátedra notes, "[w]ithout any prior planning, having barely begun the conversation, we found a problem with which to open a dialog: work in conditions of total instability" (Cátedra Experimental sobre Producción de Subjetividad, 2007, p. 134). In four countries and across three continents,

---

[30] When asked why so many of the union local members the Communications, Energy and Paperworkers Union had arranged for me to meet with were men I received this response: "[When we received your request for interviews] I think we went to a lot of the shop stewards, and there's not many women shop stewards—they're mostly men" (D. Gallant-Vautour, personal communication, April 5, 2006).

[31] There are certainly cases where an attention to gender politics acted as a catalyst for labour organizing. For example, the promotion of gender equality and workplace safety became a major campaign issue for UNITES (Union for IT Enabled Services Professionals) in India. As Stevens and Mosco (2010, p. 51) note: "UNITES has attracted public attention by bringing to light issues pertaining to inequality and exploitation in the IT/ITES sectors. One of its earliest initiatives was a Forum organised in response to the murder of Pratibha, which led to a more general campaign to draw attention to sexual harassment in the industry. After this incident occurred, Shekhar (as cited in Stevens and Mosco, 2010) asserts, 'that's when people actually started to talk to us and started looking us up, and . . . immediately there was some kind of connect between the workers, the public in general.'"

my research repeatedly confirmed that work in conditions of total instability is one of the constitutive characteristics of call centre labour and a key dimension of the workforce's composition. This precarity, or what we can define as the material and existential insecurity brought on by the flexible management of the workforce under post-Fordism (Brophy & de Peuter, 2007), is also a dimension of call centre work which unites it with the experience of workers across the economy, including interns, part-timers, and temp agency workers. As the labour researcher Guy Standing (2014, p. 1) suggests in his discussion of the "precariat," this group is "characterized by chronic insecurity" and "detached from old norms of labour and the working class." The global call centre workforce and the precariat are not identical, but they certainly overlap and constitute one other in significant ways.

Just as in the broader economy, manifestations of precarity in the call centre are many. They're captured well by the account of Laurence Peterson, who has shared his experience working at Computershare. As Peterson relates, the company

> not only relied on temps to do the ordinary, if to me, anyway, highly challenging and extremely stressful work, for a far-below median wage with no benefits; indeed, they relied on temps to supervise such work at the same rate of pay and again, with no benefits, or even the most basic workplace protections. (Peterson, 2015, para. 58)

Workforce flexibility was inscribed so completely into the company's operations that in addition to having temps supervising temps, it had three temp agencies housed on its premises (Peterson, 2015). While the example is an extreme one, precarious employment relationships—including temp work, part-time, self-employment, zero-hours, and even freelance contracts—are clearly constitutive of this form of work. The biggest complaint call centre workers in New Zealand had was the lack of control over their zero-hours, part-time schedules, which could see them commute to work only to be sent home after an hour-long shift. At Atesia, workers navigated a seemingly endless series of temporary contracts which acted as a constant reminder of how tenuous their employment was.

But the experience of labour precarity in the call centre is more widespread than a simple discussion of the contractual arrangements within these workspaces would suggest. The high level of worker turnover in the industry, even among full-time, permanent workers, is another sign of the tenuous nature of call centre employment. Moreover, the transferability of such work ensures that the experience of precarity extends to virtually everyone working in a call centre. After all, call centres are not only a cause but also (and more significantly) an effect of labour precarization. As we have seen, the rise of call centre work has been part and parcel of the restructuring of office labour under post-Fordism, through which companies sought to rid themselves of their dependence upon in-house, stable, and unionized workforces. As a result the potential for work transfer, whether it is from in-house to outsourced operations or among outsourced operations, is present in the very DNA of the call centre labour process. Thus, even when the Steelworkers successfully organized the Omega call centre in Sudbury, Ontario, Andrew Stevens (2014, p. 131) quickly pointed out that the biggest danger facing the incipient bargaining unit was the precarity of the outsourced call centre market.

The pervasive sense of insecurity these conditions produce in workers gives employers formidable clout. As the Argentine Telephone Workers and Employees' Federation (*Federación de Obreros y Empleados Telefónicos de la República Argentina*), or FOETRA puts it, "[t]he core of the problem of precarious employment for call center workers is the power that those companies have over the working conditions of their staff as a result of the process of flexibilization of labor" (Mirá quién habla, 2010).

On the other hand, however, the precarious conditions marking call centre work have also been harnessed by the campaigns described in this book and others, sometimes to devastating effect for employers. The point of departure for the Call Center Offensive campaign described by Kolinko (2002, section 6.3.c, para. 16) "was casualisation, read: the break-up of what has so far been the normal work relation (35 or 40 hour week, permanent contracts) and the creation of so-called 'a-typical' work contracts (temp work, limited contracts, part-time, trainee-contracts, pseudo self-employment ...).'' Unite's organizing in New Zealand has worked through an open-shop model of trade unionism, making precarious employment and zero-hour contracts a key plank of its union strategy and labour actions. Unite and Collettivo Precari Atesia both turned the precariousness imposed on workers back against the employer by developing flexible strikes. In India, the Young Professionals collective mobilized around the precarity affecting the industry on the subcontinent, arguing that funds equal to 2% of corporate profits should be kept aside as a contingency fund for retraining and compensation in the event that companies pack up and leave (Stevens & Mosco, 2010). Perhaps the most powerful instance of workers seizing upon precarious employment as a catalyst for aggregation was the Collettivo Precari Atesia, which turned the succession of short-term contractual agreements they were forced to endure into a public relations black eye for Atesia management and the Italian state.

Moreover, as precarious employment operates as a means to segment workforces from one another, it becomes increasingly critical to focus on organizing *across* those divisions, including those separating in-house and outsourced employees, workers employed at the same company but on different kinds of contracts, and workers at one branch of a company's transnational operations from those at another. Here my inquiries highlighted the limits of an established union's strategy, the Communications, Energy and Paperworkers Union of Canada (now Unifor), that defended unionized in-house workers but neglected the opportunity to organize precarious workers in the outsourced call centre industry—a decision which only made it more vulnerable to outsourcing.[32] On the other hand, members of the Italian rank-and-file union Cobas whose members worked in-house at Telecom Italia offered a laudable example of organizing across the divisions of post-Fordist outsourcing when they (along with other social movements) picketed Atesia for years in the hopes

---

[32] The Colectivo Situaciones points to the same problem encountered during their inquiry in Argentina: "When a union 'takes charge of a struggle,' the different labor sectors that belong to the same company become represented by that union, which goes on to manage the conflict always in relation to the company itself (the employer), without transversalizing the dynamic beyond those limits, isolating, for example, the operators in other call centers that are developing, in a more or less apparent way, similar struggles" (2006, p. 42).

that a committee would be formed at the call centre. They initiated this organizing because, according to labour organizer Domenico Teramo, they understood very clearly that outsourced work was "the other side of the coin" of the stable, full-time employment they benefitted from (D. Teramo, personal communication, May 11, 2007).

Mobile The third feature defining the composition of call centre work I identify is that of *mobility*, a term which refers to three interrelated characteristics marking the workforce: transience through different call centre and service sector jobs, labour migration (both virtual and physical), and the detached working subjectivities that do not conform to the more stable occupational identities that were cemented under Fordism.

The composition of the call centre labour force is profoundly marked by a nomadic approach to employment, often featuring short stints at call centres before quitting or being fired. In Chap. 3, we surveyed the tremendously high levels of turnover, or "churn," characterizing the sector. With the median annual attrition rate in call centres being estimated by one study at one out of every five workers per year (Holman et al., 2007), the workforce is in a continual process of being made and unmade, as workers constantly exit and enter the revolving doors of this communicative workplace. The Colectivo Situaciones describe the dizzying nature of this process as they encountered it in Buenos Aires:

> The rotation of girls and boys from one call center to another is rapid. Because you can't handle being there for much time and because the projects in the call centers open and close like the eyes of someone hallucinating. Even though many times the operators are legally contracted, when they close the offices they don't pay severance because they reassign employees to other projects. (2006, p. 32)

Much of this turnover, as has been noted above, can be seen as a manifestation of one of the most widespread forms of resistance in the face of unendurable labour conditions—quitting. As the Colectivo relate,

> [t]here is much desertion after collecting the first paycheck: after verifying the "broken promises" or the "rewards and punishments" that the wage

includes. The smile of the "always alert" worker contorts into a grimace upon realizing what she is paid for such a vital gesture. (2006, p. 32)

Even in the newly unionized Omega call centre in Sudbury, Ontario, as one shop steward related to Andrew Stevens (2014, p. 128), the workforce was still unlikely to stick around to fight for better conditions on the job because "[t]hey've gone on to other jobs. It's not the fact that they're not committed, it's that they're young, and in a call center you don't want to be there for the rest of your life, that's for sure." In India, the workforce's mobility has reportedly become so endemic that employers have collectively—if unsuccessfully—brought in measures seeking to curtail it (Carrillo Rowe et al., 2013, p. 185) such as pacts to not hire workers away from one another. The workers I interviewed over the years confirmed the finding that, as the call centre researchers Vincenzo Fortunato and Rita Palidda (2012, p. 13) suggest, "[i]n the perceptions and aspirations of those entering it, the call centre seems to take on the semblance of a job in transit."

The workforce's lack of fixedness is compounded by the call centre labour process, which as post-colonial scholars have underscored often involves a kind of virtual migration across space, borders and cultures. In addition to this virtual projection of call centre worker's subjectivity, there is also significant evidence of how the more traditional, physical form of migration marks the makeup of the workforce. As Martina Tazzioli (2013) notes, an online search of job offers in Tunisia reveals dozens of announcements in Italian for call centres in Tunis, Sousse, and Sfax, promising a monthly salary of around 900 dinars to Italians escaping the financial downturn, unemployment, and high cost of life on the peninsula. This cosmopolitan call centre composition can be found in many parts of the world where workers are able to take advantage of (or seek refuge in) labour mobility. Thomas Hastings notes that in Glasgow, Scotland, call centres serving pan-European markets often rely upon a migrant division of labour (Hastings, 2011, p. 120). Dublin also features a highly transnational workforce, often working within different divisions of the same call centre.

A broader, transnational analysis of this workspace highlights the multifaceted nature of its labour force's mobility. To be sure, the kinds

7 The Making and Unmaking of the Global Call Centre Workforce

of mobility that are available to call centre employees are distributed differently according to the privilege that citizenship confers, with workers in the global south mostly limited to virtual forms of migration across borders. Yet when all of these elements are considered together, the emergent call centre workforce can still be seen as a powerful example of how

> [t]he composition of postindustrial labor-power is characterized by a forced mobility and flexibility, deprived of fixed contracts and guaranteed employment, having to migrate from one job to another in the course of a career and, at times, in the course of a working day, and in many cases having to migrate great distances across the city and across continents for work. (Hardt & Negri, 2009, p. 289)

Lastly, the general lack of fixedness outlined here has profound effects on the subjectivity of workers. Most significantly (as we saw in Chap. 6), the mobile nature of call centre labour manifests in a workforce defined by its *lack* of identification with the employer or the work (Huws, 2009), and even in instances where there is some attachment—perhaps due to the modern, informational image of the call centre industry projected by employers and the state (see Freeman, 2000)—it is highly ambivalent. It is in this light that we can perhaps better understand management schemes to make call centre work seem "fun," or even academic discourses that aim to sell this form of employment as "knowledge work."

What's more, the unfixed nature of call centre labour and the workforce's reluctance to identify with the form of employment has serious implications not only for employers, but for established trade unions. At a very basic level, as Jack Qiu (2010, p. 89) notes in the Chinese context, mobility in call centre employment significantly affects "labour solidarity patterns,"[33] perpetually troubling attempts to organize this peripatetic

---

[33] Qiu (2010, p. 89) elaborates further: "The worst situation, in terms of labour organising, is in the emerging sectors discussed in the previous section: call centre employees, SMS or network authors and online game gold farmers. To most of these, the idea of trade unions for grey-collar knowledge workers would sound outlandish because they have never heard of such a thing; even the official ACFTU doesn't see the necessity to organise them collectively, and, because their jobs are indeed mostly transient, consisting of short-term employment created in response to rapid market changes and the constant industrial restructuring of each of these new sectors."

workforce. As the Colectivo Situaciones (2006) observed in Argentina, however, there are also more deep-seated contradictions between the mobile nature of the labour force and the rootedness of the established union movement:

> ... the very premise of the union—to assert the identity of the worker as such—comes undone because of the dynamic of the call centers. Unionism foments localization as an achievement and stability as a benefit. This does not seem to be an evident premise in the call centers: the mobility of those who are employed in these places makes it so that their most common feature is to always be temporary workers. (p. 41)

As the Cátedra Experimental sobre Producción de Subjetividad suggests, "if the classical—Fordist—syndicalism was configured on the basis of the stability of workers in their jobs, their jobs also constituted a point central to the political strategy" (2007, p. 137). Faced with a new workforce composition in which mobile subjectivities are displaying a clear reluctance to identify with their jobs, we can begin to see why established trade unions are having such difficulties in call centres.[34]

While any union organizer will tell you that labour's lack of fixedness is a serious challenge for organizing, it may also present an opportunity. The case of the Collettivo Precari Atesia offers an example of the construction of a powerful counter-subjectivity out of an endemic *detachment* from the job and the firm. Seen from a different perspective, labour's unfaithfulness and resulting mobility creates opportunities for workers to carry the

---

[34] It is also true that in some cases established unions haven't done themselves many favours with respect to their efforts to organize call centre workers. Consider Jamie Woodcock's (2013) account of his attempt to contact a trade union in London: "My attempt to build some kind of organization began by joining a trade union. I emailed over my application and did not receive a reply for a few weeks. Eventually I got an email confirming my membership, with the telephone number for a branch organizer. After missing each other a few times, due to the nature of shift work, I finally made contact with the organizer. She informed me that I had been added to a conglomerated geographical branch that covered a wide area and number of different employment types. Unfortunately I had missed the last branch meeting a few days ago, which had been cancelled anyway for low attendance. I was shocked to find out that the next meeting would not take place for three months. After a brief discussion the organizer offered to pay for a room in a pub near the workplace to host a meeting. She also offered to mail membership forms; three arrived in a handwritten envelope a few days later" (para. 44).

seeds of discontent and organization from one call centre to the next. One of the interviews I did in Ireland, where the call centre workforce is often multinational and frequently transient, was with an Italian worker who, led by labour sympathies brought from his country, was organizing his Italian, Spanish, French, and Irish colleagues, divided up as they were into divisions of the same company. Labour's mobility may, as the Colectivo Situaciones observes, change the parameters of union struggle, but it also creates an opening, most notably the chance to connect

> the possibilities of protest with the immediate experience of urban life, in which this mobility finds more affinity with an everyday life made of fragments, habituated to uncertainties and the possibility to abandon a place when the exhaustion and disgust are too much. (Colectivo Situaciones, 2006, p. 41)

The mobility of labour may in fact point to the utility of a kind of "nomadic" unionism, of the sort that Unite has deployed within the New Zealand service industry. The churn characterizing the Kiwi union's membership has already transported revolt from workplace to workplace, and even from sector to sector. A clear sign of this came when the union's Calling for Change campaign reaped the benefits of their previous organizing in the fast-food industry (in the Supersize My Pay campaign). Not only did organizers discover that a number of workers in call centres had moved on from the fast-food industry, but some of these workers had been a part of the Supersize campaign. This realization seems to have spurred some innovation in Unite's strategy as well. As Matt McCarten put it, "the workers move from one call centre to another, so you follow the workers" (personal communication, May 11, 2011). This model has notable precedents, recalling the Wobbly strategy of organizing the workers, not the boss. When we met in New Zealand, McCarten reflected on the value of having something like a lifetime membership, which could accompany workers from one job to the next and through periods of employment, unemployment, and underemployment. This kind of loose, non-workplace-based organizing model would closely mirror the composition of an unfaithful, mobile workforce. And while the organizational challenges associated with developing such a model should not be downplayed, in the case of call centres it would seem to be tremendously well suited.

Another Call Centre Is Possible: Beyond "High-Commitment" Work

> A new social subject emerging out of the condition of immaterial labour can be only this one which does not pertain to its own position in the cycle of production, but one which challenges its identity by working on its immanent, situated and embodied experiences. (Tsianos & Papadopoulos, 2006, para. 8)

Call centre executives dream of conversational bots. For many years now, the Holy Grail of companies in the sector has been a call centre run on artificial intelligence (AI), with customer communication provided by "chat-based bots" instead of humans. The automation of call centre work offers capital a tantalizing alternative to the cost and effort associated with shaping, disciplining, and supporting an often unpredictable labour force. Robots, it's hoped, won't quit, slack, or organize collectively in the same way that humans have. Dispensing with what one industry observer recently called "your most expensive touchpoint" (Burns, 2016, para. 4) is such an enticing option for call centre company executives that a cutting-edge industry has been constructed around the goal of expanding call centre automation, drawing on advances in AI, database mining, and computer-processing speed.[35] If white-collar workers "crept silently into

---

[35] By 2005, businesses were already spending over a billion USD a year on speech recognition telephone systems (Yellin, 2009, p. 76). Companies like SmartAction are moving beyond the more elementary interactive voice response systems towards offering clients "artificial general intelligence and natural language capabilities ... at less than quarter of the cost of live agents" (2013, para. 6). Not only is the labour of frontline customer service agents being targeted for automation, but the responsibilities of managers are also being encroached upon as research in the area has pursued the goals of automated surveillance and management functions. Enghouse Interactive's Quality Management Suite (QMS) will "bring more emotional intelligence to bear in their interactions with customers" with the launch of a new "real-time soft evaluator capability" (Enghouse Interactive, 2016, para. 9) in the latest version of its software, which can "assess live calls to identify incidences of cross-talking, changes in conversational tone, speech ratio balance, speech volume and the stress levels of both parties" (para. 2).

the world" as C. Wright Mills (2002) claimed, then automation has the potential to usher them out of it.

The imposition of the call centre labour process documented in this book could therefore be a prelude, some suggest, to the disappearance of call centre work altogether. History shows that once labour has been simplified, the substitution of machines for human work becomes increasingly possible, and that this process has been among the tools through which capital has sought to decrease its dependence on labour (Bellamy Foster, 1998, p. xix).[36] Widely cited reports have suggested that up to half of all jobs could be under threat of being replaced by robots (Frey & Osborne, 2013), and one needs to look no further than the telecommunications industry to find a very similar sector with a well-established history of human labour substituted by technology. The application of this process in call centres, especially when one considers the interactive voice response menus that are already a consolidated part of routing us through our communications with organizations, is already relatively advanced. At the same time, the seeming inevitability of this process is also being questioned by observers. The kind of tacit knowledge and emotional intelligence needed to guide someone through a panicked 911 call seems at the very least a long way off from being implanted into computers. Some in the industry have suggested that the cost savings offered by machines would only be gobbled up by the need to pay for much more expensive data engineers, speech scientists, and AI experts (Anadkat, as cited in Wade, 2016). But even a less extreme scenario of steadily advancing automation, which seems likely, will put significant pressure on the customer service workforce.[37]

In order to avoid dwelling on capital's fantasy scenario for frontline customer service, however, I end this book by discussing a different

---

[36] As David McNally (1993) has pointed out, mechanization has often been "the only way to break working-class resistance by establishing a rhythm of production materially embodied in the machine rather than in the skills of the labourers" (p. 39).

[37] As Laurence Peterson (2015) suggested in his account of employment within a call centre, "as long as the ranks of the underemployed and unemployed remain quite elevated, and the cost of labor-saving technology stays extremely low, existing workforces can continue to be squeezed to meet demand, especially as workplace protections continue to stagnate and quality employment opportunities to shrink" (2015, para. 64).

possibility for the "unmaking" of the call centre workforce—one that is initiated from below by workers rather than imposed from above by management. This vision of an alternative to call centres as they are currently configured imagines a communicative workplace that is subtracted from the market, with socially progressive applications (including health care, emergency services, welfare, research, and rebuilding democratic practices), and that is organized and controlled democratically by those who work within it. The model (although that is likely too strong a term) would certainly retain some of the elements characterizing contemporary call centres, but those working there would by necessity have overturned the process of proletarianization documented in this book.

Discussions of how call centres could be transformed by and for their cybertarian workforces are few and far between in academic scholarship.[38] Where management scholars have discussed working conditions in call centres changing for the better, their vision has been limited to the goal of injecting more participatory, "high-involvement" or "high-commitment" management practices into the existing labour process in order to make it more bearable for workers (Batt & Moynihan, 2002; Kinnie, Hutchinson, & Purcell, 2000). According to this model, firms dedicated to "mass customization" of communicative labour (as opposed to the "mass-production" model) adopt "a set of management practices that invest in the skills and the abilities of the workforce, design work so that employees have opportunities to use those skills effectively, and create incentives that reward effort and commitment" (Batt & Moynihan, 2002, p. 15). The concept of high commitment is somewhat nebulous, but one of the better-known studies investigating this strategy in call centres underscores that while it is "an investment" made by management with an "uncertain payback," its costs can be "minimized" by productivity and performance improvements (Kinnie et al., 2000, p. 76). Happier workers, it is hoped, work better and harder, increasing productivity and profits.

Efforts to consider improved scenarios for call centre work are laudable, but the "high-involvement" model offers a problematic and deeply

---

[38] The very fact that the subject of what a call centre might become is virtually never discussed in the academic literature underscores the degree to which scholars have been confined within a discussion of what is, rather than allowing themselves to imagine and advocate for what ought to be.

stunted vision of social change. First, it runs counter to the dominant mass-production model implemented by management in most call centres, which obeys the far simpler logic of providing the greatest amount of customer communication at the lowest possible cost. Even where they are introduced by call centre firms, such practices are highly unlikely to result in the kinds of discretion afforded to elite "knowledge workers", as Callaghan and Thompson (2002) have suggested. "High-involvement" practices are also insidious, Fleming and Sturdy (2011, p. 178) found, in that they can distract workers from boring work by injecting "non-work" themes into the labour process, but also because they offer a devious way of capturing "the emotional and social skills of workers" so as to ensure the ideal performance of emotional labour. What's more, the underlying assumption of this literature is that high-participation schemes are only "economically viable" (Batt & Moynihan, 2002, p. 15) if they add to productivity, and hence to profits. In other words, that profit is the single most important objective in operating a call centre is seen as entirely natural and unproblematic. Finally, this literature only seems to accord any kind of meaningful agency to management. Any adoption of high-participation schemes, it's assumed, will only ever be granted by an enlightened managerial class—a belief which effaces the ever-present capacity for worker autonomy, not to mention the role of progressive labour policies. Given these problems, discussing high-participation schemes as a best possible scenario for call centre workers does them a disservice, turning the fable of empowered knowledge workers "coming to life" into an aspirational scenario it is hoped employers will be magnanimous enough to adopt.[39]

Rather than letting the profit motive dictate a discussion of what kind of transformation might be possible, my attempt to sketch out a different kind of communicative workplace draws on examples of worker occupations and self-management, socially progressive call centre applications, and the visions offered in literatures produced by call centre workers and their allies in order to imagine how these workspaces could be reformed by

---

[39] High-commitment management strategies seek to mitigate the damage done to human communication and labour by the profit motive, rather than targeting the real problem—capital's valorization of communication in call centres.

and for workers. The goal of drawing together these subterranean threads is admittedly, as Harry Braverman (1998, p. 5) characterized his own views about work, "governed by nostalgia for an age that has not yet come into being." But my sketch of a self-organized, "socialized" call centre adds itself to a growing set of efforts on the left to draft proposals for post-capitalist futures (Dyer-Witheford, 2013; Mason, 2016; Srnicek & Williams, 2015) amid the utter failure of neoliberal, post-Fordist capitalism to provide an equitable or sustainable working life for the great majority of humans on the planet—including those toiling in call centres.

The means to achieve this transition are already in place in call centres across the world. The first steps are being taken every day through the mass refusal of call centre work as it is currently configured, including quitting, slacking, and acts of sabotage. These refusals have unmistakably brought the alienating and inhuman nature of contemporary call centre work to the fore, and forced the issue of changing the call centre labour process onto the agenda. (Would management scholars be discussing the need for high-commitment practices in the absence of widespread employee disavowal of this new workspace?).

The next step lies in collective organizing in the workplace in order to expand the frontier of worker control, a process for which we have just elaborated some strategic axes in the preceding section. This development of horizontal forms of association among workers, including what the Call Center Offensive described as "communication without management and telephones" (as cited in Kolinko, 2002, section 6.3.c., para. 10), will be integral to any transition. The scenario of call centre transformation discussed here is certainly not intended to replace the bread-and-butter demands of contemporary organizing efforts by workers and their unions, but rather to accompany them, to be developed within them, and to be articulated through them. We should, in fact, begin from an entirely opposite premise from the one assumed by management and industrial relations researchers proposing "high-involvement" schemes—that any meaningful improvement of labour conditions will be imposed by workers and their struggles rather than granted by management.

At the same time, collective struggles in call centres should be accompanied by a firm and growing refusal of work that has no social value. Alienating, resource-depleting labour should be resisted in principle in favour of "creative, ecological, reproductive work done in freedom" (Standing, 2014, p. 12). By this logic, most forms of outbound sales work in call centres—with all of the accompanying nagging, manipulation of consumers, and even outright theft, not to mention the flogging of useless commodities and services—must come to an end. Of all the accounts of call centre work that have been offered by employees, sales work is the most clearly alienating form of such employment, characterized as it is by a steady torrent of emotional abuse from recipients of cold calls and shot through with a general sense of futility in one's labour. Such work is one of the clearest examples of how communicative capitalism generates needless and harmful jobs, a point provocatively underscored by David Graeber (2013) when he includes telemarketers among the "bullshit" forms of wage labour which could in all likelihood disappear without causing humanity much grief. The "do not call" registries that have been implemented in many nations so consumers can elect to not be harassed by sales calls can be seen as a first, rudimentary measure of reform on the path towards the elimination of this kind of call centre work.

Workers and their unions are eminently capable of promoting a broader vision of call centre work which challenges destructive applications such as outbound telemarketing. There are plenty of examples of call centre workers refusing or resisting work in order to oppose the socially problematic applications of their labour (see Chap. 3). Here I add just two, drawn from call centre campaigns dedicated to electoral politics. In Indiana in the United States, 40 call centre workers reportedly walked off the job in 2008 rather than read a campaign script from John McCain attacking Barack Obama for being "dangerously weak on crime," "coddling criminals," and voting against "protecting children from danger" (janann1206, 2008). Call centre workers at the Responsive Marketing Group Inc., in Thunder Bay, Ontario, became concerned that the outgoing calls they were making on behalf of the Conservative Party of Canada during the 2011 election were misleading and illegal, and informed supervisors and then the police. The testimony of one call centre worker that she and her co-workers were given scripts to mislead voters into going to the wrong location to vote on election day was at the centre of a legal challenge of the election results by the Council of Canadians NGO.

There is also a strong argument to be made for more progressive forms of call centre automation which remove the simplest, most rote, and unpleasant jobs from the ones presently endured by humans. Where people on the other end of the phone need very basic, quick interactions, then automation is likely a welcome development for all parties. As Nick Dyer-Witheford (2013) suggests in his view of a socially co-ordinated digital economy,

> [i]n a communist framework that protected access to the use value of goods and services, robotization creates the prospect of a passage from the realm of necessity to freedom. It reintroduces the goal—closed down both within the Stakhanovite Soviet experiment and in the wage-raising trades unionism of the West—of liberating time from work, with all this allows both in terms of human self-development and communal engagement. (p. 15)

Some will object that call centre sales work and rote jobs, while unpleasant, at least provide a pay cheque in times of high unemployment and economic stagnation. This, however, is an inadequate justification for the existence of such jobs, akin to suggesting that new pipelines bring employment even as they hasten climate change and ecological destruction. The valid concerns over the loss of employment in call centres should rather be addressed by a long-overdue retooling of welfare systems in order to update them for an age of flexible employment and extreme income inequality. Scenarios of automation and the elimination of harmful applications of the call centre model would be at the very least drastically mitigated by the institution of a universal basic income, a now widely discussed policy reform aimed at expanding workers' security in an increasingly flexible labour market (Srnicek & Williams, 2015; Standing, 2014). A basic income would extend a meaningful floor-level income to all citizens unconditionally, the annual monetary value of which would be incrementally dispensed at regular intervals, thereby delinking income and employment. For call centre workers, not only would a basic income absorb the shock of regular bouts of unemployment, but it would diminish the necessity of taking a more exploitative job out of sheer desperation, thereby putting the onus on employers to make their jobs more palatable to workers.

7 The Making and Unmaking of the Global Call Centre Workforce   249

As Kathi Weeks (2011, p. 124) reminds us, the refusal of work is a rejection of both the key elements of the wage relation and the discourses that encourage our consent to the modes of work it imposes—but not a rejection of productive activity per se.[40] The "unmaking" of the call centre workforce I am proposing could therefore just as easily be seen as a process of what autonomists have described as the *self-valourization* of labour.[41] Instead of socially and ecologically destructive call centre activities, alternative models based around the principle of self-valourization would include and expand socially progressive orientations aimed at improving health, welfare, or political engagement. Existing social services delivered at a distance, like health advice, crisis support, and emergency services, research intended to design or gauge progressive social policy, or hotlines for reporting abuse and exploitation, all have great social value. Moreover, despite the singular focus call centre scholars have lavished upon profit-driven call centres, there are important alternative examples of worker-operated call centres to be considered, whether through the model of collectives, co-operatives, or the seizure of workplaces during occupations.

We will review some of these progressive applications and democratic forms of organization momentarily, but here I would like to briefly dwell on the ethic, or culture that might be developed within, and pervade such organizational modifications of, the call centre—one we could define more precisely as characterized by social solidarity, or mutual aid (Kropotkin, 1902).[42] Throughout this book, we have seen how the call centre employer appropriates and puts to work not only language but the capacity to make common which lies at the foundation of human communication. It is this dimension of human nature which could be set free in a call centre placed at the service of a genuinely caring and egalitarian digital society. It is no coincidence that whenever call centre workers

---

[40] As Standing suggests: "the precariat has an interest in recapturing a progressive vision of 'freedom from labour,' so establishing a meaningful right to work" (2014, p. 18).

[41] Self-valourization has been defined by Harry Cleaver (n.d., pp. 19–20) as "the positive moments of working class autonomy—where the negative moments are made up of workers' resistance to capital domination" and "a self-defining, self-determining process which goes beyond the mere resistance to capitalist valorisation to a positive project of self-constitution."

[42] See de Peuter and Cohen (2015) for an application of this concept to the projects of solidarity enacted by workers in contemporary creative industries.

actually speak of their job as being rewarding, it is usually the sense of accomplishment they feel in having connected with a customer emotionally or having genuinely been of assistance to them. It is fair to say that this experience is quite likely the exception, rather than the rule, in contemporary call centres. Often, as we have seen, moments like this occur despite rather than because of the scripted interactions imposed on workers by management.[43]

This kind of encounter could become the norm in call centres that restore human communication to its proper fullness rather than producing maimed forms of interaction designed exclusively for the production of profit. To give just a few examples of the many that could be identified in the health sector, Aman Telehealth in Pakistan is a free healthcare call center that offers diagnostic service and medical advice over the phone around the clock, seven days a week (Justice, 2013). The health support lines that have been a growing feature of public healthcare systems are another example of how valuable forms of knowledge can be shared at a distance via call centre technology. The rape crisis relief telephone lines developed within women's movements offer numerous examples of overtly political and progressive call centres dedicated to the goal of social solidarity. The Vancouver Rape Relief (VRR) and Women's Shelter's 24-hour crisis line, for example, fields thousands of crisis calls a year and is run by a feminist collective of around 20 women. The Toronto Rape

---

[43] In one of many relevant examples found in the literature, Kiran Mirchandani (2012, p. 115) describes the emotional bond created between a call centre worker and a customer in India, quoting a worker she interviewed: "Most of the time they [customers calling to make purchases from the catalogue] are very old people who are not able to shop or even walk as well. There were sometimes people who have just been discharged from hospitals ... they need a kind of dress and they are not even able to shop. There were times when people have told me their own feelings and own personal problems, and I also cried for that. One of the calls, I still remember, this old man called up. He wanted a trouser and a shirt. He bought it and he said, 'Do pray for me.' I said 'I will pray for you.' I forgot his name. Then he said, 'Do you know the reason why I asked you to pray?' I said 'no.' He said 'I am suffering from leukemia.' I said, 'I'm so sorry.' She [the customer] was just going on as if there was nobody with who she can talk. She's pouring everything into me. I said, 'OK, let me listen.' She was so glad that at the end of the call, she said: 'Why don't you come and have Christmas dinner with me?' So I said, 'I'm so sorry but you're calling in India.' She said, 'Whenever you come here, you just come to my place' and gave me her address ... That gives me satisfaction, OK, I spoke to a lady who was very elderly, of my mother's age, and I built up a relationship with her ... She wanted me to call her Granny. She didn't feel she called a call center. She feels she called someone she knows."

7 The Making and Unmaking of the Global Call Centre Workforce

Crisis Centre Multicultural Women Against Rape (TRCC/MWAR) is another progressive and democratically organized call center service, describing itself as a "grassroots, women-run collective working towards a violence-free world by providing anti-oppressive, feminist peer support to survivors of sexual violence through support, education and activism" (2016, para. 1).

A transnational example of a mutual aid-driven call centre is provided by Women on Waves who (among other services) run a safe abortion hotline for women in Ecuador, Chile, Peru, Venezuela, Argentina, Pakistan, Indonesia, Kenya, Thailand, Poland, and Morocco. Women on Waves gives advice based on research by the World Health Organisation that can help women safely self-administer abortion medication (Women on Waves, n.d.). Worker safety hotlines can be found in a number of contexts and are generally run by unions, including the BC Nurses' Union workplace violence hotline and the International Alliance of Theatrical Stage Employees safety hotline. In Asia, the China Labour Watch's worker hotline is used to inform and help workers in the Guangdong province with labour concerns including contracts, wages and working hours, female worker protection, insurance, health and safety, living conditions, benefits, and more (China Labor Watch, n.d., para. 11). The Australian Unemployed Workers' Union has instituted a national advocacy hotline to instruct unemployed workers on their rights when dealing with government agents, ask questions, and file complaints in the context of a Work for the Dole workfare scheme and a "punitive system of fines and activities" that gives government employees a large amount of power over the unemployed (Australian Unemployed Workers' Union, n.d., para. 6). Most impressively, in the summer of 2016, the Refugee to Refugee (R2R) Call Center was established in Greece, providing "cooperation and communication among people living in concentration and in isolation, away from the cities, the solidarity movement and each other, with limited access to vital information about the common struggles and related latest news" (Call Center: A Cooperative Project of Solidarity From Refugees to Refugees, 2016). The line offers information for refugees by refugees on transit routes, safe accommodation in camps, and other available services as they strive to build a better life in Europe.

It is important to point out that many of these solidarity-based organizations run their hotlines either wholly or partly on volunteer labour, a choice dictated by the lack of resources they are allocated in a market system, but nonetheless a factor which should temper excessive enthusiasm regarding the possibilities they present. In a progressively de-marketized society, initiatives like these which are broadly dedicated to social reproduction would need to be accorded expanding access to resources so as to ensure that their benefits can be extended to larger numbers of people, and those who run them are rewarded for their contribution.

Call centres that are worker-owned, run as co-operatives, or run by unions with unionized staff offer another important avenue of possibility to be explored by workers and their allies. The Co-operative Response Center in the United States is a co-operatively owned and operated call center with offices in Minnesota, Tennessee, and Texas providing services to electric utilities (Cooperative Response Center, 2013). The Ontario Co-op Association (OnCo-op) in Canada runs two hotlines to support co-operatives in the province, a 411 line for "general co-op information" and a 911 line "for urgent or more pressing issues including governance/democracy challenges" (The Ontario Co-operative Association, 2016). Credit unions also operate call centres which could offer examples of workplaces that are more empowered than "high-commitment" models might allow for. The Co-operative Bank and Co-operative Insurance Society in the United Kingdom, and the Desjardins Bank in Quebec, Canada both run call centres (*Daily Mail*, n.d.).

While progressive economic policies would have a space in co-ordinating the transition of for-profit call centres towards worker-owned and operated models with socially useful applications, the impetus could come from below as well. Although there are no mentions of this tactic in the academic literature on call centres I am aware of, the occupation of workspaces has been deployed by call centre workers in moments of labour conflict. This form of action has a rich history in worker's movements. At the outbreak of the Spanish Civil War in 1937, the telephone building in Barcelona was taken over and run by workers' organizations.[44] Closer to the present day, in Nanaimo, British Columbia, telephone workers unionized with the Telecommunications Workers

---

[44] See George Orwell (1938) for a description of these conflicts.

7 The Making and Unmaking of the Global Call Centre Workforce   253

Union (TWU) occupied BC Telephone's headquarters in the city and ran operations province-wide without disruption to customers for five days in 1981 as the takeover spread to other parts of the territory.[45] Significantly, the driving factor in the conflict for workers was the automation pursued by BC Tel management.

Call centre workers have also occupied their premises of work, often in response to news their jobs are about to be transferred. Against the backdrop of the 2001 Argentine financial crisis, 1500 call center workers unionized with FOETRA reportedly occupied two Telefónica de Argentina buildings in order to reject the restructuring plan proposed by the telecommunication companies, which included a 10% salary cut, a decrease of overtime hours, and a reprogramming of work shifts (Fernández, 2015). The Colectivo Situaciones (2006) also reports on occupations of call centres and strikes featuring the co-ordinated refusal of calls in Buenos Aires, Argentina. In Turin, Italy, workers occupied a call centre in 2010 in response to the threat of company closure (Voce Proletaria, 2011, para. 2).[46] And after a month with no wages, workers at Phonemedia in Italy occupied their call centres and organized protests (Schuetz, 2010). YouTube videos show workers chanting "occupazione, ocupazione" at one of the Phonemedia call centres in Trino, Piedmont, where they then held an assembly (post by pirati delle risaie, 2009).

Similar instances of direct action by call centre workers have been discussed in this book, such as those engaged in by the Collettivo Precari Atesia, which occupied the offices of various town councils, the Ministry of Labour, and the confederal unions to get their message across. While it would most likely be unwise for workers to occupy their workplaces in anything but the most extreme situations, it is not entirely far-fetched to imagine the infrastructure of a call centre business that skips town being appropriated by its workers and turned to socially useful ends within a worker co-operative model. There are interesting precedents here too. In Italy, 11 female operators laid off by a hospital in Legnano, close to Milan,

---

[45] See the account of the occupation offered by Bernard (2011) and also the BC Labour Heritage Centre (2016).
[46] See also Parola (2010).

set up a worker-owned and operated "telefono precario" hotline in 2009 to provide advice to precariously employed workers in the region (Unione Sindicale di Base, 2009). Supported by the rank-and-file union confederation Rappresentanze Sindacali di Base-Confederazione Unitaria di Base (RdB-Cub), the experiment ultimately failed, but it provides compelling evidence of how the feminization of labour in call centres is a process that could be redirected towards the broader purposes of social reproduction and labour solidarity. Moreover, such spaces would have the capacity, as Friends of Kolinko and Gurgaon Workers News (2012) have mused, to become the "telegraph stations" of an emerging global movement for social justice.

There is clearly the need to explore and engage with alternative possibilities for call centre organization through paying closer attention to moments of occupation, progressive, de-commodified applications of call centres, and democratic forms of worker organization within them. Such research would, in collaboration with the more active rank-and-file organizations of workers and their allies, move well beyond the limited and management-friendly vision of "high-involvement" call centre work in order to support more progressive worker goals—including, ultimately, freeing themselves from employers altogether. This is what Paolo Greco, an Italian call centre worker, hints at when he notes (in a quote that opens this book) that "inside, the worker knows that she has the capacity to run the call centre." For this to happen the global call centre workforce will need to *unmake* itself, to reverse the process of class formation, and turn it into the construction of class autonomy.[47] The practices and the desires that will be part of this unmaking, including a refusal of socially harmful work, desires for a life beyond the market, and an ethic of mutual aid, are already out there—scholars just need to pay attention to them.

---

[47] As Nicole Cox and Silvia Federici suggested so long ago in their classic, *Counter-Planning from the Kitchen* (1975, p. 39), "[w]e should not ask capitalism to change the nature of our work, but struggle to refuse reproducing ourselves and others as workers, as labor power, as commodities."

Interviews Cited

Hamed, Omar. Auckland, New Zealand, May 6th, 2011.
McCarten, Matt. Auckland, New Zealand, May 11th, 2011.
Teramo, Domenico. Rome, May 11th, 2007.

References

Amorim, H. (2014). Theories of immaterial labour: A critical reflection based on Marx. *Work Organisation, Labour and Globalisation, 8*(1), 88–103.
Australian Unemployed Workers' Union. (n.d.). *Join us.* Retrieved from http://unemployedworkersunion.com/join-us/
Batt, R., & Moynihan, L. (2002). The viability of alternative call centre production models. *Human Resource Management Journal, 12*(4), 14–14.
BC Labour Heritage Centre. (2016). *A revolution in a wire.* Retrieved from http://www.labourheritagecentre.ca/project/a-revolution-in-a-wire/
Bellamy Foster, J. (1998). New introduction by Bellamy Foster. In H. Braverman (Ed.), *Labor and monopoly capital: The degradation of work in the twentieth century* (25th Anniversary ed., pp. ix–xxiv). New York, NY: Monthly Review Press.
Bernard, E. (2011). Recipe for anarchy: British Columbia's telephone workers' occupation of 1981. In I. Ness & D. Azzelini (Eds.), *Ours to master and own: Workers' control from the commune to the present* (1st ed., pp. 338–355). Chicago, IL: Haymarket Books.
Bologna, S. (2014, December 15). Workerism beyond Fordism: On the lineage of Italian workerism. *Viewpoint Magazine.* Retrieved from https://viewpointmag.com/2014/12/15/workerism-beyond-fordism-on-the-lineage-of-italian-workerism/
Braverman, H. (1998). *Labor and monopoly capital: The degradation of work in the twentieth century* (25th Anniversary ed.). New York, NY: Monthly Review Press.
Brophy, E., & de Peuter, G. (2007). Immaterial labour, precarity, and recomposition. In V. Mosco & C. McKercher (Eds.), *Knowledge workers in the information society* (pp. 177–191). Lanham, MD: Lexington Books.
Buchanan, R. (2002). Lives on the line: Low-wage work in the teleservice economy. In F. Munger (Ed.), *Laboring below the line: The new ethnography of poverty, low-wage work, and survival in the global economy* (pp. 45–72). New York, NY: Russell Sage Foundation.

Burns, C. (2016). *Your IVR is still a CX rock star. . . don't ignore it*. Retrieved from http://customerthink.com/your-ivr-is-still-a-cx-rock-star-dont-ignore-it/

Call Center: A Cooperative Project of Solidarity From Refugees to Refugees. (2016). Retrieved from http://callcenter.coop/

Callaghan, G., & Thompson, P. (2002). We recruit attitude: The selection and shaping of routine call centre labour. *Journal of Management Studies, 39*(2), 233–254.

Carrillo Rowe, A., Perez, K., & Malhotra, S. (2013). *Answer the call: Virtual migration in Indian call centers*. Minneapolis, MN: University of Minnesota Press.

Cátedra Experimental sobre Producción de Subjetividad. (2007). Call centre: The art of virtual control. *ephemera: theory and politics in organization, 7*(1), 133–138.

China Labor Watch. (n.d.). *Our work*. Retrieved from http://chinalaborwatch.org/our_work.aspx

Cleaver, H. (2000). *Reading Capital politically*. Edinburgh, UK: AK Press.

Cleaver, H. (n.d.). *The inversion of class perspective in Marxian theory: From valorization to self-valorization*. Retrieved from https://libcom.org/files/Inversion_0.pdf

Colectivo Situaciones. (2006) *¿Quién habla? Lucha contra la esclavitud del alma en los call centers*. Buenos Aires, Argentina: Tinta Limón Ediciones.

Cooperative Response Center. (2013). *About CRC*. Retrieved from http://www.crc.coop/CRCWeb/contentPages/About%20CRC/About.aspx

Cox, N., & Federici, S. (1975). *Counter-planning from the kitchen: Wages for housework, a perspective on capital and the left* (1st ed.). Bristol, UK: New York Wages for Housework Committee/Falling Wall Press.

D'Cruz, P., & Noronha, E. (2012). High commitment management practices re-examined: The case of Indian call centres. *Economic and Industrial Democracy, 33*(2), 185–205.

Daily Mail. (n.d.). *Co-op plans 500 UK call centre jobs*. Retrieved from http://www.dailymail.co.uk/news/article-207417/Co-op-plans-500-UK-centre-jobs.html

Dalla Costa, G. (2008). *A work of love: Unpaid housework, poverty and sexual violence at the dawn of the 21st century*. New York, NY: Autonomedia.

Dalla Costa, M., & James, S. (1972). *The power of women and the subversion of the community*. Bristol, UK: Falling Wall Press.

de Peuter, G., & Cohen, N. (2015). Emerging labour politics in creative industries. In K. Oakley & J. O'Connor (Eds.), *The Routledge companion to the cultural industries* (pp. 305–318). New York, NY: Routledge.

Dean, J. (2009). *Democracy and other neoliberal fantasies: Communicative capitalism and left politics.* Durham, NC: Duke University Press.

Dean, J. (2012). *The communist horizon.* London, UK: Verso Books.

Dyer-Witheford, N. (1999). *Cyber-Marx: Cycles and circuits of struggle in high-technology capitalism.* Urbana, IL: University of Illinois Press.

Dyer-Witheford, N. (2013). Red plenty platforms. *Culture Machine, 14.* Retrieved from http://www.culturemachine.net/index.php/cm/article/viewArticle/511

Dyer-Witheford, N. (2015). *Cyber-proletariat: Global labour in the digital vortex.* London, UK: Pluto Press.

Dyer-Witheford, N., & de Peuter, G. (2009). *Games of empire: Global capitalism and video games.* Minneapolis, MN: University of Minnesota Press.

Ellis, V., & Taylor, P. (2006). 'You don't know what you've got till it's gone:' Re-contextualising the origins, development and impact of the call centre. *New Technology, Work and Employment, 21*(2), 107–122.

Endnotes. (2010, April). The history of subsumption. *Endnotes, 2.* Retrieved from https://endnotes.org.uk/issues/2/en/endnotes-the-history-of-subsumption

Enghouse Interactive. (2016). *Enghouse interactive brings emotional intelligence to the contact centre.* Retrieved from http://enghouseinteractive.co.uk/about/in-the-media/enghouse-interactive-brings-emotional-intelligence-contact-centre/

Federici, S. (2004). *Caliban and the witch: Women, the body and primitive accumulation* (1st ed.). Brooklyn, NY: Autonomedia.

Federici, S. (2012). *Revolution at point zero: Housework, reproduction, and feminist struggle.* Oakland, CA: PM Press.

Fernández, R. (2015). *Terror center: Flexibilidad laboral en los call center.* Retrieved from http://razonyrevolucion.org/terror-center-flexibilidad-laboral-en-los-call-center/

Fleming, P., & Sturdy, A. (2011). 'Being yourself' in the electronic sweatshop: New forms of normative control. *Human Relations, 64*(2), 177–200.

Fortunato, V., & Palidda, R. (2012). *Il call center in Italia: Lavoro e organizzazione tra retorica e realtà.* Roma, Italy: Carocci Editore.

Freeman, C. (2000). *High tech and high heels in the global economy: Women, work, and pink-collar identities in the Caribbean.* Durham, NC: Duke University Press.

Frey, C. B., & Osborne, M. A. (2013). *The future of employment: How susceptible are jobs to computerisation?* Retrieved from http://www.oxfordmartin.ox.ac.uk/downloads/academic/future-of-employment.pdf

Gorz, A. (2010). *The immaterial* (C. Turner, Trans.). New York, NY: Seagull Books.

Graeber, D. (2013, August 17). On the phenomenon of bullshit jobs. *Stike! Magazine*, pp. 10–11.

Gramsci, A. (1971). In Q. Hoare & G. Smith (Eds. & Trans.), *Selections from the prison notebooks* (1st ed.). London, UK: Lawrence & Wishart.

Guard, J., Steedman, M., & García-Orgales, J. (2007). Organizing the electronic sweatshop: Rank-and-file participation in Canada's steel union. *Labor: Studies in Working-Class History of the Americas, 4*(3), 9–31.

Gurgaon Workers News. (2012). *GurgaonWorkersNews no.9/52*. Retrieved from https://gurgaonworkersnews.wordpress.com/gurgaonworkersnews-no-952/

Hardt, M., & Negri, A. (2000). *Empire*. Cambridge, MA: Harvard University Press.

Hardt, M., & Negri, A. (2004). *Multitude: War and democracy in the age of empire*. New York, NY: Penguin Press.

Hardt, M., & Negri, A. (2009). *Commonwealth*. Cambridge, MA: Belknap Press of Harvard University Press.

Hastings, T. (2011). *A job worth doing? Reinterpreting control, resistance and everyday forms of coping with call centre work in Glasgow* (Unpublished PhD). University of Glasgow, Glasgow, UK.

Hochschild, A. R. (2004). *The managed heart: Commercialization of human feeling*. Berkeley, CA: University of California Press.

Holman, D., Batt, R. & Holtgrewe, U. (2007). *The global call centre report: International perspectives on management and employment*. Retrieved from http://www.ilr.cornell.edu.proxy.lib.sfu.ca/globalcallcenter/upload/GCC-Intl-REpt-US-Version.pdf

Holst, H. (2008). The political economy of trade union strategies in Austria and Germany: The case of call centres. *European Journal of Industrial Relations, 14*(25), 25–45.

Huws, U. (2009). Working at the interface: Call-centre labour in a global economy. *Work Organisation, Labour & Globalisation, 3*(1), 1–8.

Huws, U. (2014). *Labor in the global digital economy: The cybertariat comes of age*. New York, NY: Monthly Review Press.

Ipsos. (2014). *Casual home based interviewers*. Retrieved from https://www.qjumpers.co.nz/job-seeker/job-detail/11835/#.V56oDhI3laV

janann1206. (2008). Dozens of call center workers walk off job in protest rather than read McCain script attacking Obama. Retrieved from http://ireport.cnn.com/docs/DOC-126348

Justice, J. (2013). *Mobile health around the globe: Aman Telehealth call center increases access to care in Pakistan*. Retrieved from http://www.healthworkscollective.com/joan-justice/121861/mobile-health-around-globe-aman-telehealth-call-center-increases-access-care-pak

Kinnie, N., Hutchinson, S., & Purcell, J. (2000). 'Fun and surveillance': The paradox of high commitment management in call centres. *The International Journal of Human Resource Management, 11*(5), 967–985.

Kolinko. (2002). *Hotlines: Call centre, inquiry, communism*. Retrieved from http://www.nadir.org/nadir/initiativ/kolinko/lebuk/e_lebuk.htm

Kropotkin, P. (1902). *Mutual aid: A factor in evolution reprint*. London, UK: Heinemann.

Lazzarato, M. (1996). Immaterial labor. In P. Virno & M. Hardt (Eds.), *Radical thought in Italy: A potential politics* (pp. 133–148). Minneapolis, MN: University of Minnesota Press.

Linebaugh, P., & Rediker, M. B. (2000). *The many-headed hydra: Sailors, slaves, commoners, and the hidden history of the revolutionary Atlantic*. Boston, MA: Beacon Press.

Lorey, I. (2015). *State of insecurity: Government of the precarious*. Brooklyn, NY: Verso.

Marazzi, C. (1999). *I posto dei calzini: La svolta linguistica dell'economia e i suoi effetti sulla politica*. Turin, Italy: Bollati Borlinghieri.

Marx, K. (1990). *Capital: Volume 1*. London, UK: Penguin.

Marx, K. (1993, orig 1858). *Grundrisse: Foundations of the critique of political economy* [Grundrisse der Kritik der politischen Ökonomie] (M. Nicolaus, Trans.). Harmondsworth, UK: Penguin Books.

Mason, P. (2016). *Postcapitalism: A guide to our future* (1st American ed.). New York, NY: Farrar, Straus and Giroux.

Mattoni, A. (2012). *Media practices and protest politics: How precarious workers mobilise*. Burlington, VT: Ashgate.

McClintock, P. (2016). *Global 2015 box office: Revenue hits record $38 billion-plus*. Retrieved from http://www.hollywoodreporter.com/news/global-2015-box-office-revenue-851749

McNally, D. (1993). *Against the market: Political economy, market socialism and the Marxist critique*. London, UK: Verso.

Mills, C. W. (2002). *White collar: The American middle classes* (50th Anniversary ed.). New York, NY: Oxford University Press.
Mirá quién habla. (2010). *Call center: Un blog sobre la esclavitud posmoderna*. Retrieved from http://mira-Quién-habla.blogspot.ca/2010/03/la-esclavitud-posmoderna-ensayo-de-otro.html [blog became unavailable].
Mirchandani, K. (2012). *Phone clones: Authenticity work in the transnational service economy*. Ithaca, NY: ILR Press.
Morini, C. (2007). The feminization of labour in cognitive capitalism. *Feminist Review, 87*(1), 40–59.
Mosco, V., & McKercher, C. (2008). *The laboring of communication: Will knowledge workers of the world unite?* Lanham, MD: Lexington Books.
Orwell, G. (1938). *Homage to Catalonia*. London, UK: Secker and Warburg.
Parola, S. (2010). *Omnia, blitz del commissario: 'Fuori tutti, lasciate le chiavi'*. Retrieved from http://torino.repubblica.it/cronaca/2010/10/01/news/omnia_service_occupata-7612737/
Peterson, L. (2015). *Where 'talents' go to die: Diary of a US call centre worker*. Retrieved from https://rdln.wordpress.com/2015/09/11/where-talents-go-to-die-diary-of-a-us-call-centre-worker/
pirati delle risaie. (2009). *Aggiornamenti dal call center Phonemedia di Trino vc -3-*. Retrieved from https://www.youtube.com/watch?v=6x0gVmYQvzQ
Qiu, J. L. (2010). Network labour and non-elite knowledge workers in China. *Work Organisation, Labour & Globalisation, 4*(2), 80–95.
Roggero, G. (2011). *The production of living knowledge: Crisis of the university and transformation of labour in Europe and North America* [Produzione del sapere vivo.] (E. Brophy, Trans.). Philadelphia, PA: Temple University Press.
Ross, A. (2004). *No-collar: The humane workplace and its hidden costs*. Philadelphia, PA: Temple University Press.
Schiller, D. (2014). Rosa Luxemburg's internet? For a political economy of state mobilization and the movement of accumulation in cyberspace. *International Journal of Communication, 8*, 355–375.
Schuetz, L. (2010). *Country's largest call centre company facing bankruptcy: Workers fight to save 10,000 jobs*. Retrieved from http://www.socialistworld.net/doc/3999
Scott, J. (1985). *Weapons of the weak: Everyday forms of peasant resistance*. New Haven, CT: Yale University Press.
Sewell, G. (1998). The discipline of teams: The control of team-based industrial work through electronic and peer surveillance. *Administrative Science Quarterly, 43*(2), 397–428.

Skand Bhargava, K., & Menzigian, S. S. (2015). *Contact center outsourcing annual report 2015: Incumbents beware – There's no place for complacency* (No. EGR-2015-1-R-1470). Dallas, TX: Everest Group.
SmartAction. (2013). *SmartAction names new CEO Tom Lewis*. Retrieved from http://www.prnewswire.com/news-releases/smartaction-names-new-ceo-tom-lewis-213966961.html
Srnicek, N., & Williams, A. (2015). *Inventing the future: Postcapitalism and a world without work* (Verso ed.). London, UK: Verso.
Standing, G. (2014). *A precariat charter: From denizens to citizens*. London, UK: Bloomsbury.
Stevens, A. (2014). *Call centers and the global division of labor: A political economy of post-industrial employment and union organizing*. New York, NY: Routledge/Taylor & Francis Group.
Stevens, A., & Mosco, V. (2010). Prospects for trade unions and labour organisations in India's IT and ITES industries. *Work Organisation, Labour & Globalisation, 4*(2), 39–59.
Tazzioli, M. (2013). *Geografie rivoluzionate: Tunisia, due anni dopo*. Retrieved from http://www.uninomade.org/geografie-rivoluzionate-tunisia-due-anni-dopo/
Terranova, T. (2004). *Network culture: Politics for the information age*. London, UK: Pluto Press.
The Ontario Co-operative Association. (2016). *Starting a co-op*. Retrieved from http://www.ontario.coop/programs_services/coop_development/starting_a_coop#a_100
TRCC/MWAR. (2016). *Mission, vision and philosophy*. Retrieved from http://trccmwar.ca/about-us/mission-vision-philosophy/
Tsianos, V., & Papadopoulos, D. (2006). *Precarity: A savage journey to the heart of embodied capitalism*. Retrieved from http://eipcp.net/transversal/1106/tsianospapadopoulos/en
Unione Sindicale di Base. (2009). *Telefono precario: 800.03.42.35 il numero verde nazionale autogestito da RdB*. Retrieved from http://precari.usb.it/index.php?id=20&tx_ttnews%5Btt_news%5D=19396&cHash=ade1a48490&MP=63-629
Voce Proletaria. (2011). *Lavoratori dei call center Uniti a Torino*. Retrieved from http://blog.libero.it/VoceProletaria/10198680.html
Wade, J. (2016). *Call centers chase a false holy grail of artificial intelligence and full automation*. Retrieved from http://www.nearshoreamericas.com/automation-call-center-artificial-intelligence-holy-grail/

Weeks, K. (2011). *The problem with work: Feminism, Marxism, antiwork politics, and postwork imaginaries*. Durham, NC/London, UK: Duke University Press.
Winks, C. (1981). *Manuscript found in a typewriter*. Retrieved from http://www.processedworld.com/Issues/issue01/i01manu.html
Wittel, A. (2004). Culture, labour and subjectivity: For a political economy from below. *Capital & Class, 28*(3), 11–30.
Wolff, S. (2016). Behind the line: Information privatization and the reification of work in the call center of a Brazilian state-owned telecommunications company. In R. Maxwell (Ed.), *The Routledge companion to labor and media* (pp. 130–142). New York, NY: Routledge.
Women on Waves. (n.d.). *Safe abortion hotlines*. Retrieved from http://www.womenonwaves.org/en/page/2583/safe-abortion-hotlines
Woodcock, J. (2013, September 25). Smile down the phone: An attempt at a worker inquiry in a call centre. *Viewpoint Magazine*, (3). Retrieved from https://viewpointmag.com/2013/09/25/smile-down-the-phone-an-attempt-at-a-workers-inquiry-in-a-call-center/
Wright, S. (2002). *Storming heaven: Class composition and struggle in Italian autonomist Marxism*. London, UK: Pluto Press.
Yellin, E. (2009). *Your call is (not that) important to us: Customer service and what it reveals about our world and our lives*. New York, NY: Free Press.

Interviews Cited

Aliant worker 1, Moncton, April 6th, 2006.
Aliant worker 2. Moncton, April 6th, 2006.
Aliant worker 3. Moncton, April 3rd, 2006.
Aliant worker 4. Moncton, April 3rd, 2006.
Aliant worker 5. Moncton, April 5th, 2006.
Aliant worker 6. Moncton, April 6th, 2006.
Aliant Worker 7. Moncton, April 5th, 2006.
Aliant Worker 8. Moncton. April 4th, 2006.
Benedetti, Cecilia. Rome, May 8th, 2007.
Bosi, Christian. Rome, May 8th, 2007.
Brideau, Sandy. Moncton. April 6th, 2006.
Buckley, Karen. Moncton, April 6th, 2006.
Carolan, Joe. Auckland, New Zealand, May 6th, 2011.
Chaloux, Jim-Bob. Moncton, April 6th, 2006.
ex-Synovate employee. Auckland, New Zealand, May 11th, 2011.
Fatu, Arnold, & Asiata, Ross. Auckland, New Zealand, May 16th, 2011.
Gentile, Valerio. Rome, May 8th, 2007.
Hamed, Omar. Auckland, New Zealand, May 6th, 2011.
Irish worker 1. Dublin, July 24th, 2009.
Irish worker 2. Dublin, August 5th, 2009.
Leblanc, Ferdinand. Moncton, April 3rd, 2006.

© The Author(s) 2017
E. Brophy, *Language Put to Work*, Dynamics of Virtual Work,
DOI 10.1057/978-1-349-95244-1

Malone, Mark. Dublin, July 21st, 2009.
McArdle, Ian. Dublin, February 13th, 2009.
McCarten, Matt. Auckland, New Zealand, May 11th, 2011.
Minto, John. Auckland, New Zealand, May 11th, 2011.
Moase, Godfrey. Auckland, New Zealand, June 22nd, 2011.
Nastro, Rosanna. Rome, May 8th, 2007.
Oosterman, Simon. Auckland, New Zealand, May 6th, 2011.
Petricca, Alessandro. Rome, May 8th, 2007.
Portolani, Mara. Rome, May 8th, 2007.
Richard, Donovan. Moncton, April 4th, 2006.
Richard, Keenan. Moncton, April, 4th, 2006.
Roy, Philippe. Moncton, April 5th, 2006.
Sciotto, Antonio. Rome, April 30th, 2007.
Teramo, Domenico. Rome, May 11th, 2007.
Testa, Maurizio. Rome, May 8th, 2007.
Thibodeau, Josée. Moncton. April 4th, 2006.
Treen, Mike. Auckland, New Zealand, May 10th, 2011.
Unite member. Auckland, New Zealand, May 16th, 2011.

References

AES. (2013, October 4). *Are you stealing from your boss?* Retrieved from https://libcom.org/forums/oceania/are-you-stealing-your-boss-04102013

Aglietta, M. (1979). *A theory of capitalist regulation: The US experience*. London, UK: Verso.

Ahiuma-Young, V. (2011). *Nigeria: Aggrieved workers shut down Airtel's call centre*. Retrieved from http://allafrica.com/stories/201110040014.html

Alferoff, C., & Knights, D. (2000). Quality time and the beautiful call. *Are regimented forms of work organisation inevitable? Call centres and the chances for an innovative organisation of service work in Europe*, University of Duisburg-Essen, Germany.

Aliant. (1999, May 31). Atlantic business combination complete: Aliant launched; enters TSE as CDN$3B growth company. *Canada NewsWire*. Accessed via Factiva database: https://global.factiva.com/

Aliant, & Council of Atlantic Telecommunications Unions. (2004, September). *Collective agreement*.

Almiron, N. (2010). *Journalism in crisis: Corporate media and financialization*. Cresskill, NJ: Hampton Press.

Amorim, H. (2014). Theories of immaterial labour: A critical reflection based on Marx. *Work Organisation, Labour and Globalisation, 8*(1), 88–103.

Aneesh, A. (2006). *Virtual migration: The programming of globalization*. Durham, NC: Duke University Press.

Aneesh, A. (2015). Emerging scripts of global speech. *Sociological Theory, 33*(3), 234.

Annis, R. (2009). Unite union wins gains for vulnerable workers in New Zealand. *The Bullet,* (No. 216). Retrieved from http://www.socialistproject.ca/bullet/bullet216.html.

ANSA. (2009, April 3). Omnia network late with wages, protest in Turin. Accessed via Factiva database: https://global.factiva.com/

Artaria, E., Coluccio, E., Fiorenza, P., Bocca Gelsi, F., Pedote, G., Pedranti, G. (Producers), & Rizzo, F. (Director). (2008). *Fuga dal call center.* [Motion Picture]. Milan, Italy: Orda d'Oro Distribuzione.

Atento. (2015a). *Atento reports fourth quarter and full year 2014 results* (press release). New York, NY.

Atento. (2015b). *Our locations.* Retrieved from http://www.atento.com/about-atento/our-locations/

Atesia. (2007). *Chi siamo.* Retrieved from http://www.atesia.it/chisiamo/profilo.htm

Australian Unemployed Workers' Union. (n.d.). *Join us.* Retrieved from http://unemployedworkersunion.com/join-us/

Azzellini, D., & Ness, I. (2011). *Ours to master and to own.* Chicago, IL: Haymarket Books.

Bain, P., & Taylor, P. (2000). Entrapped by the 'electronic panopticon'? Worker resistance in the call centre. *New Technology, Work, and Employment, 15*(1), 2–18.

Bain, P., & Taylor, P. (2008). No passage to India? Initial responses of UK trade unions to call centre outsourcing. *Industrial Relations Journal, 39*(1), 5–23.

Bain, P., Taylor, P., Watson, A., Mulvey, G., & Gall, G. (2002). Taylorism, targets and the pursuit of quantity and quality by call centre management. *New Technology, Work and Employment, 17*(3), 170–185.

Balka, E. (2002). The invisibility of the everyday: New technology and women's work. In *Sex and money: Feminism and the political economy in the media* (pp. 60–74). Minneapolis: University of Minnesota Press.

Ball, K. (2005). Organization, surveillance and the body: Towards a politics of resistance. *Organization, 12*(1), 89–108.

Ball, K., & Wilson, D. (2000). Power, control and computer-based performance monitoring: Repertoires, resistance and subjectivities. *Organization Studies, 21*(3), 539–565.

Barker, G. (1998, February 24). Factories of the future. *The age.*

Batt, R., & Moynihan, L. (2002). The viability of alternative call centre production models. *Human Resource Management Journal, 12*(4), 14–14.

Batt, R., Holman, D., & Holtgrewe, U. (2009). The globalization of service work: Comparative institutional perspectives on call centers. *Industrial and Labor Relations Review, 62*(4), 453–488.
BC Labour Heritage Centre. (2016). *A revolution in a wire*. Retrieved from http://www.labourheritagecentre.ca/project/a-revolution-in-a-wire/
Bell, D. (1973). *The coming of post-industrial society: A venture in social forecasting.* New York, NY: Basic Books.
Bellamy Foster, J. (1998). New introduction by Bellamy Foster. In H. Braverman (Ed.), *Labor and monopoly capital: The degradation of work in the twentieth century* (25th Anniversary ed., pp. ix–xxiv). New York, NY: Monthly Review Press.
Berardi, F. (1998). *La nefasta utopia di potere operaio: Lavoro tecnica movimento nel laboratorio politico del sessantotto italiano.* Rome, Italy: Castelvecchi.
Berardi, F. (2012). *The uprising: On poetry and finance.* Los Angeles, CA: Semiotext(e).
Berardi, F. (2013). L'autonomia dell'intelletto generale: Ecco il problema. *Commonware: General Intellect in Formazione.* Retrieved from: http://www.commonware.org/index.php/neetwork/45-autonomia-intelletto-generale
Bernard, E. (2011). Recipe for anarchy: British Columbia's telephone workers' occupation of 1981. In I. Ness & D. Azzelini (Eds.), *Ours to master and own: Workers' control from the commune to the present* (1st ed., pp. 338–355). Chicago, IL: Haymarket Books.
Bibby, A. (2000). *Organising in financial call centres: A report for the UNI.* Retrieved from http://www.andrewbibby.com/pdf/fin-callcent-e.pdf
Biondi, A. (2014). *Call center, l'utile non è in linea.* Retrieved from http://www.confapimatera.it/wp-content/uploads/downloads/2014/11/sole-call-center.pdf
Bologna, S. (2014, December 15). Workerism beyond Fordism: On the lineage of Italian workerism. *Viewpoint Magazine.* Retrieved from https://viewpointmag.com/2014/12/15/workerism-beyond-fordism-on-the-lineage-of-italian-workerism/
Boltanski, L., & Chiapello, E. (2005). *The new spirit of capitalism.* New York, NY: Verso.
Bouzane, B. (2004, July 30). Union brings it home: Pickets set up at manager's houses. *St. John's Telegram*, p. A4.
Bradbury Bennett, T. (2004a, June 11). Police seek list from Aliant: Want to know who has knowledge to bring service down. *St. John's Telegram*, p. B7.
Bradbury Bennett, T. (2004b, July 21). Strikes draining food bank. *St. John's Telegram*, p. A1.

Bramming, P., Sørensen, O. H., & Hasle, P. (2009). In spite of everything: Professionalism as mass customised bureaucratic production in a Danish government call centre. *Work Organisation, Labour & Globalisation, 3*(1), 114–130.

Braverman, H. (1998). *Labor and monopoly capital: The degradation of work in the twentieth century* (25th Anniversary ed.). New York, NY: Monthly Review Press.

Braverman, H. (1974). *Labor and monopoly capital: The degradation of work in the twentieth century.* New York: Monthly Review Press.

Breathnach, P. (1998). Exploring the "celtic tiger" phenomenon: Causes and consequences of Ireland's economic miracle. *European Urban and Regional Studies, 5*(4), 305–316.

Breathnach, P. (2000). Globalisation, information technology and the emergence of niche transnational cities: The growth of the call centre sector in Dublin. *Geoforum, 31*(4), 477–485.

Brophy, E. (2009). Resisting call centre work: The Aliant strike and convergent unionism in Canada. *Work Organisation, Labour & Globalisation, 3*(1), 80–99.

Brophy, E. (2010). The subterranean stream: Communicative capitalism and call centre labour. *ephemera: theory and politics in organization, 10*(4), 470–483.

Brophy, E. (2014). Phone clones: Authenticity work in the transnational service economy, by Kiran Mirchandani (review). *Canadian Ethnic Studies, 46*(1), 225–227.

Brophy, E. (2015). Revisiting the digital assembly line: New perspectives on call centre work. *Labour/Le Travail, 75*, 211–230.

Brophy, E., & de Peuter, G. (2007). Immaterial labour, precarity, and recomposition. In V. Mosco & C. McKercher (Eds.), *Knowledge workers in the information society* (pp. 177–191). Lanham, MD: Lexington Books.

Brophy, E., & de Peuter, G. (2015). Communicative capitalism and the smartphone cybertariat. In A. Herman, J. Hadlaw, & T. Swiss (Eds.), *Theories of the mobile internet: Materialities and imaginaries* (pp. 60–84). New York, NY: Routledge.

Brophy, E., Cohen, N., & de Peuter, G. (2016). Labor messaging: Practices of autonomous communication. In R. Maxwell (Ed.), *The Routledge companion to labor and media* (pp. 315–326). New York, NY: Routledge.

Buchanan, R. (2002). Lives on the line: Low-wage work in the teleservice economy. In F. Munger (Ed.), *Laboring below the line: The new ethnography of poverty, low-wage work, and survival in the global economy* (pp. 45–72). New York, NY: Russell Sage Foundation.

Buchanan, R., & Koch-Schulte, S. (2000). *Gender on the line: Technology, restructuring and the reorganization of work in the call centre industry.* Ottawa, ON: Status of Women Canada.

Burawoy, M. (1979). *Manufacturing consent: Changes in the labor process under monopoly capitalism.* Chicago, IL: University of Chicago Press.

Burgess, J., & Connell, J. (Eds.). (2006). *Developments in the call centre industry: Analysis, changes and challenges.* New York, NY: Routledge.

Burnham, J. (2003). Why Ireland boomed. *The Independent Review, 8*(4), 537–556.

Burns, C. (2016). *Your IVR is still a CX rock star... don't ignore it.* Retrieved from http://customerthink.com/your-ivr-is-still-a-cx-rock-star-dont-ignore-it/

Call Center: A Cooperative Project of Solidarity From Refugees to Refugees. (2016). Retrieved from http://callcenter.coop/

Callaghan, G., & Thompson, P. (2001). Edwards revisited: Technical control and call centres. *Economic and Industrial Democracy, 22*(1), 13–37.

Callaghan, G., & Thompson, P. (2002). We recruit attitude: The selection and shaping of routine call centre labour. *Journal of Management Studies, 39*(2), 233–254.

Cámara de Telecomunicaciones del Uruguay. (2010). *Call center pierden competitividad y piden normas laborales flexibles.* Retrieved from http://www.telecomunicaciones.org.uy/web/index.php?option=com_content&task=view&id=285&Itemid=74

Cameron, D. (2008). Talk from the top down. *Language & Communication, 28*(2), 143–155.

Canadian Press. (2004, May 4). Union leader predicts Aliant managers will tire as strike drags on. *Canadian Press.* Accessed via Factiva database: https://global.factiva.com/

Carrieri, M. (1995). Industrial relations and the labour movement. In S. Gundle & S. Parker (Eds.), *The new Italian republic: From the fall of the Berlin wall to Berlusconi* (pp. 294–310). London, UK: Routledge.

Carrillo Rowe, A., Perez, K., & Malhotra, S. (2013). *Answer the call: Virtual migration in Indian call centers.* Minneapolis, MN: University of Minnesota Press.

Castellano, L., Cavallina, A., Cortiana, G., Dalmaviva, M., Ferrari Bravo, L., Funaro, C.,... Virno, P. (1996). Do you remember revolution? In M. Hardt & P. Virno (Eds.), *Radical thought in Italy: A potential politics* (pp. 225–240). Minneapolis, MN: University of Minnesota Press.

Castells, M. (1996). *The rise of the network society.* Cambridge, MA: Blackwell Publishers.

Castells, M. (1997). *The power of identity.* Malden, MA: Blackwell.
Cátedra Experimental sobre Producción de Subjetividad. (2007a). Call centre: The art of virtual control. *ephemera: theory and politics in organization, 7*(1), 133–138.
Cátedra Experimental sobre Producción de Subjetividad. (2007b). *From knowledge of self-management to the self-management of knowledge.* Retrieved from http://eipcp.net/transversal/0707/catedraexperimental/en
CBC News. (2004a, July 6). Aliant using outside workers: Strikers. *Canadian Broadcasting Corporation.* http://www.cbc.ca/story/canada/national/2004/07/06/Aliant_040706.html
CBC News. (2004b, July 30). Strike has cost CDN$21M: Aliant. *Canadian Broadcasting Corporation.* Accessed at: http://www.cbc.ca/news/business/strike-has-cost-21m-aliant-1.495490
CBC News. (2009, October 16). Bell Aliant to close 11 call centres. *Canadian Broadcasting Corporation.* Accessed at: http://www.cbc.ca/news/canada/nova-scotia/bell-aliant-to-close-11-call-centres-1.838216
Chakravartty, P., & Schiller, D. (2011). Global financial crisis: Neoliberal newspeak and digital capitalism in crisis. *International Journal of Communication, 4*(23), 670–692.
China Labor Watch. (n.d.). *Our work.* Retrieved from http://chinalaborwatch.org/our_work.aspx
Choudry, A. (2003). *New wave/old wave: Aotearoa New Zealand's colonial continuum.* Retrieved from http://www.voiceoftheturtle.org/show_printer.php?aid=328
Cleaver, H. (2000). *Reading Capital politically.* Edinburgh, UK: AK Press.
Cleaver, H. (n.d.). *The inversion of class perspective in Marxian theory: From valorization to self-valorization.* Retrieved from https://libcom.org/files/Inversion_0.pdf
Cohen, N. (2012). Cultural work as a site of struggle: Freelancers and exploitation. *tripleC (Cognition, Communication, Co-Operation): Open Access Journal for a Global Sustainable Information Society, 10*(2), 141–155.
Colectivo Situaciones. (2003). *Causes and happenstance: Dilemmas of Argentina's new social protagonism.* Retrieved from http://www.nodo50.org/colectivosituaciones/borradores_04_eng.htm
Colectivo Situaciones. (2006) *¿Quién habla? Lucha contra la esclavitud del alma en los call centers.* Buenos Aires, Argentina: Tinta Limón Ediciones.

Colectivo Situaciones. (2009). *Genocide in the neighborhood* [Genocida en el barrio: Mesa de escrache popular] (B. Whitener, D. Borzutzky, & F. Fuentes, Trans.). Oakland, CA/Philadelphia, Pennsylvania: ChainLinks.

Colectivo Situaciones. (2011). *19 & 20: Notes for a new social protagonism.* Retrieved from http://www.minorcompositions.info/?cat=27

Collettivo Precari Atesia. (2005a). *Alcune notizie sulla sitazione dei lavoratori.* Retrieved from http://www.slaicobasmilano.org/precariatesia.htm

Collettivo Precari Atesia. (2005b). *Corteo cittadino contro la precarietà.* Retrieved from http://www.slaicobasmilano.org/precariatesia.htm

Collettivo Precari Atesia. (2005c). *Giusto per essere chiari.* Retrieved from http://www.slaicobasmilano.org/precariatesia.htm

Collettivo Precari Atesia. (2005d). *Resoconto assemblee in Atesia.* Retrieved from http://www.slaicobasmilano.org/precariatesia.htm

Collettivo Precari Atesia. (2006a). *Ennesima truffa di azienda e sindacati diciamo no!!! In francia l'hanno fatto...* Retrieved from http://www.slaicobasmilano.org/precariatesia.htm

Collettivo Precari Atesia. (2006b). *Le lavoratrici ed i lavoratori di Atesia respingono l'accordo-truffa voluto da padron tripi e firmato da CGIL-CISL-UIL.* Retrieved from http://www.slaicobasmilano.org/precariatesia.htm

Collettivo Precari Atesia, Collettivo contro la precarietà Telecontact center, RSU Cobas XCOS, Lavoratrici e lavoratori Unicab, Lavoratrici e lavoratori autorganizzati ACI Informatica, Lavoratrici e lavoratori Alicos,... Coordinamento lavoratrici e lavoratori Roma Ovest. (2005). *Mobilitazione contro la precarietà 22 giugno a Roma: Da Atesia a COS.* Retrieved from http://www.slaicobasmilano.org/precariatesia.htm

Communications, Energy and Paperworkers Union of Canada. (2001, September 27). Aliant Inc: Call-centre workers among 800 newly-unionized phone workers. *Market News Publishing Via COMTEX.*

Communications, Energy and Paperworkers Union of Canada. (2005, September 27). Phone customers should be rebated for poor service – CEP Canada. *NewsWire.*

Cooperative Response Center. (2013). *About CRC.* Retrieved from http://www.crc.coop/CRCWeb/contentPages/About%20CRC/About.aspx

Cox, N., & Federici, S. (1975). *Counter-planning from the kitchen: Wages for housework, a perspective on capital and the left* (1st ed.). Bristol, UK: New York Wages for Housework Committee/Falling Wall Press.

Cronk, E., & MacDonald, D. (2004, July 16). *Council of Atlantic Telecommunication Unions info update: Bell contract offer & CIRB hearing.* Retrieved from http://www.cep.ca/reg_atlantic/files/aliant/040716_e.html

Cuccomarino, C. (2013). La parabola di una rivolta. Gli operatori dei call center Almaviva di Palermo. *Commonware: General Intellect in Formazione*, January 17, 2014.
Cuccomarino, C., & Pezzulli, F. M. (2012, December 13). Tra mirafiori e Bangalore: L'inchiesta politica nei call center calabresi. *Il Manifesto*, pp. 8–9.
Cugusi, C. (2005). *Call center: Gli schiavi elettronici della New Economy*. Genoa, Italy: Fratelli Frilli Editori.
D'Cruz, P., & Noronha, E. (2006). Being professional: Organizational control in Indian call centers. *Social Science Computer Review, 24*(3), 342–361.
D'Cruz, P., & Noronha, E. (2012). High commitment management practices re-examined: The case of Indian call centres. *Economic and Industrial Democracy, 33*(2), 185–205.
D'Cruz, P., & Noronha, E. (2013). Hope to despair: The experience of organizing Indian call centre employees. *The Indian Journal of Industrial Relations, 48*(3), 471–486.
Daily Mail. (2009, March 5). Thames battles union over "sacking threat". *Daily Mail*, p. 73.
Daily Telegraph. (2009, July 18). Power plug pulled. *Daily Telegraph*, p. 16.
Daily Mail. (n.d.). *Co-op plans 500 UK call centre jobs*. Retrieved from http://www.dailymail.co.uk/news/article-207417/Co-op-plans-500-UK-centre-jobs.html
Dalla Costa, G. (2008). *A work of love: Unpaid housework, poverty and sexual violence at the dawn of the 21st century*. New York, NY: Autonomedia.
Dalla Costa, M., & James, S. (1972). *The power of women and the subversion of the community*. Bristol, UK: Falling Wall Press.
David, N. (2008). *Spotlight interview with Laïla Nassimi (Morocco – CDT)*. Retrieved from http://www.ituc-csi.org/spotlight-interview-with-laila.html?lang=en
D'Cruz, P., & Noronha, E. (2007). Technical call centres: Beyond "electronic sweatshops" and "assembly lines in the head". *Global Business Review, 8*(1), 53–67.
de Peuter, G. (2014). Confronting precarity in the Warhol economy: Notes from New York City. *Journal of Cultural Economy, 7*(1), 31.
de Peuter, G., & Cohen, N. (2015). Emerging labour politics in creative industries. In K. Oakley & J. O'Connor (Eds.), *The Routledge companion to the cultural industries* (pp. 305–318). New York, NY: Routledge.
Dean, J. (2009). *Democracy and other neoliberal fantasies: Communicative capitalism and left politics*. Durham, NC: Duke University Press.

Dean, J. (2010). *Blog theory: Feedback and capture in the circuits of drive.* Cambridge, MA: Polity.
Dean, J. (2012). *The communist horizon.* London, UK: Verso Books.
Dean, J. (2014, November). Communicative capitalism and class struggle. *Spheres, Journal of Digital Cultures.* Retrieved from http://spheres-journal.org/communicative-capitalism-and-class-struggle/
Deery, S., & Kinnie, N. (2004). *Call centres and human resource management: A cross-national perspective.* Houndmills, UK/New York, NY: Palgrave Macmillan.
Deloitte Consulting. (2013). *2013 global contact centre: Survey results.* Retrieved from http://www2.deloitte.com/content/dam/Deloitte/us/Documents/process-and-operations/us-sdt-consulting-2013-global-contact-survey-051513.pdf
Direttivo CGIL, e Lazio, R., Canti, D., Taormina, A., Turi, R., & Noce, O. D. (2006, April 29). Atesia: Accordo pessimo, referendum vero. *Il Manifesto.*
Doellgast, V. (2012). *Disintegrating democracy at work: Labor unions and the future of good jobs in the service economy.* Ithaca, NY: ILR Press.
Donati, E. (1999). I call center.' una nuova opportunità di business e di lavoro nell'economia della conoscenza. *Office Automation, 3*, 2–8.
Dormann, C., & Zijlstra, F. (2004). *Call centre work: Smile by wire.* Special Issue of the European Journal of Work and Organisational Psychology. London, UK: Routledge.
Doucet, L. (2007, November 14). Upwardly mobile Afghanistan. *BBC News.*
Drucker, P. (1996). *Landmarks of tomorrow: A report on the new 'post-modern' world.* New Brunswick, NJ: Transaction Publishers.
Drucker, P. (2001). The next society. *The Economist.* Retrieved from http://www.economist.com/node/770819
Drucker, P. (2006). Knowledge workers need a new type of organization. *The Economist, 378,* 9.
Duff, M. (2008, September). Teletech 018 staff are hopping mad. *Manawatu Standard.*
Duménil, G., & Lévy, D. (2004). *Capital resurgent: Roots of the neoliberal revolution.* Cambridge, MA: Harvard University Press.
Dyer-Witheford, N. (1999). *Cyber-Marx: Cycles and circuits of struggle in high-technology capitalism.* Urbana, IL: University of Illinois Press.
Dyer-Witheford, N. (2013). Red plenty platforms. *Culture Machine, 14.* Retrieved from http://www.culturemachine.net/index.php/cm/article/viewArticle/511

Dyer-Witheford, N. (2015). *Cyber-proletariat: Global labour in the digital vortex.* London, UK: Pluto Press.

Dyer-Witheford, N., & de Peuter, G. (2009). *Games of empire: Global capitalism and video games.* Minneapolis, MN: University of Minnesota Press.

Edwards, R. (1979). *Contested terrain: The transformation of the workplace in the twentieth century.* New York, NY: Basic Books.

Ellis, V., & Taylor, P. (2006). 'You don't know what you've got till it's gone:' Re-contextualising the origins, development and impact of the call centre. *New Technology, Work and Employment, 21*(2), 107–122.

Endnotes. (2010, April). The history of subsumption. *Endnotes, 2.* Retrieved from https://endnotes.org.uk/issues/2/en/endnotes-the-history-of-subsumption

Enghouse Interactive. (2016). *Enghouse interactive brings emotional intelligence to the contact centre.* Retrieved from http://enghouseinteractive.co.uk/about/in-the-media/enghouse-interactive-brings-emotional-intelligence-contact-centre/

Farolfi, S. (2007, April 4). Call center, ride il telefono 16,000 de-precarizzati. *Il Manifesto,* p. 11.

Fatur. (2006). *Sindacato insindacabile.* Retrieved from precariatesia.altervista.org/Sfront_end/N_12.doc

Federici, S. (2004). *Caliban and the witch: Women, the body and primitive accumulation* (1st ed.). Brooklyn, NY: Autonomedia.

Federici, S. (2012). *Revolution at point zero: Housework, reproduction, and feminist struggle.* Oakland, CA: PM Press.

Fernández, R. (2015). *Terror center: Flexibilidad laboral en los call center.* Retrieved from http://razonyrevolucion.org/terror-center-flexibilidad-laboral-en-los-call-center/

Fernie, S., & Metcalf, D. (1998). *(Not) hanging on the telephone: Payment systems in the new sweatshops* London, UK: London School of Economics and Political Science.

Figiel, J., Shukaitis, S., & Walker, A. (2014). The politics of workers' inquiry. *ephemera: theory & politics in organization, 14*(3), 307–314.

Fleming, P. (2009). *Authenticity and the cultural politics of work: New forms of informal control.* Oxford, UK: Oxford University Press.

Fleming, P., & Sewell, G. (2002). Looking for the good soldier, Svejk: Alternative modalities of resistance in the contemporary workplace. *Sociology, 36*(4), 857–873.

Fleming, P., & Spicer, A. (2004). 'You can checkout anytime, but you can never leave': Spatial boundaries in a high commitment organization. *Human Relations, 57*(1), 75–94.

Fleming, P., & Sturdy, A. (2011). 'Being yourself' in the electronic sweatshop: New forms of normative control. *Human Relations, 64*(2), 177–200.
Florida, R. L. (2002). *The rise of the creative class: And how it's transforming work, leisure, community and everyday life*. New York, NY: Basic Books.
Fontanella-Khan, J., & Landingin, R. (2010, December 2). Tata unit joins call-centre rush to Philippines. *The Financial Times*.
Fortunato, V., & Palidda, R. (2012). *Il call center in Italia: Lavoro e organizzazione tra retorica e realtà*. Roma, Italy: Carocci Editore.
Foucault, M. (1995). *Discipline and punish: The birth of the prison* [Surveiller et punir.]. New York, NY: Vintage Books.
Foucault, M. (2000). The subject and power. In J. Faubion (Ed.), *The essential works of Michel Foucault, 1954–1984: Volume 3 – Power* (pp. 326–348). London, UK: Penguin.
Foucault, M. (2003). *Society must be defended: Lectures at the Collège de France, 1975–1976*. New York, NY: Picador.
Freeman, C. (2000). *High tech and high heels in the global economy: Women, work, and pink-collar identities in the Caribbean*. Durham, NC: Duke University Press.
Frenkel, S. (2005). Service workers in search for decent work. In S. Ackroyd (Ed.), *The Oxford handbook of work and organization* (pp. 356–375). Oxford, UK: Oxford University Press.
Frenkel, S., Korczynski, M., Shire, K., & Tam, M. (1999). *On the front line: Organization of work in the information economy*. Ithaca, NY: Cornell University Press.
Frenkel, S., Tam, M., Korczynski, M., & Shire, K. (1998). Beyond bureaucracy? Work organisation in call centres. *International Journal of Human Resource Management, 9*(6), 957–979.
Frey, C. B., & Osborne, M. A. (2013). *The future of employment: How susceptible are jobs to computerisation?* Retrieved from http://www.oxfordmartin.ox.ac.uk/downloads/academic/future-of-employment.pdf
Friends of Kolinko, & Gurgaon Workers News. (2012). *Burn-out in the global call centre*. Retrieved from http://www.metamute.org/editorial/articles/burn-out-global-call-centre
Fuchs, C. (2010). Labor in informational capitalism and on the internet. *The Information Society, 26*(3), 179–196.
Fumagalli, A. (1997). Aspetti dell'accumulazione flessibile in Italia. In S. Bologna & A. Fumagalli (Eds.), *Il lavoro autonomo di seconda generazione: Scenari del postfordismo in Italia* (pp. 133–170). Milan, Italy: Feltrinelli.

Fumagalli, A. (2007). *Bioeconomia e Capitalismo Cognitivo: Verso un Nuovo Paradigma di Accumulazione*. Rome, Italy: Carocci.

Fumagalli, A., & Mezzadra, S. (Eds.). (2010). *Crisis in the global economy: Financial markets, social struggles, and new political scenarios*. Los Angeles, CA: Semiotext(e).

Gandy, O. (2011). The political economy of personal information. In J. Wasko, G. Murdock, & H. Sousa (Eds.), *The handbook of political economy of communications* (pp. 436–457). Malden, MA/Chichester, SXW: Wiley-Blackwell.

Gardiner, Y. (2008, December 4). Workers will rally at park, strike today. *The Queensland Times*, p. 7.

Garnham, N. (2011). The political economy of communication revisited. In J. Wasko, G. Murdock, & H. Sousa (Eds.), *The handbook of political economy of communications* (pp. 41–61). Malden, MA: Wiley-Blackwell.

Garson, B. (1988). *The electronic sweatshop: How computers are transforming the office of the future into the factory of the past*. New York, NY: Simon & Schuster.

Gates, B., Myhrvold, N., & Rinearson, P. (1996). *The road ahead*. New York, NY: Penguin.

Ghirardi, S., & Murgia, A. (2013). Staging precariousness: The Serpica Naro catwalk during Milan fashion week. *Culture and Organization, 21*(2), 174–196.

Gill, R. (2002). Cool, creative and egalitarian? Exploring gender in project-based new media work in Europe. *Information, Communication & Society, 5*(1), 70–89.

Ginsborg, P. (1990). *A history of contemporary Italy: Society and politics, 1943–1988*. London, UK: Penguin.

Ginsborg, P. (2001). *Italy and its discontents: Family, civil society, state: 1980–2001*. London, UK: Penguin.

Glader, P. (2011, May 20). As Indian companies grow in the U.S., outsourcing comes home. *The Washington Post*.

Good, T., & McFarland, J. (2005). Call centres: A new solution to an old problem? In J. Sacouman & H. Veltmeyer (Eds.), *From the net to the Net: Atlantic Canada in the global economy* (pp. 99–114). Aurora, ON: Garamond Press.

Gorz, A. (2010). *The immaterial* (C. Turner, Trans.). New York, NY: Seagull Books.

Graeber, D. (2011). *Debt: The first 5,000 years*. New York, NY: Melville House.

Graeber, D. (2013, August 17). On the phenomenon of bullshit jobs. *Stike! Magazine*, pp. 10–11.
Gramsci, A. (1971). In Q. Hoare & G. Smith (Eds. & Trans.), *Selections from the prison notebooks* (1st ed.). London, UK: Lawrence & Wishart.
Greco, P. (2011, May 27). *Analisi di un call center*. Retrieved from http://www.uninomade.org/analisi-di-un-call-center
Grimes, S. (2003). Ireland's emerging information economy: Recent trends and future prospects. *Regional Studies, 37*(1), 3–14.
Gruppo d'inchiesta sulla precarietà e il comune. (2013a). *Boll Center n. 1: Bollettino d'inchiesta sui call center calabresi*. Retrieved from http://www.sudcomune.it/site/index.php/9-inchiesta/17-bollettino-n-1
Gruppo d'inchiesta sulla precarietà e il comune. (2013b). *Boll Center n. 2: Bollettino d'inchiesta sui call center calabresi*. Retrieved from http://www.sudcomune.it/site/images/ALLEGATI/inchiesta/Bollettino_inchiesta_call_center_n._2.pdf
Guard, J. (2003). *Manitoba's call centre explosion: A preliminary overview*. Toronto, ON: United Steelworkers Canada.
Guard, J., Steedman, M., & García-Orgales, J. (2007). Organizing the electronic sweatshop: Rank-and-file participation in Canada's steel union. *Labor: Studies in Working-Class History of the Americas, 4*(3), 9–31.
Gülsen, E. (2015). Resistance against the new working practices in the service sector in Turkey. In U. Schuerkens (Ed.), *Global management, local resistances: Theoretical discussion and empirical case studies* (pp. 135–148). New York, NY: Routledge.
Gurgaon Workers News. (2012). *GurgaonWorkersNews no.9/52*. Retrieved from https://gurgaonworkersnews.wordpress.com/gurgaonworkersnews-no-952/
Halifax Chronicle-Herald. (2004, September 9). Many striking Aliant workers to lose some strike pay, employee says. *Halifax Chronicle-Herald*.
Hardt, M., & Negri, A. (2000). *Empire*. Cambridge, MA: Harvard University Press.
Hardt, M., & Negri, A. (2004). *Multitude: War and democracy in the age of empire*. New York, NY: Penguin Press.
Hardt, M., & Negri, A. (2009). *Commonwealth*. Cambridge, MA: Belknap Press of Harvard University Press.
Harvey, D. (1990). *The condition of postmodernity: An enquiry into the origins of cultural change*. Cambridge: Blackwell.

Hastings, T. (2011). *A job worth doing? Reinterpreting control, resistance and everyday forms of coping with call centre work in Glasgow* (Unpublished PhD). University of Glasgow, Glasgow, UK.

Head, S. (2003). *The new ruthless economy: Work and power in the digital age.* Oxford, UK: Oxford University Press.

Head, S. (2004, January 2). Victims of the white-collar assembly line: ONT Edition. *Toronto Star.*

Head, S. (2014). *Mindless: Why smarter machines are making dumber humans.* New York, NY: Basic Books.

Heller, M. (2003). Globalization, the new economy, and the commodification of language and identity. *Journal of Sociolinguistics, 7*(4), 473–492.

Hendery, S. (2008, September 11). Firms plan more call centre outsourcing. *The New Zealand Herald.*

Hochschild, A. R. (2004). *The managed heart: Commercialization of human feeling.* Berkeley, CA: University of California Press.

Holman, D. (2004). Employee well-being in call centres. In S. Deery & N. Kinnie (Eds.), *Call centres and human resource management* (pp. 223–244). Basingstoke, UK: Palgrave.

Holman, D., Batt, R. & Holtgrewe, U. (2007). *The global call center report: International perspectives on management and employment.* Retrieved from http://www.ilr.cornell.edu.proxy.lib.sfu.ca/globalcallcenter/upload/GCC-Intl-REpt-US-Version.pdf

Holst, H. (2008). The political economy of trade union strategies in Austria and Germany: The case of call centres. *European Journal of Industrial Relations, 14*(25), 25–45.

Houlihan, M. (2001). Managing to manage? Stories from the call centre floor. *Journal of European Industrial Training, 25*(2), 208–220.

Houlihan, M. (2002). Tensions and variations in call centre management strategies. *Human Resource Management Journal, 12*(4), 67–67.

Huws, U. (2003). Who's waiting? The contestation of time. In U. Huws (Ed.), *The making of a cybertariat: Virtual work in a real world* (pp. 177–186). New York, NY: Monthly Review Press.

Huws, U. (2009). Working at the interface: Call-centre labour in a global economy. *Work Organisation, Labour & Globalisation, 3*(1), 1–8.

Huws, U. (2012). Bridges and barriers: Globalisation and the mobility of work and workers. *Work Organisation, Labour & Globalisation, 6*(2), 1–7.

Huws, U. (2013). Working online, living offline: Labour in the internet age. *Work Organisation, Labour & Globalisation, 7*(1), 1–11.

Huws, U. (2014). *Labor in the global digital economy: The cybertariat comes of age.* New York, NY: Monthly Review Press.

Huws, U., & Paul, J. (2002). *How can we help? Good practice in call-centre employment.* Retrieved from http://www-it.fmi.uni-sofia.bg/TOSCA/pub/leaflet/Tosca_Book_text.pdf;

Ipsos. (2014). *Casual home based interviewers.* Retrieved from https://www.qjumpers.co.nz/job-seeker/job-detail/11835/#.V56oDhI3laV

Jaimet, K. (2006, June 9). The plot to enslave New Brunswick: Did the former premier make a secret pact or was the Bilderberg just a place 'to meet interesting people'. *Ottawa Citizen.*

janann1206. (2008). Dozens of call center workers walk off job in protest rather than read McCain script attacking Obama. Retrieved from http://ireport.cnn.com/docs/DOC-126348

Jobs, C., Burris, D., & Butler, D. (2007). The social and economic impact of the call center industry in Ireland. *International Journal of Social Economics, 34*(4), 276–289.

Justice, J. (2013). *Mobile health around the globe: Aman Telehealth call center increases access to care in Pakistan.* Retrieved from http://www.healthworkscollective.com/joan-justice/121861/mobile-health-around-globe-aman-telehealth-call-center-increases-access-care-pak

Kämpf, T., & Boes, A. (2007). The nexus of informatisation and internationalisation: A new stage in the internationalisation of labour. *Work Organisation, Labour & Globalisation, 1*(2), 193–208.

Kidman, A. (2010). *10 reasons call centre work is so painful.* Retrieved from http://www.lifehacker.com.au/2010/09/10-reasons-call-centre-work-is-so-painful/

Kinnie, N., Hutchinson, S., & Purcell, J. (2000). 'Fun and surveillance': The paradox of high commitment management in call centres. *The International Journal of Human Resource Management, 11*(5), 967–985.

Knights, D., & McCabe, D. (1998). 'What happens when the phone goes wild?' Staff, stress and spaces for escape in a BPR telephone banking work regime. *Journal of Management Studies, 35*(2), 163–194.

Knights, D., & McCabe, D. (2003). Governing through teamwork: Reconstituting subjectivity in a call centre. *Journal of Management Studies, 40*(7), 1587–1619.

Knights, D., & Willmott, H. (1989). Power and subjectivity at work: From degradation to subjugation in social relations. *Sociology, 23*(4), 535–558.

Knights, D., & Willmott, H. (1999). *Management lives: Power and identity in work organizations.* London, UK: Sage.

Kolinko. (2002). *Hotlines: Call centre, inquiry, communism.* Retrieved from http://www.nadir.org/nadir/initiativ/kolinko/lebuk/e_lebuk.htm

Korczynski, M. (2002). *Human resource management in service work.* New York, NY: Palgrave.

Koskina, A. (2006). How 'taylorised' is call centre work? The sphere of customer-practice in Greece. In J. Connell & J. Burgess (Eds.), *Developments in the call centre industry: Analysis, changes, and challenges* (pp. 170–188). London, UK: Routledge.

Kropotkin, P. (1902). *Mutual aid: A factor in evolution reprint.* London, UK: Heinemann.

La Repubblica Online. (2006, December 13). Call center Atesia, raggiunto l'accordo: "Entro il 2007 assumeremo 6,500 precari". *La Repubblica Online.*

Larner, W. (2001). Governing globalisation: The New Zealand call centre attraction initiative. *Environment and Planning A, 33*(2), 297–312.

Larner, W. (2002). Calling capital: Call centre strategies in New Brunswick and New Zealand. *Global Networks, 2*(2), 133.

Lavin, D. O. (2006). *Call centres in the "new economy:" A Canadian case study* (M.A. thesis). Queen's University, Kingston, ON.

Lazzarato, M. (1996). Immaterial labor. In P. Virno & M. Hardt (Eds.), *Radical thought in Italy: A potential politics* (pp. 133–148). Minneapolis, MN: University of Minnesota Press.

Lazzarato, M. (2015). *Governing by debt* (J. D. Jordan, Trans.). Los Angeles, CA: Semiotext(e).

Linebaugh, P., & Rediker, M. B. (2000). *The many-headed hydra: Sailors, slaves, commoners, and the hidden history of the revolutionary Atlantic.* Boston, MA: Beacon Press.

Lloyd, A. (2013). *Labour markets and identity on the post-industrial assembly line.* Burlington, VT: Ashgate.

Lorey, I. (2015). *State of insecurity: Government of the precarious.* Brooklyn, NY: Verso.

Lüthje, B., Hürtgen, S., Pawliki, P., & Sproll, M. (2013). *From Silicon Valley to Shenzen: Global production and work in the IT industry.* Toronto, ON: Rowman & Littlefield.

Maass, A., & Sustar, L. (2016). *Why they won: The Verizon workers' campaign for union democracy set the stage for a successful strike.* Retrieved from https://www.jacobinmag.com/2016/06/verizon-strike-contract-deal-cwa-ibew-union-pickets/

Machlup, F. (1962). *The production and distribution of knowledge in the United States.* Princeton, NJ: Princeton University Press.

MacKinnon, B. (2004). *Aliant management answers calls during telephone worker's strike*. Retrieved from http://www.artizans.com/image/MAC960/aliant-management-answers-calls-during-telephone-workers-strike/

Macphee, N. (2004, April 13). Aliant workers could strike by Friday. *St. John's Telegram*.

Marazzi, C. (1999). *l posto dei calzini: La svolta linguistica dell'economia e i suoi effetti sulla politica*. Turin, Italy: Bollati Borlinghieri.

Marx, K. (1990). *Capital: Volume 1*. London, UK: Penguin.

Marx, K. (1993, orig 1858). *Grundrisse: Foundations of the critique of political economy* [Grundrisse der Kritik der politischen Ökonomie] (M. Nicolaus, Trans.). Harmondsworth, UK: Penguin Books.

Mason, P. (2016). *Postcapitalism: A guide to our future* (1st American ed.). New York, NY: Farrar, Straus and Giroux.

Mattoni, A. (2012). *Media practices and protest politics: How precarious workers mobilise*. Burlington, VT: Ashgate.

McClintock, P. (2016). *Global 2015 box office: Revenue hits record $38 billion-plus*. Retrieved from http://www.hollywoodreporter.com/news/global-2015-box-office-revenue-851749

McFarland, J. (2000). 1-800 New Brunswick: Economic development strategies, firm restructuring and the local production of global services. In J. Jenson & B. Sousa Santos (Eds.), *Globalising institutions: Case studies in social regulation and innovation* (pp. 53–79). Hampshire, UK: Ashgagate.

McFarland, J. (2009). Telling the story of globalization, neoliberalism and the call centre industry in New Brunswick. *Socialist Studies: The Journal of the Society for Socialist Studies*, 5(1), 24–50.

McKercher, C. (2002). *Newsworkers unite: Labor, convergence, and North American newspapers*. Lanham, MA: Rowman and Littlefield.

McLaughlin, P. (2004, September 11). Aliant workers vote on deal. *Halifax Daily News*, p. 11.

McNally, D. (1993). *Against the market: Political economy, market socialism and the Marxist critique*. London, UK: Verso.

McNally, D. (2011). *Global slump: The economics and politics of crisis and resistance*. Winnipeg, MB: Fernwood.

Mendonca, J. (2014). *Aegis plans to enter call centre markets in Japan and Korea*. Retrieved from http://articles.economictimes.indiatimes.com/2014-07-29/news/52186934_1_ceo-sandip-sen-indian-bpo-aegis

Mezzadra, S. (2010). Between centre and periphery. *Transit Labour: Circuits, Regions, Borders*, 2, 37–38.

Mills, C. W. (2002). *White collar: The American middle classes* (50th Anniversary ed.). New York, NY: Oxford University Press.
Miozzo, M., & Ramírez, M. (2003). Services innovation and the transformation of work: The case of UK telecommunications. *New Technology, Work and Employment, 18*(1), 62–79.
Mirá quién habla. (2010). Call center: Un blog sobre la esclavitud posmoderna. Retrieved from http://mira-Quién-habla.blogspot.ca/2010/03/la-esclavitud-posmoderna-ensayo-de-otro.html
Mirchandani, K. (2004). Practices of global capital: Gaps, cracks and ironies in transnational call centres in India. *Global Networks, 4*(4), 355–374.
Mirchandani, K. (2012). *Phone clones: Authenticity work in the transnational service economy.* Ithaca, NY: ILR Press.
Mirrlees, T. (2013). *Global entertainment media: Between cultural imperialism and cultural globalization.* New York, NY: Routledge.
Modimoeng, K. (2008, November 27). Airline faces strike action. *Sowetan*, p. 21.
Moodley, J. (2009, August 3). Telkom strike puts us on hold. *Daily News*.
Moody, K. (1999). Bell Canada outsources operator jobs to U.S. firm. Retrieved from http://www.labornotes.org/1999/02/bell-canada-outsources-operator-jobs-us-firm
Morini, C. (2007). The feminization of labour in cognitive capitalism. *Feminist Review, 87*(1), 40–59.
Morini, C., & Fumagalli, A. (2010). Life put to work: Towards a life theory of value. *ephemera: theory & politics in organization, 10*(3/4), 234–252.
Morning Star Online. (2009, February 18). Thames water staff vote on massive cull. *Morning Star Online.*
Mosco, V. (2004). *The digital sublime: Myth, power, and cyberspace.* Cambridge, MA: MIT Press.
Mosco, V. (2009). *The political economy of communication* (2nd ed.). London, UK: Sage.
Mosco, V. (2014). *To the cloud: Big data in a turbulent world.* Boulder, CO: Paradigm Publishers.
Mosco, V., & Lavin, D. O. (2008). The laboring of international communication. In D. Thussu (Ed.), *Internationalizing media studies* (pp. 148–162). New York, NY: Routledge.
Mosco, V., & McKercher, C. (2006). Convergence bites back: Labour struggles in the Canadian telecommunications industry. *Canadian Journal of Communication, 31*(3), 733–751.

Mosco, V., & McKercher, C. (2008). *The laboring of communication: Will knowledge workers of the world unite?* Lanham, MD: Lexington Books.

Mulholland, K. (2004). Workplace resistance in an Irish call centre: Slammin', scammin', smokin' an' leavin'. *Work, Employment and Society, 18*(4), 709–724.

Munck, R. (2008a). Globalisation and trade unions: Towards a multi-level strategy? *Work Organisation, Labour & Globalisation, 2*(1), 11–23.

Munck, R. (2008b). Globalisation, contestation and labor internationalism: A transformationalist perspective. In M. Taylor (Ed.), *Global economy contested: Power and conflict across the international division of labor* (pp. 220–238). New York, NY: Routledge.

Nadeem, S. (2011). *Dead ringers: How outsourcing is changing the way Indians understand themselves*. Princeton, NJ: Princeton University Press.

Neate, R. (2011, April 28). Orange tells call centre workers they can keep their jobs if they relocate to the Philippines. *The Telegraph*.

Negri, A. (2005). *Books for burning: Between civil war and democracy in 1970s Italy* [Libri del rogo.]. New York, NY: Verso.

NIDIL, FISTEL and CPO & Delegazione Sindacale Unitaria. (2005). *A tutti i lavoratori: Finiamola con le strumentalizzazioni*. Retrieved from http://www.slaicobasmilano.org/precariatesia.htm

NIDIL-CGIL. (2007). *Chi siamo*. Retrieved from http://www.eurofound.europa.eu/eiro/2006/06/questionnaires/it0606019q.html

Niemeijer, M. (2004, August 6). Unions slow to develop new strategies: Canadian telecom industry rocked by deregulation, competition, mergers, technology. *Labor Notes*, p. 305.

Noronha, E., & D'Cruz, P. (2009). Engaging the professional: Organising call centre agents in India. *Industrial Relations Journal, 40*(3), 215–234.

Orwell, G. (1938). *Homage to Catalonia*. London, UK: Secker and Warburg.

Outsource. (2012). *The future of rightshoring: Q&A with professor Philip Taylor, University of Strathclyde*. Retrieved from http://outsourcemag.com/qaa-professor-philip-taylor-university-of-strathclyde/

Parola, S. (2010). *Omnia, blitz del commissario: 'Fuori tutti, lasciate le chiavi'*. Retrieved from http://torino.repubblica.it/cronaca/2010/10/01/news/omnia_service_occupata-7612737/

Patel, R. (2010). *Working the night shift: Women in India's call center industry*. Stanford, CA: Stanford University Press.

Pearson, B., & Zehr, D. (2011). *Pre-commerce: How companies and customers are transforming business together*. San Francisco, CA: Jossey-Bass.

Peck, J., & Tickell, A. (2002). Neoliberalizing space: The free economy and the penal state. In N. Brenner & N. Theodore (Eds.), *Spaces of neoliberalism: Urban restructuring in North America and Western Europe* (pp. 33–57). Malden, MA: Blackwell.

Pentland, B. (1995). Information systems and organizational learning: The social epistemology of organizational knowledge systems. *Accounting, Management and Information Technologies, 5*(1), 1–21.

Persichetti, P., & Scalzone, O. (1999). *Il nemico inconfessabile: Sovversione sociale, lotta armata e stato d'emergenza in Italia dagli anni settanta ad oggi*. Rome, Italy: Odradek Edizioni.

Peterson, L. (2015). *Where 'talents' go to die: Diary of a US call centre worker*. Retrieved from https://rdln.wordpress.com/2015/09/11/where-talents-go-to-die-diary-of-a-us-call-centre-worker/

Pezzulli, F. M. (2013, July 4). La solitudine del telefonista. *Il Manifesto*.

pirati delle risaie. (2009). *Aggiornamenti dal call center Phonemedia di Trino vc -3-*. Retrieved from https://www.youtube.com/watch?v=6x0gVmYQvzQ

Pizzolato, N. (2013). The American worker and the *forze nuove*: Turin and Detroit at the twilight of Fordism. *Viewpoint Magazine*, (3).

Poster, W. R. (2007). Who's on the line? Indian call center agents pose as Americans for US-outsourced firms. *Industrial Relations, 46*(2), 271–304.

Pupo, N., & Noack, A. (2009). Standardising public service: The experiences of call-centre workers in the Canadian federal government. *Work Organisation, Labour & Globalisation, 3*(1), 100–113.

Qiu, J. L. (2010). Network labour and non-elite knowledge workers in China. *Work Organisation, Labour & Globalisation, 4*(2), 80–95.

Qiu, J. L. (2012). Network labor: Beyond the shadow of Foxconn. In L. Hjorth, J. Burgess, & I. Richardson (Eds.), *Studying mobile media: Cultural technologies, mobile communication, and the iPhone* (pp. 173–189). London, UK: Routledge.

Rainnie, A., & Drummond, G. (2006). Community unionism in a regional call centre: The organiser's perspective. In J. Burgess & J. Connell (Eds.), *Developments in the call centre industry: An overview* (pp. 136–151). New York, NY: Routledge.

Reuters News. (2008a, February 20). Strike ends at Mexico's Telmex call center unit. *Reuters News*.

Reuters News. (2008b, March 3). Union plans strike at Elisa customer service. *Reuters News*.

Richardson, R., Belt, V., & Marshall, N. (2000). Taking calls to Newcastle: The regional implications of the growth in call centers. *Regional Studies, 34*(4), 357.

Rideout, V. (2003). *Continentalizing Canadian telecommunications: The politics of regulatory reform.* Kingston, ON: McGill-Queen's University Press.

Rizzo, F. (2008). *Fuga dal call center.*

Rocker, R. (2004). *Anarcho-syndicalism: Theory and practice* (6th ed.). Edinburgh, Scotland/Oakland, CA: AK Press.

Roggero, G. (2011). *The production of living knowledge: Crisis of the university and transformation of labour in Europe and North America* [Produzione del sapere vivo.] (E. Brophy, Trans.). Philadelphia, PA: Temple University Press.

Rose, E. (2002). The labour process and union commitment within a banking services call centre. *Journal of Industrial Relations, 44*(1), 40–61.

Ross, A. (2004a). *Low pay, high profile: The global push for fair labor.* New York, NY: New Press.

Ross, A. (2004b). *No-collar: The humane workplace and its hidden costs.* Philadelphia, PA: Temple University Press.

Ross, A. (2009). *Nice work if you can get it: Life and labor in precarious times.* New York, NY: New York University Press.

Russell, B. (2008a). Call centres: A decade of research. *International Journal of Management Reviews, 10*(3), 195–219.

Russell, B. (2008b). Unions in the information economy: Info-service work and organizing in Australian call centres. *Journal of Industrial Relations, 50*(2), 285–303.

Ryan, M. (1982). *Marxism and deconstruction: A critical articulation.* Baltimore, MD: Johns Hopkins University Press.

Rynor, B. (2008, November 17). Postal workers launch strike action. *Canwest News Service.*

Schatz, L., & Johnson, L. (2007). Smart city north: Economic and labour force impacts of call centres in Sudbury, Ontario. *Work Organisation, Labour & Globalisation, 1*(2), 116–130.

Schiller, D. (1999). *Digital capitalism: Networking the global market system.* Cambridge, MA: MIT Press.

Schiller, D. (2007). *How to think about information.* Urbana, IL: University of Illinois Press.

Schiller, D. (2014). Rosa Luxemburg's internet? For a political economy of state mobilization and the movement of accumulation in cyberspace. *International Journal of Communication, 8,* 355–375.

Schuetz, L. (2010). *Country's largest call centre company facing bankruptcy: Workers fight to save 10,000 jobs*. Retrieved from http://www.socialistworld.net/doc/3999

Sciotto, A. (2006a, August 3). Atesia, vanno assunti tutti: Le conclusioni dell'ispettorato sui 3.200 co.co.pro del call center romano. *Il Manifesto*.

Sciotto, A. (2006b, October 6). Call center, un nuovo accordo che frega i cocoprò. *Il Manifesto*.

Sciotto, A. (2006c, December 8). Cos, sciopero al contrario. *Il Manifesto*.

Scott, J. (1985). *Weapons of the weak: Everyday forms of peasant resistance*. New Haven, CT: Yale University Press.

Scott, J. (1990). *Domination and the arts of resistance: Hidden transcripts*. New Haven, CT: Yale University Press.

Scott, J. (2012). *Two cheers for anarchism: Six easy pieces on autonomy, dignity, and meaningful work and play*. Princeton, NJ: Princeton University Press.

Sewell, G. (1998). The discipline of teams: The control of team-based industrial work through electronic and peer surveillance. *Administrative Science Quarterly, 43*(2), 397–428.

Sewell, G. (2005). Nice work? Rethinking managerial control in an era of knowledge work. *Organization, 12*(5), 685–704.

Shan, S. (2011). *Call center outsourcing panned*. Retrieved from http://www.taipeitimes.com/News/taiwan/archives/2011/07/27/2003509251

Sherman, A. (2013) *Telemarketing & Call Centers in the US*. IBISWorld Industry Report 56142.

Shniad, S. (2005, January 6). Lessons from the TWU-Telus dispute. *Labor Notes*. Retrieved from http://labornotes.org/node/26

Shniad, S. (2007). Neo-liberalism and its impact in the telecommunications industry: One trade unionist's perspective. In C. McKercher & V. Mosco (Eds.), *Knowledge workers in the information society* (pp. 299–310). Lanham, MD: Lexington Books.

Sitel. (2015). *Overview*. Retrieved from http://www.sitel.com/our-company/overview/

Skand Bhargava, K., & Menzigian, S. S. (2015). *Contact center outsourcing annual report 2015: Incumbents beware – There's no place for complacency* (No. EGR-2015-1-R-1470). Dallas, TX: Everest Group.

SmartAction. (2013). *SmartAction names new CEO Tom Lewis*. Retrieved from http://www.prnewswire.com/news-releases/smartaction-names-new-ceo-tom-lewis-213966961.html

Snowdon, G. (2010, September 22). Call centres benefit from rise in graduate applicants. *The Guardian*.
sp00n. (2005, May 22). *ClientLogic employment issues*. Retrieved from http://www.dslreports.com/forum/r13467423-Clientlogic-employment-issues
Srnicek, N., & Williams, A. (2015). *Inventing the future: Postcapitalism and a world without work* (Verso ed.). London, UK: Verso.
Standing, G. (2011). *The precariat: The new dangerous class*. London, UK: Bloomsbury Academic.
Standing, G. (2014). *A precariat charter: From denizens to citizens*. London, UK: Bloomsbury.
Steven. (2010, February 16). *Techy wage increase attempt at Convergys in Gurgaon*. Retrieved from http://libcom.org/library/techy-wage-increase-attempt-convergys-gurgaon
Stevens, A. (2014). *Call centers and the global division of labor: A political economy of post-industrial employment and union organizing*. New York, NY: Routledge/Taylor & Francis Group.
Stevens, A., & Lavin, D. O. (2007). Stealing time: The temporal regulation of labor in neoliberal and post-Fordist work regimes. *Democratic Communiqué*, *22*(2), 40–61.
Stevens, A., & Mosco, V. (2010). Prospects for trade unions and labour organisations in India's IT and ITES industries. *Work Organisation, Labour & Globalisation*, *4*(2), 39–59.
StopPress. (2011). *Synovate cuddles up to new global parent, changes unlikely for Kiwi outpost*. Retrieved from http://stoppress.co.nz/news/synovate-cuddles-up-to-new-global-parent-changes-unlikely-for-kiwi-outpost
Synovate. (2007). *Synovate expands footprint in Australia and New Zealand with Research Solutions deal* (press release). Retrieved from http://www.marketresearchworld.net/content/view/1700/74/
Tait, V. (2005). *Poor workers' unions: Rebuilding labor from below*. Cambridge, MA: South End Press.
Taylor, P., & Bain, P. (1999). 'An assembly line in the head': Work and employee relations in the call centre. *Industrial Relations Journal*, *30*(2), 101–117.
Taylor, P., & Bain, P. (2001). Trade unions, workers' rights and the frontier of control in UK call centres. *Economic and Industrial Democracy*, *22*(1), 39–66.
Taylor, P., & Bain, P. (2003). 'Subterranean worksick blues:' Humour as subversion in two call centres. *Organizational Studies*, *24*(9), 1487–1509.

Taylor, P., & Bain, P. (2005). "India calling to the far away towns:" The call centre labour process and globalization. *Work, Employment & Society, 19*(2), 261–282.

Taylor, P., & Bain, P. (2006). Work organisation and employee relations in Indian call centres. In J. Burgess & J. Connell (Eds.), *Developments in the call centre industry: Analysis, changes and challenges* (pp. 36–57). New York, NY: Routledge.

Taylor, P., & Bain, P. (2008). United by a common language? Trade union responses in the UK and India to call centre offshoring. *Antipode, 40*(1), 131–154.

Taylor, P., Baldry, C., Bain, P., & Ellis, V. (2003). A unique working environment: Health, sickness and absence management in UK call centres. *Work, Employment & Society, 17*(3), 435–458.

Taylor, P., Mulvey, G., Hyman, J., & Bain, P. (2002). Work organization, control and the experience of work in call centres. *Work, Employment & Society, 16*(1), 133–150.

Tazzioli, M. (2013). *Geografie rivoluzionate: Tunisia, due anni dopo*. Retrieved from http://www.uninomade.org/geografie-rivoluzionate-tunisia-due-anni-dopo/

Telelink Call Centre. (n.d.). *Answering services*. Retrieved from http://telelinkcallcentre.com/services/answering-services/

Terranova, T. (2004). *Network culture: Politics for the information age*. London, UK: Pluto Press.

Thanawala, S. (2007, October 16). India's call-center jobs go begging. *Time Magazine*.

The Economist. (2001). Will the corporation survive? *The Economist, 360*, 16.

The Economist. (2016). Call centres: The end of the line. *The Economist, 418 (8975)*, 54–55.

The Heritage Foundation. (2015). *2015 Index of economic freedom*. Retrieved from http://www.heritage.org/index/ranking

The New Zealand Herald. (2009). *Locked out call-centre staff lock managers in*. Retrieved from http://www.nzherald.co.nz/nz/news/article.cfm?c_id=1&objectid=10566554

The Ontario Co-operative Association. (2016). *Starting a co-op*. Retrieved from http://www.ontario.coop/programs_services/coop_development/starting_a_coop#a_100

Thomas, D. (2012, October 12). Telefónica to sell Atento to Bain Capital. *The Financial Times*.

Thompson, E. P. (1966). *The making of the English working class*. New York, NY: Vintage Books.
Thompson, P., Warhurst, C., & Callaghan, G. (2001). Ignorant theory and knowledgeable workers: Interrogating the connections between knowledge, skills and services. *Journal of Management Studies, 38*(7), 923–942.
Toby. (2007). *Super-size my pay*. Retrieved from http://www.metamute.org/editorial/articles/super-size-my-pay
TOSCA D1 Inventory report: Italy. (2002). Retrieved from www-it.fmi.uni-sofia.bg/TOSCA/pub/d1/Tosca_D1_IT_final.doc
Townsend, K. (2005). Electronic surveillance and cohesive teams: Room for resistance in an Australian call centre? *New Technology, Work and Employment, 20*(1), 47–59.
TRCC/MWAR. (2016). *Mission, vision and philosophy*. Retrieved from http://trccmwar.ca/about-us/mission-vision-philosophy/
Treen, M. (2014). *A short history of the Unite union in New Zealand*. Retrieved from https://d3n8a8pro7vhmx.cloudfront.net/uniteunion/pages/21/attachments/original/1431924113/A_short_history_of_Unite_web2.pdf?1431924113
Tronti, M. (2005). *Operai e capitale*. Rome, Italy: DeriveApprodi.
Tsianos, V., & Papadopoulos, D. (2006). *Precarity: A savage journey to the heart of embodied capitalism*. Retrieved from http://eipcp.net/transversal/1106/tsianospapadopoulos/en
Tutton, M. (2005, November 16). Aliant outsources 129 jobs, slashes 100 temp positions. *Halifax Daily News*, p. 13.
Tutton, M. (2006, March 8). Shakeup won't mean job cuts, CEO says. *St. John's Telegram*.
Unione Sindicale di Base. (2009). *Telefono precario: 800.03.42.35 il numero verde nazionale autogestito da RdB*. Retrieved from http://precari.usb.it/index.php?id=20&tx_ttnews%5Btt_news%5D=19396&cHash=ade1a48490&MP=63-629
Unite Union. (2008a). *Auckland call centre workers strike* (press release). Retrieved from http://www.scoop.co.nz/stories/BU0812/S00203.htm;
Unite Union. (2008b). *Calling for change: One big union agreement (campaign update #3)*. Retrieved from http://www.taikorea.co.nz/Unite/website_downloads/updateunionv3.pdf;
Unite Union. (2009). *North shore call centre workers strike at OCIS* (press release). Retrieved from http://www.scoop.co.nz/stories/BU0903/S00141/north-shore-call-centre-workers-strike-at-ocis.htm;

United Nations Conference on Trade and Development. (2004). *World investment report: The shift towards services.* United Nations Conference on Trade and Development, Switzerland.
United News of India. (2016). Thames water picks up Wipro for customer service and billing needs. Retrieved from https://www.highbeam.com/doc/1P3-4044868881.html
van den Broek, D. (2002). Monitoring and surveillance in call centres: Some responses from Australian workers. *Labour & Industry, 12*(3), 43–58.
van den Broek, D. (2004). Globalising call centre capital: Gender, culture and work identity. *Labour & Industry: A Journal of the Social and Economic Relations of Work, 14*(3), 59–75.
van den Broek, D., Barnes, A., & Townsend, K. (2008). 'Teaming up': Teams and team sharing in call centres. *The Journal of Industrial Relations, 50*(2), 257–269.
Vaccaro, A. (2004, September 22). Aliant workers wary. *St. John's Telegram,* p. D1.
Vercellone, C. (2007). From formal subsumption to general intellect: Elements for a Marxist reading of the theory of cognitive capitalism. *Historical Materialism, 15*(1), 13–36.
Viewpoint Magazine. (2013, September 30). Issue 3: Workers' inquiry. *Viewpoint Magazine, 3.* Retrieved from https://viewpointmag.com/2013/09/30/issue-3-workers-inquiry/
Virno, P. (2001). Lavoro e linguaggio. In U. Fadini & A. Zanini (Eds.), *Lessico Postfordista: Dizionario delle Idee e della Mutazione* (pp. 181–185). Milan, Italy: Feltrinelli.
Virno, P. (2003). *A grammar of the multitude: For an analysis of contemporary forms of life.* Cambridge, MA: Semiotext(e).
Voce Proletaria. (2011). *Lavoratori dei call center Uniti a Torino.* Retrieved from http://blog.libero.it/VoceProletaria/10198680.html
Vosko, L. (2005). Precarious employment: Towards an improved understanding of labour market insecurity. In L. Vosko (Ed.), *Precarious employment: Understanding labour market insecurity in Canada* (pp. 3–42). Montreal, QC: McGill-Queen's University Press.
Wade, J. (2016). *Call centers chase a false holy grail of artificial intelligence and full automation.* Retrieved from http://www.nearshoreamericas.com/automation-call-center-artificial-intelligence-holy-grail/
Wallace, C. M., Eagleson, G., & Waldersee, R. (2000). The sacrificial HR strategy in call centers. *International Journal of Service Industry Management, 11*(2), 174–184.

Warson, A. (2002, July 30). Moncton's core gets urban facelift: City's fortunes have been reversed by new businesses, prompting building. *Globe and Mail.*
Wasko, J., Murdock, G., & Sousa, H. (2011). *The handbook of political economy of communications.* Malden, MA: Wiley-Blackwell.
Weeks, K. (2011). *The problem with work: Feminism, Marxism, antiwork politics, and postwork imaginaries.* Durham, NC/London, UK: Duke University Press.
Weiss, A. (2007). Global forces and national institutions: Call centre work in Colombia. *Work Organisation, Labour & Globalisation, 1*(2), 131–154.
Wilkie, R. (2011). *The digital condition: Class and culture in the information network.* New York, NY: Fordham University Press.
Winks, C. (1981). *Manuscript found in a typewriter.* Retrieved from http://www.processedworld.com/Issues/issue01/i01manu.html
Winseck, D. (1998). *Reconvergence: A political economy of telecommunications in Canada.* Cresskill, NJ: Hampton Press.
Winseck, D. (2011). The political economies of media and the transformation of the global media industries. In D. Winseck & D. Y. Jin (Eds.), *The political economies of media* (pp. 3–48). London, UK: Bloomsbury Academic.
Wittel, A. (2004). Culture, labour and subjectivity: For a political economy from below. *Capital & Class, 28*(3), 11–30.
Wolff, S. (2016). Behind the line: Information privatization and the reification of work in the call center of a Brazilian state-owned telecommunications company. In R. Maxwell (Ed.), *The Routledge companion to labor and media* (pp. 130–142). New York, NY: Routledge.
Women on Waves. (n.d.). *Safe abortion hotlines.* Retrieved from http://www.womenonwaves.org/en/page/2583/safe-abortion-hotlines
Wong, T. (2004, July 31). Strike could hit Bell this week: Technicians give union mandate to set up picket lines. *Toronto Star.*
Woodcock, J. (2013, September 25). Smile down the phone: An attempt at a worker inquiry in a call centre. *Viewpoint Magazine,* (3). Retrieved from https://viewpointmag.com/2013/09/25/smile-down-the-phone-an-attempt-at-a-workers-inquiry-in-a-call-center/
Wright, S. (2002). *Storming heaven: Class composition and struggle in Italian autonomist Marxism.* London, UK: Pluto Press.
Yellin, E. (2009). *Your call is (not that) important to us: Customer service and what it reveals about our world and our lives.* New York, NY: Free Press.
Zecca, E. (2010). *Histórico paro de trabajadores de call centers.* Retrieved from http://www.180.com.uy/articulo/14602_Historico-paro-de-trabajadores-de-call-centers

Index

A
abstract communication, 6, 6n4, 15, 17, 87–8, 96–112, 97n15, 98n18, 120, 121, 219
abstract knowledge, 6n4, 88, 97n15, 110n26
abstract labor, 6n4, 88, 97, 98, 98n16, 99, 108n24, 120n30, 222n15
Acadians, deportation of, 88, 93
Accenture, USA, 36n14, 138
Aegis, USA, 138, 138n7, 141, 145, 155
Airtel Telecommunication, Nigeria, 73
Aliant, Canada, 17, 85, 86n1, 87–9, 94, 95, 95n13, 96–120, 119n29, 122, 123, 132, 231
Alquati, Romano, 60, 60n1
alternative call centre organization, 19, 20, 213, 244, 249, 254
Aman Telehealth, Pakistan, 250
Aneesh, A., 98, 135, 136
anti-globalization movement, 148, 149. *See also* global justice movement
Apex, Argentina, 48, 67
artificial intelligence (AI), 242, 243. *See also* automation
Assemblea Coordinata e Continuativa Contro la Precarietà (ACCCP), Italy, 189n18
assembly line, 3, 3n2, 10, 11, 38, 173, 221, 222. *See also* digital assembly line; factory; Fordism

---

Note: Page number followed by 'n' refers to notes

Association of Call Center Workers, Turkey, 19
AssoContact, Italy, 183
Atesia, Italy, 19, 143, 170, 174–6, 181, 182, 184–207, 186n15, 186n16, 189n18, 204n21, 206n22, 232, 234, 236
Atlantic Communications and Technical Workers Union (ACTWU), Canada, 95, 115–17
AT&T, USA, 32n6
Australian National Union of Workers, 18, 226, 251
Australian Unemployed Workers' Union, 251
automation, 102, 113, 143n11, 223, 227, 242, 242n35, 243, 248, 253. *See also* artificial intelligence (AI)
autonomist Marxism, 5, 5n3, 43, 43n26, 44, 44n28, 45, 45n30, 49, 62, 175, 196, 203, 213, 229, 232, 249. *See also* operaismo
Avaya, USA, 137n6

B

Bain Capital, USA, 140
Bain, Peter, 10, 36, 37n17, 37n18, 38n19, 40, 42, 62, 66, 68n8, 70, 76, 98n17, 109, 120, 173
BC Nurses' Union, Canada, 251
Bell Aliant, Canada, 8n7, 103, 118, 119, 121, 123. *See also* Aliant, Canada

Bell Canada, 71, 89n3, 94, 105, 113, 115, 118
Bell, Daniel, 8, 35, 35n11, 41. *See also* post-industrialism
Berardi, Franco, 31, 44n28
bilingualism, 17, 91–3, 100, 101, 106, 123, 159
Blu, Italy, 74
Braverman, Harry, 7, 7n6, 8, 8n8, 9, 9n9, 10–13, 13n15, 15, 17, 35–7, 39, 41–3, 70, 87, 108n23, 172, 219, 228, 246
British Telecom, 107, 120n30, 121
Burawoy, Michael, 78
burnout, 39, 99, 109. *See also* turnover

C

Call&Call, Italy, 183
Call Center Offensive (CCO), Germany, 15, 47, 77, 235, 246
Call Centre Attraction Initiative (CCAI), New Zealand, 146
call centre employment, 4, 34
  in Afghanistan, 4
  in Argentina, 4, 47, 61, 67, 73, 74, 109, 120, 139, 155, 222, 233, 236n32, 240, 253
  in Australia, 18, 38n19, 62, 67, 70, 72, 73, 131, 133, 145, 146, 150, 152, 154, 156, 157, 159
  in Austria, 71, 72
  in Barbados, 4, 222, 230, 232
  in Brazil, 139, 188, 223

in Canada, 4, 17, 38n19, 50,
    65n5, 71, 72, 79, 85, 87, 91,
    94, 96, 112, 113, 119, 120,
    123, 132, 140, 146n14, 181,
    215, 230, 232, 235, 238,
    247, 252
in Chile, 140
in China, 4, 56, 76, 188, 222,
    239
in Colombia, 137, 137n6, 140
in Costa Rica, 141
in Finland, 73
in Germany, 46, 72
in Ghana, 73
in Guatemala, 140
in India, 4, 47, 62, 64, 65, 65n5,
    68, 72, 75, 108, 108n24,
    109n25, 120, 135, 135n4,
    136, 138–42, 144n12, 158,
    203, 205, 230, 230n27,
    233n31, 236, 250n43
in Indonesia, 139
in Ireland, 4, 17, 50, 61, 63, 79,
    86, 86n2, 87, 93, 94,
    100n20, 111n27, 119, 140,
    141, 180, 215, 223n18, 231,
    238, 241
in Italy, 5, 19, 48, 50, 63, 74, 77,
    79, 93n11, 101, 108, 109,
    121, 162, 170, 171, 180–5,
    188, 194, 199, 202, 225,
    231, 232, 236, 253
in Japan, 141
in Malaysia, 141
in Mauritius, 140
in Mexico, 73, 139, 140
in Morocco, 135, 140
in the Netherlands, 4, 72
in New Zealand, 18, 50, 76, 79,
    131, 133, 134, 145, 146,
    146n14, 150, 152, 153,
    155–7, 159, 161, 181, 225,
    227, 232, 234, 236, 241
in Nigeria, 73
in Pakistan, 250
in the Philippines, 4, 76, 132n1,
    139, 141, 142
in Puerto Rico, 140
in Senegal, 140
in Singapore, 139
in South Africa, 4, 75, 139
in South Korea, 73, 139, 141
in Spain, 140, 252
in Sri Lanka, 139
in Taiwan, 76, 139
in Thailand, 139
in Tunisia, 188, 238
in Turkey, 1, 70
in the UK, 4, 10n12, 32n5,
    37n17, 37n18, 39n20,
    39n21, 40n22, 49, 59,
    64n4, 67–9, 72, 75, 76,
    91n6, 99n19, 109, 120,
    121, 135, 139, 140, 141,
    143, 143n10, 229, 238, 252
in Uruguay, 73
in the USA, 4, 33, 33n8, 38n19,
    61, 71, 103, 105, 121, 122,
    135, 138–41, 143, 143n10,
    160, 247, 252
callcentreification, 86, 96–112,
    97n14, 120, 121, 132, 218
call centre workforce
    making of, 5, 12, 13, 17, 20,
    29, 32n5, 64, 76, 85–124,
    213–54

call centre workforce (*cont.*)
  unmaking of, 213–54 (*see also* alternative call centre organization)
Call Direct, UK, 59, 60
Calling for Change campaign, 18, 134, 144–55, 158, 159, 160n23, 161, 162, 241. *See also* Unite, New Zealand
Cameron, Deborah, 6, 15
Canada Industrial Relations Board (CIRB), 94, 95, 102
Canada Post, 71
Canadian Auto Workers (CAW), 86n1, 119, 122
Canadian Customer Contact Centre Industry (CCCI), 91n7
Canadian Labor Code, 114
Canadian Radio-Television and Telecommunications Commission (CRTC), 94
Cátedra Experimental sobre Producción de Subjetividad, Argentina, 15, 15n18, 48, 61, 67, 77, 222, 223, 233, 240
China Labor Watch, 251
class, 5, 8, 8n8, 9, 11–14, 14n17, 15, 22, 22n21, 35, 43, 46n35, 60n1, 144, 171, 173, 230n27, 232, 234, 243n36, 245, 249n41, 254
  class composition, 5, 156, 169
  class formation, 7, 12–14, 14n17, 19, 47, 50, 60, 61, 77, 78, 87, 213, 222, 254
  informational underclass, 5, 9, 12, 29, 49, 76, 78, 79

clerical work, 32n6, 35n12, 88, 90, 95, 95n13, 96, 100, 102, 108n23, 112, 138
ClientLogic, USA, 104–6, 138
Colectivo Situaciones, Argentina, 16, 48n34, 67, 74, 109, 137, 155, 203, 236n32, 237, 240, 241
collective organization. *See* labor organizing
Collettivo Precari Atesia (CPA), Italy, 19, 170, 171, 174, 175, 186, 189–94, 196–200, 203, 206, 206n22, 207, 225, 226, 232, 233, 236, 253
colonialism, 135n4, 140, 141, 157
Comdata, Italy, 75
commodification of language, 30, 93, 98n17, 110, 254. *See also* language put to work
communication from below, 2, 7n5, 14, 47, 144, 225, 244, 252. *See also* horizontal communication
Communication Workers of America (CWA), USA, 71, 94n12, 123
Communication Workers' Union (CWU), Ireland, 73, 86, 111n27, 173
Communications, Energy and Paperworkers Union of Canada (CEP), 71, 86, 86n1, 94, 94n12, 95, 95n13, 96, 113, 114, 115n28, 116–19, 122, 123, 233n30, 236. *See also* Unifor, Canada

communicative capacities, 34, 88, 100, 102, 102n21, 120, 203, 223, 224
communicative capitalism, 7–12, 16–18, 23, 29–31, 33, 34, 44, 45, 50, 76, 78, 86, 96, 122, 136, 137, 157, 161, 215, 220, 221, 228, 230. *See also* Dean, Jodi
communicative labor, 3, 20, 29, 34, 38, 88, 96, 97, 97n14, 98, 102, 107, 108, 134, 136, 140, 171, 202, 244. *See also* communicative production
communicative production, 34, 38, 88, 96, 224n20. *See also* communicative labor
Confederazione dei Comitati di Base (Cobas), Italy, 178, 185, 186, 190, 206n22, 236
Confederazione Generale del Lavoro (CGL), Italy, 177
Confederazione Generale Italiana del Lavoro (CGIL), Italy, 176n7, 177, 177n9, 177n10, 178, 178n11, 186n16, 188, 195, 200–3
Confederazione Italiana Sindacati Lavoratori (CISL), Italy, 176n7, 177, 177n9, 178, 178n11, 188, 195, 203
convergence, 85, 94, 96, 104, 111
    corporate, 85, 86n1, 89, 89n3, 94, 95, 99, 102, 103, 112, 117, 120, 123, 132n1, 133, 138, 145, 185
    trade union, 71, 86, 94, 112, 117, 119–24, 177, 186n16

Convergys, USA, 68, 138, 139
Co-operative Bank and Co-operative Insurance Society, UK, 252
Cooperative Response Center, USA, 252
co-operatives, 21, 252, 253. *See also* alternative call centre organization
Coordinamento dei Lavoratori di Roma Ovest (CLARO), Italy, 189n18
Council of Atlantic Telecommunication Unions (CATU), Canada, 95, 113–16
Council of Canadians, 247
counter-knowledges, 45
counter-perspective on call centres, 7, 47, 60, 77, 78, 170, 194
counter-subjectivity, 7, 77, 170–5, 202–7. *See also* counter-perspective on call centres
creative industries, 11, 31, 204, 249n42
creative labor, 220
customer relations, 17, 18, 34, 35n12, 40n22, 76, 86, 91, 96, 145, 159, 175, 183, 188, 202, 228. *See also* customer service
customer service, 38n19, 41, 67, 70, 74, 75, 90n5, 91n7, 94, 96, 97, 99, 99n19, 100–2, 104, 107, 108, 112, 115, 120n30, 122, 132, 135, 137, 138, 142, 156, 157, 169, 218, 219, 223, 226, 226n23, 242n35, 243. *See also* customer relations

cybertariat, 5, 7–12, 14, 18, 19, 22, 85–124, 141, 161, 244. *See also* Huws, Ursula

D
Dean, Jodi, 9, 14n17, 29–31, 31n3, 33, 34, 34n9, 44, 76, 214n1, 215. *See also* communicative capitalism
Dell, USA, 138
deregulation, 85, 86, 94, 219. *See also* privatization
Desjardins Bank, Canada, 252
detachment. *See* resistance
Deutsche Telekom, Germany, 121
digital assembly line, 7, 50, 66, 71, 96, 205, 221n12, 222, 223. *See also* assembly line
disenchantment, 23, 172, 173. *See also* counter-subjectivity; detachment
dotcom bust, 21, 137, 139
Drucker, Peter, 8–10, 35n11. *See also* knowledge work

E
education, 17, 22n21, 86–8, 91, 91n6, 91n7, 100, 100n20, 101, 119, 133, 146, 159, 169, 180, 181
  call centre training, 91, 108n24, 113
  policy, 89, 91, 93, 215n3
  post-secondary, 91, 91n6, 91n7, 92, 100, 100n20

Electronic Data Systems (EDS), USA, 139
emotional labor, 10, 40, 49, 66, 109, 203, 224n20, 232, 245
Employment Contracts Act, New Zealand, 147
EuroMayDay movement, Italy, 203
Everything Everywhere (EE), UK, 132n1
Excell, 70

F
factory(ies), 4–6, 8, 8n8, 9, 10, 10n12, 11, 20, 22n21, 97, 177n9, 178, 181, 202, 217n6, 218. *See also* assembly line; Fordism
Far-EasTone, Taiwan, 76
Federación de Obreros y EmpleadosTelefónicos de la República Argentina (FOETRA), 74, 235
Federazione Informazione Spettacolo e Telecomunicazioni (FISTeL), Italy, 186n16
Federici, Silvia, 216, 216n5, 217n6, 229n26, 232n29, 254n47
feminization, 18, 20, 48, 181, 182, 228–42, 253, 254
Fight for 15 movement, USA, 160, 160n24
Fleming, Peter, 41, 65, 65n6, 224n20, 226n23, 245
flight from work, 44, 60–2, 62n3, 63–5, 99. *See also* quitting; work refusal

flows of capital, 3n2, 18, 131, 133, 139, 140, 140n8, 141, 143, 146, 157, 158, 158n20
flows of labor, 18, 132, 134. *See also* labor mobility
Fordism, 3, 3n2, 5, 7, 9, 10, 22, 35, 38, 113, 122, 132, 134, 170n1, 173–7, 186, 221, 221n14, 222, 223n17, 237, 240. *See also* assembly line; Factory
foreign direct investment (FDI), 92, 139
Foucault, Michel, 41, 42, 42n24, 43–5, 46n35, 49, 50, 172, 172n3, 174, 175n6

G

Garanti Bank, Turkey, 1–3
Gewerkschaft der Privatangestellten (GPA), Austria, 71
global call centre capital, 18, 133, 135–44, 137n5, 146, 150, 155–7, 161
global call centre market, 17, 33, 33n8, 219, 220
global call centre workforce, 4, 12, 20, 50, 122, 213–54
global division of labor, 155
global justice movement, 134. *See also* anti-globalization movement
global production networks, 157
GMB union, UK, 75
Grupo Atento, Spain, 138, 140
Gruppo Almaviva, Italy, 188, 200

Gruppo COS, Italy, 188, 198, 200, 201
Gruppo d'Inchiesta sulla precarietà e il comune, Italy, 16, 49, 63, 109
Gurgaon Workers News, India, 6, 16, 22n21, 65n5, 131, 161, 230n27, 254

H

hacking. *See* resistance
Hardt, Michael, 43n26, 43n27, 44, 102n21, 144, 215, 224n19
Head, Simon, 10, 37n18, 38n19, 39n21, 66
Heller, Monica, 93, 93n9
Hewlett-Packard (HP), USA, 133, 138
high-commitment model, 20, 65n6, 213, 242–54, 245n39
high-involvement model. *See* high-commitment model
Hochschild, Arlie, 6, 66
horizontal communication, 2, 3, 14, 15, 47, 225. *See also* communication from below
Huws, Ursula, 5, 11, 12, 12n14, 33, 91n7, 96, 97n14, 121, 132, 132n2, 137, 144n12, 174, 174n4, 215n3, 221n14. *See also* cybertariat

I

ICT Group, Canada, 117, 118
immaterial labor, 19, 20, 44, 45, 45n32, 49, 79, 87, 88, 110,

120n30, 121, 144, 214–28, 216n5, 218n7, 221n12, 232, 242. See also subsumption of labor
indigenous workers, 18, 134, 148, 150, 159, 160
Industrial Development Agency (IDA), Ireland, 92, 93
Industrial Workers of the World (IWW), 151
informal resistance, 63, 64, 68, 70, 169, 228, 228n25. See also resistance
informational development, 86–96, 92n8, 119, 137, 215, 215n3
Infosys, India, 138
Instituto per la Ricostruzione Industriale (IRI), Italy, 184n14
International Alliance of Theatrical Stage Employees, USA, 251
Ipsos, France, 155, 227
IslandTel, Canada, 89n3, 95
IWW. See Industrial Workers of the World (IWW)

K
knowledge work, 6–8, 11, 11n13, 20, 20n19, 21, 29, 35, 35n11, 36, 42, 45, 62, 77, 121, 171, 214n1, 219, 220, 222, 228, 239, 239n33, 245. See also Drucker, Peter
Kolinko, Germany, 16, 22n21, 46–7, 68, 108, 121, 132, 134, 219, 235

L
labor mobility, 18, 20, 65, 228–42. See also flows of labor; migration
labor organizing, 2, 7, 12, 15, 17–19, 21–3, 42, 46, 47, 49, 50, 59, 60, 63, 64n4, 71, 72, 79, 112, 122, 124, 144, 148, 158, 170, 170n1, 174, 175–9, 190, 206, 225, 228, 229, 233n31, 237, 239n33, 242, 246
labor process(es), 2, 8, 8n8, 10, 11, 13, 16, 20, 22n20, 29, 36–8, 40–2, 42n24, 43, 63, 64, 65n5, 87, 88, 96, 97, 97n14, 98, 98n17, 99, 100, 102–4, 107–13, 116–18, 120, 122, 132, 135, 135n4, 136, 137n6, 171, 172, 172n3, 173, 178, 186, 190, 204, 217–19, 222, 224, 225, 227, 228, 235, 238, 243–6
language put to work, 3, 5, 7, 11, 14, 17, 30, 47–8, 67, 77, 87, 88, 100–2, 109, 110, 120, 156, 169, 203, 213, 217, 219, 249. See also commodification of language
lawsuits. See resistance
Lazzarato, Maurizio, 44n28, 169, 221
L'Istituto nazionale di statistica (ISTAT), Italy, 188
Lord, Bernard, 103

M
Marazzi, Christian, 44, 44n29
Maritime Telegraph and Telephone Company, Canada, 89n3

market research, 131, 133, 137, 145, 150, 151, 157, 184, 185, 226, 227
Marx, Karl, 5, 5n3, 6n4, 8, 8n8, 14n17, 16, 45, 45n33, 62n3, 88, 97, 97n15, 216, 217, 217n6, 218, 220n10, 221, 221n13
mass intellectuality, 91, 91n7, 102n21
mass-production call centre model, 38, 97, 97n14, 98, 99, 107, 108, 120, 220, 244, 245
McKenna, Frank, 89, 90, 90n5, 91
New Economic Strategy, Canada, 89
measurement, 6, 12, 39, 40, 40n22, 87, 88, 96, 98, 98n16, 98n17, 99, 104, 108n23, 110, 110n26, 112, 116, 120, 133, 219, 221, 223. *See also* routinization; Quantification
mental labor, 7, 7n6, 8, 12, 17, 87. *See also* Braverman, Harry
Merchants, South Africa, 139
Microsoft, USA, 92n8, 137n6, 138
migration, 93, 136, 238. *See also* labor mobility
migration of struggles, 133, 134, 136, 155–62, 160n23
virtual migration, 133–44, 156–60, 238, 239

N

Nadeem, Shehzad, 62–4, 135, 135n4, 158
National Business Review, New Zealand, 147
National Communications Commission (NCC), Taiwan, 76
National Union of Workers (NUW), Australia, 131, 146, 150, 152, 154, 158
NBTel, Canada, 86n1, 89, 89n3, 90, 90n4, 95, 100, 102, 120. *See also* Aliant, Canada
Negri, Antonio, 43n26, 43n27, 44, 45, 45n31, 102n21, 144, 215, 224n19
neoliberalism, 12, 22, 22n21, 30, 33, 89, 133, 134, 142n9, 146, 147, 161, 219, 246. *See also* deregulation; privatization
network media industries, 11, 31, 31n1, 44, 45, 220
NewTel, Canada, 89n3, 95
Nielsen, USA, 151, 226
Nuove Identità di Lavoro (NIDIL), Italy, 186n16

O

occupation. *See* resistance
offshoring, 65n5, 76, 133, 135, 135n4, 138–40, 140n8, 141–3, 143n10, 144, 150, 155, 222
Omega, Canada, 235, 238

Omnia, Italy, 74, 183
Ontario Co-op Association (OnCo-op), Canada, 252
operaismo, 13, 13n16, 14n17, 44, 44n28, 46, 60, 60n1, 170n1. *See also* autonomist Marxism
Orange, UK, 132n1
outsourced call centre sector, 18, 31n1, 47, 61, 64, 65, 71–3, 75, 76, 86, 92, 96, 97, 103–10, 112–24, 131, 132, 132n1, 133, 133n3, 134–6, 138, 140–4, 146, 150, 151, 155–9, 173, 178, 180, 182, 183, 185, 186n15, 189, 190, 219, 220, 230n27, 235, 236

P

Partito Comunista Italiano (PCI), Italy, 60n1, 176
Philips, Netherlands, 138
Phonemedia, Italy, 253
picketing. *See* resistance
post-colonialism, 135n4, 136, 139, 161, 230n28, 238
post-Fordism, 3, 3n2, 5, 32, 62, 97n15, 141, 145, 190, 206, 215, 221, 231, 234–6
post-industrialism, 8, 8n7, 11, 11n13, 35. *See also* Bell, Daniel
post-operaismo, 5, 5n3, 6, 13n16, 16, 175, 175n5. *See also* autonomist Marxism
post-workerism. *See* post-operaismo
precariat, 18, 20, 21, 49, 174, 189, 234, 235. *See also* precarity

precarity, 10, 121, 123, 134, 150, 160–2, 169, 171, 175–9, 181, 183–5, 187, 189, 189n18, 190, 192, 197, 198, 202, 204, 204n21, 225n21, 228–42, 249n40, 254. *See also* precariat
privatization, 32, 73, 75, 85, 121, 138, 147, 175, 180, 185, 219. *See also* deregulation
Processed World, USA, 221
proletarianization, 11, 22n21, 78, 87, 174, 214n1, 244. *See also* proletariat
proletariat, 8, 14n17, 135n4, 229, 231. *See also* proletarianization
Public Service Alliance of Canada, 71

Q

quantification, 87, 97, 98n17, 133, 219. *See also* measurement; routinization
quitting. *See* resistance

R

racialization, 5, 12, 18, 64, 161
Rappresentanze Sindacali di Base-Confederazione Unitaria di Base (RdB-Cub), Italy, 254
Rappresentanze Sindacali Unitarie (RSU), Italy, 178
real subsumption. *See* subsumption of labor
Red Decade, Italy, 176, 206n22

Refugee to Refugee (R2R), Greece, 251
Regulation School, 3n2, 14n16, 43n26, 98n16
Research Solutions, New Zealand, 145
resistance, 7, 12–14, 14n16, 17, 18, 23, 30, 32n4, 41, 42n25, 43, 43n27, 44, 45, 45n31, 46, 47, 49, 50, 59–79, 61n2, 64n4, 65n6, 88, 99, 111, 112, 121, 131, 132, 162, 169, 175, 189n18, 215, 225, 226, 228, 229, 241, 243n36, 247, 249n41
  detachment, 60, 61, 63–6, 78, 108, 172, 174, 191, 204, 237, 239, 240 (*see also* counter-subjectivity; disenchantment)
  hacking, 67
  lawsuits, 1, 3
  occupation, 14, 21, 60, 74, 75, 178, 197, 245, 249, 252, 253, 253n45, 254
  picketing, 18, 89, 114, 115, 149, 149n16, 152, 154, 157, 197, 225n21, 236
  quitting, 14, 61, 63, 69, 77, 173, 237, 242, 246
  sabotage, 14, 17, 19, 45, 46, 60, 61n2, 66–9, 115, 149, 152, 170, 191, 205, 206, 225, 246
  slacking, 46, 61, 66, 67, 69, 77, 242, 246
  strike, 14, 17–19, 39, 46, 68, 71, 73–6, 79, 85, 86n1, 88, 89, 105, 106, 112–20, 122, 123, 132, 149, 149n17, 150, 152, 153, 157, 160n23, 170, 176, 190, 194–6, 199, 206, 225, 225n21, 236
  strike fund, 115n28, 116, 123
  theft, 61n2, 67–9, 173
  work refusal, 12, 44, 44n28, 63, 67, 68, 74, 173, 191, 205, 213, 225, 246, 249
Responsive Marketing Group, Canada, 247
restructuring, 32, 32n4, 43, 74, 85, 86, 86n1, 87–9, 94, 96, 97, 102, 107, 111n27, 117, 118, 120–3, 188, 219, 235, 239n33
Roggero, Gigi, 6, 6n4, 62, 88, 97n15, 110n26, 229
routinization, 7, 11, 15, 18, 20, 35n18, 37, 40, 41, 87, 96, 102, 106, 107, 110, 120, 120n30, 121, 143, 219, 221, 222. *See also* measurement; quantification

S

sabotage. *See* resistance
Sales-Com, Scotland, 67
Scott, James C., 7n5, 60, 61n2, 62, 169
self-organization, 19, 45n31, 77, 79, 162, 170, 170n1, 171, 175, 193, 203, 206, 206n22, 207, 213, 233, 246, 254. *See also* alternative call centre organization

self-valourization, 45, 45n31, 249, 249n41. *See also* valourization
Sindacato Unitario Lavoratori Transporto Aereo (SULTA), Italy, 198
Sitel, USA, 135, 138, 139
SKY-TV, UK, 159
slacking. *See* resistance
Snater, Italy, 199
South African airlines, 75
South African Transport and Allied Workers Union (SATAWU), 75
spatialization, 137, 137n5
Sprint, USA, 71, 122
standardization. *See* routinization
Stellar, Australia, 38n19
strike. *See* resistance
subjectivity, 13, 35, 40, 41, 47, 49, 101, 161, 171–5, 172n3, 175n6, 191, 203, 205, 222, 224, 237–40. *See also* counter-subjectivity
mercenary subjectivity, 62
subsumption of labor, 98, 217, 218n7
formal subsumption, 217, 218n7
real subsumption, 19, 120n30, 218, 218n7, 219
subterranean stream, 1–23
Supersize My Pay campaign, 148, 149, 149n17, 150, 152, 160, 161n27, 241
surplus value, 98, 110, 220, 224
surveillance, 10, 33n7, 34, 37, 39, 40, 40n22, 41, 66, 67, 70, 71, 94, 96, 102, 104, 110, 112, 120, 152, 172, 172n3, 199, 219, 222, 223n18, 242n35
Sykes, USA, 138, 139
Synovate, Singapore, 133, 134, 144–55, 151n18, 227, 227n24

T

Taiwan Labor Front, 76
Tata Consultancy Services, India, 141
Taylorism, 5, 6, 8, 10, 20, 22n21, 23, 37, 40, 48, 86, 97n14, 109, 110, 121, 148, 221. *See also* Routinization
Taylor, Phil, 10, 32n5, 32n6, 36, 37n17, 37n18, 38n19, 39n20, 39n21, 40, 42, 61, 66, 68n8, 70, 76, 98n17, 109, 120, 142, 173
teamwork, 22, 40, 70n10, 172, 222
Tech Mahindra, India, 141
Tecmarketing, Mexico, 73
Telecom Eireann, Ireland, 92
Telecom Italia, Italy, 121, 169, 180, 182, 184, 185, 190, 236
Telecom Italia Mobile (TIM), Italy, 186n15, 192
telecommunications infrastructure, 90–2, 215
Telecommunications Workers Union (TWU), Canada, 71, 113, 115, 252–3
Telecontact, Italy, 188, 190
Telefónica de Argentina, 74, 253
Telefónica, Spain, 140
Teleperformance, France, 73, 138, 138n7, 141

Teletech, New Zealand, 76
Teletech, USA, 138
Teletec, South Africa, 73
Telkom, South Africa, 73
Telmex, Mexico, 73
Telus, Canada, 71, 113, 114, 122
Thames Water, UK, 75
theft. *See* resistance
T-Mobile, Germany, 132n1, 138
TNS, New Zealand, 134, 151n18
Toronto Rape Crisis Centre Multicultural Women Against Rape (TRCC/MWAR), Canada, 250–1
transnationalization, 3, 7, 14, 18, 47, 92, 111n27, 124, 133, 133n3, 134, 135, 135n4, 136, 137n6, 138, 139, 143–5, 147, 156–8, 158n20, 203, 226, 230, 236, 238, 251
Tronti, Mario, 13, 16, 23, 23n22, 43, 44n28
turnover, 39, 41, 48, 61, 62, 65, 71, 146, 159n21, 160n25, 235, 241. *See also* flight from work
global, 62
in Australia, 18, 38n19, 62, 67, 70, 72, 73, 131, 133, 145, 146, 150, 152, 154–7, 159
in India, 4, 47, 62, 64, 65n5, 68, 72, 75, 108, 108n24, 109n25, 120, 135, 135n4, 136, 138–41, 144n12, 158, 203, 205, 230n27, 231, 233n31, 236, 238, 250n43
in Ireland, 4, 17, 50, 61, 63, 79, 85, 86, 86n2, 87, 93, 94, 100n20, 111n27, 119, 140, 141, 180, 215, 223n18, 231, 238, 241
in the UK, 10n12, 32n5, 37n17, 37n18, 39n20, 39n21, 40n22, 49, 59, 63, 64n4, 65n5, 67, 68, 69, 72, 75, 76, 85, 91n6, 99n19, 109, 120, 121, 135, 139, 140, 141, 143, 143n10, 229, 238, 252
in the USA, 4, 33, 33n8, 38n19, 61, 62, 71, 103, 105, 121, 122, 135, 138–41, 143, 143n10, 160, 247, 252

U

Unifor, Canada, 71, 86n1, 119, 122, 123, 236
UNI-Global, India, 158
UniNomade 2.0, Italy, viii
Unione Italiana del Lavoro (UIL), Italy, 176n7, 177, 177n9, 178, 178n11, 188, 195, 203
Unione Italiana Lavoratori della Telecomunicazione (UILCOM), Italy, 186n16
Union for IT Enabled Services Professionals (UNITES), India, 72, 158, 233n31
Union Network International (UNI), 72, 76
Union of Salaried Employees, Finland, 73
United Nations Conference on Trade and Development (UNCTAD), 90, 91, 138, 139

United Services Union, Australia, 73
United Steelworkers (USW), USA, 72
Unite, New Zealand, 18, 134, 147–54, 156, 158–60, 161n27, 161n28, 162, 225, 225n22, 226, 227, 241. *See also* Calling for Change campaign

V

valourization, 3n2, 5, 97, 108, 110, 217, 245n39. *See also* self-valourization
Vancouver Rape Relief (VRR), Canada, 250
Verizon, USA, 71, 121–3, 138
vernacular, 7, 7n5, 13, 60, 77, 101, 109
Virno, Paolo, 3, 3n2, 5, 5n3, 6, 8n7, 44, 44n29
virtual migration. *See* migration
Vodafone, UK, 73, 156, 159, 182, 188

W

Wind, Italy, 180, 182, 188

Wipro, India, 69n9, 75, 138, 141
Women on Waves, Netherlands, 251
worker autonomy, 10n12, 11, 14, 37, 39n20, 43, 66, 79, 120, 169–207, 175n6, 245, 254
worker inquiry, 15n18, 42–50, 68n8, 69, 229
workerism. *See* operaismo
worker subjectivity. *See* subjectivity
work intensification, 3n2, 13, 23, 37, 38, 38n19, 39n20, 39n21, 40, 69, 70, 96, 102, 104, 118, 120, 190, 226
work refusal. *See* resistance

X

xwave, Canada, 103, 105, 112, 114, 115. *See also* Bell Aliant, Canada

Y

Yellow Pages, New Zealand, 76
Young Professionals Collective, India, 158, 236

The manufacturer's authorised representative in the EU is Springer Nature Customer Service Centre GmbH, Europaplatz 3, 69115 Heidelberg, Germany. If you have any concerns regarding our products, please contact ProductSafety@springernature.com

Printed and bound by CPI Group (UK) Ltd, Croydon, CR0 4YY

23/03/2026

02076398-0003